Whitman and Burroughs
COMRADES

BOOKS BY CLARA BARRUS

The Life and Letters of John Burroughs

Our Friend John Burroughs

The Heart of Burroughs's Journals (*Editor*)

My Dog Friends (*Editor*)

Whitman and Burroughs, Comrades

WALT WHITMAN
From a photograph by Pearsall, of Brooklyn, 1872

Whitman and Burroughs Comrades

By CLARA BARRUS

WITH ILLUSTRATIONS

KENNIKAT PRESS, INC./PORT WASHINGTON, N. Y.

TO
ONE I KNEW
AND
ONE I WISH I HAD KNOWN

And this, O this shall henceforth be the token of comrades, this calamus-root shall,
.   .   .   .

... what I drew from the water by the pond-side, that I reserve,
I will give it, but only to them that love as I myself am capable of loving.

WHITMAN

His piercing and eternal cadence rings
Too pure for us — too powerfully pure,
Too lovingly triumphant, and too large;
But there are some that hear him, and they know
That he shall sing tomorrow for all men,
And that all time shall listen.

EDWIN ARLINGTON ROBINSON

ACKNOWLEDGMENT

I GRATEFULLY acknowledge the kindly aid of all who have had a hand in the compilation of this book. Chief among them, aside from John Burroughs himself, and the help from the Burroughs Whitman Collection, is Mr. Clifton J. Furness. He urged me onward in the beginning, and has aided and abetted me at every turn: has given the entire manuscript his painstaking and scholarly aid, and contributed to its accuracy and interest by research in the libraries of Boston and Harvard University, from his own voluminous notes on Whitman material, and through his access to the Bucke, Sprague, Lion, Einstein, Goldsmith, and Perry Collections. The footnotes bearing his initials are further evidence of his aid; also a large part of the bibliography. Mr. Henry S. Saunders also contributed generously to the bibliography; verified much other data; and furnished many photographs for selection. Mr. Julian Burroughs supplied the early, unfamiliar photograph of his father. Signal aid has been afforded me by items from Charles N. Elliot's Whitman Collection, and by his gift to me of typed copies of a voluminous correspondence between Dr. Bucke and O'Connor. I also gratefully acknowledge Professor Perry's courtesy in permitting me personal access to his Whitman Collection.

Of the many books consulted during the progress of this work, the most of which are frequently mentioned in the body of it, none has proved more helpful than 'The Fight of a Book for the World,' by the late William Sloane Kennedy. And I have found Horace Traubel's three volumes on Whitman a veritable mine of information.

The American Academy of Arts and Letters has extended many courtesies, as have Miss Jessie L. Whitman, Miss Bertha Johnston, Mr. Albert E. Johnston, Mrs. Frank J. Sprague, Mr. W. S. Monroe, Mr. Oscar Lion, Mrs. Stanley Worthington, Mrs. Grace Gilchrist Frend, Dr. Clyde Fisher, Mr. Glen Buck, Mr. and Mrs. H. A. Haring, Mr. Ferris Greenslet, and Mr. Francis H. Allen. I also appreciate the courteous replies received to inquiries from Mr. Robert Underwood Johnson, Mr. Charles De Kay, Mr. Ernest Ingersoll, Mr. Daniel Henderson, and Professor Emory S. Holloway.

My especial thanks are due the correspondents of Burroughs (or their representatives) for the loan of letters written by him, and for permission to use letters written to him; as well as for other letters and data germane to the work. Mrs. Edward Dowden, Miss Hilda Dowden, the late Charles E. Benton, the sons and daughters of the late Thomas B. Harned, Mrs. Horace Traubel, Miss Harriet Monroe, Mr. Richard Le Gallienne, Miss Kate Buss, Mr. Charles N. Elliot, Mrs. T. W. Higginson, the late Mrs. J. T. Trowbridge, Miss Rosamond Gilder, Mrs. Laura Stedman Gould, Mr. Johnson Brigham, and Mrs. Carolyn Wells Houghton have favored me in this connection. Thanks also to Mrs. Charles Holden for permission to quote from her letters to me. And to Mrs. Dowden for the photograph of Edward Dowden.

To the publishing firms of J. M. Dent and Company, E. P. Dutton and Company, Doubleday, Doran and Company, and Houghton Mifflin Company I acknowledge permission to use excerpts from their publications.

C. B.

CONTENTS

ILLUSTRATIONS

INTRODUCTION

WALT WHITMAN was among the earliest of writers to vision and celebrate 'the institution of the dear love of comrades'; to sing of manly attachment, athletic love, adhesiveness — that peculiar sympathy and affection which binds man to man in close bonds of fellowship — an affection which, the poet seems to hint, may find its fullest fruition beyond the bounds of time and space. In those mystical, often misunderstood poems named 'Calamus,' Whitman declares that the man he speaks for needs and rejoices in comrades. Regarding comradeship as the basis of all enduring life in humanity, in the state, in philosophy, in religion, he predicted the day when the yearning for it, latent in all men, will emerge and reveal itself in the noblest manifestations of which mankind is capable. What Whitman voiced so fervently in his poems, and in 'Democratic Vistas,' he exemplified with added fervor in his life. His yearning, affectionate nature, which drew to him many and diverse comrades, expressed itself, notably toward the soldiers of the Civil War, in rare self-sacrifice, unbounded compassion, unwearying devotion.

The main purpose of this book is to show how Whitman's conception of comradeship worked out in personal relations in life, and especially to show John Burroughs as the most complete embodiment of the Whitman ideal of comradeship. Burroughs was the unflagging disciple, ever ready to give a reason for the faith within him; ever at hand with steady, unassuming support. His unswerving loyalty to the poet was no less in evidence than his abiding affection for the man. After having put his hand to the plough, he was always there, quiet, sane, sustaining to the end. Less picturesque, less explosive, less brilliant than that earlier comrade, William Douglas O'Connor, though no more loyal (for no man could be more loyal than O'Connor); less partisan than the 'hot little prophets' that revolved around the poet in his later years, and without a vestige of the self-advertising that marred the fealty of certain rabid adherents, Burroughs illustrated in near sixty years' allegiance the 'lifelong love of comrades.' Moreover, through early and late writings, he rendered probably the most effectual aid of all Whitman's interpreters toward an understanding of 'Leaves of Grass' and its enigmatic author.

Since the wealth of material is intimately connected with so many of Whitman's American *confrères*, I have found it necessary, in tracing the Whitman-Burroughs comradeship through voluminous letter-files, to extend greatly the original scope of this volume. This, in turn, led to the question of the reception of Whitman in Great Britain and on the Continent. It soon became apparent that to present this significant comradeship in all its ramifications, I must cover a period extending from 1863 to more than a score of years beyond the life of Whitman. Thus it happens that, in essaying a delineation of the comradeship between two outstanding figures in American literature in the nineteenth century, sidelights are simultaneously thrown upon their most important contemporaries in Europe and America.

In spite of the fact that it originally aimed to picture the comrades and, later, their contemporaries, the book, consequent upon various accretions, has now virtually grown into a history of 'Leaves of Grass,' and a compendium of Whitman criticism covering the period when America was coming into her own in literature.

Out of their own mouths the literary contemporaries of Whitman and Burroughs are depicted; and if, as was often the case, many a detractor, in the attempt to write Whitman down as a nonentity, a rowdy, an uncouth singer, has written himself up as an ass, he has only to eat his own words — the vilification is mostly to the vilifier, and comes back most to him. However, many who came to scoff remained to pray, although in a few notorious instances, some who came to pray remained to scoff. But whether Whitman was a thorn in the flesh to his contemporaries, or a voice from the heights, we may learn here, from the witnesses themselves, who were his steadfast appreciators, who the persistent vilifiers, and who the vacillators.

A study of Whitman's contemporary reception leads one over a wider range of persons and interests than would that of any other writer of his day. Again and again one is struck with the poet's many-sidedness. Through his personal and artistic relations he touched all strata of society, all spheres of current activity. Does not this prove him more truly the poet of the American people, more the representative voice of his age, than is usually conceded?

Besides offering new material to illuminate the characters of Whitman and Burroughs, these pages shed light upon some perplexing Whitman problems, and make additions to what is already known of certain aspirations of the poet; for example, his lecture projects.

Along with the two main characters in this volume, a captivating figure frequently walks the boards — that ready redresser of wrongs, that glowing, ardent Irish-American, William Douglas O'Connor, the constant friend who grappled to his soul with hooks of steel Whitman and his cause. The same courtly knight rushed to the fray whenever he heard of a 'genteel female' in distress; for example, his defense of Elizabeth Akers Allen when her 'Rock me to Sleep, Mother' was claimed by one Ball, his castigation of Richard Grant White for his unchivalrous attacks upon the Bacon-Shakespeare students Miss Delia Bacon and Mrs. Henry Pott; also his defense of the Donnelly Cryptogram. In fact, all that the militant O'Connor needed was to learn of an unfair fight under way, and in a twinkling he was armed to the teeth, and to the tip of his eloquent tongue. And how he fought! One is often struck by the contrasting methods of Whitman's two chief defenders — the staid and sturdy Burroughs, keeping it up quietly and unrelentingly for almost sixty years, and the ardent and learned O'Connor, of eloquent tongue and pen, who, in scoring his brilliant points, excoriated the Enemy mercilessly whenever he reared his venomous head; who marshaled the literature of all time to back up his Poet, the while he gleefully 'lambasted' the unbelievers, and shot telling darts at smug sitters in the seats of the scornful.

'Leaves of Grass' has probably been more discussed, pro and con, than any other work by an American author. Indeed, the multiplying of books about it seems without end, some fifty having been published in the last decade alone. In July, 1930, it reached the seventy-fifth anniversary of its publication, while the first book ever written about it, 'Notes on Walt Whitman as Poet and Person,' by John Burroughs, reached its sixty-third. For brevity this book by Burroughs will be designated in these pages as 'Poet and Person.'

In his Introduction to 'Poems of Walt Whitman,' in the Modern Library (Boni and Liveright, 1921), Mr. Carl Sandburg says that 'Leaves of Grass' is 'the most highly praised and the most deeply damned book that ever came from an American printing-press as the work of an American writer.'

In that first decade of the Whitman-Burroughs comradeship, which began in Washington, D.C., in 1863, Burroughs lived and moved and had his being in Whitman. It was an obscure but highly significant period in the lives of both men, and, without doubt, the most significant to Burroughs in his whole career. He was stirred to the depths by both the man and his work. Little wonder that it marked the gestation of his first book. That book was, however, preceded by a preliminary study — an essay called 'Walt Whitman and his "Drum Taps,"' published in the 'Galaxy,' December, 1866. That essay has the distinction of being the first in appreciation of Whitman to be published in the United States, although three somewhat favorable reviews of the 'Leaves' had previously appeared, one by Charles Eliot Norton in 'Putnam's Monthly,' September, 1855,[1] one by Edward Everett Hale in the 'North American Review,' January, 1856, and one by Moncure D. Conway in the 'Dial,' August, 1860. This last I have not seen. Norton's review spoke of the 'Leaves' as a 'curious and lawless collection of excited prose broken into lines.' He characterized it as 'gross, yet elevated, superficial, yet profound — this preposterous, yet somehow fascinating book.' Since he quoted generously from the 'Leaves,' his notice had, on the whole, a favorable effect. Hale reviewed the book with discrimination. The author, he said, had printed it himself and left it to the winds of heaven to publish. As he read, he enjoyed the 'freshness, simplicity, and reality' of it, 'as a tired man, lying on the hillside in summer, enjoys the leaves of grass around him.' Referring to the 'thumb-nail sketches' it contains — an expression much used by Whitman in later years — Hale declared the book to contain things 'so real we wonder how they came on paper.' Still he thought it 'a pity that a book where everything else is natural, should go out of its way to avoid the suspicion of being prudish.'

O'Connor's stirring pamphlet, 'The Good Gray Poet,' had pre-

[1] See K. B. Murdock: *A Leaf of Grass from Shady Hill.* Harvard Press, 1928. C. J. F.

ceded Burroughs's 'Galaxy' article by a year — a piece of brilliant special pleading, a valiant vindication of the maligned poet. O'Connor attempted no evaluation of Whitman's work, no æsthetic analysis. His philippic, as is well known, was called out by the dismissal of Whitman from his post in the Indian Bureau upon the discovery by the Secretary, James Harlan, that the large, picturesque, slow-moving clerk in his bureau was the author of a book which he, the chief, considered indecent.

Burroughs was, as Whitman would say, 'eligible,' not only to appreciate the 'Leaves,' but to qualify as the comrade of comrades long before encountering either book or man. His early notebooks prove this. The following passage is from one kept when he was but twenty-one years of age. In thought it is curiously like a passage in 'Poet and Person,' written when he was twenty-nine or thirty:

My author must suggest and define, convey by accurate analysis and definition, and by casual hints and imperfect revelations.... Some paths he must go with me the whole way, but leave the by-roads and intersecting trails for me to follow through at my own leisure.... When he is showing me any particular constellation.... I love to be permitted to look through to remote stars, or nebulous fields of light beyond....

Again, four years previous to meeting Whitman (and probably it was of Emerson he was then thinking), he wrote:

That man is my pilot who has traversed the seas before me; that man is my master in whom I can see my own green, crude feelings and grub instincts ripened and hanging upon him like apples, absorbing the rich golden autumn sunlight. Hence men become leaders only by greater power of expression; by affording a free passage to that which is choked and obstructed in others. They shape into notes and cadences the music that, unexpressed, is ravishing other souls. That man is our hero who is more ourselves than we are; who beats us at our own game; who surpasses us in our own direction.

Apropos of the influence of both Emerson and Whitman on the plastic youth, one recalls that in 'Whitman: A Study' (1896) Burroughs has said that Whitman was Emerson translated from the abstract to the concrete. There he also said:

My absorption of Emerson had prepared me in a measure for Whitman's philosophy of life, but not for the ideals of character and conduct which he held up to me, nor for the standards in art to which the poet perpetually appealed.

The soil thus prepared, by reason of Burroughs's own philosophical nature, and by his reading of Emerson, the long foreground of their comradeship received further cultivation when, in 1859 or 1860, Burroughs came upon some stray poems by Whitman, and soon after learned from his friend E. M. Allen details of the poet's appearance and ways. Still later, in the autumn of 1862, when on a nutting excursion with Myron B. Benton, a young rural poet and philosopher living at Amenia, New York, Burroughs had his first dip into the 'Leaves' itself.[1] There, in the shelter of Mulberry Rock on the old Dutchess County farm, Burroughs and Benton read from that strange book which puzzled, repelled, and fascinated them by turns. Thereafter the new poet's words itched at their ears. As Burroughs said in later years, 'I picked out what I could understand and let the rest go till I grew to understand it.'

Earlier proof than that already given of Burroughs's eligibility for comradeship is found in the Allen-Burroughs and the Benton-Burroughs correspondence. Burroughs's attachment to these young men was an earnest of the greater comradeship awaiting him with the poet. A letter from Allen to Burroughs, May 1, 1862, reveals their *camaraderie*:

MY DEAR JOHN,

... If you were here now I should be happy, for you are my twin-spirit. We are like two lovers, are we not? Do you remember how we used to lie on the rock by the brook in the twilight? You ought to be a woman, John, or I. In this soft, sweet air of spring, when the bloom of the peach tree, and the white blossom of the other trees are snowed down on the grass, and the golden stars of the dandelions shine out in green nooks, and sweet earthy scents fill the air, I seem to see your spirit in all these things. You are so associated in my memory with the spring and summer, and your nice observation of the phenomena of nature, and your fine appreciation of the Beautiful as it is gradually unfolded over the hills and valleys, has so identified you in my mind, with these sweet seasons, that I cannot help thinking of you when I feel the dreamy influence of spring,

---

[1] In an article, 'Whitman and Burroughs as Comrades' (*Yale Review*, October, 1925), I confused certain data, incorrectly placing that nutting party in New Jersey with Allen, whereas it was with Benton at 'Troutbeck,' Amenia, that Burroughs first read the 'Leaves.' It was, however, Allen who sent Burroughs the first copy he ever owned of the 'Leaves.'

and long to be with you. I imagine you exclaiming to yourself at this point, 'Why, Allen has made a mistake in directing this to me — it is a love letter to some fair friend of his!'...

For comparison see Burroughs's first venture into verse (except for still earlier lines to the sweetheart who became his wife), addressed 'To E. M. A.' — verses printed in the 'Saturday Press' in the late summer of 1860. As the summer wanes, identifying his friend with the scenes amid the Catskills, Burroughs writes in wistful reminiscence:

> A change has come over nature
> Since you and June were here;
> The sun has turned to the southward
> Adown the steps of the year.

Then, after enumeration of the seasonal changes, he concludes:

> But a change has come over nature,
> The youth of the year has gone;
> A grace from the wood has departed,
> And a freshness from the dawn.

A still closer communion bound Burroughs and Benton, which lasted almost forty years. I quote from an essay by Burroughs describing a camping party in the Adirondacks in 1863, when Allen, Benton, Burroughs, and one 'Jaspar from Jersey,' made up the group. Giving Benton the fictitious name 'Richard,' Burroughs writes of their camp-fire loungings:

In the twilight 'Richard' and I made our bed on a gentle slope nearly overshadowed by a huge pine, where the moss was peculiarly thick and soft, and fell into one of our discursive, easy-going talks — the sport and play of the mind rather than the deliberate application of its powers. Rich and rare old 'Richard'! What depths there are in thee, and what heights! what quaintness, what subtlety, what clearness of vision, and what Norseman sturdiness and vigor! How we have tugged at the old problems, seeking again the unknown quantity whose symbol is not x, but the visible universe! Loafing and inviting our souls in forest and field, by lake and river and mountain, what converse we have had, what questionings, what glorious metaphysical wrestlings, what uplifting and liberation of spirit!...

This capacity for comradeship made Burroughs, when a mere lad, cleave to a boy cousin much younger than himself. All his life he remembered his bereft feeling when the boy's visit had ended. When in California in his seventy-second year, he made a special trip to San Francisco to find that grown-up boy, lured by the glamour which had enveloped the memory of him down through the years. In young manhood his dearest companion had been a nephew, Channy B. Deyo, a winsome, affectionate lad — 'both son and brother and dear comrade to me.' Channy had shared his rambles, and he had directed the lad's reading and studies with fond concern. He mourned Channy's early death all his days. When, during the last three years of his own life, he became strongly attached to the young poet John Russell McCarthy, first attracted by his verses, later by a deep congeniality, Burroughs said fervently, 'He is the dearest man friend who has come to me since Channy B. was taken.' Another deep attachment from early manhood to the end was for his 'soldier comrade,' Aaron Johns, with whom he camped in the wilds. Aaron wrote, after the passing of Burroughs: 'Heaven has granted me but few more grateful memories than our companionship and affection.'

With Burroughs's rich capacity for comradeship, one understands the sudden flowering of affection that marked his meeting with Whitman. One notes his unperturbed chronicling of the fact, 'Walt kissed me like a girl.' This act, which would have ruffled, perhaps estranged, most men, making impossible the bond of comradeship, found ready comprehension in Burroughs. His own large endowment of affection, amativeness, and potential 'adhesiveness,' was like a huge dynamo charging him and his associates with propelling force, yet was always controlled by the intellect, thus admirably complementing Whitman's less disciplined emotional nature. In this connection I am reminded of a passage in one of his letters to me, from New York City, in the early nineteen-hundreds. Writing of having had his head examined by a phrenologist, who had told him he had the largest development of the 'bump' of philoprogenitiveness on record — that faculty which ensures love and friendship — he added whimsically, 'And now I am going back to Slabsides to be alone with Silly Sally.' Despite the craving for companionship, he had soon wearied of the city throng, and the balance in his make-up led him back to his woodland retreat, and to the company of his pet cat. That same balance rendered him peculiarly adjustable: he could companion richly emotional natures like Whitman, volatile ones like Allen, reserved ones like Benton; and could understand and admire men like O'Connor, like John Muir, like Roosevelt, enjoying a considerable degree of fellowship with each; although his fullest communion was with those in whom a wordless companionship was possible. This is why he constituted so perfect a comrade of Whitman.

Let me recall that memorable description in 'Specimen Days' — 'An Ossianic Night — Dearest Friends.' The strange effects of sky, moon, and river, as the poet crossed and recrossed the Delaware by ferry at midnight, somehow suggesting his absent friends, he fell to musing on them: 'William O'Connor, Maurice Bucke, John Burroughs, and Anne Gilchrist — friends of my soul — staunchest friends of my other soul — my poems.' Burroughs once said, when speaking with me of his love for Whitman:

We were companionable without talking. I owe more to him than to any other man in the world. He brooded me; he gave me things to think of; he taught me generosity, breadth, and an all-embracing sympathy. He was a tremendous force in my life. It was really Walt that drew me to Washington — through Allen's letters.

Before meeting Burroughs in 1863, Whitman had heard much of him from E. M. Allen. It is probable that he had even been favorably impressed with his writing, since a clipping of his essay — 'A Thought on Culture,' from the 'Saturday Press' of July 21, 1860 — preserved from those early years, is among Whitman's papers in the Bucke-Whitman Collection.

In one of his volumes on Whitman in Camden, Horace Traubel reports the poet as saying of Burroughs:

He was so equable, buoyant, happy — so like a strong helpful stream of water — all eyes for joyous assurances — a grown man with a boy's soul... so wise, so gay, though never boisterous.... We were thrown much together in Washington — were like chips of the same block, members of a common family.

It seems impossible to exaggerate Whitman's influence upon Burroughs during that formative period between his twenty-sixth and thirty-sixth years when, both of them in Government employ, they were in almost daily communication. In later years, although seeing much less of each other, Burroughs often visited Whitman in

Camden, and Whitman visited him thrice in his river home on the Hudson. They also met many times in New York and Philadelphia. In 1881, I think, together they visited Whitman's birthplace, and in September, 1883, the two spent a happy holiday at Ocean Grove, New Jersey. Burroughs frequently sent the poet the fruits of his vineyard for delectation, and sometimes the fruits of his pen for criticism. Their correspondence was maintained throughout the years, and Burroughs, as his readers know, continued zealous in the Whitman cause to the end, ever quick to defend both the man and his book.

Among the many services which he rendered the 'Leaves' is that of his youthful testimony in refutation of the charge of its indecency. In his first book he avowed the 'Leaves' had strengthened his faith; had taught him the dignity of the body, and the sanctity of sex; had been a 'constant invisible influence toward physiological cleanliness and strength, and a severance from all that corrupts and makes morbid and mean.' Truly, as Whitman has said, all architecture — yes, and all poetry, and all life — is what you do to it when you look upon it. Some have looked upon the 'Leaves' and found it indecent; Burroughs saw it all as good — a breadth of conception which enabled him to catch the drift of the book before he could grasp its full meaning. Hence his sturdy espousal of it long before the bandages dropped from the eyes of most of his contemporaries. Today it is no longer necessary to defend Whitman or his book. His stanchest supporters, if living, could now drop the chips from their shoulders. But the way was long and disheartening. It is not to be wondered at that the few who saw 'face to face' felt constrained to witness emphatically to the splendor of the vision vouchsafed them.

While tracing Whitman's influence upon Burroughs, one must remember that, to some extent, Burroughs also influenced Whitman. He contributed to at least two of Whitman's poems: his description of the hermit thrush supplied the poet with the bird used so effectively in his threnody on Lincoln; and his account of the mating eagles (a mating which Whitman never witnessed) enabled the poet to write 'The Dalliance of the Eagles.' Furthermore, a letter from Burroughs to Whitman, describing a stalwart, Viking-like farmhand (quoted in 'Specimen Days'), was incorporated by Whitman as his own, in a publication to be indicated later. Whitman also borrowed the title of Burroughs's third book, 'Winter Sunshine,' as caption of a letter to the 'Philadelphia Times' of January 26, 1879. And, too, it seems probable to me, as will be further considered, that in many of his detailed observations of Nature in 'Specimen Days,' Whitman was largely indebted to Burroughs. The poet's forte was not the study of details, but of wholes. That is why the comrades, far apart in age and temperament, were so congenial — they fully complemented each other. The one sought the truth of detail, the other that of ensemble; the one was keenly observant of every phase of Nature; the other, given rather to the leisurely contemplation of her. Still their interests tallied far oftener than might be supposed. Burroughs, intent on the facts gleaned from Nature, was always investing those facts with the witchery of the ideal; while Whitman, with his comprehensive glance, came more and more, as seen in 'Specimen Days,' to seek special knowledge about the birds, the flowers, the trees. On the other hand, concerning their attitude to science, what Whitman felt from the first, Burroughs came also to believe. For example, Whitman said:

> Your facts are useful, and yet they are not my dwelling,
> I but enter by them to an area of my dwelling.

Late in life Burroughs came to hold more firmly to what he had written in an early notebook:

Only when we look at the stars without recalling the figures and calculations of the astronomers, but when these things may be inferred from our wonder and admiration and appreciation, has science passed from a formula to become sight and volition....

In coming upon this and much other writing on astronomy in Burroughs's early manuscript notebooks, Mr. Clifton J. Furness was impressed with the striking resemblance therein to the basic thought in Whitman's poem, 'When I Heard the Learn'd Astronomer' (first printed in 1865); so much so that in his 'Walt Whitman's Workshop' (page 221) he comments on the likelihood that Burroughs suggested the leading thought of the poem to Whitman. At that time the two friends were in the habit of taking long walks together at night in and around Washington. It was probably on such walks as these that they had the interchange of ideas from which Whitman caught the germ of his famous poem. This surmise by Mr. Furness is reënforced by a passage in Burroughs's Introduction to a volume of selections from Whitman, called 'The Rolling Earth,' edited by Mr. Waldo R. Browne:

I remember that often in our walks by starlight, he would suddenly stop and gaze long and intently at the sky....

Starting, as this book did, with so simple an original plan, it has grown to almost unmanageable proportions, owing to the enormous mass of source material. The 'thumb-nail sketch' type of work is particularly difficult to handle. It could be made more readable if connected throughout by a thread of narrative, and by digests of lengthy original documents, but, as a rule, I have preferred not to sacrifice the flavor of the originals by summarizing them, and, in order to economize space, have often omitted comments, letting the documents speak for themselves.

Being essentially a collection and digest of the most important contemporary criticism of Whitman, this book should prove serviceable to students. With this in mind, I have striven for accuracy in matters of fact, giving dates when ascertainable, and, as a rule, indicating sources, even at the risk of seeming meticulous. In fact, I have tried to spare future students much of the arduous work I myself have been unable to escape owing to writers so often disregarding the principles of careful editing. In transcribing from original sources, I have allowed faulty spelling and other errors to stand. Apology is perhaps due the general reader for presenting so many footnotes and cross-references, which seem unavoidable when considering the convenience of special students. Despite earnest efforts at accuracy, many errors may have crept into this work. If I seem ungracious in pointing out occasional mistakes and inaccuracies met with in the work of certain critics and biographers of Whitman, this has not been done in a carping spirit, but because, having come upon them in my own research, I have hoped, in correcting them, to smooth the path for future students. In matters open to various interpretations, I have tried to reach an unprejudiced evaluation of the evidence, although I am aware that my own zeal and interest in the principal characters may sometimes have led me to fall short. Where doubt about actual circumstances exists, I have given the available evidence on both sides, leaving it to the reader to form his conclusions. I have not suppressed evidence, and have tried to help clarify some of the tangles and conflicting opinions that center around Whitman's complex personality.

One aim in assembling these contemporary records has been to dispel certain misconceptions and misrepresentations still persisting about the poet. Many prejudices and erroneous opinions about him still prevail, owing to ignorance of some facts and to the garbling of others. Certain mistakes are doubtless due to the modern tendency in biography to assume the virtue of truth if truth is wanting; to advance fictitious episodes, absurd and unwarrantable conjectures, and even malicious rumors, in order to heighten interest in the story. Gross liberties have been taken by several writers with phases of Whitman's life about which little or nothing is known. In effect this is highly mischievous. The uninformed reader, owing to the dramatization of imaginary episodes, is led to think he is reading of actual events. Wild guesses and wilder anachronisms, fearfully and wonderfully mingled in certain books purporting to interpret Whitman's life, have grievously maligned the poet and some of his most devoted friends. But, as Whitman said, with more of truth than poetry, 'There will always be plenty of embroiderers.' In his boundless charity he would not 'exclude' even these. Books about Whitman in which unwarrantable romancing has been substituted for the truth have received scant mention in these pages beyond the antidotal presentation of authenticated facts.

It is hoped that certain data offered here will serve to dispel the persisting impression that Whitman led a dissolute life. Whatever of youthful indiscretion, or failure to conform to the exactions of the 'unco guid,' Whitman may have manifested prior to 1862, a cloud of witnesses aver that his life thereafter was exceptionally clean and wholesome. Testimony to this effect is admirably summed up by Mr. Bliss Perry in his 'Walt Whitman.' Still the opposite impression obtains in the minds of many. Even during the early Bohemian days at Pfaff's, when the poet was supposed to be living 'jolly bodily,' as described by himself, he is said by Howells to have emanated 'an atmosphere of purity and serenity.' This, taken in connection with the statement of Sir Edwin Arnold (who visited him in 1889), that Whitman was the most beautiful old man he ever beheld, should give pause to any one inclined to credit rumors of libertinism. Men do not gather grapes from thorns, nor figs from thistles. It should be remembered, however, that Whitman himself is partly responsible for spreading impressions as to his licentiousness and debauchery, since, in speaking for his human brothers and sisters, he takes upon himself all the sins of erring humanity. His poetic avowals, misinterpreted by the literal-minded, have often been regarded as actual confessions.

Abundant evidence is offered here that Whitman held women in the highest regard, never tolerating light or lewd talk about them, and setting his face sternly against all violation of the sanctity of the family. Moreover, it testifies to his scrupulousness in the discharge of his debts; and to the donation of his scanty savings and the lavish use of time and strength for the needs of the soldiers, from early 1863 till long after the close of the Civil War.

It has pleased certain writers to belittle Whitman's hospital services, and to criticize his easy-going ways in office work while drawing pay from the Government; but we are assured by those who knew that for whatever of laxity he may have shown in his clerkship, he compensated a thousand-fold in ministry to the war veterans. A recent writer, in casting aspersions on that ministry, has asserted that Whitman's connection with the Washington hospitals was 'either wholly imaginary or very greatly exaggerated.' He states further that he himself does 'not discover that any of Whitman's friends at the time of the Civil War, or later, accompanied him frequently on his hospital visits, or knew about them, except as they learned from him.' Adroitly worded. Of course his friends did not 'accompany him frequently,' and of course they did learn from him — from seeing him at the work itself. In these pages it is shown conclusively that Burroughs and O'Connor, and their respective wives, and E. M. Allen, Charles W. Eldridge, and J. T. Trowbridge, to name a few reliable witnesses, knew from personal observation of Whitman's untiring devotion in this particular. And it was because of James Redpath's personal knowledge of these services that Emerson, and others in Boston, Providence, and New York, sent substantial contributions to aid Whitman in supplying comforts to the soldiers. Thomas Donaldson, in his book called 'Whitman, the Man,' has a valuable chapter on the poet's services to the Union Cause (although Whitman's beneficence included the boys in gray as well as the boys in blue). Furthermore, it would seem that the poet's homely, human letters written to his mother during his ministrations (edited many years later by Dr. Richard Maurice Bucke in a book named 'The Wound Dresser') should forever silence ignoble insinuations as to Whitman's war service even in the most hostile critic. There are still other evidences of the value of those services: August 26, 1871, Richard J. Hinton, in the 'Cincinnati Commercial,' gave a glimpse of Whitman as hospital nurse while he himself was a wounded patient in the wards.[1] And John Swinton, in a letter to the 'New York Herald,' April 1, 1876, testifies to having accompanied Whitman again and again on his hospital rounds. Swinton was a friend of the poet's dating from the Washington period on through life. Burroughs quotes Swinton's letter in full in 'Whitman: A Study,' pages 41–42.

Another competent witness, Dr. D. W. Bliss, surgeon in charge of the Armory Hospital, wrote in a letter, January 27, 1887:

From my personal knowledge of Mr. Whitman's labors in Armory Square, and other hospitals, I am of the opinion that no one person who assisted in the hospitals during the War accomplished so much good to the soldiers and for the Government as Mr. Whitman.

Throughout this work, including its bibliography, it will be seen how completely Burroughs submerged himself in the Whitmanian sea. Eloquent of the poet's pervasive influence upon him from first to last is the fact that as Burroughs's very first book had Whitman for its subject, so also had the last essay in the last book to be published by him during his lifetime, namely, 'The Poet of the Cosmos,' in 'Accepting the Universe.' And further, his final volume, a posthumous book named 'The Last Harvest,' contains many quotations from Whitman, and comments about him, among which the passage to follow contains the last words about the poet which Burroughs ever wrote for publication:

I have always patted myself upon the back for seeing the greatness of Whitman from the first day that I read a line of his. I was bewildered

---

[1] Hinton also published a letter of his reminiscences of Whitman in the *New York World*, April 14, 1889. He is presumably responsible for an article, 'The Poet Walt Whitman — His Fame and Fortunes in England and America,' in the *Rochester Express*, March 4, 1868. C. J. F.

and disturbed by some things, but saw enough to satisfy me of his greatness.

Another quotation from 'The Last Harvest,' when compared with Burroughs's initial views in 'Poet and Person,' proves the consistency of his early and late estimates of the poet:

It is his tremendous and impassioned philosophy suffusing his work as the blood suffuses the body, that keeps 'Leaves of Grass' forever fresh. We do not go to Whitman for pretty flowers of poesy, although they are there, but we do go to him for his attitude toward life and the universe; we go to stimulate and fortify our souls; in short, for his cosmic philosophy incarnated in a man.

CLARA BARRUS

ROXBURY-IN-THE-CATSKILLS

Whitman and Burroughs
COMRADES

Whitman and Burroughs
COMRADES

I

THE CALL TO COMRADESHIP
(1861–1865)

I perceive one picking me out by secret and divine signs,

. . . .

Some are baffled, but that one is not — that one knows.

WHITMAN

THE comradeship of Walt Whitman and John Burroughs began in 1863 and ended at Whitman's death in 1892 — if such a 'real reality' does end with the 'mask of materials.' The first news of a personal nature about the poet had come to Burroughs through his friend, E. M. Allen, a young man of congenial literary tastes with whom Burroughs had formed a friendship while teaching in Newark, New Jersey, in 1859–60. Having seen a stray poem or two by Whitman in the New York 'Saturday Press,' the youths had become both curious and eager for concrete information about the strange poet. They had a hint of him from Bayard Taylor, who, through their instrumentality, had lectured in Newark, but to their inquiries, as Burroughs told me years later, Taylor had only commented patronizingly, 'Oh, yes, there is something in him, but he is a man of colossal egotism.'

Early in February, 1861, when teaching at Marlboro-on-the-Hudson, Burroughs received a letter from Allen lamenting the decease of the 'Saturday Press' which left 'such a void in the literary world.' Allen wrote of seeing its 'set' in New York, at Pfaff's Restaurant:

Walt Whitman was there — rough, hairy, and 'gray-necked'; he had his hat on, looking reflective, listening to a nicely dressed young fellow who sat next him, which might have been Aldrich...

Aldrich, Howells, 'Artemus Ward,' George Arnold, Ned Wilkins, and Fitz James O'Brien were among the frequenters of Pfaff's in those days.

In the fall of 1862 Burroughs visited New York hoping himself to get a glimpse of Whitman, but succeeded only in meeting some of the clever Bohemians then writing for the 'New York Leader.' To Myron B. Benton he wrote of meeting the editor, Henry Clapp,[1] and 'Ada Clare,' the Queen of Bohemia, and of getting news of another brilliant writer, 'Agnes Franz,' whose 'short pithy reviews' had attracted both Benton and Burroughs. In the excerpt to follow, from an October letter to Benton, Burroughs tells of the literary Bohemians:

Of course I called on the 'Leader' folks and pumped all the information out of them I could. And herein chiefly will my letter be of interest to you.

If you feel the least bit spooney, my dear Myron, about 'Agnes Franz,' get over it at once, and turn your thoughts in a different direction — which direction I will indicate presently. 'Agnes Franz' is a *nom de plume*, the lady bearing it lives in Albany and is *married*. She is very poor, and for some reason or other does not choose to reveal anything of herself. They pay her three dollars per article, which is the only money they pay out at present for contributions....

'Ada Clare' is Clapp's favorite, and toward this star I want you to look. When I asked Clapp about her he said she was young, pretty, unmarried, and had a boy. When I pressed him about the boy he said he believed it was an immaculate affair; but finally told me an unvarnished tale of Ada's life. She is a native of Charleston, and, when about 18, fell in love with a young fellow by whom she had this boy (a strangely beautiful child, Clapp says); he [finally?] discarded her and she went to Paris. After a year or two she came to New York where she has since lived. She possesses a competence and writes for the 'Leader' just for the pleasure of the thing. Clapp said she was very beautiful and, he believed, entirely virtuous. He said if I were to come on Friday night at 6 o'clock I would see her. So I dropped in. She is really very beautiful; not a characterless beauty, but a singular, unique beauty. When you go to New York, if you call at the 'Leader' office on Friday night, you will be most certain to see her. You will also be more apt to see Mr. Clapp on Friday than any other day.

Walt Whitman is at Pfaff's almost every night. He lives in Brooklyn,

[1] Traubel, in his *With Walt Whitman in Camden* (first volume, Boston, 1906, page 236), quotes Whitman saying to him, May 30, 1888: 'Henry Clapp was always loyal.... Henry Clapp stepped out from the crowd of hooters — was my friend: a much-needed ally at that time (having a paper of his own) when almost the whole press of America when it mentioned me at all treated me with derision or worse.'

is unmarried, and 'manages,' Clapp says, to earn 6 or 7 dollars per week writing for the papers. He wrote a number of articles for the 'Leader' some time ago, on the Hospitals. Do you remember them? I do not like to believe that he can write in any other style than that of 'Leaves of Grass.'

On November 14, again writing Benton of his gleanings concerning literary folk, Burroughs tells of a visit to James Brownlee Brown at Newburgh, New York. He quotes from and comments upon that 'son of Emerson,' for Brown had admitted that he 'had been fertilized by the Emersonian pollen.' Burroughs adds:

He frankly confesses his obligation to Emerson — says 'he is the father of us all.' He thinks when a man gets through the crust of things, and stands face to face with the ineffable mysteries of the Universe, he necessarily expresses himself somewhat after this style — which I know is very near the truth. He has visited Emerson twice, and told me much about him....

He has known Walt Whitman for a number of years and admires him hugely. Only the other day he met him at Pfaff's.

'Ada Clare,' he says, is virtuous after the French fashion, namely, has but one lover at a time! Walt told him this story about her:

A recent lover of hers was a young man from the country; he was engaged to a very fine young lady who wrote him affectionate letters and seemed deeply attached to him. In Ada's presence his rustic love fell clear out of mind, and he took counsel with Ada how to rid himself of her. After Ada had read her letters she spoke to him after this fashion:

'Now I will tell you what to do: Do you go back to the country and *seduce* her; you can do it. Any woman that writes such letters as that can be seduced. It will do you good. You will both learn something; and then you may come back to me.'

Walt said that was not fair, and was very severe on Ada because of it.

So, dear Myron, I beg you not to take to heart the advice I gave you touching Ada; I take it all back, and will not presume to advise you again. [Henry] Abbey declares if he ever sees her again, he is bound to squeeze her, and I think he would if he got a chance. O, Ada! I had half-suspected it of you!

This denunciation by Whitman of the fair frail lady's counsel puts him in quite a new light to many, yet it is the attitude toward these questions which his personal friends declare him to have consistently maintained.

W. S. Kennedy, in his 'Fight of a Book for the World,' gives the real name of 'Ada Clare' as Mrs. Julia Macelhinney, but the 'New

York Herald' at the time of her death, which followed a bite from a dog, gave it as Mrs. Ada A. Noyes. She was an actress. Writing of her death to Mrs. O'Connor, Whitman said:

Poor, poor Ada Clare — I have been inexpressibly shocked by the horrible and sudden close of her gay, easy, sunny, free, loose, but *not ungood* life.

In early February, young Allen, then employed in Washington, had begun writing Burroughs stirring war news, and news of the literary folk there. The letters which gave glimpses of Emerson and Whitman interested Burroughs the most. Allen had heard Emerson lecture and was delighted with the noble production on American Civilization. All that Allen wrote of Whitman during the ensuing months put a keener edge on Burroughs's curiosity, so that by autumn, when he began reading the 'Leaves' in earnest, after having been intrigued for some time by an occasional poem, Whitman's pull on him grew almost irresistible.

Early in '63 Burroughs was incensed to see an abusive article about his hero in the London 'Saturday Review,' which said that Whitman was 'strong only as an onion is strong in an obscene rowdy.' The obvious unfairness of such criticism only strengthened his interest in the poet for whom he had already begun to feel a personal attachment. Allen's letter of May 5, put his correspondent on the *qui-vive*:

... Between Walt Whitman and me has passed the bond of beer, and we are friends. He calls in occasionally and chats, but I am so occupied in the day that I do not get much time to talk to him. He was in a little while today. A broad-chested old fellow, with gray beard and moustache radiating from a broad, ruddy face. He has the mildest of clear blue eyes, far apart, and one of the most sympathetic voices I ever heard in a man. He wears a broad-brimmed soft hat well back on his head... and collar well open on the chest. His dress and air is very farmer-like, and he walks the streets with an easy stride, his hands in his pockets, and always seems to be musing. He does not talk much on literature. He lent me some letters from some of his young friends in New York. They call him 'Walt,' and by reading you would judge him to be a young fellow, and indeed, he is young, with his perfect health and youthful tastes.

From these letters I learn that Pfaff's has come into partial disuse, so many of the 'good fellows' who used to frequent the place have been scattered by the vicissitudes of war, and the rest have found some other places. Walt says he will take me around when we are both in New York sometime. He tells me he likes Emerson better than he did; he thought he was too refined, but now he does not think so; his experience in the hospitals with poor suffering humanity, he says, has refined him some.

I was speaking to him of Abbey one day, when he said he had no sympathy with that school of Poetry, but thought there was some promise in him. I asked him if he did not admire Tennyson; he said, 'Ah, yes! he is a great artist'; but he thought our poetry ought to partake of the vastness of the country, the great lakes and wide prairies.

This damning of Abbey with faint praise must have reached Abbey's ears, for Benton, to whom Burroughs had reported Whitman's opinion of Abbey, wrote that the latter reciprocated, thought but slightingly of the 'Leaves,' and had dubbed its author 'our poetical Nebuchadnezzar.'

Still the news about Whitman kept coming from Allen, augmenting Burroughs's discontent with school-teaching. The previous November he had tried philosophically to still his unrest, having then written the poem 'Waiting,' in which he assured himself

> ' Nor time, nor space, nor deep, nor high
> Can keep my own away from me.'

But now the waiting was growing irksome, though he could not yet see his way to venture into an unknown field. Allen's letter of May 23 said, in part:

Walt was in the other day and I had quite a talk with him. He has a volume coming out soon called 'Drum Taps.' He told me some of his plans and what he intends to 'celebrate,' as he terms it. I'll not dwell on him now, but will defer it till another time.

Allen was then full of his courtship with Elizabeth Akers, the widow of Paul Akers, the sculptor. Her poetry, published under the pen-name 'Florence Percy,' had attracted him before he had come under her personal spell. Owing to this new interest, Whitman got scantier mention than he would have otherwise, yet Allen sends on this welcome glimpse:

Walt strolled in today as he frequently does. The whole front of our store is open and shaded with an awning, and is a cool pleasant place, coming in from the street. Sometimes when I am busy I'll see Walt's picturesque form in one of the many camp-chairs, a fan in his hand; and then, after a while, he is gone. When I am not busy I sit down and talk with him. He says he is going to give me a book of Thoreau's which the author sent him some years ago. I would prize it highly. We projected an excursion for Sunday up the Branch to the same woods where Florence and I went. I wish you could be with us.

On June 18, Allen writes of looking out on the Avenue and seeing a forest of glistening bayonets, then long lines of artillery, moving heavily, next a black regiment with burnished arms and glittering shoulder-pieces, and then:

Walt just passed with his arms full of bottles and lemons, going to some hospital, he said, to give the boys a good time. He was sweating finely; his collar and shirt were thrown open, showing his great hairy throat and breast. I asked him about Brown and Thoreau some time ago: 'Fine fellows, fine fellows!' he said. That was all. He never gives a literary opinion of any one, but always speaks of him in a personal sense. In fact, he is very reticent on book matters. He knew Thoreau and liked him much. I shall not forget that book of the Hermit's which he promised me.

'Florence Percy' and the War now fill Allen's letters, but early in July a few sentences about Whitman creep in:

Walt and I quaffed beer today from great goblets that would become the halls of Walhalla. Walt is much interested in you, and I sketched your history some to him. He would like to know you. He is a good fellow, and although over fifty, belongs to the present generation. He was much interested in our trip to the Beaverkill which I detailed to him.

Allen was mistaken as to Whitman's age, then but forty-four. Later came this tantalizing glimpse of a comradeship Burroughs longed to share:

While Walt and I were beering it the other evening, I read some of your letters to him and he was much interested. He sends his compliments and says if you ever come anywhere near him you must find him out and give him a call.

In August, when Allen, Benton, and Burroughs camped out together in the Adirondacks, the two now avid readers of the 'Leaves' plied Allen with questions about the poet. Everything they learned augmented their desire to come face to face with him. On returning to Washington in September, Allen sent on this account of Whitman:

Walt was in to see me two or three times, but I was busy and could not talk much. But last night after closing up the store, as I was meandering down the Avenue toward my lodgings, about half past nine, what should I see in the dimness but the picturesque form of my friend the poet?... He grasped my hand with a cordial, 'How are you, my boy?' He, good man, was just returning from some hospital where he had been doing the sort of good which a kind heart and noble soul can do, performing those sweet, balmy ministrations which win the sinking spirit from the very borders of the Dark Realm — his large active sympathy reaching down to the home-sick soul shivering within a shattered body, and lifting it into light and warmth and love.

Late in October, unable longer to resist the call, Burroughs suddenly abandoned school-teaching and went to Washington, avowedly to get nearer the War, and nearer Whitman. Evidently but a few days passed before the memorable meeting took place, for on November 8 he wrote his wife, 'I have seen Walt and think him glorious.'

Burroughs was six and twenty, and Whitman forty-four, when they met. For several previous evenings the younger man had hung around, expectant, in the army supply store of Allen, Clapp and Company, hoping for Whitman to stroll in. At last, one evening on entering the store, he spied the poet in the rear leaning back in a big canvas lounging-chair.

'Walt,' said Allen briskly, 'here's the young man from the country I told you about.'

As the young man from the country shyly approached, in a state of seething emotion which made him blush and stammer, he felt his fingers enveloped in the large soft hand extended to him, the poet at the same time bending upon him 'a look of infinite good nature.' What Burroughs thought of Whitman at that first meeting may be gleaned from his notebook excerpts and his letters to Benton; what Whitman thought of him is hinted in his comment to Allen — 'His face is like a field of wheat.' Even those who knew that face only in its later years, with its snowy hair and beard, its hue of health, its perennially young eyes, and its quick reflections of changing moods, can appreciate the apt comparison of the youthful face to a field of wheat. It was ever a face of vigor and promise, with flowing lines, and a mobile response to the slightest emotional breeze.

The poet was soon calling Burroughs 'Jack,' and 'Jack,' calling him 'Walt.' Thus began the tie, the two clinging together throughout the years.

In his notebooks of that period Burroughs wrote that the first reading of the 'Leaves' had been as if some one had dumped South Africa at his door, but that amid the elephantean trampling upon all the amenities and proprieties of literature, the lusty exulting in life and health, the appalling egotism, he had also found sanity and wisdom, solemnity and grandeur, and a sublime faith in man — all of which had made him long to get nearer the man and take his weight and measure. He then describes the poet's large benevolent look, his neat appearance, the shaggy appearance of the free open throat, his look of infinite good nature and contentment, and the curious blending of youth and age in his expression; also the transparent skin which allows the summery, motherly nature to shine through, and the rich, mellow voice, indicative of deep human sympathies and affinities, and of the finest blood and breeding. Summing up he adds: 'A gentle, strong, cultivated soul.' This early appraisal will be compared with interest with a later description in 'Whitman: A Study' (pages 52–53).

Although after that first meeting, Whitman and Burroughs met several times in Allen's store, it was not till they encountered each other along a footpath under the trees, of a Sunday afternoon, that they really found each other. Whitman was on his way to an army hospital with haversack slung over his shoulders, that and his pockets stuffed with gifts for the soldiers. Burroughs eagerly accepted the invitation to accompany him. In years to come he spoke of the effect of that first hospital visit. Unused as he was to witnessing suffering, it was almost more than he could bear. Then, and on many a subsequent day, he gained a realization of the loving kindness of the man, as he watched him moving among the maimed, the low-spirited, and the dying, cheering and invigorating by gifts and timely services and all-embracing sympathy.

In those early weeks in Washington, when, poor and forlorn, Burroughs was looking for work, eating his bread with tears, he wrote his wife of his various makeshifts to keep down expenses — sleeping on an army cot in Allen's store, washing out his socks and handkerchiefs, dining off a piece of pie — none of which seemed a hardship, since he could be near Whitman:

... I go up to the Capitol often and walk through its marble halls and down its long colonnades, and listen to the senators and representatives, or saunter with glorious old Walt and talk of the soul and immortality.

JOHN BURROUGHS
In the late Washington period
From a photograph by P. B. Marvin

The Washington of those days, he said, was like a country village, the population only about sixty thousand. Many of the streets were unpaved, the mud and dust frightful:

Ah! the glamor of those days! Walt and O'Connor, Allen, and Eldridge, Parnell, Dr. Baker, Piatt, and Aaron Johns — of all those friends, only Aaron and I are left.

The Dome of the Capitol — we could see it from all points of the landscape, rising above the hills like a cloud. I used to walk over on the old Marlboro road, off beyond Georgetown, and on beyond to Cabin Johns. I've seen whirlwinds there carry up a cloud of dust that blotted out the Capitol.

From my window in the Treasury Building I used to see Lincoln stepping over the piles of lumber with his long, lank legs. When he wanted to see Seward he took that way to avoid the crowd. I saw him often, but never spoke to him but once, and then briefly — at a reception at the White House. I passed along in line with hundreds of others. When my turn came I lingered a little, but was pulled along — I can feel yet the pull of his great hand as he drew me along past him to make room for those coming after. I used to see John Pierpont, the poet, often in the corridors. He was very old then — a clerk in the Treasury.

Burroughs spoke often of those walks and talks with Whitman, and of the picture Whitman made coming leisurely down the Avenue, feeding his hunger for faces — 'lover of populous pavements' that he was. He could detect, many blocks away, the large, gray-clad figure with broad-brimmed hat looming above the crowd. The tears would well up in his eyes when speaking of that scene, in the spring of '64, when, standing by Whitman's side at the corner of Newspaper Row, opposite Willard's Hotel, he watched Burnside's army flow through the streets all day long on its way to the Battle of the Wilderness. Every little while a soldier in the ranks, recognizing Walt, would wave to him. Sometimes one would break away, step to the curb, greet Walt with a kiss and draw him along a few steps, after which Walt would drop back and rejoin Burroughs, still following the boys yearningly with his eyes.

The following account of Whitman during the Civil War was written in 1911, by John James Piatt in response to a request for his recollections of Whitman and O'Connor. It is transcribed here through the courtesy of its recipient:

WHITMAN IN WAR TIME, BY JOHN JAMES PIATT

To Charles N. Elliot, Ketchikan, Alaska

MY DEAR MR. ELLIOT:

I first met Walt Whitman on New Year's Day, 1863 — the day on which President Lincoln's Proclamation freeing the slaves was issued, and the day on which Whitman himself had first arrived in Washington. We had chanced to cross the street in front of Willard's Hotel when we encountered William D. O'Connor, then a friend of two years' standing, accompanied by a large, gray-haired, gray-bearded man, dressed rather shabbily, in what might be called 'country clothes.' They had come from the direction of the White House, whither we ourselves were going to attend the annual levee of the President.... He at once introduced his companion to us. I did not need to be told who Whitman was. For some years I had known of him through reviews of his 'Leaves of Grass.'... Though little was said, our greeting was cordial, and, on the whole, I was pleased at meeting him.

Afterward, during that year and the following one,... I occasionally met him at the house of O'Connor and that of our common friend Arnold B. Johnson, who was then the private secretary of Charles Sumner.

On one occasion, perhaps in the spring of 1864, I happened to visit O'Connor's house, where I found Whitman helping Mrs. O'Connor hang window shades, an exasperating service at which he showed unusual good humor. This was at the time when Whitman was making his memorable visits to the hospitals at Washington previous to his service in the Interior Department, whence he was dismissed by Secretary Harlan.

Afterwards, I occasionally met him when he was going home on the street-cars at night and had some talk with him; also, once or twice, I encountered him walking through the public grounds north of the White House among the moonlighted trees, of whose beauty he spoke.

Early in the spring of 1864... I had a long and serious attack of typhoid fever. O'Connor at this time assisted in nursing me,... sometimes sitting up at night with me. Whitman also offered to help nurse me, which offer I have always gratefully remembered.

After Whitman's dismissal from the clerkship which he held in the Interior Department, O'Connor read to me from the manuscript of his pamphlet called 'The Good Gray Poet,' in which he defended Whitman from the attack made on him by Secretary Harlan. When it was published, I reviewed it, sympathetically, in a letter contributed to a Columbus newspaper, 'The Ohio State Journal.' My review was warmly appreciated by Whitman. O'Connor put this review away in his scrap book, and told me, the last time I saw him before we went to Europe, that he still kept it, and I remember to have heard Whitman himself say, as he was walking out of O'Connor's rooms at the Light-House Board with a copy of the paper containing it in his hand, that it was the best thing he had yet received on the subject.

John Burroughs, in his little book called 'Walt Whitman as Poet and Person,' included one or two paragraphs from my article, particularly one describing Whitman's personal appearance as he walked on the Avenue in Washington.[1]

Thenceforward, I used to meet Whitman when he was walking on the Avenue, and at the band concerts at the White House on Saturday afternoons....

Our relations were always friendly, though he never regarded me as one of his disciples, and, after his death, Mr. Burroughs told me in a letter that he always spoke of me and mine in a friendly way.

Before Whitman's arrival in Washington, in 1863, E. C. Stedman (he and I were rooming together at the time) used often to talk of Whitman's work, commending especially letters of his which had appeared in the newspapers, referring more or less to the war and his own Hospital experiences. These he praised as good strong prose, but showed comparatively small appreciation of Walt's so-called poetry.

As to the influence of Walt Whitman on the younger generation of writers, it has, on the whole, certainly been bad, especially upon a certain class of women who admire and do not hesitate to 'gush' over him.

Personally Whitman had some fine manly qualities, and his Hospital record is a monument to his memory that deserves to endure.

To recur to O'Connor. He was on friendly terms with Stedman and myself and he sometimes visited our rooms and discussed with us Whitman's claims as a poet. I first met O'Connor in the company of Mr. William D. Howells, who was staying with us while receiving his instructions as consul to Venice. Mr. Howells had met O'Connor (in the city) who came to visit him at our house, and Howells then introduced me to him. Afterwards I often called on O'Connor at his office at the Light-House Board, and our acquaintance and friendship continued through his lifetime.

O'Connor was considered a remarkably handsome man, and to strikingly resemble the Chandos portrait of Shakespeare....

I happen to recall that one morning I was calling on O'Connor when he told me that Hawthorne had been in to see him and was going down stairs. He asked me if I had met him.

I did not intend to say anything more of Whitman, but I remember that I used to meet him at the home of my friend Mr. E. M. Allen (where he sometimes came to tea), who made a medallion portrait of him, of which he gave me a copy. Whitman was then revising his 'Drum Taps,' referring to Lincoln and the war.

December, 1911   J. J. PIATT

Piatt's 'we' doubtless refers to himself and wife, Sarah M. B. Piatt. Both were versifiers of some vogue in their day. He was a

[1] See *Poet and Person*, pp. 84, 85. J. S. Redfield, New York, 1867, 1871.

journalist, and librarian of the House of Representatives, later consul at Cork. As to Piatt's comment that Whitman was shabbily dressed, he undoubtedly was. He had left home suddenly for the South a few months before, to seek a wounded brother, had but little money on leaving, and had been robbed on the way of that little by a pickpocket. Tarrying in Washington after finding his brother, he began his ministry to the boys in the hospitals, eking out the wherewithal for his support — helped out by the generous O'Connors — by writing for the newspapers until, becoming depressed and homesick, he was, through O'Connor's offices, given a free pass North for a brief stay. John Hay had secured the pass. Hay remained a staunch friend of the poet through life, and a keen appreciator of his poems.

I am reasonably sure that in his paragraph about the Allens, Piatt's memory played him false. He was seventy-six when he wrote the reminiscence. He probably met Whitman often in Allen's store, but certainly never in his home: Allen and Elizabeth Akers were married from the home of Burroughs, October, 1866, leaving Washington shortly after to live in Richmond, Virginia. Furthermore, as will be seen later, Elizabeth Akers held a fixed prejudice against Whitman. She tried to discourage Allen's intimacy with him before their marriage, and never became friendly thereafter. She surely never offered him a cup of tea in her own home. I think Piatt is also mistaken about Allen having made a medallion of Whitman. Allen was not an artist, although in young manhood he had shown some facility in drawing, as well as in versifying.

In a letter which Burroughs wrote Benton in 1865, he spoke of Piatt as 'unpretending and modest... though his soul is not robust enough.... He has not much zeal for our own favorites, and seems to be no hero-worshipper, which is not good in a young man.'

To Charles W. Eldridge, formerly of the Boston publishing firm, Thayer and Eldridge, in a letter dated November 17, 1863, Whitman shows prescience as to his own future. 'William and Nellie,' of whom he writes, are the O'Connors, who, with Eldridge, were among his earliest friends at the Capital. The letter, only a part of which is quoted here, was given by Eldridge to John Burroughs:

I feel to devote myself more to the work of my life, which is making poems. I must bring out 'Drum Taps.' I *must* be continually bringing out poems — now is the heyday — I shall range along the high plateau of my life and capacity for a few years now, and then swiftly descend. The life here in the cities, and the objects &c of most, seem to me very flippant and shallow since I returned this time....

The great recompense of my journey here is to see my mother so well and so bravely sailing on amid many troubles and discouragements like a noble old ship — My brother Andrew is bound for another world — he is here the greater part of the time.

Charley, I think sometimes to be a woman is greater than to be a man — is more eligible to greatness, not the ostensible article, but the real one. Dear Comrade, I send you my love, and to William and Nellie, and remember me to Major.

'Major' doubtless refers to Major Hapgood, Paymaster, in whose office Whitman was given a desk. Eldridge was a clerk there at the time.

On returning to Washington, Whitman resumed his volunteer nursing. The friendship between him and Burroughs, interrupted by his visit North, progressed by leaps and bounds. By the nineteenth of December the intimacy had reached the point described by Burroughs in a letter to Benton:

I have been much with Walt. Have even slept with him. I love him very much. The more I see and talk with him, the greater he becomes to me. He is as vast as the earth, and as loving and noble. He is much handsomer than his picture represents him, goes well-dressed, and there is nothing *outish* in his appearance, except, it may be, his open throat. He walks very leisurely, rather saunters, and looks straight forward, not down at his feet. He does not talk readily, but his conversation is very rich and suggestive. He regards Emerson as one of the great, eternal men, and thinks there is not another living, nor has lived for the last two or three centuries.

I am convinced that Walt is as great as Emerson, though after a different type. Walt has all types of men in him, there is not one left out. I must write you all about him, but cannot now. If I get settled here I want to give an account of him in the 'Commonwealth.' If you can get a 'New York Times' of date October 4, 1863, you will find a letter of his which is one of the finest pieces of writing I have ever seen. It is just like Walt.

Once in reply to my inquiry as to what this newspaper letter was about, Burroughs said he thought it described the unfinished Capitol — the Dome. Years later, among the mementoes he had saved of the Washington period, I found, in mice-nibbled copies of the

'New York Times' for February 26, August 16, and October 4 (1863), these very Whitman letters. Below is an excerpt from one describing the melancholy part played in the street panoramas of Washington by the ambulances:

You mark the forms huddled on the bottom of the wagons; you mark yellow and emaciated faces. Some are supporting others. I constantly see instances of tenderness in this way from the wounded to those worse wounded.

From the 'Times' of October 4 is here transcribed a paragraph or two of the letter so much admired by Burroughs. Whitman, after having written of the architects putting the Genius of America away up there on the top of the Dome of the Capitol, thus comments about the Dome:

All the great effects of the Capitol reside in it. The effects of the Capitol are worth study, frequent and varied; I find they grow upon one. I shall always identify Washington with that huge and delicate towering bulge of pure white, when it emerges calm and lofty from the hill, out of a dense mass of trees. There is no place in the city, or for miles and miles off, or down or up the river, but what you see this tiara-like dome quietly rising out of the foliage. (One of the effects of first-class architecture is its serenity, its *aplomb*.)

A vast egg-shell, built of iron and glass, this dome — a beauteous bubble, caught and put in permanent form. I say a beauty and a genuine success. I have to say the same, upon the whole (after some qualms, maybe) with respect to the entire edifice....

In connection with what the Dome meant to Whitman in the old days, let me quote a passage from one of Burroughs's letters written to me from Washington, nearly half a century later:

The one thing I see here as I go about that looks like an old friend, almost like the face of a member of my own family, is the Dome of the Capitol. This alone is unchanged. It looks like Walt. It suggests my native hills. It has figured in my dreams since I left Washington. Once I dreamed of it as covered with farms and homes where some of my people lived. How many times I have seen it rising over the hills as I have tramped over the surrounding country, from all points of the compass; it has been the one part of the city that I have seldom lost sight of.

During those years the Comrades met chiefly in Allen's store of an evening; at Harvey's Restaurant for an occasional luncheon, where, perched on high stools, they held oyster-eating orgies; along

Rock Creek and Piney Branch where they sauntered; in the home of the O'Connors for Sunday suppers and conversations; and in the Burroughs home for Sunday breakfasts. Sometimes Burroughs would call at Whitman's bare little room in Four and One-Half Street, where the poet lived frugally mostly on bread and tea, that he might spend all he could scrape together for his 'maimed darlings,' whose sufferings wrung his great heart.

In Burroughs's notebooks of those early Washington years are many brief jottings about Whitman, which afford fleeting glimpses of the poet, for example: 'There is something indescribable in his look, in his eye, as in that of the mother of many children.'[1] And, more significant still:

Notwithstanding the beauty and expressiveness of his eyes, I occasionally see something in them as he bends them upon me, that almost makes me draw back. I cannot explain it — whether it is more, or less, than human. It is as if the Earth looked at me — dumb, yearning, relentless, immodest, unhuman. If the impersonal elements and forces were concentrated in an eye, that would be it. It is not piercing, but absorbing and devouring — the pupil expanded, the lid slightly drooping, and the eye set and fixed.[2]

This reminds me of an expression of Emerson's, quoted by Conway to O'Connor (1866) in a letter in the Perry Whitman Collection, in which Emerson spoke of Whitman's 'terrible eyes.' Burroughs said O'Connor described the unique look as 'draining.' To Burroughs it was as if the soul drew things to itself through sympathy and personal, rather than intellectual, force.

The following jotting from the notebook was probably after one of Whitman's Sunday breakfasts in the Burroughs home:

One delicate test by which he knew he had eaten too much of my wife's good victuals was that he did not spring (with a peculiar motion of the hand) and respond buoyantly to such a scene as was before us — as we came down back of the Capitol.

Apropos of nothing, this bit is salvaged, perhaps from one of their rambles:

Walt says he is awed and overwhelmed by the thought of the infinite number of identities — in the earth and air and waters, yet no confusion or

[1] See Furness: *Walt Whitman's Workshop*, p. 222. Cambridge, 1928.
[2] Compare this with what he wrote thirty years later in *Whitman: A Study*, p. 62.

collision, or running foul of one another, and no sign of Nature exhausting herself.

And this, perhaps after one of his vigils with a dying soldier:

Death, he says, is a great mystery and fills him with awe. In its presence he is dumb; he walks up and down the room and sees the flame of life hover and flicker, and words are a profanity. . . .

This record of one of their rambles was fortunately preserved by Burroughs:

Sauntering with him one day along by the Capitol, we met a soldier — dirty, travel-stained and ragged, with a very friendless, care-worn expression — not a loiterer, but one evidently bent on some long journey, whom Walt kindly accosted. I shall never forget how the soldier altered the tone in which he was about answering him, as he looked Walt in the face.

He had evidently been spoken to often, but not in this fashion, and the sympathy and deep, yearning love that spoke in this man's voice, and beamed in his face, completely disarmed him. And in a blushing, bashful way he answered Walt's questions. I stood a little apart and thought I had never seen anything so human and good. The soldier looked down at his boots and began to be ashamed of his appearance, since here was some one who took an interest in him. He was a Western boy and there was some curious history connected with his story and appearance.

Walt, in his tender, curious way, asked him if he should not help him a little — not enough to hurt him, but enough to get him a bit of food, for he looked hungry. The soldier did not know how to meet this charge and came near breaking down outright; and as Walt placed some small notes [1] in his hand and turned away, he found his tongue to say, in that awkward, constrained way, that he hoped he would have good health and keep well. I saw how deeply he responded to this act of kindness, and how poorly his words expressed what he felt.

That youth will not forget, as long as he lives, the great kind man that accosted him under the walls of the Capitol, and spoke the first words of human sympathy and tenderness, perhaps, he had heard since his mother bid him farewell.

Walt said he had probably been guilty of some misdemeanor, perhaps was a deserter, or a returning rebel. But I saw that this incident would do more to strengthen and encourage him, and help restore his lost manhood, if so it was, than all the sermons and homilies and tracts that have ever been preached or printed.

In early January, 1864, by which time Burroughs had obtained his appointment in the Treasury Department (which he held till

---

[1] The fractional currency — denominations of ten, twenty-five, and fifty cents — then in use.

resigning ten years later), he wrote cheerfully to his friend Benton of his growing friendship with Whitman, having that day spent two or three hours with him. Still later in the month he wrote:

When I called on Walt this morning I found him *en dishabille*, reading 'Walden.' 'My impression of the book last night,' he said, 'was rather poor; I thought it puerile. But this morning, after I had sipped my coffee, I found it more satisfying. I opened near the end and found it so good that I turned back and commenced again.'

He thinks Thoreau's translations from Anacreon, in the 'Week' far the best he ever saw; so good that he tore the leaves out that contained them, and put them among his choice tid-bits. He thinks Thoreau a very sweet, pure soul, but by no means a number one man, as Emerson is. He was too timid and afraid of the world; did men and things injustice; was too exclusive; and not enough of a cosmopolitan.

The more I see of Walt, the more I like him.... He is by far the wisest man I have ever met. There is nothing more to be said after he gives his views. It is as if Nature herself had spoken. And so kind, sympathetic, charitable, humane, tolerant a man I did not suppose was possible. He loves everything and everybody. I saw a soldier the other day stop on the street and kiss him. He kisses me as if I were a girl. He appreciates everybody, and no soul will get fuller justice in the next world than it gets at his hands here.

I related to him our Adirondack trip, the deer-shooting, etc., which so pleased him that he said seriously he should make a 'leaf of grass' about it. I related to him other country experiences which he relished hugely. In the spring he wants to go out to my home with me to make sugar, and get a taste of that kind of life.... He also wants to go up to the Adirondacks and spend a season at the Upper Iron Works. He says a trip to Europe would be nothing compared to it.

He bathed today while I was there — such a handsome body, and such delicate, rosy flesh I never saw before. I told him he looked good enough to eat, which, he said, he should consider a poor recommendation if he were among the cannibals.

I have often told him of you, but without exciting any remark from him till the other day, without any provocation, he commenced to ask me about you, how you lived, and if you were 'a good fellow' (the highest praise he ever bestows upon a man). I told him what you had written. He said he did not want to hear about your poetry, but about you — what your type and temper and hair were, etc. So I fell to portraying you — a pleasant task — and Walt was much interested, and for all I know may immortalize you in a 'leaf of grass.'...

About this time Burroughs began to enlist the interest of several friends in Whitman's lecture projects, having become enthusiastic from listening to the poet's plans about them. He writes to Benton in mid-January:

> Walt has agreed to lecture here in Washington if I will take the matter in hand and arrange things, which I am going to do somewhere about the 20th or 25th. If we succeed here, he proposes going North to New York, Brooklyn, Boston, etc.
>
> Now if it is a success here, why cannot you have him come up there somewhere, say to Poughkeepsie, if at no nearer place, and then go with him to Newburgh, making the thing pay expenses? Write me just what you feel about it. I am sure he will lecture magnificently, and eclipse every one in the field. Everybody will love him, and I predict a great success.

Although both Myron Benton and his cousin Joel, a minor poet and reviewer, also interested themselves, the lecture project did not then materialize. This ambition of Whitman's

To inflate the chest, to roll the thunder of the voice out from the ribs and throat,

·   ·   ·   ·   ·   ·   ·   ·   ·   ·   ·   ·   ·   ·   ·   ·

To lead America . . . with a great tongue,

which showed itself so early in the habit of reading aloud, and 'spouting' on the seashore, has been emphasized by Mr. Furness as probably the origin of the fluent, orotund style of Whitman's poetry.[1] Burroughs's later attempts to further the lecturing are shown on pages 74–76.

Writing to Benton on March 13, Burroughs says:

> Walt is as glorious as ever and, as usual, looks like a god. He expects to bring out his 'Drum Taps' pretty soon. He discoursed with me an hour the other day on his plans and purposes. He anticipates a pecuniary success with his book. By and by he expects to make himself felt lecturing. He is quite ambitious. Allen calls him the Old Goat. I tell him I wish I was an Old Goat.

By another month the zealous disciple is getting critical of the friends who fail to accept Whitman in his own whole-hearted way. Of a new friend, Charles D. Akers, he writes Benton:

> Akers has got a clerkship in the War Department. I like him much. He is somewhat after our own hearts. . . . He has good sense and good taste, though he is quite overpowered by the old masters, and lacks faith in the

[1] Furness: *Walt Whitman's Workshop*, pp. 27–32, 196–98.

present and the possibilities of today. Walt's continental and sidereal proportions appear quite small to him! Allen has become childish in his denunciation of Whitman, and is falling hugely in my estimation. He is too weak. That feathered edge of his can stand nothing. I hope he will not turn out to be capable of no other edge but a feathered, artificial one....

Walt and I meet two or three times a week over a mug of ale or a peck of oysters. Often his talk is so rich and suggestive that he sets every feeling and faculty in me on the alert.

During the summer of 1864 the intense strain under which Whitman had been in his ministry to the soldiers began to tell on him. In June, while Burroughs was away in the Catskills, Whitman experienced frequent attacks of deathly faintness which alarmed his friends who, until then, had seen him only in superb health. He went North to recuperate. While in Brooklyn, he received the following letter from Burroughs, written from the Treasury Department, August 2:

DEAR WALT,

I am disconsolate at your long stay. What has become of you? On returning, the 7th of July, I found you had gone home sick. You have no business to be sick, so I expect you are well. I was so unlucky as to be sick all the time I was home — and most of the time since I came back. I am quite well now, however....

Benton and I looked for you at Leedsville, as I wrote you to come. If you have leisure now you would enjoy hugely a visit up there.

I hope you are printing 'Drum Taps,' and that this universal drought does not reach your 'grass.' But make haste and come back. The heat is delicious. I have a constant bath in my own perspiration.

I was out at the front during the siege of Washington and lay in the rifle pits with the soldiers. I got quite a taste of war and learned the song of those modern minstrels — the minie bullets — by heart.

A line from you would be prized.

Truly yours

JOHN BURROUGHS

From Brooklyn, October 8, 1864, Whitman writes to Eldridge as follows:

... I am perhaps not so unconscionably hearty as before my sickness. We are deprest in spirits here about my brother George — if not killed, he is a prisoner — he was in the engagement of Sept. 30 — on the extreme left —

My book is not yet being printed. I still wish to stereotype it myself. I could easily still put it in the hands of a proper publisher then and make better terms with him.

If you write to William I wish you to enclose him this letter — I wish him to receive again my faithful friendship — while health and sense remain I cannot forget what he has been to me. I love him dearly —

... The political meetings in New York and Brooklyn immense. I go to them as to shows — fireworks, cannon, clusters of gas lights, countless torches, banners and mottoes. 15, 20, 50,000 people — Per contra I occasionally go riding off in the country, in quiet lanes, or a sail on the water, and many times to... Coney Island.

All the signs are that Grant is going to strike farther, perhaps risk all. One feels solemn when one sees what depends. The military success though first class of war, is the least that depends.

Good by, dearest comrade....

WALT

The spring of 1865 found John Burroughs and his wife keeping house on Capitol Hill in a quaint red-brick house which stood where the Senate Offices now stand. There, on an acre of ground, after office hours, the Treasury clerk hoed his potatoes, looked after his chickens, and turned Chloe, the cow, out to grass on the common near the Capitol, for in those days cows had the freedom of the city, goats cropped rosebushes through fence pickets, and pigs dreamed dreams under many a garden fence. Writing Benton of their venture in housekeeping, Burroughs urged him to come on for Lincoln's Inauguration:

We have a spare bed and would be delighted to have you come. Walt is here, Spring is here, the Bluebird and Robin are here. The Spirit says Come, the flesh says Come, Wife says Come, 'Abe' says Come, *so Come!*

Charles E. Benton, a brother of Myron, and a young officer in Sherman's army, visited Burroughs that summer. In the evening Whitman dropped in. Writing me of that visit more than half a century later, and recalling his own bashfulness in the presence of those literary men, Mr. Benton told of his surprise to find the author of the 'much-berated Whitman stuff' such a 'kindly and courteous old gentleman.'

It was at this period that Whitman began breakfasting on Sunday with Burroughs.

Walt was usually late for breakfast [said his host], and Ursula, who was as punctual as the clock, would get in a pucker. The coffee would boil, the griddle would smoke, and car after car would go jingling by, but no Walt. The situation at times verged on the tragic. But at last a car would stop, and Walt would roll off it and saunter up to the door — so cheery, and so unaware of the annoyance he had caused, that we soon forgot our ill-humor. He always said Ursula's pancakes and coffee couldn't be beat.

Although Mrs. Burroughs disapproved of poets and 'scribblers' in general, and of Whitman in particular (chiefly for his unpunctuality), she obligingly made his shirts. She was the only one, he said, who would make them loose enough to be comfortable. And she could sometimes be wheedled into making pies and doughnuts for his soldier boys. Later on, after his first stroke of paralysis, she carried him delicacies, darned his socks, and took him for an occasional drive.

Both during and after the Civil War, Burroughs sometimes accompanied Whitman to the army hospitals. The poet's pockets and knapsack would bulge with gifts for the boys. 'Jack' would look on, deeply moved, while 'Walt' walked the wards tossing to the sick boys a flower, an orange, tobacco, a newspaper — the special need of each determining the gift — and tossing also cheer and comfort as he passed. Recalling those scenes in later years, Burroughs said: 'He brought father and mother to them, and the tonic and cheering atmosphere of simple, affectionate home life.' He described Whitman's manner in the wards as 'quiet and easy, as though he had just happened in. He would wave to one, "Howdy" to another, toss some little gift here and there, and when a soldier looked particularly eager, would stop and chat with him.'

After their Sunday breakfasts, the friends would have a long confab on 'the cataract of marble steps of the Capitol.' In their rambles past the White House, Walt would bring forth from its hiding-place in an old fence-post a smooth round stone which he would toss from hand to hand as they went on, tucking it away in its niche on the return walk, there to remain till they came that way again. 'What wouldn't I give for that stone now!' Burroughs used to say, then sigh regretfully at having kept so few records of those memorable walks.

Doubtless the hue and cry raised against Whitman in that eventful year had its effect in producing the scornful attitude which Mrs. Burroughs showed in later years when speaking of Whitman. For

Mr. Julian Burroughs, in his boyhood recollections of his father, describes the asperity with which Mrs. Burroughs was wont to name 'Walt Whitman, poet and *person*,' with disdainful emphasis upon the 'person.' Yet, besides her many kindnesses to the poet in the Washington years, she welcomed him later to 'Riverby,' though doubtless was still tried by his tardiness to breakfast. The fact is, as Burroughs often pointed out, women who disapproved of Whitman as poet, found their disapproval vanish in his presence. Elizabeth Akers was a case in point. Being a writer of correct, rhythmical verse, she looked with disfavor upon Whitman's 'uncouth lines.' And, too, misled by the candor of his poems, like many others, judged him loose in life and morals. In telling of her enforced meeting with Whitman, Burroughs said:

It pleased me hugely, yet I felt awkward, as I always do, at another's discomfiture. She had repeatedly refused to meet Walt, but one day when calling at our house, she came tripping down the stairs to meet me, and there was Walt, too! I laugh whenever I think of her look of dismay when she saw him. Walt saw it, too, but appeared not to notice it. He laughed about it afterwards. Of course she couldn't help liking him — no one could — and soon surrendered to his personality, though she wasn't big enough to accept his poetry.

Shortly after this encounter, when Burroughs was on vacation in the Catskills, Mrs. Akers wrote him:

I was very agreeably disappointed in Whitman. But for the fact that I detest his avowed principles, and that his course of life has been such as I could never endorse, I admit that I should be more than ordinarily pleased with him. His photographs are base slanders. He looks a thousand times better than any of those pictures. I can see how I might feel a great interest in him, and much pleasure in his speech and presence, but for his free-and-easy notions regarding women. I never can pardon him those. I couldn't forgive them in a man whom I loved dearly else. And I suppose my prejudices make very little difference to Walt. He has the view now that I am an extremely flighty and flirty and flippant person. Let him keep it.

This lady never came to a friendly footing with Whitman, and in later years, after sorrow, reverses, and thwarted ambition had embittered her, wrote almost venomously about him, repeating the unwarranted impressions held during all the years. How different her opinion of Whitman's attitude toward women from that of

Harriet Prescott Spofford! I recall once seeing a letter of O'Connor's in which he wrote that 'Dick Spofford' said his wife insisted Whitman was the only poet who had ever done complete justice to women.

Whitman's compelling charm is again seen in the account which William Sloane Kennedy gives of the first meeting of his wife and the poet.[1] She had not been especially drawn to him from his work, but on seeing him burst into tears — 'the majestic old man, chair-bound, sunny-hearted... radiating magnetism, kindness and power.' To a friend later she wrote, 'I felt as if I were in the presence of a god.'

Something of Whitman's reverence for women may be gleaned from his friendly letters to and about them, and from the fine types of women that he admired. His letters to Mrs. O'Connor always breathe tender consideration and *camaraderie*. The most of his letters in the Perry Whitman Collection are undated, but from some in the eighteen-seventies to Mrs. O'Connor are found such expressions as these:

It does not surprise me that Mrs. H—— meets emergencies, and so splendidly expands to greater womanly beauty and development — I always thought it in her to do so.

Of Miss G. H.:

She is a good, tender girl — true as steel.

Again:

I went over to Philadelphia yesterday and had a nice, good, I may almost say, *happy* afternoon with dear Mrs. Lesley, Kate Hillard, and the two Miss Lesleys, daughters — us four only, no men critters but me — I was there some four hours, filled with animated talk.... Mrs. Lesley a fine, gentle, sweet-voiced handsome black-eyed New England woman....

He comments further on the jolly, hearty Kate Hillard, and her sprightly conversation and fine mind. Writing of his brother's household, he says:

We have a fine old Irish woman (an old maid, not so very old, either) who cooks nicely and runs the domestic machinery for George, Eddy and self. She little knows how much good she does me with her great splendid coarse face and great figure, and warm-blooded and simple ways.

[1] Kennedy. *The Fight of a Book for the World.* Stonecroft Press, 1926 (in the Dedication).

In a mid-September letter to Benton, Burroughs gives further glimpses of his growing comradeship with the poet. He speaks of a talk with him on the recently published Thoreau 'Letters':[1]

His letters on Walt are capital.... Walt says Emerson told him that Thoreau was forever talking about the 'great democrat.' Walt's book will be out in a week or two. He comes up to see me two or three times a week. If I were a Boswell I could make the best biography ever written....

He is deeply interested in what I tell him of the Hermit Thrush, and says he has used largely the information I have given him in one of his principal poems.[2]

I have just finished my case of birds and it is the admired of all admirers. Walt says it is quite a poem....*

[1] Thoreau's *Letters to Various Persons.* Boston, 1865.
[2] The requiem on Lincoln, 'When Lilacs Last in the Dooryard Bloomed.'

II

'THE GOOD GRAY POET' VINDICATED

(1865–1866)

Liberty is to be subserv'd whatever occurs;
There is nothing that is quelled by one or two failures,...
Or the show of the tushes of power...
What we believe in waits latent forever through all the continents
... sits in calmness and light, is positive and composed,
Knows no discouragement,
Waiting patiently, waiting its time.

WHITMAN

What place is besieged, and vainly tries to raise the siege?
Lo, I send to that place a commander, swift, brave, immortal,
And with him horse and foot, and parks of artillery,
And artillery-men, the deadliest that ever fired guns.

WHITMAN

AS is known to the point of satiety to Whitman students, the poet was removed from his post in the Department of the Interior on June 10, 1865, by James Harlan, the Secretary of that Department, because Harlan deemed 'Leaves of Grass' an immoral book. Important side-lights are thrown upon this historic episode by the documents here transcribed, the most of which have not before been printed. The following letter from James Harlan to Dewitt Miller, dated July 18, 1894, from Mount Pleasant, Iowa, was published in Harlan's biography in 1913, by the Iowa State Historical Society. It is reprinted here in order to allow the chief witness to speak for himself.

DEAR SIR: —
I am in receipt of your letter of the 14th inst. requesting me to give you the reasons for the removal of Mr. Walt Whitman, in 1865, from a Clerkship in the office of the Commissioner of Indian Affairs, and the Department of the Interior.
You must pardon me for suggesting that it has not been usual for the heads of Departments of the National Government to assign to the public — nor to individuals for public use — their reasons for such official action. And that if they should so far forget the proprieties as to do so, such thoughtlessness would in many cases injure the reputation of the persons thus dropped from the public service, without being beneficial to any one.

But in this case — impelled by a desire to gratify your wishes — I think I may so far depart from a commendable usage as to say generally that when I entered the Department of the Interior as its Chief, I found on its payrolls a considerable number of useless incumbents who were seldom at their respective desks. Some of them were simply supernumerary, and some of them were worthless.

Deeming it my duty to administer the business of the Department economically as well as efficiently, I endeavored, with the aid of the heads of bureaus, to weed out the needless and worthless material.

Under this order, Mr. Walt Whitman, and a considerable number of others were, from time to time, removed, as the same were reported to me by their respective chiefs, for my action in the premises.

It would not be possible for me now, after the lapse of about twenty-nine years, to recall in detail the reasons reported to me by their respective heads of Bureaus, for their discontinuance in the public service, even if it were desirable and proper to recite them after many of them like Whitman have passed to the other side. It is, therefore, deemed needful only to say in relation to his removal, that his Chief — Hon. W. P. Dole, Commissioner of Indian Affairs, who was officially answerable to me for the work of his Bureau — recommended it, *on the ground that his services were not needed.* And no other reason was ever assigned by my authority.

You are kind enough to tell me that the reasons given for his dismissal by his friends are favorable to him and unfavorable to me.

I need only say on that point, that, according to my recollection, the same could be said truthfully of every one so removed by me during my incumbency of the office of Secretary. The least worthy usually raised the greatest clamor; making it clear to my mind that any one who would be seriously disturbed by such querulousness ought not to accept the position of the head of a Department where he must necessarily perform such unpleasant duties.

> With great respect,
> Your obedient servant,
> JAS. HARLAN

On the first reading, this dignified letter seems to score in Harlan's favor, but things not so admirable appear on further examination: a very subtle insinuation occurs in two passages, as to damaging things which might be offered about Whitman's reputation. Further, it seems to shoulder upon Dole, the head of the Bureau, the responsibility of Whitman's discharge. But, most important, it evades and hedges as to the real question. Harlan knew that Whitman's official dismissal merely said that his services after that date would be dispensed with, but for him to offer as excuse for failing to give Mr. Miller the real reason for Whitman's dismissal, that it wasn't possible, after the lapse of twenty-nine years, to recall in detail the reasons reported to him for all the dismissals (when only the dismissal of Whitman was in question), is preposterously evasive. After the hue and cry raised at the time (and echoing down the years) by O'Connor's ringing pamphlet, for Harlan to plead those twenty-nine years as an excuse for not recalling the reason for the poet's discharge, seems the height of insincerity and absurdity as well. Through the influence of J. Hubley Ashton, then Assistant Attorney-General, to whom the irate, persuasive O'Connor appealed in Whitman's behalf, Whitman was almost immediately appointed to a clerkship in the Attorney-General's department, which he held until failing health obliged him to relinquish it. At such a crisis in his career this prompt rehabilitation to another Government post had a profound bearing upon him and his work, and consequently upon American letters.

In 1902, when Burroughs was trying to persuade himself to supplement his 'Whitman: A Study' by writing a biography of Whitman, Charles W. Eldridge wrote him, June 14, 1902:

I see you are to write a 'Life of Walt Whitman.' At my suggestion J. Hubley Ashton has written out his recollection of all the circumstances attending Walt's removal... and his subsequent immediate appointment in the Attorney General's office. This he owed, as you will remember, to Mr. Ashton's position and influence... but primarily to the personal appeal made to him by William O'Connor, Ashton's old friend. His account of the interview with Harlan is very interesting.... I think it ought to go in your book.... It is the only *authentic* account of one of the most important events of Walt's life....

The Ashton letter follows:

PACIFIC BUILDING
WASHINGTON, D.C., *June* 13, 1902

Charles W. Eldridge, Esq.

DEAR ELDRIDGE:

I received your note with the prospectus of the new edition of Walt's Works, for which I am obliged.

I was not aware that Dr. Bucke's book, the only one I have of the books you mention, contained the account I find in it of my interview with Secretary Harlan about Walt Whitman after his dismissal from the clerkship in the Interior Department to which I had originally been instrumental in having him appointed. Dr. Bucke's report of the conversation appears to be substantially correct as far as it goes. Dr. Bucke does not expressly mention, however, that I was at the time Assistant Attorney General of the United States; nor does he state the circumstances, perhaps he did not know them, under which I appeared before Secretary Harlan for the purpose of vindicating our friend against the aspersion intended to be cast upon him by that officer, and which have some interest as showing that whatever benefit Walt derived from my intervention and action in respect to his dismissal by Mr. Harlan, was primarily due to the devoted friendship of William D. O'Connor.

I observe that Dr. Bucke speaks of the events to which he refers as 'an occurrence in 1865.' They constituted, properly speaking, an important crisis in the life of Walt Whitman. It would have been the greatest possible misfortune, I think, if he had been driven at that time from the public service with the stigma upon his name and character involved in the order of dismissal, and had been compelled to earn his living with his pen or in some other way in one of the great cities of the country. Secretary Harlan was essentially a good and kind man, but he was capable of bitter prejudices and strong resentments, and he had, of course, great power and influence in the Government at that time. My great apprehension was, as I remember, not merely that he would refuse, as he did, to recall the dismissal of Walt Whitman, but that he would set his face against Walt's appointment to any place under the Government in Washington. If he had done so, it would have been difficult, and might have been impossible, for me, against his opposition, to secure for Walt such a vindication as he received by his appointment to the clerkship he held for several years in the Department with which I was connected. My intervention with Secretary Harlan had the effect at least of modifying his prejudices against Walt which had been created by his examination of the copy of 'Leaves of Grass' he found in Walt's room in the Indian Bureau, and finally inducing him to say that he would not attempt to interfere with any arrangement that might be made for the transfer of our friend to the Attorney General's Department.

I remember as if it were yesterday the day in the summer of '65, on which O'Connor came down to my office from his room above in the Treasury Building, where the Attorney General's Department was then located, with Secretary Harlan's letter to Walt in his hand, and his terrific outburst against the Secretary for his act of infamy, as he described it, when he put the letter on my table.

Everybody who knew William O'Connor and has read 'The Good Gray Poet' can imagine the scene in my office. I fancy that there never was before such an outpouring of impassioned eloquence in the presence of an audience of *one*. The wrong committed, as O'Connor said, was the ignominious dismissal from the public service of the greatest poet America had produced, an offence against the honor and dignity of American letters, and against humanity itself as consecrated in 'Leaves of Grass.' I agreed

WILLIAM DOUGLAS O'CONNOR

that the wrong was a great one, and it seemed to me of the highest importance that the Government of the United States, through the Secretary of the Interior, should not range itself among the enemies of Walt Whitman by dismissing him from its service as an unworthy person. The practical question was whether and how the wrong that had been done could be righted, and that I endeavored to ascertain through my interview, on the same day, I think, with Mr. Secretary Harlan. The conversation in his office was a protracted one, much longer than as represented by Dr. Bucke in his account of it, and by no means so stiff and formal. I had great misgivings, at the time, as to the final fate of our friend in connection with the Government. The Secretary declared that he would not restore Walt Whitman to his place in the Interior Department if the President himself asked him to do so, and it was even difficult to obtain his express assurance that he would refrain from opposing the appointment of Whitman to another position in the public service in Washington; but happily he gave that assurance before the interview came to an end, and I then mentioned to the Secretary frankly the plan I had in view for the transfer of our friend to a suitable position in the Attorney General's Department. The Attorney General, Mr. James Speed, gave his ready assent to my plan, and the result of it all was that the Government finally became the friend and protector, instead of the enemy and persecutor, of our poet.

In September, 1865, William D. O'Connor published that courageous and impassioned pamphlet in vindication of Walt Whitman against the assault of Secretary Harlan, entitled 'The Good Gray Poet,' which assigned to Whitman his place in the hierarchy of letters.

The clerkship Walt received he retained during the administration of Attorney General Speed, and during a part, at least, of that of Attorney General Stanbery, who always reminded Walt, as he often said to me, of Ralph Waldo Emerson, to whom Mr. Stanbery seemed to me also to bear a most striking resemblance. It is a pleasure to mention that Mr. Stanbery, in his intercourse with Walt, was invariably as kind and cordial as Mr. Emerson himself could have been. The great lawyer and the great poet, although wide apart, were more nearly kin than either of them knew, as I doubt not.

The position Walt received in the Attorney General's Department, in 1865, enabled him to bring out with comfort to himself the 4th, and, I think, the 5th, edition of 'Leaves of Grass,' and my impression is, 'Drum Taps' also. I believe that he was engaged in preparing the 4th edition of his book for the press when he was removed from the Interior Department.

My understanding is that the period of Walt's service in the Attorney General's office was in many respects the happiest of his life. He was free from pecuniary cares. He pleasantly saw his friends, and many of them at that time were people from abroad who came to visit him. As his work was light, he was able to devote a good portion of his time to his corre-

spondence and the revision of his writings. He had the gratification of
seeing then the dawn of the day of his great fame.

Faithfully yours
J. HUBLEY ASHTON

Subsequently, June 26, 1902, Charles Eldridge wrote Burroughs
further on the Harlan matter:

... While Walt was in the Attorney General's office, Stanbery, who
seemed to be very fond of him, offered him the position of Pardon Clerk,
then vacant. Walt told me this himself. Walt met many of the applicants
for pardon while at his desk there, and became much interested in many of
the cases. He used to tell me about them. Walt said such a position was
an impossible one for him, as he would be sure to recommend everybody's
pardon, so he declined it, wisely, I think.

On April 28, 1910, Mr. Johnson Brigham, State Librarian of
Iowa, writing John Burroughs of his own forthcoming 'Life of
James Harlan,' protested against a severe arraignment of Harlan
published in a de luxe edition of Whitman's works. Two paragraphs
from his letter to Mr. Burroughs are given here:

The late Charles Aldrich, curator of our historical department, in an
article in the 'Annals of Iowa' several years ago, expressed the belief —
held by me from a study of the man's character — that there was nothing
secretive and underhanded in his [Harlan's] make-up. Mr. Aldrich states
on information that Whitman never made any public complaint as to the
treatment he received.... Was he correct in this?...

I am led to add a word of apology for Secretary Harlan.

(1) He was not in our present-day sense a civil service reformer, and in
response to pressure made many vacancies in his department, not a few of
them with excellent cause. (2) Recalling a time when I was yet in my sins
in my attitude toward Whitman, and knowing the Puritan nature of
Harlan's early education, I can readily see how he might greatly miscon-
ceive Whitman's character, and the trend of his book, as a whole, especially if... some one interested in making another vacancy should bring to
his attention certain isolated passages of 'Leaves of Grass.' But we have
gone over all this, and... are in full agreement as to Whitman's soul
quality. All I want is either confirmation of the Aldrich statement... or
a reference to any allusion made by him to his discharge.... Can you aid
me?

On May 11, Burroughs replied:

... You will not find an apologist for Secretary Harlan in me. I believe
he did what has been charged against him in regard to 'Leaves of Grass.'

To be sure Whitman made no public complaint, but his friends did. Have you read O'Connor's 'Good Gray Poet — a Vindication'? If not, do so. Assistant Attorney General Ashton went to Harlan, after Whitman was discharged, and remonstrated with him, but Harlan said that the author of 'Leaves of Grass' could not have a place in his department. Harlan was guilty of a mean cowardly act. Probably it was the one thing by which he will be remembered.

On November 14, 1910, Mr. Brigham writes again to Burroughs, referring to Harlan's already quoted letter to Dewitt Miller, and enclosing a copy of it, adds:

... It coincides with the record made by the Washington correspondent of the New York Herald at the time, namely, that Mr. Harlan found a large number of men on the pay-roll, some of whom were newspaper correspondents, who had been given place in the Department in response to the influence of newspapers they represented, that their expenses might be paid from the government treasury; thus relieving the newspapers of all, or a large part, of the expense of maintaining correspondents in Washington. Others held places in the Department because of their service to the public in literature, in the war, and in other ways. At one time — about the time Whitman was relieved, eighty clerks were similarly relieved, the heads of Bureaus having been directed to cut down the force to the minimum. I also enclose such quotations as are at hand, from the 'Herald,' covering the Whitman case.

Viewed from your standpoint and thought of Whitman, I can see, as Whitman himself saw (I quote from his diary entry of March 29, 1888), that it is 'easy to be unjust to a man like Harlan.' [1] From my standpoint, I can see how easy it was for 'the more or less anonymous young writers and journalists of Washington' to be 'greatly incensed,' making Whitman's cause their own. Quoting farther from the same entry, Whitman says speaking of these anonymous writers: 'They write almost violently about it; but the papers generally as well as literary people either ignored the incident altogether or made light of it. This was the hour for O'Connor....'

From my standpoint, it is, as I have said before, absolutely unthinkable that Harlan should play the sneak, opening Whitman's desk during his absence, purloining a copy of his book, reading it, and then putting it back. Whatever may have been Harlan's faults, they were not of that petty nature. I know of no man in public life who despised underhandedness more than he. I have only to point to your statement of May 11, that 'Whitman *made no public complaint*' to illustrate the ease with which the mind slips a cog. In Traubel's 'Walt Whitman in Camden,' Whitman is quoted as saying: 'I have been making a few notes today on the subject

[1] Traubel: *With Walt Whitman in Camden*, vol. I, pp. 3–4.

of my removal from the Interior Department,' and in volume 2, page 3, he speaks of having gotten 'ready a little manuscript not originally intended to go into the book — notes made in Washington in August and September, 1865, and a brief statement on the Harlan case not *before* printed.' On page 25: 'W. said the Harlan piece sent to the printer the other day was his "*first public expression* in that matter."' This only proves how easily one can be mistaken as to events occuring in the past.

I cannot now place my hand on the words, but clearly recall Whitman's' deprecatory words concerning O'Connor's extreme partisanship.[1] I can see how Harlan could have said the words attributed to him afterward, when he was remonstrated with; but O'Connor and the whole tribe of 'literary fellers' who after the general discharge combined to write him down, cannot convince the thousands of personal friends of Harlan that he would perform the despicable act attributed to him by O'Connor — the accusation repeated without proofs by nearly, if not quite all, of Whitman's biographers.[2]

My dear Mr. Burroughs, I am not sending you this with any thought or desire to provoke controversy: I do not like controversy, and especially with a friend, but I do want you to see how natural it was that a Western man, free from literary traditions and associations, and desirous of making a record for reform and economy, should do exactly what Harlan did, namely, direct Commissioner Dole to cut down the list to the minimum, sparing not even Whitman, and that when put upon his defense, he might easily have made the mistake which even Nicolay, Hay and Emerson made at the time — that of regarding 'Leaves of Grass' as an immoral book. [!]

I will not enter into an argument to disprove your concluding statement that probably Harlan's 'cowardly act' is ' the only thing by which he will be remembered': I will only say in closing that the man whom Sumner and Seward, in 1865, hailed as a young giant in debate, the man who fearlessly led the forces against Buchananism in '61, the man who did more than any other man in his speech in reply to Sumner and Schurz to save Grant from humiliation, in connection with the Santo Domingo affair, the man who did more than any other Senator to secure the passage of the Homestead law, and to bind the Atlantic and Pacific together by railroad ties, and the man who was early made a confidant of Lincoln, and, later, was chosen by Lincoln to succeed Usher in his Cabinet, has

[1] In refutation of Mr. Johnson's recollection of Whitman having criticized O'Connor, we have this statement from Whitman:

'To me William is self-justified in the truest sense of the word. He is intense, overwhelming — when he wrote the " Good Gray Poet," when he wrote the letter for Bucke's book, he was excited and indignant to a degree; but we must remember what it was that called forth his wrath — the consciousness of a great wrong: an inexcusable offense which demanded a corresponding emphasis of resentment....' (Traubel: *With Walt Whitman in Camden*, vol. 2, p. 240.)

[2] See Traubel: *With Walt Whitman in Camden*, vol. 3, pp. 472, 473-75.

other claim to place on the pages of History than that given him by O'Connor.

I cannot now turn to the page, but somewhere in Traubel's work, Whitman states that one authority for the statement as to Harlan's despicable act was based upon the statement of a clerk in the President's office — this is as I remember it. I have no question whatever, but that the clerk either lied outright, or made the statement on misinformation. I would as soon think that you would pick my pocket, as that Harlan would do the deed charged to him. All this in the interest of justice to a man whose death all Iowa mourned, and who, after all these years, still holds his place firmly as first in the triumvirate of Iowa statesmen — Harlan, Grimes, Kirkwood.

Pardon this infliction and accept my assurance that I have written not to stir up controversy, but simply in the hope that my friend alive may not longer do injustice to a friend who is gone....

Yours very truly
JOHNSON BRIGHAM

The three following quotations from the 'New York Herald' of 1865, enclosed by Mr. Brigham, are offered as germane to this question:

WASHINGTON, May 30, 1865
[HERALD, May 31, 1865]

The Secretary of the Interior has issued a circular to the heads of bureaus in the department, to report as to the loyalty of each of the employés under him, and also whether there are any whose fidelity to duty or moral character is such as to justify an immediate dispensation of their services.

WASHINGTON, July 2, 1865
[HERALD, July 3, 1865]

Quite a commotion has been kicked up in a quiet way by a portion of the clerks in the Interior Department in consequence of the dismissal of some of their number by Secretary Harlan. Walter Whitman, A. L. Stevens and Judge Jesse Connard of Indiana (rep.), are reported among those with whose services Mr. Harlan has concluded to dispense.

WASHINGTON, July 11, 1865
[HERALD, July 12, 1865]

Secretary Harlan seems disposed to make very extensive changes in the Interior Department. The Superintendent of the Census has been followed into retirement by the Commissioner of Indian Affairs, and other changes in the heads of bureaus are spoken of. Many removals of clerks have been made, and a large proportion of those who remain feel anything but secure in their places. The Secretary evidently regards the Interior Department as a sort of Augean stable, which it is his herculean task to clean out. Of course this cannot be effected without exciting much complaint and remonstrance among the victims and their friends; but the Secretary calmly pursues his task, and doubtless has good reason for the belief that new men, even though lacking in experience, can better administer the affairs of the department than those who have grown gray and rusty in the service.

Burroughs sent on Mr. Brigham's letter to me in the autumn of 1910, on which he penciled:

I wish you would write Brigham some time and quote Ashton's letter, which you have, about Walt's dismissal.... J. B.

This closed the incident so far as Burroughs and Mr. Brigham were concerned.

In connection with all this, one reads with special interest what Horace Traubel quotes Whitman as saying in later years. The passage which Mr. Brigham referred to is found in volume 1, pages 3 and 4, and is given more fully here to show Whitman's fair-mindedness:

... It is easy to be unjust to a man like Harlan. He was of the sincere fanatic type, given to provincial views, ignorant of literature, in many ways that I consider, ignorant of life. To Iowa as Iowa, Walt Whitman as Walt Whitman was not easily digestible, so Whitman the author of an indecent book had to go....

Whitman says much more on the whole question in this same passage which any one wishing to sift the evidence should read. In concluding his comments at that time, Whitman told Traubel that 'one of the newspaper fellows in St. Louis' said that, long afterward, Harlan acknowledged, 'The removal of Whitman was the mistake of my life.'

For the convenience of those who wish to look further into this vexed question, I refer them to 'With Walt Whitman in Camden,' vol. 2, pp. 20, 21, 25, 26, 27; and, more particularly, to vol. 3, pp. 470, 471, 472–77. One of the most delicious things about the whole matter is what Whitman said of Harlan in summing up, after discussing the dismissal:

... There was only a dim light in his noddle; he had to steer by that light; what else could he do?... yet he had the courage of his convictions;

he didn't allow Ashton's eloquence to shake him; he threw me out; his heart said, 'Throw Walt Whitman out,' so out I went. I have always had a latent sneaking admiration for his cowardly despicable act....

O'Connor's story of Whitman's dismissal, told with such fire and eloquence in 'The Good Gray Poet,' was written early in September, 1865, and issued in a pamphlet with the imprint of Bunce and Huntington, New York, January, 1866. Not alone for its splendid defense of the poet and his 'Leaves' has it won deserved fame, but also for its earnest, scholarly plea for freedom in letters. Wendell Phillips, Burroughs told me, wrote O'Connor that he thought it 'the most brilliant and vigorous effort' that he knew of in controversial literature, and urged him to marry his style to the living voice 'and we talkers will all take back seats.' Henry J. Raymond said it was 'the most brilliant monograph in our literature'; and even the hostile R. H. Stoddard, in the 'Round Table,' January 20, 1866, characterized it, perhaps somewhat equivocally, as 'one of the most extraordinary things we have ever encountered.'

The following letter from O'Connor to Burroughs, January 6, 1866, marks the beginning of the friendship between these two staunch defenders of Whitman:

My DEAR Mr. BURROUGHS:

Many thanks for your letter of this date, which I have just read with great satisfaction and the glow that sincere praise kindles. Your words, and the words of such as you, will go far with me in my per contras to the abuse I shall presently receive (undoubtedly) from the representatives of 'American' literature.

My little book is but the beginning of much I shall have to say, I hope, of Walt's writings and of the topics I broach — the preliminary skirmish of a war which will be fought under many flags for many years on many fields. If we fellows should ever have a magazine of our own —!

I sympathize deeply and agree perfectly with all you say about WW. Yes, I have had good times with him — immortal times, and I only regret that I have not, as you tell me I ought, made full record of what to the future will be 'dearer than Plutus' mine, richer than gold.' A Diary of our days together during the War would have lasted as long as the world lasted and been the delight and comfort of generations. And your thought is also mine — he is an incarnation. That is the word. Out of that word spin volumes, as out of the sun dart rays. I hope yours will take such form that I can hail it as one of them.

You must come with Walt and see us. He will show you the way. I never force an acquaintance or friendship, believing it an uncanny thing to do, but let it grow itself — and you must come to help grow this one!...

Faithfully yours
W. D. O'CONNOR

JOHN BURROUGHS ESQ.

Following this, Burroughs used to drop in at the O'Connors' of a Sunday evening where Whitman and the host would hold a symposium, with Professor Baird of the Smithsonian, Count Gurowski, Burroughs, Eldridge, and others as listeners. Never, said Burroughs, had he heard talk to equal that between the two — O'Connor with his Irish wit, ardor, eloquence, and deep learning, and Whitman with his own wide, assimilated reading, and the vision of what had been and what was yet to be. 'When Walt got warmed up,' said Burroughs, 'he met O'Connor as a foeman worthy of his steel.'

In August, Burroughs wrote Benton:

I see O'Connor much. He is a tip-top fellow, but awfully learned, and sharp, and smooth-tongued.

Among the Washington mementoes preserved by Burroughs is a letter in bold, original script, from a youth who had been deeply stirred by Whitman and by Harlan's dismissal of him. Probably Whitman gave the letter to Burroughs. A striking letter, startlingly outspoken for that time, and now offered as an illustration of the reactions of a college-bred youth of the day to the author of the 'Leaves.' It is dated February 21, 1866, from Williamstown, Massachusetts.

WALT WHITMAN,

I want to write to you of yourself. It is better to translate you than Epictetus or Marcus Antoninus. To translate you one must be in sympathy with you. I think I am in sympathy with you. I can see that you are a limpid man, a realist, one who looks through all words and shows and bearing into the secret nature with a terrible perception. You look inward, inward at the soul of things. You are terrible for finding a way into the depths. Your poetry is of a new order. You breathe the Modernesque, nothing of the Antique in you. Something flows in your veins warmer than ice-water. Conscientious, earnest, you talk plain words, and command your publisher not to alter a line. Thus, some of your passages seem profane, sometimes blasphemous to the world — you do not hesitate to shock any weather-worn creed or belief.

Damn your critics!

Hear this what I say —

You are a greater Stoic than Xeno or Scævola or Xenophanes, greater, because nothing of impurity clings to you. You are a man whose core and whose breath is conscience, and now I say that not one of these critics (?) not one of the old giants of literature, not one of Europe's best but could come to you and say *Peccavi*.

I have lived twenty-one years and society has just begun with me. *You* I have found and with you I talk. I am in moods and anxieties, but you elevate me. And when I am above them, and in those grand still moments in which one sees infinite things, even then I find you far above, and out of your experience and helpfulness looking down at me.

How long have I been a stranger to this foreign land in which I have wandered — foreign, and yet within my own heart? For when most you talk to me of yourself, then most do you talk to me of myself. Is this not true?

Emerson told me to seek you. 'You shall find much of genius there,' said he, in his kind, quaint way; and Thoreau, you know how he speaks of you in his 'Letters.' But Emerson did not say the best thing. I find Genius here, indeed, but so I can find it in Shakespeare, and Mrs. Browning, and in the effete books.

But human heartedness, but self-giving, but brave sense, mettle, hard and heavy force, laconic energy, when books swim in loquacious impotence, how shall I seek them elsewhere? All lives beside are comparatively objectless and dull and dreary in the prospect. Amid all shame and falsehood around and in me, in you I ever find clearly acknowledged and outspoken the truth.

You are of great practical value.

You are a royal fellow.

Can I serve you?

God damn Sec'y Harlan!

One word of myself: I am twenty-one. Twenty-one looked venerable to me six years ago. And, alas, nothing looks venerable to me now. I am pressing the vintage just now for the wine of hell and stammer curses pretty well. I think there was a devil born in me. I have got the dual existence the Germans tell us about, body at night, and mind in the morning, you understand. I am in this village a thousand miles from home, trying to study and write verse. But enough of me.

I look at your picture in 'Leaves of Grass.' I fancy you are growing old and (is it but fancy) that you suffer.

Will you trust me with one line of yourself. I know you are a poet, older than I, and we are strangers. But if you could see me you would trust me, for I swear there is congruity between us.

Your earnest, unique, lyrical words — God bless you for them!
I love you.
(A friend has defended you with a pamphlet has he not. I endeavor in
vain to get it. Will you not tell me where to send.)

CHARLES WOODBURY

WALT WHITMAN, *Vir.*

On the envelope young Woodbury has inserted the initial 'J' in
his name. He is the same Charles J Woodbury who wrote an
article called 'Emerson's Talks with a College Boy,' in the 'Century Magazine,' February, 1890, later incorporating it in his 'Talks
with R. W. Emerson,' published by Baker Taylor and Company,
1890.

In the 'Century' article, Woodbury quotes Emerson as saying:
'"Leaves of Grass" by Walt Whitman is a book you must certainly read. It is wonderful. I had great hopes of Whitman until
he became Bohemian.' In his book he writes: 'I remember he
[Emerson] returned from New York and told me that Mr. Walt
Whitman, by invitation dining with him at the Astor House, had
come without his coat.' Whitman flatly contradicts this in 'Lippin-
cott's Magazine,' March, 1891. Mr. Clifton J. Furness tells me
that there is a letter in the Bucke Collection, written by Charles J.
Woodbury to Whitman, apologizing for his paragraph about
Whitman in his 'Talks with Emerson.' This letter is in reply to
Whitman, who had evidently taxed him with his misstatements.
Also a letter from Whitman to Dr. Bucke, August 14, 1890, reads:
'Suppose you got what I sent about that ridiculous Prof. Woodbury
... the fool dies hard & dying fights or living fights.' And again,
August 18, Whitman writes Bucke: 'The contemptible little
Woodbury shirt-sleeve story (being piquant and a lie) is copied
and circulated everywhere.'

It is difficult to reconcile these puerile stabs at Whitman as
coming from the same young man who wrote the foregoing letter to
him, but between the ages of twenty-one and forty-five much may
happen.

Writing to Benton in January, 1866, Burroughs inquires how he
likes O'Connor's 'Good Gray'; says he knows O'Connor for a good
fellow, and hopes Benton will review the pamphlet.

Benton replies on March 17:

I should like right well to happen along on occasion of some of your 'immortal evenings.' Mr. O'Connor is a very enthusiastic champion. 'Drum Taps' is full of exquisite things. How rich some of his lines are! I wrote a little review of the volume for the 'Radical,' but guess it has got crowded out.

Later Benton quotes to Burroughs passages from a letter from Moncure D. Conway, written from England, April 25, 1866:

I received your letter of March 30 and its valuable photograph of Whitman, and thank you very heartily. I had rec'd 'Drum Taps,' and O'Connor's gallant defence of its author. I have much faith in Walt, and am persuaded that his powerful priapism is the raw — perhaps *very* raw — material from which some stronger warp is to be drawn than any one finds in the emasculated poetry of the present day.

> 'In a cleanly, sober mind
> Heaven itself full room doth find,'

sings Dr. Beaumont, and he might have added, 'earth also.' As polished columns have griffins' claws, etc., underneath, so I see a shaft (ahead) resting on the wild vitality and biblical virility of Walt. And I mean to have some of his good things in the little Album of 'American Poets' Leaves,' if it ever gets published.

Once, in speaking with me about Conway, Burroughs made the following statement which I noted down at the time:

Conway was an early abolitionist. He wrote on Emerson, Carlyle, Hawthorne, etc., etc. He was a prolific essayist and lecturer. Lived much in England. Preached in London. He took me to see Carlyle and the Rossettis. His 'Earthward Pilgrimage' was eloquent and finely done; also a sacred Anthology he compiled. He was not always reliable in what he wrote. He drew the long bow — a picturesque statement, even though wanting in truth, was too much of a temptation to him. Imagine Walt's trying to look the sun out of countenance, as Conway said he did! That was in his article, back in the sixties, in the 'Fortnightly Review' — an eloquent article — a taking one — one of the first that appeared about Whitman[1] — but it told untruths about him. Walt said it did; for example, his telling about Walt at Coney Island, flat on his back, gazing at the sun. Walt laughed at the absurdity of such a theatrical thing.

Dr. R. M. Bucke, in his 'Walt Whitman,'[2] says that the authentic parts of Conway's 'Fortnightly' article had been con-

[1] Conway's article was in the *Fortnightly Review*, October 15, 1866. He had previously had a review of the *Leaves*, and a defense of Whitman in *The Dial*, August, 1860.

[2] Bucke: *Walt Whitman*. David MacKay, 1883.

tributed by O'Connor, but that Conway had greatly altered the material sent. O'Connor, in a letter to Trowbridge, called it 'a frightful mess of misstatement and fiction, redeemed by Conwegian good nature and good intentions.' W. S. Kennedy points out that Conway confused events, mingling reports of two visits to Whitman, in 1855 and 1857. A letter in the Bliss Perry Whitman Collection, from O'Connor to Freiligrath, dated November 11, 1868, states that Conway's article is 'an incredible mixture of dream and error.' He instances details about the situation and personnel of the poet's home, the furniture in the room, the drawings of Silenus and Bacchus — that Conway asserted he saw there — all a 'monstrous fable.' For special ridicule he holds up Conway's saying he saw Whitman lying on his back, on an excessively hot day, the temperature at 100° F., staring at the noonday sun, and that Whitman then confided to him that it was one of his favorite places and attitudes for composing his poems. Rossetti quotes from this part of Conway's article in the Prefatory Note to his 'Poems by Walt Whitman,' which he edited and selected, and which were printed by Hotten in London in 1868. Evidently Conway was later taken to task for these exaggerations, for in volume 1, page 218, of his 'Autobiography,' written many years later, he modifies his account, saying, 'I found him at the top of a hill [before he had said it was on the hot sandy beach], lying on his back and gazing at the sky.' In 1906, Conway, writing to Mr. Bliss Perry, complained of his quoting from O'Connor's letter to Trowbridge in his 'Whitman' (page 180). He had thereby, he averred, been seriously wronged, perhaps harmed, by Mr. Perry's 'stab in the back.' He bolsters up his former position by declaring, 'Every statement in my "Fortnightly" article, every anecdote, is true and exact.' Who shall decide? Whitman himself, in 1888, speaking to Traubel [1] of the Conway article, is reported as saying:

I can't help feeling a little suspicious of Conway's lack of historic veracity. He romances. William says he lied, but 'romances' will do.

An amusing corroboration of the correctness of Burroughs's early opinion of Conway's 'romancing' is to be found in Mr. David

[1] Traubel: *With Walt Whitman in Camden*, vol. 3, p. 16.

Alec Wilson's book, 'Carlyle to Threescore and Ten,' page 516: Mr. Wilson there quotes from Conway's 'Autobiography,' volume 2, page 112, an account of a visit he and Burroughs had with Carlyle (1872): Conway reports Carlyle as telling them of an Arabian legend about Solomon's temple having been built amid the chirping of thirty thousand sparrows. Burroughs, in 'Fresh Fields,' page 201, describing the same conversation, quotes Carlyle as numbering those chirping sparrows at ten thousand — evidently a fair sample of Conwegian exaggeration.

III

BURROUGHS ENTERS THE LISTS

(1866–1870)

Because of my tender and boundless love for him I love,
and because of his boundless love for me.
WHITMAN

THE comradeship between Whitman and Burroughs was growing apace, apparently more concerned with everyday affairs than with literary matters. Still Burroughs was making good his expressed intention of taking the weight and measure of the poet, and was filling his notebooks with reports of their 'confabs,' and with his own ruminations on 'Leaves of Grass.' Entries from those significant notebooks, and a reissue of Burroughs's earliest published writings on Whitman, long out of print, will be published in the near future, in a volume sure to be welcomed by the student of Whitman.

In the summer of 1866, when Burroughs was absent from Washington, Whitman wrote him, July 2, one of his homely, human letters telling of having just been up to his house to see if all was well there; of finding things growing first-rate in the garden; and of receiving a favorable report about his cow; and continuing:

John, about coming, I am not able to say anything decisive in this letter.... Up in your Bureau all seems going as usual.... John, I send you the July Atlantic....

I am feeling well and in good spirits — go around more than usual — go to such doings as Base Ball matches and the music performances in the Public Grounds — Marine Bands, &c.... I hope your parents are well — I wish you to give them my love — though I don't know them, I hope to one of these days — remember me to the wife also.

I am writing this by my window in the office — the breeze is blowing moderate, and the view down the river and off along Virginia hills opposite is most delightful. The pardon clerks are middling busy — I have plenty of leisure as usual — I spent yesterday afternoon at the hospital and took tea in the evening at O'Connor's.

Piatt is trying to get transferred to New York, to the Custom House — Well good bye for present, you dear friend, and God bless you and wife, and bring you both safe back.

WALT

WALT WHITMAN
From a wood engraving after the photograph taken by
Kurtz in the *Brooklyn Eagle* office, 1873

Speaking to me of this letter, in 1907, Burroughs said:

That was when we lived on Capitol Hill. I must have been on vacation at Roxbury. Walt lived on M Street then…. No, Walt never got to Roxbury. He took Sunday suppers at O'Connor's for years and years. Charles Eldridge was then in the Paymaster General's Office…. John James Piatt was a poet who wrote for the Atlantic then. He and Howells had a book called 'Poems by Two Friends.'
Oh, those Washington days! How it brings it all back! I can see the Monument when I shut my eyes, the Potomac gleaming, and the Virginia hills beyond, through the shimmering sunlight.

On September 10, the same year, Whitman wrote Burroughs from New York that his book was being delayed by the printers, was only about half done, and that he must stay to see it through. It was the 1867 edition of the 'Leaves,' which came out in 1866. He asked his friend, if convenient, to send him a draft for $100, giving explicit directions about sending it. He wrote further:

The book is going to suit me pretty well — it will make a volume of 500 pages, size and style &c fully equal to 'Drum Taps' — I shall feel glad enough when it is completed — I have a constant struggle with the printers — They are good fellows and willing enough — but it seems impossible to prevent them making lots of ridiculous errors — it is my constant dread that the book will be disfigured in that way — though we have got along pretty well thus far….

Burroughs commented on the foregoing:

I had offered to lend him money. I was then getting $1400 a year and had saved some. He was then in the Attorney General's office and got $1200. He sent a good deal home to his mother, and spent a good deal on the soldiers. There were many left over in Washington then, and he still went among them, ministering to them. Walt paid me back at intervals for the loan. Sometimes he borrowed from me, and sometimes I borrowed from him. Walt was always punctilious in returning every cent he borrowed.
O'Connor was then a clerk in one of the departments. He and Walt had known each other since 1860, I think….

It was during this absence of Whitman in New York that Burroughs had written his essay on 'Drum Taps,' which Whitman did not see till it came out in the 'Galaxy,' December, 1866. This was the first article about him that had appeared in the United

States, and Whitman, being eager for his mother to see it, wrote her, November 23, to have Jeff or George get the magazine:

It has a piece about me — I think it is very good — John Burroughs is a young man from Delaware County, New York — he lives here now, is married — I am well acquainted with him and he and his wife have been very hospitable and friendly to me.

Whitman must have felt his stock rising when, on December 2 of that year, O'Connor had a long article on 'Drum Taps' in the 'New York Times,' preceded by an editorial by Henry J. Raymond. A notice of 'Drum Taps' in the January (1867) 'North American Review' must have been less gratifying. This said that Whitman's view of America smacked of 'We can lick all creation'; but added, with fairness, that his 'braggart patriotism' proved its genuineness during the War; it also spoke appreciatively of many fine phrases in the poems, and quoted choice passages, including the Lilac dirge, which it styled 'remarkable.'

Burroughs had been profoundly impressed with 'Drum Taps.' He had seen some of its poems growing for two years and more. Walt would sometimes stop in the street and jot down the germ of a poem, sometimes would drop into Allen's store and make a note of some episode he had just witnessed, the tears still dimming his eyes. Burroughs wrote Benton that no poems in the language went into him like some of those. Outlining to him his article on 'Drum Taps,' on which he was at work, he wrote later that it was one of a series that he contemplated putting in a book. Still later he gave the plan of the book itself,[1] and said that its drift was to show Whitman to be a return to nature, and 'Leaves of Grass' an utterance from nature, and opposite to modern literature which is an utterance from art; that Whitman gives the analogies of the earth, and is the only modern or democratic man who has yet spoken, and our only hope of rescue from utter literary inanition.

By June of that year, Burroughs writes Benton that his book is substantially done, but he intends to lay it aside and see how it reads in the fall, when he hopes to publish it. But his hopes were not realized. The book still dragged. He wrote Benton that it had grown amazingly on his hands, and that he had rewritten it a good

[1] Burroughs: *Notes on Walt Whitman as Poet and Person*, American News Company, New York, 1867.

many times. He thought there were some things in it that would
make Benton open his eyes. He believed he had revived and illustrated a principle that was entirely obsolete in that age, but which,
if carried out, would revolutionize modern literature.

By mid-February (1867) he wrote that he was 'getting up' the
plates of his book in Washington, and should try for a publisher in
New York. He enclosed a strip of galley proof that Benton might
see how it would look. Expressing himself well pleased with the
book, he thought the main idea so prominent that no reader could
escape it. 'Of course,' he added, 'I expect great things from it.
But I expect to wait.'

By the time his little book did come out, and Benton had set the
seal of his approval on it, Burroughs had begun to feel less confident of its merits. On June 19, he replied to Benton:

> ... I really hope the 'Notes' have got life and enthusiasm in them. I was
> afraid they were too quiet and tame. I wanted to make a book with warm
> blood in its veins, and as unruly and revolutionary as possible. I hardly
> expected you to make a notice about it.... Make my regards to Joel and
> tell him if he feels like reviewing the book not to spare me. I am by no
> means sanguine about the immediate success of the book. I am fortified
> against any indifference on the part of the public and literary men
> generally....

In letters to Edward Dowden, quoted later, Burroughs credits
both Whitman and O'Connor with aid in the preparation of 'Poet
and Person,' but shortly after he had launched that work, he
showed signs of breaking away from the domination exercised by
those advisers; for example, he reversed or greatly modified what
he had said in his book about Wordsworth and Tennyson. In fact,
while still at work on the book, he evidently differed with some
objections raised by O'Connor, who had read his manuscript, as is
seen in his letter to O'Connor, dated January 4, 1867:

> He, in my opinion, is either more and different from any other poet, or
> he is a ridiculous failure. I am fully persuaded that he belongs to an
> entirely new class of geniuses which has no type in the past; and that he is
> to be justified and explained on entirely new grounds. You can never
> make people believe, till the day you die, that Walt is like other poets, and
> we have got to show new grounds, new issues, new ends in literature by
> which to try him, or we will be forced to admit that he is a tremendous

humbug.[1].... And more than that, I do not think that either you or I, or both, are the guardians of Walt's fame, or that we can make or unmake it.

Although by now Burroughs had himself become a bold swimmer in the Whitman sea, he still felt some hesitation as to others striking out too boldly. He would at least offer them a plank to cling to. The following letter of January 5, 1867, to a bird-student correspondent, Miss Sarah Adams, is a case in point:

I hasten to warn you against an act so rash as the procuring and attempting to read 'Leaves of Grass.' You do not know what is before you, or what an *awful* book it is — the very antithesis of the sweet and charming productions of the current poets. Read a literal description of Michael Angelo's 'Last Judgment' and you will get a hint of the principle involved in the construction of 'Leaves of Grass.' Read 'Drum Taps,' but do not attempt the 'Leaves' yet awhile. Yet perhaps I am wrong in this, for, by some marvelous insight or higher spirituality, women often see clearly and instantly where men falter and stumble; and I have known those who made no pretence to literary ability or critical acumen — mothers of families, and, in one case, a lady who had long been an invalid — who yet saw at a glance, in reference to this book, what it has taken me years to figure out.

In less than one month I shall astonish you with a little book on the subject, the conclusions of which will astonish you more than the book itself. After reading it, you may be somewhat prepared for the 'Leaves' themselves....

In late February, Burroughs reports to Benton a recent conversation with Whitman:

You remember those letters of Thoreau addressed to 'W.'[2] Conway said they were addressed to Walt, and so I thought till yesterday, when Walt laughed at the idea. He said it reminded him of the young man who seriously advised him to study Addison to improve his style! It is true Walt's poems have not the finish and outside polish of the works of the popular poets, which fact might be taken by a careless observer as evidence of want of skill or culture from books, but which in reality constitutes, or is inseparable from, their transcendent merit....

---

[1] A curiously similar statement made by O'Connor to Burroughs years later is found on page 132.

[2] Two letters of Thoreau's to a 'Mr. W.,' December 12, 1856, and April 26, 1857, giving advice on reading Oriental philosophy, have been cited as directed to Walt Whitman because they were published by Emerson without identification of the addressee. They are shown conclusively to have been directed to B. B. Wiley, however, through editorial researches of F. B. Sanborn. See *The Writings of Henry David Thoreau*, vol. VI, *Familiar Letters*, Boston, 1906, p. 298. C. J. F.

Conway had first met Whitman in 1855, introduced by Emerson. In his 'Autobiography' [1] he says that Whitman told him he was the first man to visit him because of his book. On July 13, shortly after the publication of 'Poet and Person,' Conway wrote Burroughs:

Your book is not only the best on its subject, but the best critical work ever produced in America. The proof you sent me has been read by many with delight.

If you were pleased with the 'London Review' article [2] (and we can hardly hope to have John Bull at his best see Walt as we see him), how much more will you be delighted with Rossetti's article [3] which I am about sending you! I fancy I see the glow of O'Connor's eyes when he reads it. More will come. Rossetti tells me he was misquoted by Swinburne in thinking that there was anything in 'Leaves of Grass' that couldn't be published in England.[4] Our Cause, as you well call it, gains continually. The editor of the 'Pall Mall Gazette' told me he had been reading it and thought it one of the most wonderful productions of any age.... I have met a good deal of Philistinism here in this matter, but a great deal of insight, too. We can afford to wait, for Walt is as sure to be recognized as the sun.

Give my love to the old youth, and tell him I hope to see him over here yet before I return; and remember me to O'Connor.

I am writing weekly now for the 'Tribune,' and you will now and then see some sly mention of what we are interested in.

In a letter to Burroughs, dated August 2, Benton comments about O'Connor's 'gallant championship' of 'Poet and Person' in the 'Times,' and speaks of notices in the 'Tribune' and the 'Commonwealth,' and of his own intention of sending one soon to the 'Radical,' whose editor, Morse, esteems Whitman highly. He tells of having seen an extract in the 'Times' from the 'London Chronicle' in which Whitman was placed on a pedestal as high as Homer and Shakespeare. In replying, a few days later, Bur-

---

[1] Conway: *Autobiography, Memories, and Experiences*, vol. I, p. 217. Houghton Mifflin Company, 1904.

[2] June 8, 1866.

[3] Rossetti: *Walt Whitman's Poems*. *London Chronicle*, July 6, 1867.

[4] Checking up on this statement of Conway's, I submit what Mr. Bliss Perry says in his *Walt Whitman*, page 185, to the effect that on April 30, 1867, Conway reported to O'Connor a consultation, at which he was present, with Swinburne, Rossetti, and Hotten, the publisher, when it was agreed that to publish the *Leaves* in England without modification of a few passages 'would bring a legal prosecution on any publisher.'

roughs shows how completely he is making Whitman's cause his own:

My book has not excited much comment yet, though its reception has been much more favorable than I had expected. The 'Citizen,' 'Leader,' and 'Evening Post' have had eminently friendly notices in it. Mr. Rossetti in his article on Walt in the 'London Chronicle' speaks in commendatory terms of it; so did the article in the 'London Review' some time ago. Conway, in a letter which I received a few days ago, says it is the best critical work ever produced in this country, which, of course, I take with a grain of allowance.

The 'Chronicle' article is magnificent, and has had a profound effect. The 'Round Table' completely goes back on its statement of a year ago. Church of the 'Galaxy' is trying to get a poem out of Walt for the October number of his magazine, and I guess will succeed. Subject, the Harvest which the returned soldiers have sown and gathered.... The editor of the 'Pall Mall Gazette' says 'Leaves of Grass' is the most wonderful work he has ever read, of any country or age. The victory is ours beyond all doubt.

Charles Warren Stoddard wrote Burroughs rather effusively from San Francisco, August 8 of that year, praising his little volume on 'the glorious Walt Whitman,' and saying he had tried hard to learn something of him, but could get no replies to his letters, so was grateful that Burroughs's book supplied the need. Regarding Burroughs as a go-between, he begged for a line from him, and some expression as to whether his book of verses, soon to be brought out, would be acceptable to Whitman. When giving this and other Stoddard letters to me, Burroughs explained: 'Stoddard was a college professor and lecturer, a young man of twenty-four when he wrote those letters. He wrote "South Sea Idyls," and "Summer Cruising in the South Seas."' [1]

Benton's review of 'Poet and Person' came out in the November 'Radical.' Thanking him for it in a letter of November 12, Burroughs said:

It is better than I deserve. It will keep the ball moving. There is little or no sale of the book — not fifty copies have yet been disposed of, which is proof, I think, that the book has something in it.

I hear from Conway occasionally. He says my book irritates and interests Matthew Arnold, who has written Conway a letter about it.

[1] Other letters from Stoddard to Whitman himself in regard to the 'Calamus' theme of Whitman's poems are in existence. Whitman undoubtedly refrained from answering for the same reason that he later pursued the policy of evasion in a similar connection during the famous correspondence with John Addington Symonds. — C. J. F.

Some months later, Burroughs wrote Benton that his notice of
the book in the 'Radical' had been the means of selling at least one
copy of 'that illustrious work.' A man, Greene, from Rochester,
Wisconsin, he said, had seen Benton's notice, sent for the book,
and liked it much. This probably refers to Calvin H. Greene, of
Rochester, Michigan, a correspondent of Thoreau.

In a late December letter Benton comments:

I read Walt Whitman's answer to Carlyle with great interest.[1] It
exhibits him in a new phase. I had no idea that he was so conservative.
His poems are so intense — making such extreme statements — that it is
very pleasing to see this admirably cool and wise statement. It is excellent.

And I have just read also Mr. O'Connor's very interesting story of the
Good Gray Carpenter; and I took a fancy that 'Faulkner' was Mr. O'Connor himself; at any rate, I picture the gentleman in my fancy as somewhat
like that charming young fellow.

Abbey's two volumes, which he has published, I understand were about
as profitable pecuniarily as your 'Notes.' But he is not disheartened.

While Burroughs was still living on Capitol Hill, O'Connor had
occupied for a time an attic room in his house and had there written
his story 'The Carpenter,' in which the Christlike carpenter bears
an intentional resemblance to Whitman in person and character.
After office hours, and far into the night, O'Connor wrote feverishly
on his story, stimulated by coffee and tobacco. Burroughs protested
against this suicidal way of working, and, when hoeing below in the
garden, would throw up plums into the open window to divert
O'Connor from his task. The story was first published in 'Putnam's
Magazine,' January, 1868, later in the book 'Three Stories' by
Houghton, Mifflin & Company. Despite its perfervid style, it is
such a moving tale that one wishes it could be rewritten and shorn
of certain faults. Years later (in 1880) O'Connor gave his own estimate of it to Dr. R. M. Bucke. After commenting on a still earlier

---

[1] The *Galaxy*, December, 1867, pp. 919-33, contains a paragraph (p. 926) which undoubtedly refers to Carlyle's attack in 'Shooting Niagara.' Whitman says in part: 'such
a comic, painful hullabaloo and vituperative caterwauling as this about the "Niagara
leap," etc.... I never yet encountered.' Later in life, Whitman's view of Carlyle was
more tolerant. He writes to Dr. Bucke, September 8, 1888, of 'the refreshing, natural old
fault-finder of everything and every person and writing including his own utterances
(that cursed book he calls the *Frederic*).' — C. J. F.

story of his own — 'Harrington' — as being 'monstrously crude, written under contract, and in a terrible hurry,' he added:

Like 'The Carpenter,' haste spoiled it. After the second feat of this sort, I made up my mind never to write anything to order, or in a hurry, again. It's the slow brew that makes the sweet malt, the English brewers say. I have never really written anything except on the spur, or for some occasion, hence nothing of any moment.

One is glad that O'Connor waited at least nine weeks after the provocation before writing his 'Good Gray Poet.' His ability may be gauged more accurately by that brilliant pamphlet than by the stories referred to here, although, in time, O'Connor became very critical of that work also.[1]

Late in 1867, Burroughs began building a dwelling-house, a substantial brick building, in what was then the north edge of the city. The house is still standing, Number 1332 V Street. Whitman dubbed it 'The house that Jack built.' There Burroughs had a small fruit and vegetable garden in which he worked after office hours, when not occupied with what Emerson termed his 'other garden.' The O'Connors occupied half the house for a time. It was of this V Street house that Whitman wrote his mother, January 26, 1868:

Well, I have been out to John Burroughs (the naturalist) again to breakfast this morning — we have a nice hot breakfast, buckwheat cakes, etc. — It seems to be the regular thing almost every Sunday morning — Then we sit and talk and I read the Sunday morning papers till about half past 10 o'clock — & then I walk down here to the office, about a mile and a half — Mother I have not much to write about, only the same old story — I believe I told you some time ago I had been applied to by an English magazine, 'The Broadway,' to write something for them — Well, I have lately sent them a piece of poetry — If they accept it I shall get pay for it.

How earnestly Burroughs threw himself into Whitman's affairs may be gathered from this excerpt from a letter of February 29 to Benton:

Walt will have a poem in the 'Broadway' soon, called 'Whispers of Heavenly Death.' The publishers wrote him soliciting one. They pay him $50 in gold for a short piece. His stock has gone up immensely. He has another piece (prose) called 'Personalism,' the mate and complement to

[1] See page 207.

'Democracy,' which Church will publish in the 'Galaxy' in May. He is to write one more, making a trilogy, called 'Literature,' in which he says he shall bring his heaviest guns to bear.[1]

After the publication of his book on Whitman, Burroughs could not cease writing on him and related matters. Many questions which had taken possession of him while his book was on the ways kept him ruminating and endeavoring to answer them. Concerning this experimental writing, he wrote Benton in March:

... I have spent nearly the whole winter writing upon the subject of Art — literary art — with a view to settle in my own mind the question as it relates to 'Leaves of Grass.' The more I have explored the matter, the stronger has become my conviction that this poem fulfills all the conditions of great art. One of my foundation stones is this: that a work of art differs from a didactic or philosophical treatise in this, that it is not a thought, but an act, as Creation is; it is the deed transferred to a higher plane, and implies a like totality of the human being. The grand artist is not merely the knower or sayer, he is the doer.

No modern production certainly compares with 'Leaves of Grass' in this respect. No other poet *so moves one.* Again, I have settled to my own satisfaction that the antithesis of Art is Science. Both aim at truth, but with this difference: Science aims at truth in detail, Art at truth of *ensemble.* The results of Science, relatively to its aim, must be parts and pieces, but Art must give the whole in every act; not quantitatively, of course, but qualitatively. Hence, I have no difficulty, after lifting the subject out of the petty, superficial grounds of finish and lineal regularity, in proving 'Leaves of Grass' to be in the highest sense a poem and a work of art.[2]

... I have been re-reading Carlyle. The only two living writers with whom I do not get disgusted are Carlyle and Emerson. With all those Boston wits — with Lowell, Higginson, Wasson, Howells — I am thoroughly sick, I cannot read a line Wasson writes nowadays. In my piece ('Before Genius') I speak of Carlyle as having a fuller measure of the great religious artist-mind than any of his contemporary poets. He has more of that which makes a man of action, and has injected into his pages more of the stuff of which strong manly characters are made.

'How are the mighty fallen!' There had been a time when the youthful Burroughs had regarded David A. Wasson as only a little

---

[1] Whitman wrote the article, 'Orbic Literature.' His letter to the *Galaxy* editors proposing that it be used, July, 1868, is given in Traubel's *With Walt Whitman in Camden,* vol. 3, pp. 454–55. But the article never appeared in the *Galaxy,* nor is it found listed among Whitman's prose periodical publications in the *Cambridge History of American Literature.*

[2] 'I haven't outgrown this opinion,' Burroughs said years later; 'I got hints of it from Lessing and Goethe.'

lower than the Sage of Concord, which may be seen by his correspondence with Wasson in 'Our Friend John Burroughs,' pages 164–72.

Two March letters to Trowbridge give further light on Burroughs's championship of Whitman, as well as on his own views on poetic art:

The result of my scribblings and cogitations upon Art, of which I told you when you were here, is a brief essay which I think of offering to some magazine. To help it with editors, at least not to hinder it, I have not discussed the question of 'Leaves of Grass' as a work of art, but have only touched upon it incidentally.

It has occurred to me to ask you if it would be in your way to put the piece in the hands of Mr. Fields, in case I should send it to you? I know very well what would be its fate if I send it in the regular course, and it falls into the hands of his subs; but with Fields himself, I think, the piece would stand a good chance. I think the 'Galaxy' or 'Putnam' would publish it, but the 'Atlantic' is much to be preferred.

And a little later:

I am quite of your opinion about the probable fate of the essay if I sent it to the 'Atlantic.' On looking it over again, after I had written you, I saw it was not the thing they would like.

The most I say directly about Walt is this; that he is an artist in this at least, that he has not preached Democracy as a doctrine, but has predicated his poems upon it as a living, dominating fact, which I claim to be the method of all first-class artists. Also that in making himself the staple of his poems, he is strictly artistic, since it is himself only in his universal human attributes, and not in his local or accidental traits at all. I claim that any obtrusion of himself in the character of *poet*, or *artist*, or as a person with a point to make, or theory to divulge, would be the height of the inartistic. My notion is that the artist, ideally, is the universal man, or that Art aims at the universal, the All, and that its antithesis is science....

I shall give the piece one or two more revisions, and, if it keeps well, send it to the 'Galaxy,' or to 'Lippincott's.'

Rossetti's edition of Walt's poems is out. It looks first rate, and, save two or three very absurd and stultifying statements in the introductory essay, is all that we had expected....

Concerning Whitman's 'Personalism' in the May 'Galaxy,' Burroughs wrote Benton:

There is meat in it, and bone, too. I do not object to the style. I think we all write too smoothly and flippantly. The need of literature always is for something deep-cut and characteristic. Alcott writes Walt that he and

Emerson are enthusiastic. He says he (Walt) is on the road to empire. My little squib in the 'Galaxy,'[1] stirred them up considerable. (I regret the name — 'The Manhood Test,' it should have been called.) Higginson was exercised to the point of writing me a letter. I am letting him have it right and left, though, of course, good-naturedly. There are many things in heaven and earth not dreamt of in his philosophy. The article is only a chip from what I hope is a real log, though one can hardly tell, at the time at least. As I told you before, it is something about Art. Church praises the article, but thinks it too soon to publish it.

The crossing of mightier weapons than swords between Burroughs and T. W. Higginson will be seen in excerpts from letters quoted here. On March 28, Higginson wrote, in part:

May I take the liberty to express the interest with which I have read your article in the last 'Galaxy'?

That character ranks before genius or culture is a point of which we cannot be too often reminded in America. Specially at this time, when the tonic of great moral enterprises is being withdrawn, and increased wealth opens the way to the lower influences of foreign example, we need this lesson. You have put it with undoubted freshness and vigor.

Having said this much, I may venture a step further and say that there seemed to me to be a slight tinge of undue antagonism in the tone of the essay; as if it were assumed in advance that there were advocates of culture who would vehemently oppose what you say. If there are, they must be foolish advocates. Your general position is impregnable.

I think it is a mistake to assume that there is any incompatibility between native force and high polish — any more than between manliness and refined manners, or personal strength and personal grace. All that could be criticized in the tone of your essay is a slight tinge of this particular assumption. The little hit at 'Eastern' ways, seems to me a part of the same tone. For myself I have been in most of the states of the Union and found the conditions of human life essentially the same, only that the older states are necessarily at a slightly different stage of the common problem, *viz.*, to combine a cosmopolitan culture with indigenous strength. I entirely agree with you that if we must sacrifice either, it should be the former; but can we not be men enough to unite the two?

The only objection I have to your favorite, Walt Whitman, is that he seems to me not to have been quite strong enough to do this; but that with all his remarkable gifts he has stopped short with being a phenomenon, when he might have accomplished something much greater. In saying this I do not wish to try him by any petty standard, but by the standard of Aeschylus, which you would admit. But I say again, I am happy to learn from one who appreciates Nature and Emerson and Aeschylus and

[1] Burroughs: 'Before Genius,' the *Galaxy*, April, 1868.

Thoreau as you do.... Your only two great Americans are Emerson and Whitman; mine are Emerson and Hawthorne: I am glad to have even fifty per cent of agreement with one who writes so heartily.

Cordially yours

THOMAS WENTWORTH HIGGINSON

Mrs. Higginson writes me that Burroughs's reply to the foregoing cannot be found, but we may get an inkling of it from the next letter from Higginson, of April 24:

Thank you for your letter, which I read with much interest; also for the book, of which I had heard before, though I had not seen it. I am glad to know more of you and of Walt Whitman.

His poems I read on their very first appearance, and with some disappointment; the attacks on them made me expect more from them than I got. This, you would say, was my fault; perhaps it was — at any rate, I like your loyalty to your friend. Afterwards I met the author, and was gratified to see his fine physique, that being rather a hobby of mine. In other ways he did not make so favorable an impression — seemed a little self-conscious and egotistical, I thought — though here, again, I may have done him an injustice. Several times I have gone back to him, trying to do him justice. Believing most heartily myself in whatever is broad, hearty, American; having found the roughest forest and border society palatable (to say nothing of the camp), I cannot quite understand why it is that he still seems to me crude, turgid and even morbid.

When I read a single line or passage it sometimes seems the preface to something very fine; but when I follow it up, I always wish that he had ploughed it all in and waited for a better crop which, in that rich soil would surely come. But Time will show the truth. As to the general question, the difference between us seems to be that you think only one great want exists, and I think there are two: original manhood and culture. That you should select such a book as 'Kathrina' as a type of cultivated reading in any sense, indicated to my mind that you had not quite done justice to the side of culture, for I should not say that it had been read by cultivated persons at all; its great circulation has been at the West, a region which you think the superior. (For myself, I deprecate local disparagings in literature; and also class allusions in which I think you and WW. deal too much: 'Sprung from the common people' — as if we were not all such!)

I think we need good-natured, hearty coöperation from all sorts and conditions of men to make a nation or a literature. I think with you that genius must precede culture, and character genius. But I am sure that genius and character together without culture will not make a great or enduring literature; and far from seeing any tendency to overrate, there seems to me the greatest disinclination to allow its claims at all.

One almost thinks that the urbane Higginson has had the last word until one reads the rejoinder, copied from a rough draft of Burroughs's letter, dated June 10, which he had fortunately preserved.

... I appreciate your candor and friendliness, and would reciprocate. I believe we agree pretty nearly in theory at least. I can hardly see how two reasonable persons can differ materially on so important a subject as culture, when they come to understand each other. Of course we must have culture. We can be nothing without it, either as a nation, or as individuals. We do not want crab apples in literature, or politics, or religion, or manners, but the fullest fruit Nature can bring forth. I should differ with you perhaps as to the relative value or importance of artificial culture (culture from books, art, society, exclusively) in the production of a national literature, and the broader culture of life and real things. The question with me now is not what will conduce to the production of scholars, or a class of witty, elegant, accomplished *littérateurs*, for such obscure the true ends of literature, as the priests pervert religion; but what comports with grand, primary bards upon whom a nation can build. I think of Homer's teachers, and of Shakespeare's, and of all monumental, everlasting men, and I see how little what is now called culture had to do with what they were, or what they achieved.

Whether or not we have culture enough in America, it is plain that there is as yet no full fruition of culture here, no triumph of the man-quality in our literature over the conventional, and, what is worse, there is not likely to be.

The matter often shapes itself in some such formula as this: the first step in culture is marked by a love for, and an acquiescence in, the artificial; the second step shows a revolt against the artificial, as in Byron; the third and last step, which not one poet in a century takes, shows no revolt against society, or civilization, or art, but an absorption of them, and a rising above them.

I do not see that any of our popular poets have ever taken the second step, the step which disturbs and unsettles and presages new things. To me, Longfellow, sweet and gentle spirit that he is, is no more tonic than confectionery is. Lowell's whip has got a good snapper on it, and he knows how to make it crack like a pistol, but is that enough? I think Emerson has taken the highest step in morals and religion; but the only modern who has taken it in Art, according to my judgment, is Walt Whitman. From the standpoint of culture I regard 'Leaves of Grass' as a supreme work. It shows a maturity of the man beyond any other modern poem — the man done with toys, done with ornaments, done with criticism, and solemnly confronting the terrible beauty and majesty of things.

You must allow me the frankness to say that I think you do not under-

stand it. You look into it for what the poet had no design of putting there
— at least of making the main thing — namely, gems, specimens, 'fine
things,' highly wrought, intellectual porcelain ware. It must be understood at the outset that this poem does not enter into competition with
other modern works with reference to these things. It differs from them
just as the landscape differs from a flower-garden. It is absolutely new,
both in the theory of art upon which it is based, and in the ends which the
poet had in view. This theory of Art I have attempted to suggest in my
book. It is briefly this: that Nature affords the only adequate standard
for a first-class modern artist. That to elaborate is of no avail, but to
hint, to stimulate, to vitalize, to set going, is everything. Nature is
perpetual transition. Everything passes and presses on; there is no pause,
no completion, no exhaustive elaboration. To produce and multiply endlessly, and commit herself to no end or scheme, is the law of Nature.
Something like this is in 'Leaves of Grass' — a hint, a word, a significant
look, and on the author goes, follow who can.

I am as little in love with crudeness and awkward or bungling workman-
ship as you are, or with acrid, unripe fruit; and any such thing in W. W.
would be to me his instant condemnation. Against any such charge I set
the fact that his most hearty recognition, both in this country and in
Europe, has been from men of the most liberal and ample culture. To
partially cultivated people, he is meaningless and repulsive.

You are wrong in saying I think the West superior to the East as respects literature and general culture. It would be silly to affirm such
a thing. I think the West *prospectively* superior to the East. I think a type
of character is forming there which will eclipse anything that has yet
appeared in the Atlantic states, though that character may yet be a long
way off from literature. Neither did I wish to be understood as referring
to 'Kathrina' as a work of true culture. It perhaps represents the average
culture of the schools and churches, and its author has doubtless been
cultivated fully up to his capacity for culture.

I appreciate the need of good nature and hearty coöperation among
literary men as much as any one, but we must be aware what price we are
paying for them. I think Lessing's example as a critic a good one for
young men to emulate; and that soft words may not always be best. The
class of poets who aspire to foster and lead public taste in this country is
intensely obnoxious to me, because I see such are the sworn enemies of
any large, generous growth. The great standards, and the principles of
universal Nature, need to be revived and enforced at all hazards.

Let me call your attention to Whitman's article on 'Personalism' in the
May 'Galaxy,' which I think contains the deepest, largest word ever
spoken on the subject of culture.

Burroughs and Higginson met some months later, and many
times in after years. Despite Higginson's personal charm, he con-

tinued to be a thorn in the flesh to Burroughs because of his repeated gibes at Whitman. After their first encounter, Burroughs wrote to Benton:

I spent an evening not long since with Higginson.... He is bright and witty in conversation, and no doubt a good fellow. I feel the same want in the man that I do in the author — a want of unction, heartiness, common and broad grounds of character. The god of his idolatry is a well-turned sentence. Higginson will make a graceful, but not a deep and lasting mark.

Great was the rejoicing in the Whitman camp in 1868 when Ferdinand Freiligrath in Germany, and Robert Buchanan and Swinburne in Great Britain, hailed Whitman as a new order of poet. Buchanan had a eulogistic review of the 'Leaves' in 'Broadway' that year. Rossetti names W. J. Fox, too, as one of the few discerning ones in Great Britain to call attention to Whitman. Swinburne's appreciation and depreciation will be commented on in later pages.

While Burroughs was North on holiday in late June, he wrote his wife of having called on Whitman's mother in Brooklyn: 'A spry, vivacious, handsome old lady, worthy of her illustrious son.' In October, Whitman wrote Burroughs from Providence, Rhode Island, of having had a good time there in a quiet way as guest of Thomas Davis, a manufacturer, formerly a member of Congress. O'Connor, not then very well, he said, had been there also.

Once, when speaking to me of Myron Benton and the mellow quality of his mind, induced by a loving study of the best literature, Burroughs said: 'But Myron only nibbled at the edges of Walt. He looked mostly for dainty morsels here and there, which is to miss the main matter — like going to the sea merely for the pretty shells along the shore.' However, recalling Benton's attitude toward the poet as gleaned from their later correspondence, one wonders if Burroughs was quite fair to his friend's grasp of Whitman.[1] Still Burroughs was as critical of himself as of his friends: Once when discussing his early book on Whitman he said to me:

I was too ambitious. Think of the audacity of my trying to write on Walt at that time! I had just begun to get hold of my pen. I was like a young bird just out of the nest — my flights were short and awkward.

[1] See p. 165.

We find him giving advice to Benton, and to himself, in a letter written in January, 1869:

... You need to work like Jehu, and to let yourself out. The great trouble with men of your temperament, and my temperament, is that we are too reserved, too cautious. We do not get up heat and motion enough. Such men as O'Connor and Victor Hugo err in the other direction. They beat the air wildly. Their writing is a conflagration. I constantly feel that I need more swing. We want nothing sensational, but a work cannot be too striking and deep-cut.

Most of Burroughs's writing at this period contained either an allusion to, or a direct mention of, Whitman. In an essay, 'More About Nature and the Poets,' in 'Appleton's Journal,' September 10, 1870, after having taken Victor Hugo, Byron, and others to task for not dealing honestly with Nature, he ends with a characteristic passage:

Where is the poet who strikes his roots down deep and draws up for us some of the rude vigor and freshness of the earth itself? a poet in whom Nature wells up full and lusty, overriding and keeping under all mere prettiness and excrescence, and making his words rank and savory, and an insult to our dainty euphemisms, and to the sentimental gallantries with Nature?

If we except Walt Whitman, a bard certainly aboriginal and virile enough, and one thoroughly Greek in his attitude toward man, who else is there?

IV

APPRECIATION ABROAD AND AT HOME
(1871–1876)

This moment, yearning and thoughtful, sitting alone,
It seems to me there are other men in other lands yearning and thoughtful.
. . . .
And it seems to me if I could know these men I should become attached to them as I do to
men in my own land.

WHITMAN

IN the pages immediately following are many evidences of the overseas appreciation of Whitman, as well as that of those at home who, having put their hands to the plough, remained steadfast. A little ground was gradually being gained in new fields.

O'Connor and Burroughs, and of course Whitman himself, were cheered in the early eighteen-seventies to learn through Professor Dowden that his esteemed *confrère* Professor Tyrrell had given an address on Whitman in Dublin University, marked by 'strong though discriminating admiration.' On the other hand, O'Connor and Burroughs were roiled at Alfred Austin, who, in his 'Poetry of the Period,' wrote of Whitman's 'grotesque, ungrammatical and repulsive rhapsodies' which he compared to 'the painful ravings of maniacs' dens.'

Eighteen-seventy-one was an eventful year for Burroughs in that he then brought out his second edition of 'Poet and Person,' published his first nature book, 'Wake-Robin,' and made his first trip to Europe. One is puzzled to see him pronouncing O'Connor's poem 'To Fanny,' in the February 'Atlantic,' 'a great success of its kind' — such a piece of learned sophistication for a Whitman disciple to approve! He writes Benton that Howells is delighted with it, and explains that while, as a rule, he himself is 'down on such affectations,' he welcomes 'anything that breaks through the primness and prettiness of most poems.' He loves, he says, 'to see a poet kick up his heels like a wild horse.'

In a notebook entry dated March 9, 1871, the pupil is seen trying to step in the footprints of his teacher. The following passage of rhythmical prose, occurring along with other comments on March weather, is so in the manner of Whitman that I searched the 'Leaves' to make sure it was not a transcription from Whitman. The resemblance is more apparent from my having arranged it here in verse form:

O, West Wind! wind of high-sailing clouds,
Wind of blue sky and fair weather;
Dry, intermittent wind, clear-off wind, wind of the mountains and the spheres!

South Wind! moist, wooing, fragrant wind,
Streaming, musical wind from the Gulf, loaded with vapors;
Wind of the low-hurrying clouds, rolling over the mountains,
Resting on their tops, drenching the land with rain!

Southwest Wind! with your long processions, your caravan of clouds filing across
    the sky,
Great fleets and armadas — black-hulked, white-sailed; water in their bellies, and
    lightning in their shrouds;
Swooping up the dust, silvering the leaves, making the flags leap, and the sails
    careen!

This one instance is in marked contrast to Burroughs's other flights in the poetical field, for example in the poem, 'Waiting,' and in his collection of verses in 'Bird and Bough,' where he flocks with the conventional poets.

He reports a conversation with Whitman on Joaquin Miller in his journal, August 1, 1871:

... He has seen only some extracts — thinks we ought to lean to the favorable side.... In the first place, Miller had saturated himself through and through with Byron and the stormy, passionate poetry of that school, but had had the good sense, or luck, to graft, or get grafted, upon this stock, fresh subjects — miners, hunters, etc. from Mexico and California. He said there was a dash and spirit in the book, and freshness, but it would not bear trying by any high, serene standards. He said that beneath the conventionality of English aristocracy there was a chord that vibrated to the wild-horse business — roughness, danger, courage — that Miller had had the luck to strike it, and John Bull was tickled.

From London, in September, Moncure Conway writes Burroughs approvingly of a letter in the 'Cincinnati Commercial,' August 26, 1871, by R. J. Hinton, about Whitman as a hospital nurse. He comments on Dowden's 'Westminster Review' article — 'The Poetry of Democracy — Walt Whitman,' in the July number — as very valuable and telling, though he regards the Honorable Roden Noel's 'A Study of Walt Whitman' (which he had read in manuscript) as a better piece of detailed criticism.[1] Conway adds: 'I sometimes yearn to mingle with your little circle of true-souled seers at Washington, and wonder that Destiny should have made such a mistake as to cast me in that city fifteen years too soon.'

One of Burroughs's 'splendid, off-hand letters' — 'a superb example of let-go,' as Whitman characterized it to Traubel, years later, was written from London, October 3, 1871:

DEAR WALT: I am writing you on the spur of the moment in hopes it will bring me to my senses, for I am quite stunned at the first glance of London. I have just come from St Paul's and feel very strange. I don't know what is the matter with me but I seem in a dream. St Paul's was too much for me and my brain actually reels. I have never seen architecture before. It made me drunk. I have seen a building with a living soul. I can't tell you about it now. I saw for the first time what power and imagination could be put in form and design — I felt for a moment what great genius was in this field. But I had to retreat after sitting down a half hour and trying to absorb it. I feel as if I should go nowhere else while in London. I must master it or it will kill me. I actually grew faint. I was not prepared for it and I thought my companions, the Treasury clerks, would drive me mad, they rushed around so. I had to leave them and sit down. Hereafter I must go alone everywhere. My brain is too sensitive. I am not strong enough to confront these things all at once. I would give anything if you were here. I see now that you belong here — these things are akin to your spirit. You would see your own in St Paul's, but it took my breath away. It was more than I could bear, and I will have to gird up my loins and try it many times. Outside it has the beauty and grandeur of rocks and crags and ledges. It is nature and art fused into one. Of course time has done much for it; it is so stained and weatherworn. It is like a Rembrandt picture, so strong and deep is the light and shade.

It is more to see the Old World than I had dreamed, much more. I thought art was of little account, but, now I get a glimpse of the real article, I am overwhelmed. I had designed to go on the continent, but I shall not stir out of London until I have vanquished some part of it at least. If I lose my wits here, why go further? But I shall make a brave fight. I only wish I had help. These fellows are like monkeys. I have seen no one yet but shall try to see Conway tomorrow.

[1] Noel's paper was printed in the *Dark Blue Magazine*, October–November, 1871, and reprinted in *Essays on Poetry and Poets*, London, 1886.

I write this, dear Walt, to help recover myself. I know it contains nothing you might expect to hear from me in London, but I have got into Niagara without knowing it and you must bear with me. I will give facts and details next time. Go and see Ursula.

With much love

JOHN BURROUGHS

Oct. 4 I went today to see Conway but he was not in — so I went back to St Paul's to see if I really made a fool of myself yesterday. I did not feel as before, and perhaps never shall again. Yet it is truly grand and there is no mistake. It is like the grandest organ music put into form.

On the 20th of October, still in London, Burroughs writes Benton:

I have dined with Conway and the Rossettis, and spent an evening at the house of Carlyle, and drunk tea with the glorious old Scotchman. He was in the best of moods — gentle and grandfatherly, and entertained us (Conway and me) for two and a half hours with reminiscences of Scotland and Scott and Goethe, all of which I will tell you at some future time.

And to the same, on the 15th of December:

In Dublin I made the acquaintance of Professor Dowden of Trinity College.... He is a grave, serious young man of English descent, but of Irish birth and brogue, and I like him immensely, and his wife — a cultivated, enthusiastic Irish woman — also.

Walt has many fervent readers in Dublin, and I should have met more of them but for an indisposition caused by a rough passage over the Channel.

Among the fervent readers of Whitman in Ireland at this time, as seen in 'Edward Dowden's Letters,' were his brother, John Dowden, John Todhunter, J. B. Yeats, R. L. Nettleship, Edwin Ellis, Bertram Dobell, Standish O'Grady, and Professor Tyrrell.

On reaching home, early in December, Burroughs sent Dowden a batch of Whitman material: his own 'Poet and Person,' O'Connor's pamphlet, and several critiques and reviews. He wrote, in part:

... I intend, as soon as I can find a copy of it, to send O'Connor's story called 'The Carpenter.' Walt's poem, 'O Star of France,' I have been unable to procure in print, so I made him give me the original manuscript draft of it, which I enclose.

Whitman just told me that the editor of a Danish magazine [1]... had

---

[1] Rudolf Schmidt: 'Walt Whitman, det Amerikanske Democratis Digter,' *For Ide og Vickelighed*, February, 1872. (Reprinted in *In Re Walt Whitman*.)

EDWARD DOWDEN
About 1874–75

written to him for some facts and points about himself and works, stating that he was preparing an article on his poems.... So you see the ball is rolling. I believe the name of the publication is, in English, 'The Real and the Ideal.'

Replying on December 28 to the foregoing, Dowden writes:

... It was especially good of you to ask for, and of W. Whitman to give, 'O Star of France.' I need not say how much I value this live piece of paper — not with a collector's spirit as 'autograph of a great poet,' but as a living thing, animated by Whitman's breath, and so kindly made over to me. The poem itself is full of light and fire and music.

I was glad to hear of the forthcoming Danish review. I wish the *Revue des Deux Mondes* could be got at in some way. Robert Browning's friend, M. Milsand, would perhaps be a likely person to write such an article. Rossetti or Swinburne might be able to get it written. Would it not be worth your while when you are writing to Rossetti to speak of this?

Whether Dowden's suggestion bore fruit or not, an article favorable to Whitman came out in the French review, June 1, 1872, entitled 'Un Poète Américain,' by Mme. Blanc ('Thérèse Bentzon'). Burroughs comments on this some years later in 'The Flight of the Eagle.'[1]

Dowden writes in the same letter:

Have you seen that the article against Rossetti [Dante Gabriel], signed W. Thomas Maitland ('The Fleshly School of Poetry,' in 'The Contemporary Review') was really by Buchanan? It was a grievously dishonest, ill-tempered article, and I do not see how either Buchanan or Strahan, the publisher, can come well out of the matter. Rossetti's vindication of his poem in 'The Athenæum' I thought most complete, and written in an admirable spirit.

(However, I fancy you will so far agree with Buchanan — and so do I — in thinking D. G. Rossetti's poems overestimated.... They try to give 'Beauty without the lion.' That whole passage of your book, quoted by O'Connor, seems to contain the piece of criticism most wanted at the present time.)

I have to give a lecture in Cork in April, and think of lecturing on Whitman. If I should do so, I shall get very much that is suitable for my purpose from what you have sent....[2]

[1] *Birds and Poets*, p. 190. Boston, 1877.
[2] The correspondence between Edward Dowden and John Burroughs is the property of the American Academy of Arts and Letters — the joint gift of Elizabeth Dowden and Clara Barrus. Some of the letters here quoted from that correspondence have already been printed in the *Letters of Edward Dowden*, and in *The Life and Letters of John Burroughs*.

Speaking of Buchanan in later years, Burroughs said:

He wrote of Walt, but treated him in a jaunty sort of way — he didn't appreciate his greatness.

From Burroughs's journal for 1871 three significant entries pertaining to Whitman are here transcribed:

Dec. 21, 1871.... Walt said he supposed it was some kink of his that he could not so fully accept the piece as I did ('Wayside Pikes'). He said a mild, delicate flavor of that kind, like the natural smells — hay, leaves, flowers, etc. — was good, but when put too strong was not good. He said he found himself getting his back up when those large, coarse, illiterate and homely characters were treated from a supercilious, foppish point of view; and he instanced *Tristram Shandy* as the right, the only permissable way to do the thing. Here is humor, and character, and juice, he said, and real humanity and affiliation. This is as it should be. It is this, he said, that takes the edge off Bret Harte. He is a sharp, bright fellow, but entirely cut off from what he writes about by having cultivated foppishness and superiority.

.　　.　　.　　.　　.　　.　　.　　.　　.　　.　　.

Walt said a friend of his, Mr. Marvin,[1] met Emerson in Boston the other day. When Walt was mentioned, 'Yes,' said Mr. Emerson, 'Walt sends me all his books. But tell Walt I am not satisfied — not satisfied. I expect — him — to make — the songs of the Nation — but he seems — to be contented to — make the inventories.'

Walt laughed and said it tickled him much. It was capital. But it did not disturb him at all. 'I know what I am about better than Emerson does. Yet I love to hear what the gods have to say.' And continuing, he said, 'I see how I might easily have wandered into other and easier paths than I did — paths that would have paid better, and gained me popularity; and I wonder how my feet were guided as they were. Indeed, I am more than satisfied with myself for having the courage to do what I have.'

Dec. 23. With Walt. Taking up an ancient atlas, I remarked, 'How strange the world must have seemed to the ancients!' 'Yes,' said Walt, in a musing kind of way, 'I wonder what advantage their ignorance was to them — in stimulating their imagination. No doubt, very much, for all the old literature may be said to be founded upon fable.'

I observed that the bump of wonder seems to have died out and become extinct, like certain bodily organs that the anatomist finds the rudiments

---

[1] I am uncertain what Marvin this refers to. There seem to have been two Marvins especially friendly with Whitman. One was Joseph B. Marvin, formerly a Unitarian clergyman, who had an article on Whitman in the *Radical*, August, 1877, and who was also on the *Radical* staff at one time. He was later employed in the Tax Revenue Bureau in Washington. Fred Marvin, of whom Whitman speaks in Traubel's book 'as a consistent friend,' is also mentioned often by Whitman.

of. 'No,' said Walt, 'but the human mind has not yet adjusted itself to the new lights, to science — the vast fields and expansions laid open to us in astronomy, geology, and the like. The staple of all our literature is an emanation from, or in some way, the result of, the long age of fable and myth. Our poets more or less still play at the old game. My book is the first attempt at an expression in poetry of a knowledge of the earth as one of the orbs, and to give the wonder and imagination a new and true field — the field opened by scientific discovery.'

Emerson lectured in Washington and Baltimore in the latter part of 1871, shortly after Burroughs's return from Europe. To Benton, with whom Burroughs and Donald G. Mitchell had first met Emerson at West Point, in 1863, Burroughs wrote of this second meeting:

I had hardly got settled back into the old routine here when along comes Emerson and unsettles me for a week, my planet showing great perturbation in its orbit whenever such a body comes in my neighborhood. He was advertised to lecture in Baltimore, and away I go, dragging Walt with me, to hear him, and, as fate would have it, he enters the vestibule of the hall just as we do, and we have a little talk in one of the reception rooms. Walt introduced me to him and he received me quite warmly, unusually so, Walt said, and, to my consternation, proceeded to put me at once on trial for a remark I had made about an observation of Thoreau's (in my essay, 'With the Birds'). I defended myself as well as I could, and explained how I had left it out of the book ['Wake-Robin'] because I had not been to the Maine Woods, etc. He was good-natured about it. Said he had 'Wake-Robin' on his table, and had looked into it with a good deal of interest. Thought the title a capital one — expected to see an older man in me, etc.

Evidently Burroughs did not remind Emerson that they had met before. Continuing, Burroughs tells Benton of seeing Emerson again, of waylaying him at the station in Washington:

He was alone and had ten or fifteen minutes to spare, so I got him aboard the train and sat down beside him. He has not changed much since we saw him, except perhaps his nose is a little more hooked, and his hair a little thinner. I drew him out on Walt and found out what was the matter. He thought Walt's friends ought to quarrel a little more with him, and insist on his being a little more tame and orderly — more mindful of the requirements of beauty, of art, of culture, etc. — all of which was very pitiful to me, and I wanted to tell him so. But the train started just then and I got off. However, I wrote him a letter telling what I thought, and sent him my book. I do not expect to hear from it, but I was determined to give him a shot.

Viewed in the light of the wants or needs of the American people today, and of the great questions and issues about us, nothing can be more irrelevant or pitiful than these lectures he is now delivering. It is like a wriggling of thumbs. I am utterly tired of these scholarly things, for my part. Night before last he lectured here on 'Homes,' and I heard him again. It was a good talk, but hardly seemed worth while for him to speak, or us to hear. He came and went the same night, and I did not seek him this time.

What a contrast, this account, with all that Burroughs had felt on meeting Emerson eight years before! [1]

Burroughs's letters to Myron B. Benton were given to me in 1912 by Charles E. Benton. On reading them with me that summer, in explanation of his comments in the foregoing letter, Burroughs said:

It was during the reconstruction period after the War. Emerson's lectures were full of idealism, but they seemed unsuited to our needs. In a book they would have been like a star, but on a lecture platform they were rather ineffectual. But they were all right, in a way — Emerson couldn't unhitch his wagon from a star to drag our little burdens to market.

One wonders if it was of this same lecture by Emerson that Burroughs was thinking when he wrote in his essay on the Sage that audiences were coming to resent a little the lecturer's indifference to their moods, and when he pointed out that, even if we take the ground that Emerson was casting pearls before swine, 'the swine may safely demand some apology from him who offers them pearls instead of corn.' Whitman also had his fling at Emerson when writing Dowden of the Baltimore lecture, January 18, 1872: [2]

He draws on the same themes as twenty-five years ago. It all seems quite attenuated (the first drawing of a good pot of tea you know — and Emerson's was the heavenly herb itself — but what must we say to a *second*, and even third or *fourth* infusion?)

On forwarding Conway's 'Earthward Pilgrimage' to Benton, which Burroughs had brought over from England, he characterized it as 'extremely clever and valuable — the first chapter perfectly delicious'; but added:

I cannot help but feel that Conway is a little deficient in the heart of

---

[1] See Barrus: *Life and Letters of John Burroughs*, vol. I, pp. 72–73.
[2] From the Bliss Perry Whitman Collection.

him. I fear he is not finally to be relied upon, or is liable to make some great blunder or mistake.

As already shown, Burroughs adhered to this opinion, in spite of a certain bond of fellowship consequent upon their ardent Whitman discipleship.

When Professor Dowden, on February 23, 1872, acknowledged the receipt of 'Poet and Person' which its author had sent him, he wrote, in part, as follows:

Your book has really served to bring Mr. Whitman near to me, and to the others who have read it — not that it has altered my impression, but confirmed it and filled up the outline which already existed. One good effect it has had is that it has made me feel more strongly — what indeed I felt from the first — that such an official, inhuman way of looking at Whitman as that of my 'Westminster' article, however true and up to a certain point valuable, is little fruitful compared with the more personal relation which your book originates from. The vital nourishing contact with a great man is with his personality, not with the man 'attenuated to an aspect' (J. H. Newman's phrase). And some such attenuation was inevitable in a study from the point of view chosen by me.

The portion of 'Beauty' (besides much else) seems to me written in the very highest manner of criticism; some passages I had read before in Mr. O'Connor's review of your 'Notes.'

The one point where I feel unable to follow you is in the passage about Wordsworth on p. 47. I quite agree in thinking Whitman's cosmic conception and feeling of nature 'tallies' the world and its varied forces more adequately on the whole than Wordsworth's. But I cannot consent to call Wordsworth simply a rural and metaphysical poet. *Fear* (using the word in a high sense), as a part of the emotion passing between the world and man is felt by Wordsworth, and pain and joy. But Wordsworth in proportion to the mounting of his mind becomes calm — the composure of his whole being is always in proportion to the mass and high-wrought quality of his emotion. It seems somewhat out of place for me to find fault with you on a subject such as this, when so much that you have written bears witness to the possession in so rare a degree of what one may indicate by that wretched phrase 'a feeling for nature' — but it is not your 'feeling for nature' I question, but whether you have got into entirely true relation to Wordsworth. What I would urge is that there is in Wordsworth all you say — but much besides. If he lived I do not doubt he would be a glad accepter of Whitman's poetry. I mean the *young* Wordsworth, and I even think Wordsworth as an old man could not have failed to admit Whitman's beauty and power, though he would probably have added qualifying sentences.

Here Dowden speaks of sending Burroughs a volume of lectures, and continues:

Mr. Graves, who wrote the lecture on Wordsworth,... has recently been reading Whitman, and has taken to him very warmly — he is over sixty years of age, but has never ceased to grow, a man of most perfect character, sweet and strong.... 'Democratic Vistas' has in particular delighted him.

I had an exceedingly kind and lengthy letter from Mr. Whitman. He says he would like to come over to England and Ireland. I wish you could persuade him to change the wish into a fact. He would see much that would interest him, and his visit, I am sure, would help to make his poems understood and appreciated. Yesterday I received from him a newspaper containing his 'Mystic Trumpeter' from the Kansas magazine.... It has the freedom of a great vista, backwards and forwards, yet entire definiteness; music and picture become one in it.

In replying, March 9, to the foregoing letter, Burroughs retracted the position he had taken in 'Poet and Person' as to Wordsworth, and to Tennyson as well:

Your letter sent a warm glow through me, under the influence of which I took out my little book and read parts of it over for the first time in a long while. In the light of your approval it seemed better than it had ever seemed before. Mr. Whitman himself likes the book, and thinks it will stand; so does Mr. O'Connor; and I am indebted largely to both of them for aid in getting the matter into shape. But the book has had no audience in this country. I sent it to most of the critics and literary men, but they said not a word. The 'New York Tribune' gave me a good notice, but the other journals steered clear of it. Less than a hundred copies have been sold.

I have myself never been satisfied with the passage on Wordsworth, and it never would have been allowed to stand had not Whitman and O'Connor both commended it highly, neither of whom, I have since made up my mind, do Wordsworth justice.

I read Wordsworth a good deal, and find my own in his pages, and shall soon attempt an essay on him. The right word about him I have not yet seen spoken, nor has it come to me to speak it.[1] I think he is the first and the highest of the modern solitary poets, and that he speaks or sings, warmly and genuinely, even grandly, out of that solitude which lurks by mountain lakes, and broods over lonely moors. He is to me the greatest of the interpreters of this phase of nature, but I do not recognize the creative touch in him. Wordsworth expresses to me that delicious companionship which I have with the silent forms and shows of rural nature, and which I am half ashamed I do not have with men, and with towns and

[1] See Burroughs: 'In Wordsworth's Country,' *Fresh Fields*, pp. 147–58. Boston, 1884.

cities. I think it is something of the 'homesickness' that Schiller speaks of; while Whitman expresses to me the life and power of the globe itself, and lets me into the secrets of creation. His poems rival the elemental laws and the great dynamic forces. They are *deeds* and not *thoughts*, and have the same intimate direct personal relation to himself that a man's proper act has to himself.

I am not satisfied with my allusion to Tennyson, either, though it is doubtless true in that connection. But I think Tennyson a noble poet — he has the real 'fluid and attaching character,' and will live. He does not belong to the morning of the world, like Whitman, but rather to its sunset; but this phase has its place also.

Whitman has been absent in New York over a month, bringing out another edition of his books. Do you know John Addington Symonds? He writes Whitman some very appreciative letters, and has sent him quite a long poem in print, inspired, he says, by Whitman's 'Calamus.' It is lofty and symphonous, and reminds of Shelley....

I am not going to allow you to disparage your article in the 'Westminster.' At that distance from Whitman it is a marvel to me how you could grasp him so completely. I am sure I could never have written my book, had I not known Whitman intimately and long. There is no distinction between the man and the poet, and to know one is to know the other. The article is very lofty and effective, and the first half of it is positively a new contribution to the science of criticism. It makes a new and for us immensely important classification.

The only thing in the article I regret is the comparison to 'the beasts,' which I think is injustice to the beasts and unfair to our poet. In my opinion Whitman is to be accepted or rejected entire. He is that vital, and his works bear that direct relation to himself that one cannot sort and sift. He does not stand apart from his poems — never goes out of his way to say anything — never lets the *littérateur* or the conscious maker of poems emerge and show himself, but it is the man, Whitman, that you get on every page.

I think his treatment of the sexual part of man perfectly consistent with his scheme, and no more bold and unconventional or inartistic than his treatment of any other part. Poetry must be as pure as science, and the subject, if handled at all, must be handled without reserve, or insinuation, and solely with reference to offspring. If people are shocked — and they *are* shocked — I was shocked — it is because we are not used to cold water upon this subject, but expect something much more sweet and spicy....

I should like much to have Walt make a trip to Ireland and England. I think we would get another great poem out of him. At present he belongs there more than here, and I know he would be deeply moved by what he would see.[1]

[1] See *Edward Dowden's Letters*. London, 1914.

Concerning Burroughs's many adverse references to Tennyson in his early notebooks, and in 'Poet and Person,' he became self-critical in later years. I have often heard him say, in substance, that while much that he had said of Tennyson was true in the comparisons he had drawn, he had by no means adequately summed him up. To him Tennyson meant ripe and mellow England, and the gorgeous sunset of feudalism. He responded to his rich, sumptuous beauty, and often quoted lines of haunting melody, and commented on their simple, inevitable beauty. In fact, he overcame the prejudiced view of his youth. How much Tennyson's admiration and friendliness for Whitman may have had to do with Burroughs's change of heart, one cannot say, but that Tennyson spoke of Whitman as 'a Great Big Something,' and invited him to visit him, and said unequivocally that he was the only poet America had produced, certainly was no drawback to Burroughs in ultimately reaching a truer appreciation of him. In 'Whitman: A Study,' pages 252–53, he does tardy justice to Tennyson. There he links him and Whitman together as the only noteworthy poets of our day who have drawn inspiration from science, and who view the universe through the vistas which science opens.

Symonds's poem, 'Love and Death,' referred to in the foregoing letter by Burroughs, is printed in 'In Re Walt Whitman,' edited by Whitman's literary executors, Horace Traubel, Dr. Bucke, and Thomas Harned. Frederick Meyers, a fellow of Trinity College, was, according to Mr. Bliss Perry, the one who introduced the 'Leaves' to Symonds, by reading to him from it; and Symonds has said somewhere in print that as he listened he was thrilled to the very marrow of his bones.[1] Mr. W. S. Monroe, who has looked carefully into the data, tells me that Meyers was probably the first Englishman to visit Whitman; that he called on him in his attic room in Washington in 1865. He also says that John Morley came in 1867, Justin McCarthy in 1871, and Edmund Yates in 1872. Later British pilgrims visited Whitman in Camden — Lord Houghton, Edward Carpenter, Sir Edwin Arnold, Oscar Wilde, Dr. J. Johnston, J. W. Wallace, Henry Irving, Bram Stoker,

[1] Conway claimed in a letter to Professor Perry to have been the one who introduced the 'Leaves' to Symonds, at which time he gave him his own 'precious copy of the second edition.'

Ernest Rhys, H. W. Haweis, Edmund Gosse, Mr. Summers,[1] and others. Gosse testified to the 'peculiar magic' which Whitman could exercise upon one who was no worshiper — who went to see him unwillingly, not as a disciple, but as 'a stiff-necked and froward unbeliever'; adding that 'the unbeliever walked away, after a brief talk, with his heart full of affection for the beautiful old man.' Yet Gosse, while granting that Whitman is 'rich above almost all of his coevals in the proprieties of poetry,' considered him 'for want of a definite shape and fixity,' 'doomed to sit forever apart from the company of poets.' Apropos of British appreciation of Whitman is a note by the editor of 'Progress' in the issue for April 5, 1879:

I became quite an object of interest at Lady Hardy's in London more than a year ago, when, at one of her literary soirées it was stated that I knew the author of 'Leaves of Grass.' Swinburne, Rossetti, Justin McCarthy, Henry T. Byron, Henry Irving, and others clustered to hear what sort of a being he was. They all wished to see him in the old country, which he has never visited.

Symonds said in 1889, and again in 1893, that the reading of the 'Leaves' at the age of twenty-five had influenced him perhaps more than any other book except the Bible; more than Plato, more than Goethe. Among his contributions about Whitman are his lines in 'Studies of the Greek Poets' (1873), his 'Essays, Speculative and Suggestive' (1900) — which contains a chapter on Democratic Art and Whitman — and his 'Walt Whitman: A Study' (1893).

It is interesting to come upon Dowden's confession (December 1, 1875), to John Todhunter, another Whitmanite, that in talking to the 'Fortnightly' folk about Whitman he had assumed a cool nonchalance toward him, since the whole truth would not then have been profitable nor possible. So he had 'kept a prudent mask of common sense' over his face ('which in reality,' he confessed, 'flushes and pales more than a strong, sober person's ought').[2]

Pleasant indeed is it, at this point, to come upon a memento preserved by Burroughs which affords a charming glimpse of the

---

[1] In the *Pall Mall Gazette*, October 28, 1888, is an account of Mr. Summers, a member of Parliament, visiting Whitman. C. J. F.

[2] *Edward Dowden's Letters*, p. 86.

Washington circle in 1872. It is an invitation to a May picnic on the Potomac, sent by Dr. Frank Baker, of the Smithsonian Institution, to John Burroughs, a clerk of the Treasury: the picnic to be held on High Island; the picnickers to make the trip in a canal-boat. Under the heading 'The Floral Fragrance' are, among others, the names of May Cole, later Mrs. Baker, and Nelly O'Connor, the wife of W. D. O'Connor. (As the name of Ursula Burroughs is not here, it is probable she was away in the Catskills at the time.) Opposite each young woman's name is placed that of one of the early wild flowers. 'Lunch Consumers' is the prosaic designation for William O'Connor, John Burroughs, Frank Baker, Colonel Stone, and Walt Whitman, for whom the fair 'Hepatica,' 'Spring Beauty,' 'Arbutus,' and other sisters of Flora, were doubtless to provide. Below the names are quotations in the spirit of the occasion — from Shakespeare, Emerson, and Whitman. One from Whitman reads:

> Now I see that the secret of the making of the best persons
> Is to grow in the open air, and to eat and sleep with the earth.

Coming upon the little sheet with the idyllic summons, one's thoughts play wistfully about those merry-makers of long ago. Better than eating oysters with 'Walt' at Harvey's, better than sauntering with him on populous pavements, or along Piney Branch, or than accompanying him on his errands of mercy, would have been that May-day on High Island when he and his young friends, enamoured of growing outdoors, leaned and loafed at their ease, rejoicing in one another, and in the 'rich apple-blossomed earth.'

Another example of other than literary aid rendered by the comrades to each other is found in the records for the summer of 1872. Burroughs was on holiday in the Catskills. Whitman wrote from Brooklyn that he had been over to New York and looked up his missing trunks, and had made sure they were on their way to Roxbury. He added:

I am home here in Brooklyn, having the usual sort of time — Mother is only middling this summer — My brother George and his wife at Camden, N.J., are so strenuous for mother to break up housekeeping and go live with them, that I think she will go next September —

I expect to be on hand at Hanover on Wednesday, 26th — it is middle or latter part of the afternoon I am to be on exhibition — shall hope to see you, dear friend, on the great occasion —

WALT WHITMAN

This refers to Whitman's reading of his poem 'As Strong Bird on Pinions Free' at the Dartmouth Commencement, on June 26. Burroughs wrote to Benton early in June that he wanted much to go, to hear Whitman deliver his poem to the students, but feared he could not. And he did not, doubtless owing to the expense of the journey. The following condensed letter, from Whitman to Eldridge, dated July 19, Friday afternoon [1872], and sent by Eldridge to Burroughs, describes the summer jaunt, including a mere mention of the stopover at Hanover. Although Whitman was usually particular to mention the day of the week, the month, the day of the month, and often the time of day, in his letters, he frequently failed to name the year. In case of omissions, as here, where the contents enable one to supply the year, it is printed in brackets.

... Charley, I went leisurely up the Connecticut valley, by way of Springfield, through the best part (agriculturally and other) of Massachusetts, Connecticut, and New Hampshire, June 24th and 25th by daylight — 26th and 27th at Hanover, N.H. — 28th and 29th slowly up the White River valley, a captivating wild region, by Vermont Central RR, and so to Burlington, and about Lake Champlain, where I spent a week, filling myself every day (especially mornings and sunsets) with the grandest ensembles of the Adirondacks always on one side, and the Green Mountains on the other; sailed after that down Champlain by day, stopt at Albany over night, and down the Hudson by boat, 4th of July, through a succession of splendid and magnificent thunderstorms (10 or 12 of them), alternated by spells of clearest sunlight. Then home — some five or six days immediately following I was ill, real ill — I suppose the excessive heat, etc. etc. — but am now feeling all right.

Upon the whole, I have stood the unprecedented heat pretty well. Mother is not very well — has spells of weakness — has rheumatism, then good days again — will break up from Brooklyn in September and go with George at Camden — as they are vehement for it.

My sister Martha at St Louis is better far than one would expect after the alarm of two months ago — she has since no trouble with the cancer (or supposed cancer) — Jeff and the children well — My sister Hannah in Burlington I found better than I had anticipated — *everything much better* —

Charley, who do you think I have been spending some three hours with today, from 12 to 3 — (it is now 4½) — Joaquin Miller. He saw me yesterday toward dusk in 5th Av., on a stage, and rushed out of the house and mounting the stage gave me his address, and made an appointment. He lives here.... I am much pleased (upon the whole) with him — *really pleased and satisfied* — his presence, conversation, atmosphere, are infinitely more satisfying than his poetry. He is, however, mopish, ennuyéed, *a California Hamlet*, unhappy every way — but a natural prince, maybe an illiterate one — but tender, sweet, and magnetic.

Love to you, dear Charley, and to all — I will soon be with you again.

WALT

To Edward Dowden, in Dublin, August 16, Burroughs makes overtures in Whitman's behalf:

Walt Whitman is back again from his brief summer vacation but I am sorry to say is not as well as I should like to see him. The heat has been very severe here, and then he is really stagnating for want of a change and some wholesome excitement. What would you think of the idea of his coming to England and giving public readings from his own poems? It has occurred to me as something worth considering. It would afford him just the change he needs, and I have no doubt could be made to pay him a handsome sum — enough at any rate to pay expenses and several hundred dollars to boot. There is no probability he will ever come over to you who understand him so well, unless it is on some such enterprise. On this, I feel sure he would come. I should like to know how the idea strikes you. Whitman reads his poems in a peculiarly impressive manner, and I think would have great success with your audiences. I have written to Rossetti to see what he thinks. I am anxious that our poet should see his mother country, and see you all, and that you should see him, and I am sure that if the matter can be brought about, it will be a satisfaction all around.

A similar letter evidently went to W. M. Rossetti. Excerpts from Rossetti's reply of September 2, follow:

I was glad to see your handwriting, and the important subject matter of your letter has given me a good deal of thought since then. I confess I hardly know what to say as to the prospect of success or otherwise, were Whitman to come here and give readings of his poems. I am not a sanguine man, and (partly perhaps on that account) I doubt whether it would be a success. There is no precedent, I think, for such a form of public appearance here: it is a thing that Tennyson, Browning, Swinburne, etc. or, at an earlier date, Hood, Leigh Hunt, Campbell, Coleridge, etc., have never, I think, done — the reading of their own poems. The only sort of reading that I know of (apart from regular lectures, etc.) is dramatic readings, chiefly Shakespeare, by highly-trained actresses; or there were Dickens's readings, the subject matter and the man being enormously popular, and immense crowds of people prepossessed with the wish to see and hear him personally. Then there are slighter and very miscellaneous reading *séances*, at Mechanics Institute, etc. — such as Tennyson's 'May Queen,' followed by a comic monologue by Mrs. Gamp, or a scene from Box and Cox, winding up with the soliloquy of Hamlet, or Satan's apostrophe to the sun.

Whitman's proposed reading would be unlike any of these recognized modes of appearance, and I don't know what would be the upshot. Though there are a considerable number of *individuals* in this country who heartily admire and honor him, one can't say that the mass of the nation, or even the ordinary run of reading people, know him in the sort of way that w'd induce them to come and hear just because it is Whitman. In default of this source of attraction, there w'd remain the attraction of the poems themselves. Certainly I w'd be the last person likely to underrate this; but I am not prepared to say that large audiences w'd present themselves, considering (1) that such a mode of bringing poems before the public is not practiced here by even the most widely popular poets, and (2) that W's poems are not known, or else not liked, by the rank and file.

I can indeed easily think that, if once a large popular, democratic audience c'd be assembled, the poems would prove highly impressive to them, and the foundation of a solid success by their reading w'd be laid; the difficulty is to manage that first step — and I apprehend it to be a very serious difficulty.

Please understand, however, that I have no practical experience whatever in these matters — never having delivered, nor expecting ever to deliver, any sort of lecture or reading, and the fewest of times attended any such.

I have not had any opportunity of consulting any one on this important subject — the great majority of people are out of town now. It strikes me that Conway would be the right man for you or Whitman to address, if the thing comes near to taking a practical shape; he is constantly lecturing, etc., all over the country, and doubtless understands every detail of lecturing organization and tactics — to me totally unknown.

I am truly concerned that your letter gives an unfavorable account of Whitman's health. You know, and I am sure he knows, how much delighted and honoured I should be in seeing him in this country and house. Please remember me to him with all respect and affection, and believe me always,

Very truly yours
W. M. Rossetti

My selection of American poems, dedicated to Whitman, and containing several of his compositions, is now just finished printing; its publication can't be very distant, but I dare say two or three months may yet intervene. All this is the publisher's affair.

One recalls here an allusion to Rossetti's 'Poems of Walt Whitman' selected by him from the 'Leaves,' which J. B. Yeats made in a letter to Edward Dowden. Yeats tells of R. L. Nettleship having paid nearly his last three guineas for a copy of the 'Leaves' which 'had not been bereaved of its indecencies.'

The foregoing letter, from the conscientious, conservative, cultured Englishman, makes an interesting contrast to that from the equally conscientious and cultured, but more ardent, Irishman. Dowden wrote from Montenotte, Cork, September 3, 1872:

... First to answer the important part of your last letter — the chance of getting Whitman over is one to be valued so much that whether he were to succeed as a reader or not we should be tempted to urge him to come. But I do believe he could count on a decided success — of course I speak only of Dublin. He would probably come to us after having been in London (it would be the right order to begin at the centre). He is already known, and I think favorably known, to a good number of Dublin folk, and we have what Rossetti calls 'Whitmanites' connected with three principal Dublin newspapers, who would make it their business duly to make known his intended readings. It would be a very great happiness to my wife and myself if Whitman would stay with us — he could either see people, or see nobody, as he liked.

(I have been compelling myself to write soberly about Walt Whitman's coming over, and our seeing him, but in reality I feel overjoyed by the possibility — my wife, too, who was always a lover of his poems, has recently been quite conquered in a new way by them. I feel this myself also — after 'Leaves of Grass' has been going about for two or three months, from hand to hand; when it comes back to me, and I look into it again, it has grown something new and more powerful.)

I trust there is no serious failing of Whitman's health; you say nothing of yourself and I suppose I may infer that you are well. This has been with me an unusually unsuccessful year as far as health is concerned. I came down here to Cork in April, very far from well, hurried up (from your book, and my own article) a lecture on Whitman; had a good audience, and succeeded in one thing — carrying them away with the poems I attempted to read....

After commenting at some length on George Eliot, and his lecture about her, which he is sending on, he speaks of his own profound admiration for her, though he 'by no means lives in oneness with the spirit of her teachings.' He adds:

Her enforced calm, and noble self-surrender and sweet austerity, I think I understand and sympathize with, but it is better to show how life can be great and joyous (Whitman) than how life can be great and sad (G. Eliot).

He says further:

I do not know whether it is you or him [Whitman] I have to thank for the paper containing the *Revue des Deux Mondes* criticism. It was forwarded to me and the cover taken off previously in Dublin. It is very unsatisfying, but still will rather do good than harm. You will have read, I am sure, before this reaches you, Swinburne's last deliverance on the poet in his 'Under the Microscope.' I should say, in answer to it, that in the writings of every poet of the first order, who deals with truths and the meanings of things, there are tracts of ground which would be prose if they were not included in and hung over by a heaven of poetry — witness notably Dante.

An adhesion given to Whitman which was interesting to me was that of Alexander Strahan, the publisher, indicated by a casual reference to W. in a memorial article on Norman Macleod in the 'Contemporary Review.' ('One of the truest poets of our day,' or some such phrase.) It was interesting to me because my 'Westminster' article was in print for the 'Contemp,' and just about to appear, when Strahan and Dean Alford had a talk over it and decided it was too 'dangerous' to appear; and Dean Alford wrote to me in a contemptuous way of Whitman's work as poet. (I fear poor Dean Alford died in his sins — he always loved the safe and the mediocre — but Strahan is converted by, I suppose, Buchanan.)

Apropos of what Dowden said in the foregoing letter about Dean Alford is the light he threw on that gentleman's 'genteel' mind in a letter to his brother John, February 2, 1866. It seems that sensitive gentleman required Dowden, in his article on 'French Æsthetics,' to change the word 'nude' to 'unclothed' — 'nude' being too indecent for Alford, the prude, to countenance. Small wonder that Dowden's article on Whitman was excluded from the 'Contemporary Review,' and forced to seek shelter in the 'Westminster'!

Whitman's lecture plans were not yet abandoned, as seen in Burroughs's letter of January 12 to Dowden; although, owing to the serious break, a few weeks later, in the poet's health, fruition of the long-held plan was deferred for many more years. Burroughs writes Dowden:

I have delayed answering your letter all this long time hoping I should have something definite to tell you about Walt's coming to your country. All I can say now is that he has I think fully made up his mind to come, but when I cannot say. If his health had been as good as usual I think he would have started this winter. He will come prepared to lecture also. On the whole, I think the lecturing phase is the best. He has a lecture on President Lincoln, and on the Soldier, and on Democracy, which would perhaps please a larger number than the reading of his poems. I have little doubt you will see him inside of a year, and maybe much sooner.

Burroughs tells Dowden of having recently finished an essay, 'The Birds of the Poets,' [1] in which he gives much of Whitman's mockingbird song in the 'Word out of the Sea.'

[1] *Scribner's Monthly*, vol. 6, p. 565, September, 1873.

V

'THE VOYAGE BALK'D'

(1873–1875)

The clouds already closing in upon me,
The voyage balk'd, the course disputed, lost,
I yield my ships to Thee.

WHITMAN

WHITMAN'S superb health and high hopes suffered a sudden collapse when on the 23d of January, 1873, in his fifty-fifth year, he had his first stroke of paralysis. Premonitions of a break in his health had come about ten years before, but, in his unconquerable optimism, he believed that, having weathered that gale, he would still sail on triumphantly. With the sudden disaster, the timbers parting, while he was buffeting the waves, there came to him the separation from his two dearest friends: John Burroughs resigned his clerkship in the Treasury Department, in the beginning of the year, and returned to his native State; and William Douglas O'Connor — 'Douglas, tender and true,' (as Whitman called him)—became estranged for a period of several years. Other sorrows followed thick and fast upon him. It was, in his personal history, such as that dire year in the Nation's history, of which he had written in 1865, 'Year that trembled and reel'd beneath me.' With the gloom darkening around him, even he must have had his moments of asking:

Must I change my triumphant songs? . . .
Must I indeed learn to chant the cold dirges of the baffled?
And sullen hymns of defeat?

Although Burroughs resigned his Washington position at this time, for some years he continued in the employ of the Government, being retained as bank-examiner in certain sections of New York State and in the South. From this time onward, occupied with the banks, and later with building his house on the Hudson, with operating his fruit-farm, and writing his nature essays, he wrote less of Whitman (at least for a few years). But the records are available for tracing the course of their comradeship, even during those busy years. A letter which Burroughs wrote to Whitman on January 12, from Middletown, New York, marks a milestone in their Road of Friendship — the end of the decade spent together in Washington.

DEAR WALT: I have thought of you very often since I have been up here, but have hardly had time to write and tell you so. I left Washington in great haste, and since I have been here have been in the midst of a very maelstrom of business, all new, all strange, and very mixed. But I am now fairly master of the situation, and though I do not expect my troubles are over, yet I am better prepared to meet them. I have got a good account- ant, a competent attorney, a balance in the bank, and ought to be happy. But it cost me a pang to leave W. I was so warm and snug, and my nest was so well feathered; but I have really cut loose, and do not expect to return except briefly. I can make more money here, be much freer, be nearer home [meaning his native home at Roxbury, N.Y.] and have a new field for duties. My greatest loss will be in you, my dear Walt, but then I shall look forward to having you up here a good long time at a stretch, which will be better than the crumbs I used to get of you in W....

With much love
JOHN BURROUGHS

After Burroughs had left Washington, Whitman would drop in occasionally to see Mrs. Burroughs, who had stayed on for a while. Sometimes he brought her a magazine containing an essay by her husband, perhaps being rewarded with a piece of her pie or cake, for which he had a weakness. After Whitman's paralytic attack, Burroughs's letters to his wife make frequent mention of Whitman. He urges her to keep a sharp eye on him, to nurse him up well, if he comes up, and to go often to see him. In one letter he wrote: 'I see the "Nation" gave my "Galaxy" article a big puff last week, but I hate the "Nation" for all that.' He hated it because it was unfriendly to Whitman.

From Mrs. Burroughs, on February 23, her husband received the following:

I called to see Walt yesterday and he is still confined to his room; he felt so much better he went out last Monday just across the street, thinking it would do him good, but I fear it has been an injury to him, for he has not been so well since. He says its not only been a stroke of the muscles but also of the brain, and will be a long time perhaps before he entirely recov- ers. As soon as he is able he intends to go home. I asked him if he did not

think he had better come up here and stay with me, and I rather urged him
to come for I felt sorry for him and told him I would do the best I could,
but he said no and seemed to think he had better stay there, so I proposed
to take him out riding as soon as he was well enough, and he seemed
pleased with the offer, and said he should like to go very much. I am
going down Tuesday to see how he is and when he can go. He had just
heard of the death of his sister in St. Louis, which I think was the cause of
his being depressed, and he thought so too. She died last Wednesday and
was buried yesterday.

This was Martha, the wife of his brother Jeff, of whom he was
very fond. To this letter Burroughs replied:

I was glad to hear about Walt, and that you are so kind to him. Love
me, love Walt.

During this period, on February 26, Whitman wrote his mother:

I expect Mrs. Burroughs here probably today with a carriage to take me
out riding — so you see I am beginning to sport around.

And on March 2, Mrs. Burroughs wrote her husband that she never
saw Walt enjoy anything so much as he did the drive they had
taken a few days before. She said he was much better, and was
then going daily to his office. Whitman himself wrote Burroughs
on April 30:

DEAR JOHN BURROUGHS,
    I rec'd your letter and was glad to hear from you — I am still in a pretty
bad way — I am writing this over at the office at my desk, but feel today
more like lying down than sitting up — I do not walk any better, and my
head has frequent distress — Still, for all that I slowly gain strength, very
slowly & *shall yet get well as ever* —
    Everything goes on about the same in the sphere of my affairs, as when
I last saw you [Burroughs saw him in Washington in March] — Mother is
at Camden — mopes and worries a good deal about me — I don't feel like
leaving here, for visiting or any purpose, until I get so I can move about —
The doctor is applying electricity every other day.... I anticipate benefit
in a while, but it makes no perceptible difference yet — How and where is
'Sula — I wish I was where I could come in and see her and you often —
(those nice breakfasts were bright spots & I shall not forget them) — if I
could just get 'round and sit an hour or so for a change, and chat with
'Sula and you, two or three times a week, I believe it would do me good —
but I must take it out in imagination....
    — I got a long letter from Dowden — he mentions you — As I sit I look
over from my office window on the President's grounds — the grass is

green enough — they have already been over it once with the cutter, and Saturday there were men out in their shirt-sleeves raking it up — I have a bunch of lilacs in a pitcher in my room....

With all Whitman's optimism, he was cautious and foresighted. On May 16 of that year he made and executed a will, one copy of which he gave into the keeping of Charles W. Eldridge, then in Washington. To read the carefully worded and naïve document is to feel your heart warm to the dutiful son and brother who here endows his kin with all his worldly goods, confirming and adding to his former will, he says, made in 1872. He had $950 in one savings bank, and $550 in another. These sums, and the plates of his books; the copies of his books; any returns due him from the booksellers in London and New York; and a balance of $63.43, due from the New York bookseller; any salary or moneys due him on the payroll from his clerkship in the Solicitor's office; his clothing, books, watches, furniture, and all personal property whatever; he bequeathed to his mother, Louisa Whitman, in trust for his brother, Edward L. Whitman, to be used for his support and benefit. In case of her decease (or for other cause), he named his brother, George W. Whitman, as trustee and executor in her place. He expressed the wish that his dear mother, or his dear brother (if executor), pay to Peter Doyle $89, a sum due him from himself. He willed his friend Peter his silver watch — Appleton-Tracy movement, hunting-case — and wrote, 'I wish it given to him with my love.' The oil portrait of himself by Charles Hine he gave to his brother George; also 'the old oil painting, with old frame; also the portrait in oil of Mother, by Jacobs, small size.' His open-face silver watch he willed to James Cornwall Whitman, son of his brother Andrew.[1]

Burroughs used to speak of Doyle as 'a mute inglorious Whitman.' When Doyle died, it brought Whitman and the old days back again so vividly that, Burroughs said, it was 'almost like losing Walt anew.'

Whitman's tenderness and solicitude for his brother Edward, a defective, were always in evidence. His savings and provisions kept this brother's present and future needs steadily in view. He

---

[1] Charles Eldridge gave John Burroughs his letters from Whitman, and the copy of this will, from which the foregoing digest was made.

also nursed and provided for an elder brother, Jesse, who lost his mind in adult life, and who died in 1870. But his special care was for Edward, who outlived him.

Seven days after Whitman executed the will here digested, his mother died. He had reached her side three days before the end. Only those who understand the close bond between that mother and son can divine what a blow her death was to him in his already stricken condition. He wrote to Peter Doyle, 'It is the greatest cloud of my life.'

But, broken as he was, he returned to Washington shortly after and tried to resume work. The letter from Charles Eldridge to Burroughs, written on June 26, explains the situation:

... Walt returned here about a week after the funeral in a very depressed condition and complaining more in regard to himself than I have ever heard him do since he got sick. He was not content to stay at his room so he availed himself of the invitation of the Ashtons and went up there and staid for ten or twelve days.... The change to Ashton's was good for him as there were women and a baby, and he had more agreeable surroundings. He thought he was decidedly improving before he went away, but I have had a letter from him this week which is not so encouraging. He still has those distressed spells in the head quite often, and his locomotion is no better. He has two months' leave of absence from June 15. Barfield behaved very handsomely. '

The fact is, I begin to doubt whether Walt is going to recover, and I am very apprehensive of another attack.... He is a mere physical wreck to what he was.... It is a terrible misfortune, one of the saddest spectacles I have ever seen. His mental powers seem to be as vigorous as ever, which is the brightest part of his case, but to be stricken with such physical weakness that he cannot walk a block without resting — it is very pitiful. Such vigor, health, and endurance to be so changed, is a melancholy thing; and if it should continue for any length of time, I think it would prey upon his spirits and make him hypochondriacal. The doctor fears this, but hopes to restore him to a condition of comparative health. Walt himself believes that he is going to get well, and we all do as much as possible to encourage that belief — for it is his sheet anchor.

Whitman's letter to Eldridge, written from his brother's home, 322 Stevens Street, Camden, New Jersey, on Monday afternoon of June 23 (but without further date, though clearly of 1873), gives further particulars:

I have now been a week here.... My head does not get right... the feeling now being as if it were in the center of the head, heavy and painful, and quite pervading. Locomotion about the same — no better. I keep pretty good spirits, however, and make my calculations on getting well....

Charley, I rec'd your letter Saturday with the one enclosed. (It was a very kind sympathetic note from Kate Hillard.) I have written to Harry Douglas, my fellow-clerk in the office, asking him to send me my letters here under frank from the office, till July 1st.... Please hand her [Nelly O'Connor] this letter to read.

— Nelly, I still feel that I shall pull through, but, O, it is a weary, weary pull — and when I have these spells in the head... it requires all my phlegm....

Remember me to Dr. Drinkard if you see him, and if you have a good chance read to him what I have said of my case — if he has any suggestions, write me —

Charley, I have amused myself with *Kenelm Chillingly*, read it all — like it well — Bulwer is *such a snob* as almost redeems snobdom — the story is good, and the style a master's — Like Cervantes, Bulwer's old age productions are incomparably his best. Send me a 'Chronicle' occasionally.

WALT

Whitman's letter to Burroughs, dated June 29, much condensed here, gives a look into his heart:

My dear friends John and 'Sula Burroughs:

I am here again in Camden, stopping awhile with the intention, as soon as I can move with comfort, of getting to the seaside, probably Atlantic City — about an hour and three quarters from here by rail —... have now brought round again to where I was six or eight weeks ago.

Mother died here on the 23d of May. I stood it all better that I would have expected — I returned to Washington... but I was very restless and dissatisfied there,... obtained two months' leave of absence & (after almost making up my mind to go into quarters at a hospital, as boarder, but was persuaded out of it).... Here I am... occupying the rooms in which my mother died — waiting for time to restore my health, which I still think it will — but the blank in life and heart left by the death of my mother is what will never to me be filled —

I am comfortably fixed here, have great kindness. I try to compose myself to writing at some of my themes already outlined, but it don't amount to much yet. 'Sula, O, how I wish you was near by, keeping house — I should consider it such a privilege to hobble there for an hour or two every day while I am in this condition....

John, I don't think I have any news of Washington, or of literary affairs, nor have I heard anything since from abroad. I hope you will write me soon and spread yourself about gossip, about self and 'Sula, and the place, and everything — a letter written when you are in the mood, and let your pen run — I depend much on letters, as I am tied up here and it is pretty lonesome.

WALT

An unsigned, undated letter to Eldridge, in Whitman's hand, in the Burroughs Whitman Collection, probably belongs here. His name and address are stamped with a rubber stamp on the envelope. He writes hopefully; says he is enclosing a post-office order which Eldridge is to cash and please pay Godey. Walter Godey was his substitute during this leave of absence. His attention to Godey's pay is one of many available refutations of the unjust charge that Whitman's debts rested upon him lightly, a charge which John Burroughs always indignantly denied, stressing Whitman's punctiliousness in this particular.

In September, when Burroughs was planning the building of his house on the Hudson, on the estate which he named Riverby, where he lived the rest of his life, Whitman wrote him news of himself, discussed the proposed house, told of the new house his brother had built, and said how helpful Burroughs would find a talk with his brother George, a natural carpenter. Adding:

... There is his old Brooklyn partner... who is also a natural builder and carpenter (practically and in effect) architect.... My brother thinks (and I think so, too) that if you have not committed yourself, you could not do better than to get Smith to plan and supervise and practically work with you... an honest, conscientious, old-fashioned man, a man of family ... youngish-middle-aged — you would like him — I do — ... If you need him, & he will go, he is your man.

John, I think 'The Birds of the Poets' your best article, in many respects — it has a jaunty air, *in a perfectly natural way* — flits and hops and soars and sings around in a birdish way itself.

In later years, commenting on this letter, Burroughs said:

I was then boarding in Middletown and working on the bank affairs. I began building the house at Riverby in the fall of '73. I think I did not look up Walt's carpenter. 'The Birds of the Poets' came out in the 'Century' — the old 'Scribner's.' Yes, Walt sometimes got substitutes even before that attack — Channy B. substituted for him for two months in December and January, 1871–72, copying letters, while Walt went home to publish his book.

More letters passed between the friends about the new house, of which Burroughs sent him the plans, and photographs of a cardboard model. Whitman showed a practical knowledge of building in his comments, and said he had no doubt that Burroughs would cipher out the sum himself, and that the result would be something cozy and natural.

That month, with his brother's family, Whitman moved into the new house at 431 Stevens Street, from where, on October 3, at 3.30 in the afternoon (the year unrecorded, but clearly 1873), he wrote Eldridge of his condition:

The bad spells in my head continued at short intervals all through Tuesday, Wednesday and Thursday. Today there is a sulking sort of lull — have not had any actual blurs, but all the while ready to have them, and pretty sick and sore and bad, especially in head, confusing me, and affecting my eyes. I have rewritten my Will, with some slight changes and additions, and placed it in the pocket of my trunk here.... Ate my breakfast like a man this morning. I don't go out any.

Have been reading Dr. Adam's speech before the Evangelical Alliance in today's 'Tribune.' My eyes gave out before through.

... Charley, I think I fully appreciate my situation and the possibilities and contingencies — and honestly think yet I shall come round — that this is a pretty bad flurry, but one which will pass over....

... We like the new house.

Again to Eldridge he writes at half-past 1 P.M., October 13 [1873]. Note the meticulous care enjoined:

MY DEAR FRIEND,

I am having quite a good spell today (if only it will last) — I wish you, in conjunction with Peter Doyle, would go over to my room at Dr. White's and unlock the big trunk (the one that is strapped) and take out

My gray suit, coat, vest, and I think there are two pairs of pants, both alike,

My *black overcoat*, quite heavy — it is the one in the trunk —

Black felt hat (there are two black hats, this is the lightest, most flexible one — not the big fellow)

The *pair of old buckskin gloves*, with sheepskin cuffs, and do them up in a bundle — I think you can get three or four large sheets of *very strong brown paper* for wrapper, *tied securely*, with very strong cord — direct plainly to me — 431 Stevens Street, cor. West — here — put duplicate directions on — and send by Adams express — I wrote today to Peter Doyle, same request as this, and asking him to meet you at Milburn's bet. 3½ and 4, this afternoon — if not today, tomorrow (or next day, or next still) will do just as well, as I am in no particular hurry. Pete put the things in the trunk for me and will know about them. Then lock and strap the trunk again, and return the key to me — There are two locks, both of which this key unlocks....

After the bundle is dispatched to express office, write me a line — (As I have said, I am in no particular hurry — use your convenience).

Was there ever another poet who gave such attention to details? One almost accuses the dear man of having a touch of 'the mania of owning things.'

In May, 1874, the 17th, from his new place, Riverby, on the banks of the Hudson, eighty miles north of New York City, Burroughs wrote his comrade:

DEAR WALT:

I rec'd a magazine (the 'Galaxy') from you yesterday, which I have been peeping in a little today, but the day has been so beautiful, and the charm of the open air so great that I could not long keep my eyes on the printed page. The season is at last fairly in for it, and the fruit trees are all getting in bloom. My bees are working like beavers, and there is a stream of golden thighs passing into the hive all the time. I can do almost anything with them and they won't sting me. Yesterday I turned a hive up and pruned it, that is, cut out a lot of old, dirty comb; the little fellows were badly frightened and came pouring out in great consternation, but did not offer to sting me. I am going to transfer a swarm in a day or two to a new style of hive. I spend all my time at work about the place and like it much. I run over to Middletown to look after bank matters for a day or two, then back here. The house is being plastered and will be finished during the summer. The wrens and robins and phoebe birds have already taken possession of various nooks of it, and if they are allowed to go on with their building I must stop mine. During that snowstorm the last of April the hermit thrush took refuge in it. We are surrounded with birds here and they are a great comfort and delight to me.

Your room is ready for you and your breakfast plate warmed. When will you come? I know the change would do you good, and your presence would certainly do us good. We are counting on your coming. Do not disappoint us. I will meet you in New York if you will tell me when. Let me hear from you soon. Ursula sends love.

As ever

JOHN BURROUGHS

When, in 1888, Whitman handed this letter to Horace Traubel to read, he said:

That is like a visit to John; it is just as if I took a trip with him into the woods. I can taste his fruit — I can hear the birds sing. It is an old letter — it has been about this room now many a year. John was fresh at Esopus[1] then; he had a tussle there at first, but he has won out; he is a master vine-dresser these days; and all the time his grip on himself has grown firmer — his intuitions have grown 'cuter. . . .

[1] Later a post-office was established at West Park.

And later:

John's power is in his simplicity. He writes well because he does not try to write.... He never bowls you over with any vivid passion of speech — it is not in him to do it — but he calms and soothes you — takes you out into the open where things are in an amiable mood. John might get real mad — his kettle boil over — but his language would remain conciliatory. William O'Connor, under the same excitation, would blow fiercely and leave his mark on the landscape.

Traubel quotes Whitman further concerning Burroughs:

He is so calm, so poised, so much at home with himself, so much a familiar spirit of the forests.... He is a child of the woods, fields, hills — native to them in a rare sense (in a sense almost of miracle).

We have already had illustrations of the marked influence Whitman had on young men — on Allen, Burroughs, Charles J. Woodbury, C. W. Stoddard, and others, and shall see in the letter to follow what a pull he had on Chauncey B. Deyo, a nephew of Burroughs, to whom the latter was tenderly attached. 'Channy B.' as Burroughs called him, had substituted for Whitman in Washington, for two months, a few years before, during the poet's absence in New York. The letter, dated March 25, 1874, written from Long Island College Hospital where Channy was studying medicine, gives a glimpse of 'a youth... silently approaching' who was more than content to be near the poet, 'speaking little, perhaps not a word.'

DEAR UNCLE JOHN,

I went and [saw] Walt Whitman Saturday as I told you I intended, and felt a thousand times paid. He told me that he was not feeling quite so well that day as usual, though he was cheerful and glad to see me and talked a good deal with me. How good it seemed to be with him. Then I was happy, if ever. Every word seemed to go to the spot. To look at him inspired my soul. I do not see how any one can help but love him. It seems to me that he is the perfection of the fruit of the earth. I remember that once while looking at him when he was still, I wondered how he had lived the calm and easy life he had — how it happened that he had not been a great general, or king, or shaken the nation or world in some way, and then I thought of his writing, and how that had been his work — that instead of commanding armies and conquering worlds, as Napoleon or Cæsar, he had written poems, and I believe, as sure as the earth rolls, they will yet help America more, far more, than Washington helped it, or Napoleon France, or Cæsar Rome.

It seemed hard to see the great man afflicted, bowed down, and I could not suppress my tears, and cannot suppress them now.... His death would be a heavy, heavy blow to me. Oh, Uncle John, I can't think of it without crying, as I do now.

(I could not write any more then, after writing the above.)

I am sometimes afraid, after consulting my books, that he will never be much better. He seemed to be hopeful though, and to think that he would get well again. Yet he told me when we were walking out that sometimes when he did not feel so well he said to himself, 'Damn you, you ain't so sure you are going to get well yet,' seeming to be very unconcerned about it.

My visit seemed to cheer him. He said it did and that he wished he could have a young fellow like me two or three hours every day. He may come up and stay a spell with me. He thought perhaps he would.... I think the change would do him good, and mean to have him come if possible. He talked about you. Said I must write you that you must be sure and come and see him, as you said. He gave me one of his pictures — a wood engraving — which I think is his best. I told him what I thought of it and he said he liked what I said about it. He intends it for his 'Leaves of Grass.' I have it before me all the time....

C. B. Deyo

Some weeks later several eloquent letters came from this youth to his uncle, full of dreams and visions. Letters which show the seething emotion of adolescence carried to a state of abnormal exaltation, precursors to a sad *dénouement*. One written at a railway station records the impressions from the passing throng — girls, boys, old men bowed with care, carpenters and other sturdy workmen. The young mystic reads their souls as they pass. Something, he says, is exchanged between him and them in the quick glances. It is like a letter from an inarticulate Whitman. Is almost as though we had a glimpse of Whitman himself at that age:

I catch the eye of a girl. Her look produces its impression upon me, and my look produces an impression upon her. Nothing... can produce the impression that the eye produces. By no other means do we come so near each others souls.... I catch the eyes of men and boys. It is good. I love them, but there isn't that affinity, that love, that sympathy. Such cannot be. It is contrary to nature.... How good it is to see such men.... Oh, that we could feel our indebtedness to them! that we could feel the deepest reverence for the large brawny arms, the coarse tough hands, the tanned, sweaty faces!

Whitman's letter of June 5 refers to the death of this youth, of which Burroughs said: 'It almost cut me in two. I had set such store by him. He was only twenty-three — such a modest, gentle, affectionate character....'

DEAR FRIEND,

Your second letter, with sad news — following the sad, sad, inexpressibly sad news of the first — has just reached me.

I will not write any of the usual condolences — Channy's malady and death seem to be of those events sometimes mocking with unaccountable sudden tragedies and cross-purposes all of us & all our affairs....

WALT

It was in March, 1874, that Whitman first published his 'Prayer of Columbus,' his real swan song. Although he lived to write many lesser things for some twenty years, he never again reached the sublimity of that poem in which, old, poor and paralyzed, and thinking the terminus near, the voyage of his spiritual adventure balked, the course disputed, lost, he yielded his ships. Identifying himself, in that dark hour, with the great Genoese, he lifted his eyes to the steady, ineffable Light, and glimpsed the shadowy vast shapes of better worlds across the distant waves.

In August of that year, the 18th, he wrote Burroughs of his formal discharge from government service, it then being clear that he would not be able to resume work:

DEAR JOHN AND 'SULA BURROUGHS,

The interval of some weeks (or is it months?) since I last wrote you has passed on, bringing no decided change in my condition.... I 'most think the end is not far off — but I get over them and my natural buoyancy reaserts itself — (& in the main keeps control of the helm) — though to a man of my lazy-activity this whole condition and sickness of mine is very wearing —

Today I am feeling very comfortable, sitting here in the front room by the open window writing this — eat this morning quite a respectable breakfast, bread and tea — and at about 3 shall make a light, moderate bite of dinner — no supper — I find I get along best with *one pretty fair meal only*, and that I make breakfast. The gastric and dyspeptic trouble has been serious and perhaps is so yet — ...

John Swinton came down from N.Y. and spent Sunday with me — told me lots of N.Y. newspaper news, &c — it was a very welcome visit to me

I was discharged from my clerkship on the last of June, by B. Wilson the new solicitor of the Treasury — (it is all right) —

— All questions of *what I shall do* are to me so subordinate to the question of whether I shall soon or ever get well (or partially well), that I hardly entertain them seriously — I enclose you Tennyson's latest letter to me — also a slip Swinton gave me — Send them both back in your next letter —

...Best love to you both, & I shall be with you yet, I have no doubt.

WALT

Commenting to me on this letter in 1907, Burroughs said:

John Swinton, an Englishman, was a friend of Walt's — a newspaper man, a come-outer, a reformer who despised most things that men worship. He died about 1904, I think. I last saw him a few years before that at a Whitman dinner. He made a speech that annoyed us all, a kind of rasping speech. He was soured. His note of protest and criticism may have been wholesome amid so much praise. It came out clear, before his speech was over, that he was all right, but some things in it annoyed us a good deal. He was a brilliant man, but he never made much stir. There were two brother, John and William; their names were known in journalism. Swinton's school books were much used.

In December, at 11 P.M., the year not stated, but unquestionably it was 1874, Whitman wrote:

DEAR JOHN BURROUGHS,

I have had another severe spell the last five weeks — ... but ... am venturing out a little now — hope and quite expect to get at least as well as I was before this spell — Eldridge made me a call... seems to be nothing very new among our friends.... Marvin[1] has written me twice — has been reading your 'Notes' and is quite possessed with them — also 'Dem. Vistas.'

I am writing very little — have a piece, a *mélange*, prose and verse, in the 'Christmas Graphic'... in which I say a brief word about Emerson....

Do you get in the new house? Write me a good long letter. I wish I was with you —

WALT

Burroughs visited Whitman at least in December of 1874, and in April, 1875, as seen by letters from him to Dowden.

The following excerpt from a letter written in April, 1875, by R. W. Clifton to Edward Dowden, was sent by Dowden to Whitman, and by Whitman to Burroughs:

I wrote to Chatto and Windus, according to your instructions, for 'Leaves of Grass.' In reading this I was tempted at first to throw the book

[1] See note I, p. 64.

away as the production of a madman (you had forewarned one of the possibility of arriving at that conclusion in your letter to Magill) and utterly unintelligible, but by degrees all seemed to clear away and spite of the eccentricity of method (or rather the utter want of it) the wonderful power and reach of the man's mind unrolled itself and *now* I cannot say how much enjoyment I get from his poems.... I cannot help marvelling however how it is that any one can fail to perceive his coarseness and undisguised animalism to be the most direct and indeed the only means strong enough to combat the mock modesty and false notions of propriety of the age; it seems to me far better to speak out thus and have done with it, nor need Walt Whitman ever fear *real* modesty or *real* decency will join in the howl against him. That many will misunderstand him wilfully, or fail to interpret him aright, he will of course expect — it is the fate of all originality — and he bears much the same position in letters as Wagner does in music. I was particularly pleased with the critique from a lady's pen [1] among those you sent. One would naturally be curious to know how such writing as WW's would be looked at from a woman's point of view.

Testimony is abundant of the peculiar drawing power of Whitman, through his 'Leaves.' Among the mass of letters saved by Burroughs is one which Whitman had sent him in 1875 from a cotton-planter, John Newton Johnson, of Alabama — a fervent admirer of his poems. The letter, dated February 19, was doubtless sent Burroughs because the correspondent asked to be introduced to him that he might thank him for his eloquent treatise on Whitman. In the same letter, Johnson tells the poet that he would be proud even to be his bootblack. He gives details of his family and his life 'in order to show you the strong spiritual likeness between us two.' One paragraph reads:

I would not have you think I meant you to believe that I was able to understand everything in your writings at once. No. At first I found good things scattered about among some which I resolved to leave for future unravelling, and some there were which I thought it charity to allow that you yourself could understand them! Continually there comes to me a revelation of the meaning of some one more passage. I will now admit, without charge for the admission, that you understood it all when you wrote it.

He then relates an anecdote of an old soldier who had 'hooked' some sugar from the enemy's supplies and announced, 'I'll be dad-

[1] Anne Gilchrist's 'A Woman's Estimate of Walt Whitman,' *The Radical*, May, 1870.

slapped, if I hain't got sugar enough to do me a week.' He added:
'So it is with me: I'll be dad-slapped if I hain't got Philosophy and
Poetry and Sugar and Salt enough in "Leaves of Grass" to do me a
year or two. But don't think it is in any considerable degree the
oddity of what I find there that pleases me so much. It is the
pathos, deep feeling, enthusiastic benevolence, apprehension of the
sublime in Nature.'

The whole letter, naïve and racy, must have heartened Whitman
in those years when his work was so generally misunderstood.
W. S. Kennedy, in his 'Reminiscences of Walt Whitman' (pages
18–21), tells of this zealous disciple, in 1887, after thirteen years
of correspondence, traveling from Alabama to Camden, and hanging about for more than a month in order to see his hero often at
close range. Whitman told Kennedy that Johnson knew more
about his poetry, and more of it, than any other man living, and that
he felt highly complimented at the devotion shown in his coming
so far to see him. Nevertheless, he failed to satisfy his disciple's
hopes. Later, Johnson wrote Kennedy that he had found the poet
less 'friendly and flowing' than he had hoped to find him. Kennedy
explains that Johnson resented the changes in text which Whitman
had made in recent editions, and could not understand why
Whitman could not be drawn into a discussion of his reasons with
so zealous a follower. Kennedy points out that the disciple's visit
fell during a season when Whitman was bothered with an influx of
visitors, and was suffering from an aggravation of the mental and
physical inertia which so often overtook him and prevented him
from engaging in prolonged conversations. Well as the racy old
cotton-planter had read his 'Leaves,' he had not taken to heart the
poet's warning:

> Are you the new person drawn toward me?
> To begin with take warning, I am surely far different from what you suppose.

After an April visit to Whitman, Burroughs wrote Myron
Benton:

> I am not reading anything now-a-days. These April days keep me out of
> doors all the time. I have even fallen away behind in the Beecher trial, and
> see no prospect of ever catching up. Walt Whitman told me the other day
> that the sight of the paper made him sick — when I saw him before he was
> reading eagerly every word.

On May 2, Whitman wrote of hearing from Dowden, and of how thoroughly fine he was finding his 'Shakespeare: A Critical Study of his Mind and Art.' He added, 'I have underlined passages on every page.... Dowden advances, expands, or rather *penetrates*.'

To Dowden on May 4, Burroughs writes, in part:

... I have rather thought you would come over to this country and see us by this time — you and Rossetti both. Rossetti thought, when I saw him, he should come in three or four years, and I remember you cherished some such plan. You ought to come, both of you, while Whitman is living and not put off the day too long. He may live yet many years but I fear his sun is getting very low in the horizon, and you of all men should see and know him in life. For the past year a dark dread has beset my mind whenever I have thought of him. He is so unspeakably dear to me that the earth would not seem habitable if he were gone. And yet he does not seem to be getting worse. I saw him for a few hours about the middle of April and thought him fully as bright and hopeful as when I saw him in December. He told me with a reassuring laugh that his physician had said he was not as ill as he (W) thought he was. It was at night and near eleven o'clock, he walked out with me for several squares as I left, and his voice and manner were like the old times in Washington.

He looks as well as ever, only a little more bleached in his hair and beard. His brother with whom he lives thinks he is slowly gaining strength.

I have great hopes of having him up here with me part of the summer, and great expectations of benefit to him by the change of air and scene.

Writing to Burroughs from Camden in mid-December, Whitman said:

I have been back here two weeks and over — my Washington jaunt occupied some seventeen or eighteen days and was a very pleasant one for me — started out with the idea of a two days visit only. Am perhaps now lately not so well... still I keep up about the same (and get mad at myself for grunting)....

My new edition is nearly ready — two volumes [1] — will give you early advice of their appearance — only 100 copies issued —

Is the 'Winter Sunshine' out? Eldridge called to see me.... Marvin has gone to England with a Treasury squad. He has called on Mrs. Gilchrist. M. D. Conway called on me, Lord Houghton also.

We have great times in this house — a baby has arrived, now five weeks old (he has been named Walt) — just now, though, he is quite sick, but I opine will get along — The rest are all very well except my sister, the mother, is part of the time only middling.

[1] The so-called Centennial Edition (6th edition) of his works.

I hear young Walt raising his song in the room overhead as I conclude my letter. Love to you as always, my friend.

WALT

Burroughs explained that 'young Walt,' a child of George's wife, Lou, died July 12, 1876, much to Whitman's sorrow. He said that with the death of James, Andrew's child (in 1892), the name of Whitman went out among their kin, as Jeff's children were girls. Lord Houghton (Richard Monckton Milnes), Burroughs explained, published a volume of poems of some note, and was 'a Whitman-ite in a small way.'

In the early part of the following year, Burroughs tried persistently to persuade Whitman to come and live near his river home. He said that, for a time, he had cherished a plan of building Whitman a little hermitage at Riverby, overlooking the vineyards and the Hudson. 'Oh, if that dream could have come true! But Walt, with all his love of the country, was more at home in a city, among many people.'

VI

O'CONNOR AND WHITMAN ESTRANGED

(1872–1882)

> Alas! they had been friends in youth,
> But whispering tongues can poison truth,
> And constancy lives in realms above,
> And life is thorny and youth is vain,
> And to be wroth with one we love
> Doth work like madness on the brain.
> And thus it chanced, as I divine,
> With Roland and Sir Leoline;
> Each spake words of high disdain
> And insult to his heart's best brother,
> And never either found another
> To free the hollow heart from paining.
> They stood aloof, the scars remaining,
> Like cliffs which had been rent asunder.
>
> COLERIDGE

THE estrangement between William Douglas O'Connor and Walt Whitman, which began in 1872, and lasted about ten years, originated, John Burroughs told me, in a heated argument over the Fifteenth Amendment of our Constitution.

O'Connor became enraged at what Walt said about the unfitness of the negroes for voting. They were in the habit of goring each other in argument like two bulls, and that time Walt was, I guess, rather brutal and insulting. It was in O'Connor's home. O'Connor fired up and turned on him. Walt took his hat and went home in a pet. Then when they met on the street the next day, Walt put out his hand; but William shied around and went on past. The iron had entered his soul. But when Walt was in trouble — over the Osgood affair — William rushed to the rescue. He opened the correspondence, and right away they got back to the old footing. He came to see Walt in '88, I think, and staid a week or more.

O'Connor was an ardent abolitionist, while Whitman's primary concern at that time was for the preservation of the Union. One can imagine the fiery scorn and sarcasm which O'Connor poured upon Whitman, but it is difficult to imagine the placid Whitman being 'brutal and insulting.' Whatever the provocation, O'Connor's must have been a withering blast to make the tolerant Whitman withdraw in dignified silence. And what a curious experience for the 'Good Gray' to see the guns, hitherto (and later also) trained on others in his defense, now belching out their wrath upon him!

Let us see what Whitman said in reference to their differences during and after the Civil War. Talking with Traubel, November 11, 1888, he said, in part:

O'Connor was warm, earnest, eager, passionate, warrior-like for the anti-slavery idea.... This in some ways served to keep us apart — though not really apart — (superficially apart). I can easily see now that I was a good deal more repelled by that devotion in William — (for with him it was the profoundest moral devotion) — than was justified. With these latter-day confirmations of William's balance... — the later succession of events — there has come to me some self-regret — some suspicion that I was extreme, at least too lethargic, in my withdrawals from William's magnificent enthusiasm... some things I did not see then I see now. After all I may have been tainted a bit, just a little bit, with the New York feeling with regard to anti-slavery; yet I have been anti-slavery always — was then, and am now; and to all other slaveries, too, black or white, mental or physical.

And later, in the same conversation:

... He would go for me in the fiercest way, denounce me — appear to regard me as being negligent, as shirking a duty.[1]

On December 21, 1888, in the volume containing the foregoing excerpt, Whitman is quoted, on page 353, as commenting thus upon O'Connor's anger:

William storms and blows and rains and snows and freezes and roasts you all at once; goes for you tooth and nail... leaves nothing of you for the dogs — not a bone.

And then:

O how divine that passion in William has always seemed to me! His uncompromising love of justice! his eagerness to court any danger, to accept any peril, to go to any trouble, endure anything... for a cause which he considered sufficiently lofty.

J. T. Trowbridge wrote Burroughs, December 27, 1873, concerning 'the sorrowful conclusion to such a friendship' as had existed so long between Whitman and O'Connor, adding:

I honor Walt for his offers to make up the quarrel; should think some mutual friends of the two might bring about a reconciliation.

[1] Traubel: *With Walt Whitman in Camden*, vol. 3, pages 75–76, 77–78. New York, Mitchell Kennerley, 1914.

Again, May 20, 1874, Trowbridge asks Burroughs:

Are Whitman and O'Connor on any better terms? I can't quite reconcile my mind to that feud.

Two years later, Burroughs evidently referred to the matter in his letters to O'Connor, when, though still apparently estranged, O'Connor was proving himself a sturdy champion of Whitman. A passage from O'Connor's letter of May 4, 1876, in reply to what Burroughs must have said, reads:

I am sorry you felt about me as you did. It never was deserved. It is better that Walt and I should not meet. But I have no feeling for him but affection and sorrow, and there never has been any time when I would have let harm I could prevent come to him or his belongings. You speak of 'neglect,' but this English testimonial grew from me, and I have always done what I could, though quietly. As for my letter in the 'Tribune,' [1] it is, as service, just nothing, and nothing should be based upon it.

It is an awkward subject to write about, and I hope you will keep what I have said to yourself. The trouble between us I have never circulated, but it has been used against me by others, as reconciliation would be, and the matter is better as it is. Walt and I know our own feelings for each other, which is the best on my part, as I think it is on his; and here I rest. On reflection, you will agree with me, especially when you bear in mind that the interference of others gives the matter a complicated premise. Say nothing to any one.

I find myself somewhat mystified by this letter, unable to understand why a reconciliation could be used against O'Connor, and why so apparently trivial a matter should have had the long-continued result. Passages in Eldridge's letters to Burroughs, which follow, fail to solve the puzzle. It would seem that there must have been more to the affair than the known facts disclose. Speaking of his proposed Reminiscences of Whitman, Eldridge writes Burroughs, March 7, 1896:

Of course I shall have to practice a degree of reticence about some matters.... For instance, how shall I treat that matter of his quarrel with William? Shall I ignore it, or just allude to it, or give all the details? There are just three courses open to me. What do you advise? Please think it over and let me know when you can find time to write to me.

And on April 4, 1896, Eldridge writes:

I was glad to hear what you thought about the quarrel of William and

[1] *New York Tribune*, April 22, 1876.

Walt, in regard to its treatment by me in my Reminiscences. I shall undoubtedly follow your advice, and will probably send you the whole manuscript for criticism and suggestion before I publish anything.

One would be glad to get track of what passed from Burroughs to Eldridge on this point, but all efforts of mine, thus far, have been fruitless.

In view of the fact that Professor Holloway, in his 'Whitman,' page 302, speaks of the Osgood affair (to be discussed later) as 'the occasion of a partial reconciliation with O'Connor,' and the fact that some other writers on Whitman have taken the same stand, it seems advisable to show here how complete the reconciliation really was. Ellen Calder, formerly Mrs. William D. O'Connor, stated in an article in the 'Conservator,' May, 1906, that the Osgood defection, wherein Whitman's need of O'Connor was urgent, was the means of forever dispelling that old misunderstanding between the friends. We shall see later how valiantly O'Connor rallied to the Whitman colors in 1876 and 1882, and that he bore them aloft to the very end. It is also well to note what Whitman himself wrote to Burroughs, in a letter dated August 13, 1882:

... O'Connor sent me a copy of your letter about visiting Rossetti (O'C and I correspond now quite often, and just on the same terms as of yore).

Moreover, Whitman's fervent comments about O'Connor, scattered all through Traubel's three volumes which deal with the poet's last years in Camden, serve forever to refute statements as to a 'partial reconciliation.' The breach was completely bridged over.[1] To O'Connor, whose fervent comradeship had begun in 1860, and which lasted till his death in 1889 (notwithstanding the scar of that sundering decade) may well be applied Whitman's lines from the 'Calamus' poems:

O here I last saw him that tenderly loves me, and returns again never to separate from me.

Traubel quotes Whitman in 1888 or 1889 as saying to him, when naming O'Connor, Burroughs, Dowden, and others, in connection with what their loyalty had meant to him, 'The thought of them

[1] Whitman paid a fine tribute to O'Connor in his preface to O'Connor's *Three Tales*, Boston, 1892.

almost chokes me with gladness.' And when Ernest Rhys was going back to England without having seen O'Connor, excusing himself to Whitman by saying that since he had seen him and Niagara he felt he knew America, Whitman deplored the 'woful omission.' To Horace Traubel he declared, 'Two hundred thousand Niagaras wouldn't make up to me for one O'Connor.'

The valiant services rendered Whitman by O'Connor in his later years are proof of his unabated affection for the Good Gray Poet he had so staunchly championed early in his poetic career. That affection is well illustrated in a letter from him to Whitman, dated May 20, 1882. Traubel quotes the letter on pages 12-17, volume 2, of 'With Walt Whitman in Camden.' Of another O'Connor letter, long after the reconciliation, Whitman said, 'I carry it about in my heart — and William, too.' He is quoted by Traubel, January 8, 1889, as saying of O'Connor, 'I feel that he has always been more than my friend — has sworn his big oath in my interest, and battled for me without reservation.'

Even without the abundant documentary evidence that the friends buried the hatchet forever out of sight, is the thing that counts most of all — when Whitman needed him, O'Connor flew to the rescue. Whitman gratefully accepted his aid, and the friendship was resumed on the old terms —

'Reconciliation — word over all, beautiful as the sky.'

VII

WHITMAN PULLED AND HAULED

(1874–1882)

Apart from the pulling and hauling stands what I am,
Stands amused, complacent, compassionating,...
... curious what will come next,
Both in and out of the game and watching and wondering at it.

Backward I see in my own days where I sweated through fog with
      linguists and contenders,
I have no mockings or arguments, I witness and wait.

WHITMAN

I HOPE in this chapter to contribute something toward off-setting what seems to me an unfair tendency in certain critics to overemphasize Whitman's 'self-puffery' at the expense of his sterling and monumental qualities. Examples of the criticism I have in mind are found in Harvey O'Higgins's 'Alias Walt Whitman,' in 'Harper's,' May, 1929, and Professor Holloway's 'Whitman as His Own Press-Agent,' in the 'American Mercury,' December, 1929.

That Whitman was at considerable pains, particularly at the beginning of his poetic career, to keep his work (and himself as the embodiment of it) in the public eye through anonymous book notices, reviews, and descriptions of his looks and ways, is incontestably established. Sundry writings have been unearthed in recent years and traced directly to him. Their style is so characteristic as to make one smile at his ostrich-like naïveté in thinking himself hidden. To get at the motive back of this deliberate self-revelation, it seems necessary to approach the facts in a somewhat different attitude than that adopted by those who seem intent only on rending the poet's thin disguise, thus exposing what appears superficially to have been inordinate personal vanity.

It is perhaps irrelevant to state that Whitman was by no means unique among writers of his day (or of our own day either), in resorting to such means to boost his own work, since his critics stress not so much the means taken as the inconsistency exhibited;

for, while declaring his willingness to wait for his audience, Whitman does appear to have labored surreptitiously to drum up an audience. But he disarms us on this point, having long ago disclaimed that virtue of little minds — consistency:

> Do I contradict myself?
> Very well, then, I contradict myself.

But what of the anonymous celebration of himself, in itself? It is necessary, in this connection, to remember the difficulties he encountered five and seventy years ago in trying to root 'Leaves of Grass' deep in American soil. His fate was that of all geniuses born ahead of their time. Today, with his place so firmly established, it seems futile to dwell unduly on the early and persistent hostility he experienced, yet the younger generation needs the reminder of that long struggle for comprehension and tolerance that the revolutionary 'Leaves' had to undergo. With the narrow concepts of the time, the tyrannical conventions, and the almost universal habit of blinking the facts of life, the wonder is that the poet's few appreciators did not drift to the seats of the scornful. Here and there, in Europe and in America, was a reader who divined that the poet's words held, well enfolded, the meaning of life and the universe. But even such were mystified and sometimes repelled by certain passages, though, for the most part, having once espoused the cause of the 'misunderstood poet,' the faithful few continued zealous to the end. Among the foremost of these defenders of the faith, one thinks of the two whose names so often appear in these pages, William Douglas O'Connor and John Burroughs.

One remembers how the New England *literati* greeted with derision the mention of Whitman's name when Edward Carpenter, who had come over from England in 1877 just to see Niagara and Whitman, had spoken with enthusiasm of the 'Leaves.'

Down the years the gibes at Whitman have been so bandied about as to give them far more importance than they deserve. The author of 'Leaves of Grass' was dubbed a 'literary Nebuchadnezzar' by one (Henry Abbey) who thought himself a poet, but whose name was writ in water. Arthur Stedman's anthology compiled from the 'Leaves' was commended because its compiler 'knew the tufts of grass from the bales of hay.' Certain writers of the hour whose names are scarcely known to the present generation, shot many an arrow of outrageous abuse at the poet. He was styled a 'cumbrous, lumbering absurdity,' his verses, 'snorts of a hippopotamus.'[1] Sidney Lanier characterized him as 'poetry's butcher,' his lines as 'huge raw collops slashed from the rump of poetry.' (William Hayes Ward quotes this from Lanier in the Preface to Lanier's poems.) Yet Lanier had written Whitman in 1878 that he had spent 'a night of glory and delight' with the 'Leaves'! and that Whitman was to count him among his most earnest lovers. Stevenson jumped first one side, then the other, and finally got caught and was held straddling the fence, in company with other vacillators. Even Emerson, who had so promptly characterized the 'Leaves' as 'the most extraordinary piece of wit and wisdom that America had yet contributed,' registered some veerings. On the whole, however, he remained steadfast to his original course. Probably if the truth were known, he had a sneaking admiration for Whitman for adhering to his own conviction, and refusing to eliminate certain lines which offended the 'little ones.'

Most of Emerson's criticisms of Whitman had the saving grace of humor — such as calling him 'half song-thrush, half alligator.' W. S. Kennedy states in his 'Reminiscences,' page 78, that Sanborn told him that Emerson characterized the 'Leaves' as a mixture of the Bhagavad Gîta and the 'New York Herald.' In his Journals Emerson quotes Whipple with evident relish as saying that the 'Leaves' contains every leaf but the fig-leaf, but Kennedy says Whipple only quoted Wendell Phillips, who originated the remark.[2]

Much as both Burroughs and O'Connor revered Emerson, they were highly incensed at his omission of Whitman from his 'Parnassus.' (He also omitted Poe, of whom he spoke slightingly in his Journal as 'the jingle man.') Freeing his mind of Emerson's slight on Whitman, O'Connor announced that 'Emerson's Parnassus isn't Apollo's, not by a long shot.' And Burroughs, freeing his mind to Myron Benton, wrote, 'I think Walt can afford to be overlooked by Emerson, but I don't think that Emerson can afford to overlook *him.*'

Bayard Taylor poked fun at the Good Gray Poet's Good Green

[1] Edgar Fawcett: 'Walt Whitman,' *Collier's Weekly*, March, 1898.
[2] Kennedy: *The Fight of a Book for the World*, p. 125.

Friends, who were 'sleeplessly on the watch for slights to their master.' But the verdancy of some of them has, unfortunately, shone with a livelier hue than the goodness — a result foreseen by Whitman when he enjoined,

I charge you forever reject those who would expound me.

When one reads the efforts of avowed appreciators to reconstruct some of Whitman's most intimate experiences from the meagerest of known facts, one is reminded of the *title* of an early, unreclaimed poem of his — 'Wounded in the House of Friends.' Such 'friends' and conjecturers apparently regard themselves as Cuviers in the biographical field — able to reconstruct an entire creature from one tiny metacarpal. But Walt in his all-embracing tolerance has 'celebrated' even these —

There will always be plenty of embroiderers.

So much for the adverse conditions amid which the 'Leaves' struggled for growth. As to the poet's efforts at self-exposition: It hardly seems necessary to remind the discerning reader that it was not Whitman himself — the man — that he 'celebrated,' but Walt Whitman as spokesman for the typical American he predicted. His 'I celebrate myself' includes you and me, our souls no less than our bodies, our bodies no less than our souls — and all besides that has led up to the 'acme of things accomplished,' all that encloses 'the things to be.' In fact, his 'Walt Whitman' was widely comprehensive — 'I am large, I contain multitudes' — just as, under the symbol of the universal grass, he sang exultantly of everything on this good green earth, and on every sun and planet in the cosmos.

The ability to make so unusual a book as the 'Leaves' presupposes the author's recognition of its unusualness, and of the need for a right approach to it. Clearer than another he saw the necessity for spreading correct ideas about it, for helping to create the understanding by which it could be adequately judged. Knowing himself to be a fitter judge of his own aims than another could possibly be, he evidently preferred to do a generous share toward expounding them. Moreover, he appears always to have regarded himself and his work in a curiously detached way. Only so could he have written with such utter candor and un-selfconsciousness. Apart from the pulling and hauling of critics and reviewers, and curious as to what would come next, he stood amused, 'both in and out of the game, and watching and wondering at it.' Believing, as he did, in the high destiny of These States, and that it had been given him to help realize that destiny, even though he had declared his willingness to wait, he was not averse, on occasion, to hoisting a guiding light to penetrate the fog spread by 'linguists and contenders.' And so, 'without mockings or arguments,' but with finger-posts here and there, he witnessed, and then waited for his words to bear their destined results. Trust in Allah! yes, but '*Tie your horse* and trust in Allah.'

Whatever may be justly charged as to Whitman's occasional violation of current standards of taste in this respect, is it not clear that back of his elucidation of himself and his work was the conviction of the sacredness of his message? that his furtherance of it was a charge he felt constrained to keep? and that in that furtherance he furnished a superb illustration of his injunction to every individual: 'Rest not till you rivet and publish yourself of your own Personality.'

With the attitude here indicated toward Whitman's anonymous contributions about his own work, I now offer what contrary-minded persons may consider still another evidence of his self-exploitation, but which, I trust, many will regard quite otherwise. On February 14, 1874, Whitman wrote Burroughs as follows:

I enclose you an article from the 'Nation' of Jan. 29.[1] How will the MS. article I have scratched off do, in the main, as an answer to it (to help keep the pot-aboiling)? Do you feel like making up an article out of said MS. — adding or excising what you see fit — signing your name to it, & sending it to Mr. Nation man?

The enclosure, a manuscript of eight pages of script in Whitman's hand, is entitled 'Is Walt Whitman's Poetry Poetical?' The pages are numbered in blue pencil, and one sheet has Whitman's blue-penciled instructions to the printer as to paragraphing and the use of smaller type for the quoted verse. At the end of the article, also in blue pencil, is written the name of John Burroughs, although it is not one of Burroughs's unmistakable signatures, and may have been written by Whitman. Beneath the title, in ink, unmistakably in Whitman's hand, is written, 'Middletown, N.Y. February 17,

[1] A review of Joaquin Miller's poems, in which Whitman is criticized.

1874.' That was where Burroughs was residing at the time, and the date affixed was evidently the one on which Whitman assumed that Burroughs would submit the manuscript. Numerous erasures occur throughout the article, but not a single word, except the possible signature, is from Burroughs's hand.

I have thoroughly searched through the files of the 'Nation,' and also through the indexes to current periodicals, and fail to find this article appearing anywhere over the signature of John Burroughs. If Burroughs ever did submit it to the 'Nation' (which is possible, assuming the appended signature to be his, instead of having been written in by Whitman), it must have been returned to him, rejected. On the other hand, even after signing, if he *did* sign it, he may have changed his mind about submitting it. If he did send out the manuscript *as is*, expecting the unfriendly 'Nation' to accept it as by him, one can but smile at his ingenuousness — it so clearly emanated from Whitman.

In transcribing the article, I have copied the first page exactly as it appears in the manuscript, showing Whitman's erasures and emendations; but as that makes laborious copying, and laborious reading, the corrections thereafter are only occasionally indicated, the text being given rather as finally intended to be printed.

Presumptive evidence that Burroughs never used the article lies in the fact that I often heard him say that, after his first little book on Whitman, in 1867, he had a lull for about ten years of writing on him, and was then goaded to resume by an article in the 'New York Tribune' in 1876. His rejoinder to that 'Tribune' editorial was printed in that paper, April 13. This will be commented on in later pages. Two years following that 'Tribune' article, when writing his essay on Whitman named 'The Flight of the Eagle' ('Birds and Poets'), he there made a reference to Professor Clifford similar to the one made by Whitman in the article here transcribed. He also referred to the same foreign critics, or publications, cited here by Whitman, i.e., the Danish and French journals, and the translations by Freiligrath. These, however, are references in his own phraseology, and such as he would naturally marshal in an essay of that character.

Whatever opinion is held as to Whitman's so-called self-exploitation, it were a pity to lose the accompanying comments on his own work, and on the newer and freer forms of poetry to come of which, he thought, his own might be the germ. And one must respect the earnestness, dignity, and self-knowledge with which he writes, and yet the detachment — 'Both in and out of the game, and watching and wondering at it.

IS WALT WHITMAN'S POETRY POETICAL?

Middletown, N.Y. Feb. 17, 1874

~~I take issue with you~~

To the Editor of the Nation:

As I suppose — or rather know — that your paper is open to statements and views, even opposed to your own, if duly put, I would like to take up your_∧~~notice mostly~~ review — that part of it devoted to analyzing Walt Whitman, which appears to be the main part of the notice of Mr. Miller's last volume of poems, given in the *Nation* of Jan. 29 — and offer something ~~further and~~ on the other side. Your idea of the *ad captandum* character of Whitman's verse is quite certainly the reverse of well-founded; ~~it is~~ the almost universal testimony is that_∧~~it~~ 'Leaves of Grass' at first harsh and offensive, needs study, and more than one perusal, to give up its meaning, and confer pleasure. The author's theory_∧has evidently been_∧from the ~~first~~ outset, based upon the ~~famous~~ deep axiom 'it is ~~always~~ reserved for first-rate poems ~~not to~~ never im- to does not lap in sweets or graces but mediately_∧ gratify.' Whitman_∧is eminently an exercise, a stimulus, an inexhaustible suggestion._∧and An Italian critic complains that there is something cold and severe behind every piece. He nourishes, if and by a sort of harshness.⌉ at all, by removes and indirections⌈He is not sugar or cake ͚or any cosseting,⌋ or ornament,͚ or a warm bath, or any spiced liquor or special cookery, for a banquet. He is not even (at least apparently), art, or beauty, or melody, as those are technically construed. He construes them differently, and forms his verse thereon. To carry out the figure, he gives homely beef and bread and fruit, and water to quench thirst. His theory is that the prettiness and artificial graces and *concetti* of verse have been exhausted — have indeed become over-plentiful and nauseating; and that, for modern and popular purposes, here in America, and to express the Democratic spirit, the simple, the natural, the perennial, the familiar, and the practical (henceforth ignoring the mythologies, all the lyrical lay-figures, and the diamonds, feathers, silk, and the fine gentlemen and ladies of the saloons), must be permanently returned to and called upon and used; and these he merges in his pages. He is never a garden with regular beds and walks, and a marble fountain; but frequently the stretching landscape and distant sky — the rushing river, or briny sea — or perhaps the common and general road.

I grant you also that the so-called intellectual elements of poetry are not prominent in Walt Whitman's verse. Yet it is singularly emotional; probably no one has so daringly and freely carried 'manly attachment' into expression as this author. The 'rapture in being,' and in the physical existence of things is also vehement, beyond example. Cheerfulness overarches all, like a sky. Out of his apparent materialism, an unerring spirituality always and certainly emerges. A distinguished scientist in Washington [1] told me not long since, that, in its tally and spirit, Whitman's was the only poetry he could mention that is thoroughly consistent with modern science and philosophy, and that does not infringe upon them in a single line.

During some ten years formerly, the principal charge against *Leaves of Grass* was its offensively outspoken amativeness. The Danish critic and admirer, Rudolf Schmidt, speaks of this as 'like the roar of a wild beast in rutting time,' yet considers it not disproportioned to the magnified and vehement possession, by the ideal subject of these poems, of all the passions. But of late years, since the author's plan has expanded, and his edifice has been carried out to fuller and fuller proportions, that particular section of it has become less conspicuous, or perhaps has been seen to form, in Whitman's scheme, an honest and integral part of it. That point of attack has therefore been abandoned; and I notice you do not mention it in your analysis of the 29th.

I am not sure but now the principal trouble is in the '*shirt sleeves*.' Our poets each and all seem conventionally determined (like an Englishman in Jamaica or Ceylon), to wear the cloth coat of society, and stiff stock and hat, if they die for it; but Whitman, roaming the fields or cities in July or August, or whenever he has active work to do, is pretty sure to throw off his superficial broadcloth, and unloosen his neck-buttons. It cannot be denied that this unfits him for the dress circle of the opera, or a Saratoga ball room, or a State Dinner at the White House. But for my part, I feel refreshed by an imaginative literature which escapes from all merely genteel associations, and their standards. I think such escape (with something to make up for it), is what we all now most want, in poetical composition.

The foreign recognition of Walt Whitman's poems is by no means the mere flash in the pan inferred by your criticism. The long and very searching article some months since [2] in the *Westminster Review*, entitled 'The Poetry of Democracy — Walt Whitman,' by Professor Dowden, of Trinity College; the article on 'Leaves of Grass,' in the *Revue des Deux Mondes*, by Mme. Barthon [Bentzon], pronouncing 'Drum Taps' unapproached in

[1] Probably Professor Clifford. See 'Flight of the Eagle,' *Birds and Poets*, p. 218.

[2] Dowden's *Westminster Review* article was published July, 1871 — 'some [27] months since,' to be exact.

its vivid pictures of American Campaigning, and as modern war poetry; the splendid eulogiums of Freiligrath in his German translations of the 'Leaves,' and life of their author; the reproduction in Denmark, in the *Ide og Virkelighed* (the Copenhagen magazine, 'The Idea and Reality'), of these poems with great enthusiasm; their rendering in Hungarian, at Pesth-Buda, and reception with equal enthusiasm; with several lectures on the new American, by poets, scholars and divines, in Great Britain, and on the continent; these, I submit, are signs and accumulating proofs, steadily enlarging and deepening, of Whitman's *permanent* reception in Europe.

Then a serious principle, far beyond the merits or demerits of this individual writer, is involved. The question is not whether Walt Whitman, tried by the technical and ostensible literary standards, is a poet — as Tennyson, Longfellow, Poe, and even N. P. Willis, undoubtedly are. The real question is of a new theory and standard, discarding the old, restricted selection of the beautiful, discarding exact metre and rhyme (not rhythm), and branching out for themes into all quarters, including the modern practical and industrial ones, idealizing democracy, and finding, as Whitman himself puts it, that

'— not face alone, not brain alone, is
worthy for the Muse;
The Form complete is worthier far.'

By those ostensible, until lately current standards, tightly drawn, it is probably doubtful whether indeed he is a poet. The question remains, and must remain for the future to settle, whether in him and by him are not planted the hardy germs of a new and grander stock, and a new and freer form for poetry — certainly not less than the old, any more than our Science and Philosophy are — but necessitated by our vaster conditions of Democracy, and expressing them. In the cultus of our race, every really new, original, first-class exemplification in poetry (as in religion, politics, or anything), is a battle, a campaign, a fury, a parturition-throe of bitterness and revolt.

Finally, I would ask, on the great subject of Poetry, do we not need the introduction of the new vein which has been opened by modern thought for the treatment of Language, Religion, History, and so on — what is called the Comparative Method — into this subject also? In fact, is it not becoming indispensable, in order to get beyond narrow and sectarian views? Suppose the Comparative Method applied to such a theory and practice of poetry as Walt Whitman's, and floods of light are forthwith thrown on what would otherwise be puzzling and dark. Largely considered, great and true poetic expression is a growth (and a signifying portrait also), of clime, age, cultus, race — even of species and crises, and politics.

The immortal Hebraic poems — Homer's, Virgil's, and Juvenal's compositions — Dante's, Shakespeare's, and even Tennyson's — from the highest point of view — are all and each such characteristic yet generic growths. Walt Whitman is the same in my opinion. The physiognomy of a race — of each race in the past — has the same old generic type, and yet is markedly different, and is characteristic only of itself.

Burroughs valued highly Whitman's criticism of his work, and, as will be found in these pages, availed himself of it in the late sixties and occasionally in the seventies and eighties, always, he said, profiting by the elder writer's strictures and suggestions as to prunings and emendations. Unfortunately Burroughs's candor as to the aid given him by Whitman in his first book has subjected him to unjust and sweeping inferences on the part of certain writers who accuse him of having accepted far more aid than was the case.

Certain passages in 'The Flight of the Eagle,' as will be seen on pages 162, 163, of this volume, were contributed by Whitman.

As to whether or not a violation of ethics was involved in this coöperation between the friends — in Whitman's offering, and in Burroughs's accepting and weaving into his own writing such emendations as are indicated here and elsewhere — each person must decide for himself. Certain it is that Burroughs's essay just referred to, as well as all else he has written about Whitman, could have stood proudly without Whitman's aid; and assuredly Whitman's renown was not dependent upon his self-interpretation, however much the emendations helped in elucidation. Whatever opinions are held as to the ethics, there can be no doubt as to the value of the matter contributed, not only for its content, but especially for the light it throws upon Whitman's personality.

The correspondence between Burroughs and Whitman shows that the latter sometimes made suggestions about essays by Burroughs which bore no relation to himself. Other chapters in 'Birds and Poets' than the 'Eagle' chapter, were read in proof and criticized by Whitman, as seen in his letter to Burroughs, dated February 27, 1877:

I have gone over the chapters — got quite in the spirit of them — added and suggested a few lines or words, here and there — and pruned a few passages, even pages, remorselessly.

I like them all — they are very *living* — the Beauty chapter I think especially fine. Do you say the final chapter is already in print? the one about me? If so, *send me the proof*, which I will return by next mail....

Again, on August 29, 1879, Whitman writes Burroughs that he has jotted down a paragraph which he may use or not, as he sees fit. On the enclosure, he queries, 'How will this do to work in the essay you mention in your last? — the Nature and the Poets article?'

The enclosure runs thus:

Whitman is not remarkable in details or minute finish. But in spirit, in reverence, in breadth, *ensemble*, and in his vistas he stands unmatched. Through all that fluid, weird Nature, 'so far and yet so near,' he finds human relations, human responsions. In entire consistence with botany, geology, science, or what-not, he endues his very seas and woods with passion, more than the old hamadryads or tritons. His fields, his rocks, his trees, are not dead material, but living companions.

To him all Nature's objectiveness holds a cognizant lurking something, without voice, yet realizing you as much as you realize it. No wonder Addington Symonds, the young Hellenic scholar of England, says, 'Singular as it may appear, Walt Whitman is more thoroughly Greek than any man of modern times!'

Transcribed here is the passage from 'Nature and the Poets,' [1] that the reader may see how much, or rather how little, of Whitman's contribution Burroughs used:

Whitman is less local than the New England poets, and faces more to the west. But he makes himself at home everywhere... and identifies himself with men in all states and conditions on the continent. Like the old poets, he does not dwell upon nature, except occasionally through vistas opened up by the great sciences, as astronomy and geology, but upon life and movement and personality....

Everywhere in nature Whitman finds human relations, human responsions. In entire consistency with botany, geology, science, or what not, he endues his very seas and woods with passion, more than the old hamadryads or tritons. His fields, his rocks, his trees, are not dead material, but living companions. This is doubtless one reason why Addington Symonds, the young Hellenic scholar of England, finds him more thoroughly Greek than any other man in modern times.

As late as 1882, as seen by the following letter, Whitman offered Burroughs still another bit of critical aid:

I have run over the Carlyle proof and being in the mood have thought best to mark (of course for your consideration — you may have something behind which I do not see) *out* certain passages just as they summarily

[1] See *Pepacton*, pp. 119-20.

impresst me — clearly though rapidly feeling as I went along that the article would be bettered and more unitary without them.

What you set out mainly to say, and have to say, seems to me very well said indeed, and *I like the article* — What you have to offer as the Carlyle foil, in defence of America, I don't like so well — besides, it is unnecessary anyhow — unless one has got something outsmashing Carlyle himself — a battering-ram that batters *his* ram to the dust.

Speaking of this letter, years later, Burroughs said: 'That article came out in the "Century." I guess I struck out most of what Walt marked — I usually did. He was a wonderful critic.'

We may well apply to Whitman's anonymous elucidation of his own work, a comment which Edward Dowden made concerning Wordsworth, in a letter to J. B. Yeats: [1]

The poem once written became to him a piece of work detached from himself, which he could pronounce good as he could say, Skiddaw is so many feet high. This, I think, must be the feeling of great artists about their work. It was certainly Goethe's, who compares himself to Shakespeare,... just as a remote critic might have done.

It is interesting to see how Whitman defended himself on the self-exploitation charge when being badgered about it by Traubel. I quote from Traubel's third volume, pages 559, 560:

'Walt, some people think you blew your own horn a lot — wrote puffs on yourself — sort of attitudinized and called attention to yourself quite a bit.'...

'Do they say so? Do they? Who are "some people"? what are "puffs"? I have often talked of myself as I would of you — blamed and praised just the same; looked at myself just as if I was somebody else. I am not ashamed of it. I have never praised myself where I would not if it had been somebody else; I have merely looked myself over, and repeated candidly what I saw — the mean things and the good things. I did so in the "Leaves"; I have done so in other places — candidly faced the life in myself — my own possibilities, probabilities; reckoned up my own account, so to speak. I know this is unusual, but is it wrong? Why should not everybody do it? You, anybody? If you did it for the sake of aggrandizing yourself, that would be another thing, but doing it simply for the purpose of getting your own weight and measure, is as right done for you, by yourself, as done for you by another.'

'O rare Walt Whitman!' wrote James Redpath in 1860. This chances to be quoted on the same page with the foregoing frank

[1] See *Edward Dowden's Letters*, p. 47.

avowal. *How high is Skiddaw?* was clearly Whitman's concern. And although he may have asked and answered this question rather oftener than some of his critics approve, it is 'sure as the most certain sure' that the 'picturesque giant' never added one cubit to the height. Today the mountain looms so majestically that we give scant heed to inconsequential irregularities on its mighty slopes.

In this connection a passage from a letter of Thoreau about Whitman addressed to Harrison Blake seems apropos:

Since I have seen him I find that I am not disturbed by any brag or egoism in his book. He may turn out the least braggart of us all, having a better right to be confident.

Well may we leave to Time the settling of this moot question. Our puerile pullings and haulings, our dragging to light of his blemishes, and supposed blemishes, the hostile criticism obviously born of personal animus, the misrepresentations, intentional or otherwise, of his would-be interpreters, all are but the dancing fireflies of a summer night. When these darken there remains the light of the stars.

VIII

A GREAT SUCCORING LOVE

(1876)

Forever I shall love old England. It all comes over me now, and always does when I think of it, like a great succoring love. .

Whitman

WHEN Sidney Morse was making a bust of Whitman in Camden in 1887, the sitter, referring to the timely aid his British friends had tendered him in 1876, said it was a thing he could never forget. To the above quotation he added: 'With no discounting of friends at home, I must say that English business stands apart in my thoughts... — the money and the friendliness of it all.'

Before the concerted action was taken by Whitman's friends and readers in Great Britain, two of his keenest appreciators overseas, Edward Dowden and Anne Gilchrist, had already taken steps to add to the poet's scanty resources, as excerpts from the following letters show. Writing to Dowden in mid-October, 1875, Burroughs replies to Dowden's anxiety as to Whitman's pecuniary needs:

... You ask after his means, etc. I believe he has not much money, yet is not in want. He lives with his brother, who is comfortably off. Each edition of his book is sold in a few years, which must pay him some profit. He has earned a good deal of money, but it never stays with him long. He has given the greater part of it away to poor obscure people. When I first knew him in Washington he lived in an attic in the rudest, simplest way, preparing his own breakfast of bread and coffee, and dispensing nearly all the money that came into his hands among the soldiers....

On October 19, 1875, Mrs. Gilchrist also sends to Burroughs the letter here transcribed. This letter was copied from the mice-nibbled original given by Burroughs to Elizabeth Porter Gould [1] and given by her to the Boston Public Library. The words enclosed in brackets have been supplied by Mr. Furness as the prob-

---

[1] Elizabeth Porter Gould: *Anne Gilchrist and Walt Whitman*. David Mackay, 1900. *Gems from Walt Whitman*, also edited by Elizabeth Porter Gould. David Mackay, 1889.

able ones deleted by the mice. Was aid ever proffered more graciously than in this letter which Mrs. Gilchrist sent on from London:

DEAR MR. BURROUGHS,

It seems to me that I may, though personally a stranger, write to you as friend because of the deep feeling we have in common toward Mr. Whitman. For certainly to recognize what he really is, to understand and delight in his great poems is such broad ground of sympathy as to constitute an actual bond of friendship between those whom distance and strangeness sever.

It is of Mr. Whitman that I write and would fain hear from you. For his friends and admirers in England are full of solicitude for his protracted illness and consequent retirement from his government office which was probably his main source of income. And they think — Mr. William Rossetti, Prof. Dowden, & many others, I believe, besides myself, — that it is an opportune moment to join together and try to give some tangible embodiment, however inadequate, some visible token at least of their deep gratitude and affectionate admiration, if Mr. Whitman will honor them by permitting it. Perhaps friends in America have already some plan in view, in which we might be permitted to cooperate, or perhaps they would join us or advise us as to the best way of realizing our wishes. Mr. W. M. Rossetti thinks that if we might buy an edition or print an edition according to the one already issued, of 'Leaves of Grass,' and present copies to all the public libraries, it would combine very wide diffusion of Mr. Whitman's works, with our special aim, and also (which he seems to relish considerably) give a 'slap in the face' to detractors. But he says the weak point of his scheme is that in not a few, perhaps in the greater number of cases, the managers of the libraries might be just such people and so have power to frustrate the plan. Perhaps however they would not do so if the forthcoming 'Two Rivulets' were chosen for diffusion? For my own part, I should be well content with this latter book. Let the 'Two Rivulets' reinforce the weak-flowing [streams of man]y lands, mak[ing the land fertile and rende]ring the soil ready [for the ma]terial of 'Leaves [of Grass,' not for vain sh]ow, but that those who are capable of enjoying the one will hasten to possess themselves of the other. Perhaps however you from your knowledge of Mr. Whitman, and of all circumstances, may suggest some better plan?

I have spent some pleasant half hours over 'Wake-Robin.' [As I spend] the greater part of the year in London, it brings the fresh, moist atmosphere of the woods, the ways of its denizens, the delightful sense of outdoor life, very enjoyably home to me. Also the glimpses of the scenery round Washington are full of interest to me. Please accept all good wishes and kindly regards.

ANNE GILCHRIST

Not long after this a public controversy started by Robert Buchanan in the 'London Daily News,' March 13, 1876, resulted in an outpouring of British sympathy for Whitman. Buchanan's letter to the London paper had been called forth by the reprint of an article from the 'West Jersey Press' of January 26, 1876, which appeared in the 'London Athenæum,' March 11, 1876.[1] This letter, which it is now known was written by Whitman himself, was again, in turn, quoted in a letter from the London correspondent[2] in the 'New York Daily Tribune,' March 28, 1876. It was the 'Tribune's' editorial comment (by Bayard Taylor) upon the London correspondent's letter, in the same issue, that goaded Burroughs to write the letter of April 13, to the editor of the 'Tribune' — a letter headed 'Walt Whitman's Poetry,' reprinted on pages 125–28 of this book.

Buchanan's eloquent, if somewhat indiscreet, letter, which stung the American writers and editors, is here transcribed:

This is certainly the time, and your columns are possibly the place, for an expression of English indignation against the 'orthodox American authors, publishers and editors' who greet such a man as the author of 'Leaves of Grass' with 'determined denial, disgust, and scorn.' One can understand the publishers, for American publishers have been justly described by Whitman himself as 'mostly sharks'; one can forgive the editors, for all men know of what pudding a typical Yankee editor's brains are made; but as for the 'orthodox American authors' and the 'established American poets' — orthodox perhaps in the sense of their affiliation to the church of English literature, and 'established' truly in their custom of picking the brains of British bards — there is but one word for them, and that may be lengthened into a parable.

He who wanders through the solitudes of far off Uist or lonely Donegal may often behold the golden eagle sick to death, worn with age or famine, or with both, passing with weary waft of wing from promontory to promontory, from peak to peak, pursued by a crowd of prosperous rooks or crows, which fall screaming back whenever the noble bird turns his indignant head, and which follow once more, hooting behind him, whenever he wends again upon his way. The rook is a 'recognized' bird; the crow is perfectly 'established.' But for the Eagle, when he sails aloft in the splendour of his strength, who shall perfectly discern and measure his flight?

[1] See Furness: *Walt Whitman's Workshop*, pp. 245–47; also p. 158.

[2] This was under the head 'Anglo-American Topics,' written from London, March 16, and published in the *New York Daily Tribune*, March 28, 1876. In O'Connor's book of clippings concerning this episode, now in the Perry Collection, he has written under the London letter, 'G. W. Smalley — Appropriate name!'

Perhaps, after all, the so-called 'established poets' of America, despite their resemblance to the birds that blacken the fallows and stubbles of English literature, may claim to be at least as indigenous as the loon, the snow-bunting, and the whip-poor-will, birds well 'established' in popular liking. For such denizens of the Bostonian pond or farm-rail to crouch down in disgust and scorn when the King of Birds passes overhead is no more than natural. It is less conceivable that that other eagle of American literature, aquiline of breed, but born and degenerated in captivity, should see in silence the sufferings of his freer and sublimer brother, should utter no word of warning or of sympathy, should seem to approve by tacit and implicit silence the neglect and scorn of the little New England songsters who peck about his cage. It was the voice of Emerson — a noble and a reverbatory voice then and now — which first proclaimed the name of Whitman in America, in words of homage such as not twice in one century is paid by one poet authenticated to another obscure. It is the voice of Emerson which should be heard again for the vindication of the honour of America, now likely to be tarnished eternally by the murder of its only remaining prophet. It cannot be that a long captivity in the cage of respectability, and daily association with the choir of hedgerow warblers, has so weakened the heart of Emerson that he falters from his first faith, that he no longer recognizes the wild eagle, his kinsman, because that kinsman's flight is far off, and *his* wings, though old and feeble, are still free. There is in England no sincerer admirer of Emerson than the present writer, who awaits with anxiety the moment of explanation and justification.

Besides the foregoing letter, Buchanan wrote two other letters in Whitman's defense, a second one in the 'London Daily News,' March 15, 1876, and one in the 'New York Daily Tribune,' September 14, 1884, this last written while Buchanan was in America.

A digression may be pardoned here, relative to Buchanan's forcible figure of the eagle as applied to Whitman, and the use of the same figure a little later, by Burroughs, in his essay, 'The Flight of the Eagle.' On reading this letter of Buchanan's, one would naturally infer that Burroughs had received from it his hint for so naming his essay, were it not that at the very beginning of that essay Burroughs gives a clue to another, earlier source, namely, the Danish writer, Rudolf Schmidt, from whose essay (1872) he quotes a passage which clearly suggested the felicitous title. The sentence furnishing the hint runs thus:

His wings do not glitter in their movement from rich and varicolored plumage, nor are his notes those of the accustomed song-birds; but his flight is the flight of the eagle.

And were these two sources not so obviously the ones suggesting the title, one might go back to Burroughs himself, where, on page 49 of 'Poet and Person,' he speaks of the poet ascending with his loftiest themes, 'soaring high and cleaving the heavens.' Or, we might even go back to Whitman's lines —

> Birds tallying the ocean's roar and the
> Swooping eagle's scream.

or to

> I have abandoned myself to flights, broad circles,
> . . . .
> I have felt to soar in freedom and in the fullness of power.

Of course Buchanan's letter aroused a great hullabaloo among British and American songsters, some of the reverberations of which may be heard in these pages. Dowden followed up his inquiry of the previous autumn by another to Burroughs on March 26, 1876, in which he says:

We have been made anxious and unhappy about Whitman of late, not solely on account of his broken health, but through the fear that he may have less means of providing for all needs and comforts than he ought to have. The article from the 'West Jersey Press'[1] describing the true state of affairs was copied into our 'Athenæum'; thereupon Buchanan wrote a long and passionate letter on Whitman and the neglect of him by America in the 'Daily News.'[2] Rossetti wrote to say he was in communication with Whitman to ascertain whether it was his wish that his English friends should now move on his behalf. Thereupon the 'Daily News' had a leading article on Whitman, admitting his excellence as a man, but depreciating his work as a writer,[3] and the 'Saturday Review'[4] published a vile column of rancorous abuse of Walt Whitman, man and writer. Such is the latest aspect of things here. You probably saw the article in the 'Gentleman's Magazine'[5] some time since, by O'Grady, a friend of mine, with its warm appreciation of W; and 'Peter Bayne's' hostile review the same month in the 'Contemporary Review.'
I stayed all proceedings in Whitman's favour when I learned that it would — at that time — be probably unpleasing to him,[6] though I was in

[1] Three articles appeared in that paper, January 26, March 15, and May 24, 1876.
[2] March 13, 1876.   [3] March 14–17, 1876.
[4] March 18, 1876.   [5] December, 1875.
[6] Whitman, in reply to Rossetti's inquiries, March 17, had mentioned selling his own books, and had said: 'And *that* is the way I should prefer to glean my support. In that way I cheerfully accept all the aid my friends find it convenient to proffer.'

communication with Rossetti on the subject of some less substantial expression of his English friends' admiration and regard — and we had thought of several kinds of slighter gifts which might be taken as a token of our feeling towards him. Now this appears very insufficient and out of place.

Ought not the American government be moved to give W. a pension for the rest of his life in consideration of his services as Hospital nurse? It seems to me as if such an arrangement would be honorable to both the government and to Whitman. I hope you will soon write to me and tell me what you think of all this. But in the meantime Rossetti will have got W's answer.

Eight copies of his Autograph edition are either come or coming to Dublin — probably more will be taken. My own copy has reached me. I am greatly interested and contented by his preface (except that I think 'L of G' more for the *soul*, as well as the body, than W. quite admits); and the 'Memoranda of the War' held me close to them for long.

Before Burroughs had received the foregoing letter from Dowden, he had written him on April 9 as follows:

MY DEAR DOWDEN,

I presume you have seen what a stir Buchanan's letter to the 'London News,' in behalf of Whitman, has created. I do not see the British journals but it set the geese to cackling here beautifully. The papers all encouraged themselves with the remark that Robert Buchanan was quite unknown in this country, but the ado they have made over his letter is astonishing.

If you see him, or correspond with him, tell him that there is one man in America at least who is grateful to him for what he has done. I wish he would shy another missile into our barnyard the first opportunity that offers. Our fowls are getting too complacent. The papers have nearly all made his letter an excuse to attack Whitman, and it is pitiful and humiliating to see the littleness and cur-dog spite and bluster exhibited. Such papers as the 'New York Tribune,' of which we had some hope, has an article every day or two full of abuse of Whitman, and of lies about him.[1]

What makes it doubly annoying is that his friends can make no reply — the papers and journals are all closed to them. If we only had an organ you would see the fur fly and something under the fur. It makes me bloodthirsty to have to stand by and see and hear such things. A scalping-knife would feel better in my hand than a pen.

You can hardly understand, from your distance, what a miserable, puling set of editors and poets we have in this country. Such an utter absence of anything manly, broad, robust, is disheartening. They say that the

---

[1] Burroughs said that these were written by Bayard Taylor. See editorials March 28 and 30, and April 12, 1876.

reason that Whitman is more popular in England than here is that the Englishman has grown *blasé*, sated with order and conformity, and craves the wild and lawless. But the real reason is that we are a race of pigmies, and, in comparison, your authors and reviewers are a race of giants. All our rising literary men in this country are of the superfine sort — very knowing, very quick, bright, smart, but without any port, or stomach, or bowels, or carnality, or sexuality, or proper manliness. I heartily wish some British reviewer would take them up fairly, dispassionately, and show how they all run to mere refinement, mere finger-tips, and that in trying so hard, as the 'Tribune' says they are, to get away from the conditions represented by Whitman, they are getting away from the only sources of power and fresh inspiration. I should like to furnish the names and facts, etc., for such an article.

I see by a paragraph in the 'Tribune' that you have been reviewing Lowell's 'Study Windows.' I hope you smashed some of them in. I can't endure the man. The harshness and rawness as well as the brightness of the New England climate has come to a head in him. His seems to me one of those minds that never get ripe, but are crude and puckery to the last. He has great verbal brightness and smartness, and that is all. There are incessant fire-fly flashes of wit over a dull prosy ground. He is an 'embroiderer.' It is a kind of torture to me to read him. Such an absence of tone, of mellowness, of harmony, of poetic quality from a man of his ability, is remarkable.[1]

I saw Walt Whitman in January. My impression was that he had mended decidedly since I had seen him in the spring before. His brother also told me that he thought he was very slowly picking up. I dare not hope that he will ever be well again but think he may be spared to us yet many years.

Have you seen his 'Two Rivulets'? The prose parts are very noble and the Hospital Sketches priceless, but I do not care much for the new poems. They have not the leaven of poetry as have his old pieces. I wish you felt like reviewing it in the 'Academy.'

I sent you a little book of mine some months since which I trust you rec'd. I have written an essay on Emerson which the critics (miserable scoundrels) have commended, and which I will send you....

On April 10, Burroughs followed with another letter:

MY DEAR DOWDEN,

I received your very welcome letter today after having mailed one to you this morning.... What you say about my little book goes to my heart....

I saw the article in the 'Gentleman's Magazine' on Whitman while

[1] In 1914 Burroughs said to me of this early dictum, 'That is pretty severe — an exaggerated truth.'

visiting him last January. He was much pleased with it, as he might well be. It was a noble tribute. In his remarks upon the significance of the Calamus or friendship pieces the author turned new and deep ground, and set me to thinking a long while. In fact, he broke new soil all through the piece. 'Arthur Clive,' then, is only a *nom de plume*? The article was not reprinted here as, of course, stupid Peter Bayne's was. What a real leather-head Bayne is!

I think if Whitman's friends in England feel like doing anything for him in the shape of pecuniary aid, it would not be amiss and would be rightly rec'd by him. I should recommend taking the difficulty by the horns boldly and a point-blank gift of money, and no beating around the bush at all. As soon as I can bring it about I shall make no apologies at all for sending him my check. He is not in want so far as food, shelter, raiment etc. goes, but I suspect he has little or no money. A few years ago some wretch picked his pocket of $400, which made a sad hole in his savings. We expected he would have had a position in one of the Departments at Washington again before this, as it was promised last winter, but nothing seems to come of it yet. Yes, the government ought to pension him, but the only way it can be done is by a nominal place in one of the executive Departments. There is no law under which he could be pensioned, and you know we do things according to law in this country!

Parts of both the 'Daily News'[1] article and the 'Sat. Review'[2] article were reprinted and gloated over by the 'New York Tribune,' and I don't know how many other papers. If you think any one could be found who would work over and father an article I might write, and publish it in some leading journal I should like to set the ball going again, just for its effect here. My soul burns with indignation over the blindness and littleness of my countrymen. I have had some hopes of Emerson till recently but he is evidently in his dotage.[3] He seems to have at last settled down upon the drawing-room as the proper standard to try things by. I gave him a touch or two in my essay upon him (which I send by this mail) but if I had it to do over again, in my present state of mind, I should lay it on a good deal harder. Emerson is no doubt at heart a snob. A good raking down he never has had and it would do him good. I see fully his great service, but he cannot afford to ignore Whitman as he has done in these latter days....

[1] London *Daily News*, March 14–17, 1876.

[2] *Saturday Review*, March 18, 1876.

[3] Burroughs was evidently unaware of Emerson's mental failure at that time. Cabot's 'Emerson' states that his address at the Concord Centennial in 1875 was the last piece he had written by his own hand. By 1878, although he was reading his own lectures in public, he had no recollection of having seen them before.

Apropos of Burroughs's comments about the article by 'Arthur Clive,' anent the Calamus poems, the following excerpt is introduced here: [1]

... Of the new ideas which Whitman has cast as seed into the American brain the importance which he attaches to friendship is the most remarkable. This appears to have been a subject over which he brooded long and deeply. It is not possible that Whitman could have written as he has upon this and kindred subjects if he were merely a cultivated brain and nothing more. A thin-blooded, weak-spirited man may, doubtless, like Swedenborg, strike profound truths through sheer force of intellect, or may use violent and swelling language with little dilation in his spirit; but there is a genuineness and eloquence in Whitman's language concerning friendship which precludes the possibility of suspicion that he uses strong words for weak feelings. It must not be forgotten that, though now latent, there is in human nature a capacity for friendship of a most absorbing and passionate character. The Greeks were well acquainted with that passion, a passion which in later days ran riot and assumed abnormal forms; for the fruit grows ripe first, then over-ripe, and then rots. In the days of Homer friendship was an heroic passion. The friendship of Achilles and Patroclus was for many centuries the ideal after which the young Greeks fashioned their character. Nowadays friendship means generally merely consentaneity of opinions and tastes. With the Greeks it was a powerful physical feeling, having physical conditions. Beauty was one of these conditions, as it is now between the sexes. In the dialogues of Plato we see the extraordinary nature of the friendships formed by the young men of his time, the passionate absorbing nature of the relation, the craving for beauty in connection with it. There can not be a doubt but that with highly developed races friendship is a passion, and like all passions, more physical than intellectual in its sources and modes of expression.
[Many lines quoted from Whitman's 'Calamus.']
This is strong language and doubtless genuine. Pride and love, I have said, Whitman considers the two hemispheres of the brain of humanity, and by love he means not alone benevolence and wide sympathy and the passion that embraces sexual relation, but that other passion which has existed before, and whose latent strength the American poet here indicates as a burning and repressed flame. He speaks of the sick, sick dread of unreturned friendship, of the comrade's kiss, the arm around the neck, etc.

When the British testimonial materialized, well did Whitman speak of it as 'the blessed gale from the British Isles,' the pecuniary aid and heart-warming cheer which it wafted to him were 'deep

[1] Arthur Clive (Standish O'Grady): 'Walt Whitman, the Poet of Joy,' *Gentleman's Magazine* (December, 1875), vol. 15, p. 705.

medicines.' The two-volume Centennial Edition of his work cost ten dollars the set, and many of his British friends paid twice and thrice the cost for a set. Among the long list of subscribers to the fund were the familiar names of Ford Madox Brown, Robert Buchanan, Edward Carpenter, Moncure D. Conway, Edward Dowden, John Dowden, Anne Gilchrist, Percy Gilchrist, Edmund Gosse, A. B. Grosart, Hubert Herkomer, Lord Houghton, G. H. Lewes, Justin McCarthy, Standish O'Grady, D. G. and W. M. Rossetti, Ruskin, T. W. Rolleston, George Saintsbury, W. B. Scott, W. J. Stillman, Tennyson, and Professor Tyrrell.

IX

'LOVE ME, LOVE WALT'

(1876–1877)

... Together, through life, through dangers, odium, unchanging, long and long,
Through youth and through mid-age and old age, how unfaltering, how affectionate and
faithful they were!

WHITMAN

AS we follow Burroughs through the years in his relation to
Whitman we find it was ever with him, as he had reminded
his wife, years before, 'Love me, love Walt.' In advanced
years he admitted that in his early partisanship he had decried
many an author of whose worth he became later well aware. He
had spoken superiorly of the Tennysonian wine which had gone to
the heads of our younger poets, all unaware that he himself was
half seas over with the Whitmanian vintage. Let a writer damn his
hero with faint praise, or damn him without praise, and Burroughs's sarcasm was forthcoming, his sentence severe. In his
correspondence with Dowden, and elsewhere, we find Burroughs
qualifying as one of the 'hot little prophets,' the term Mr. Bliss
Perry applied to the Camden group of Whitmanites. Doubtless, if
challenged, Burroughs would have excused himself for his sturdy,
sometimes vehement, championship of Whitman much as O'Connor
did in his splendid early defense — 'When, on grounds of taste,
foes withhold detractions, friends may withhold eulogy.'

On February 24, 1876, Burroughs's friend Myron Benton shows
how much he also is exercised on Whitman's behalf. He writes
Burroughs:

Did you see that review of Whitman in 'Littell's'? [1] I don't exactly go
with Walt through thick and thin, but this 'Peter' is too dense, and it
will take more than one cock-crowing to wake up his slumbering faculties.
The idea of trying to square the impassioned tropes and figures of poetry
with the dry scientific statements of Darwin is too delicious. Some of the

---

[1] Peter Bayne: 'Walt Whitman's Poems,' *Contemporary Review* (December, 1875),
vol. 27, pp. 49–69. Reprinted in *Littell's Living Age* (January 8, 1876), vol. 128, pp.
91–103.

passages quoted are just the ones I have long thought particularly fine —
but Peter, poor Peter, takes them as examples of the preposterous and
utterly ridiculous.

To this Burroughs replies:

Yes, I read 'Peter's' article in the 'Contemporary,' which Henry Abbey
sent me. He is a hopeless old granny. A noble article on W. W. appeared
about the same time in the 'Gentleman's Magazine,' by Arthur Clive,[1]
that pleased me immensely. Of course Littell's Fossil Age, as O'Connor
calls it, would not reprint that....

And now, stirred by the 'New York Daily Tribune's' response
to Buchanan's letter (which letter is quoted in the preceding
chapter, pages 116, 117), Burroughs takes up the cudgels in Whitman's defense, after a lull of almost ten years in writing about him.
Considering the provocation, his letter is remarkable for its quiet
restraint:

WALT WHITMAN'S POETRY

An Estimate of its Value

To the Editor of *The Tribune*,
   SIR: As one of the friends and admirers of Walt Whitman in this country
I deeply regret that you should have felt obliged, in repelling the attack
of Robert Buchanan upon the guild of New England authorship in Tuesday's 'Tribune,' to throw the weight of your great journal so decidedly
against the literary claim of the American poet.
   It has been my good fortune to know Whitman long and intimately,
and I owe him a debt of gratitude I can never hope to repay. As a young
man I have obtained no such moral and intellectual gifts, as some one has
aptly named this kind of service, from any other source as from his poems
and his contact and conversation. He has been a help to me, as I know he
has been to others, in a way and to a degree that mere literature can
never be — a help like that one gets from primitive sources, and from the
great sciences. Hence I felt personally aggrieved over your indorsement
of the critical estimate of him pronounced by 'The London Daily News'
— all the more aggrieved because I know it to be sincere and inspired by
no craft hostility.
   'The News,' no doubt, speaks the opinion of a large number of its
readers, and perhaps the opinion of the majority of British literary journals, but not the opinion of a majority of the rising men in the fields of
English poetry and criticism, as you are doubtless aware. There is Mr.
Buchanan himself, who has certainly earned the right to be heard, and

[1] 'Walt Whitman, the Poet of Joy,' *Gentleman's Magazine*, December, 1875.

who said of Whitman nearly ten years ago, that 'in actual living force, in gripe and muscle, he has no equal among contemporaries.' And I will say here that this is very nearly the opinion of our poet pronounced by the French journal, *Revue de Lundi*, on the occasion of the publication of his 'Drum-Taps.' But before Mr. Buchanan, Wm. M. Rossetti, the accomplished London poet and critic, had come out strongly on behalf of Whitman, calling his 'Leaves of Grass' 'the largest poetic enterprise of our age.' Next came Prof. Dowden of Trinity College, Dublin, with an article in the 'Westminster Review,' in as noble and lofty a strain of welcome as was ever called forth by any poet. Roden Noel, the relative of Byron, himself a poet and an ex-M.P., has also enrolled himself among the champions of 'Leaves of Grass.' Prof. Clifford of the Royal Institute welcomes its author as the poet of all others whose utterances are most in harmony with modern science. J. Addington Symonds, an eminent Greek scholar, author of 'Studies of the Greek Poets,' and a poet himself, says Whitman is more truly Greek than any other man of modern times. Mr. Swinburne's admiration of him is well known. Arthur Clive celebrates him in 'The Gentleman's Magazine' as the 'Poet of Joy'; and George Saintsbury,[1] one of the critics of 'The Academy' and 'The Contemporary Review,' has lent his trenchant pen in his defense. The attitude of Tennyson toward him is eminently cordial and sympathetic. In every literary gathering in London, or Edinburgh, or Dublin, I am informed, there is always a large sprinkling of admirers of Whitman, and it would appear that no man is so much discussed and championed. Then what shall we say of Freiligrath's welcome of him, and of the reception given his works by the Danish and Norwegian poets and critics?

Is it only a possible, or is it an actual, poet that has thus met with a reception abroad never given to any other American singer? I am aware that there are dissenting voices in Great Britain, but they are for the most part feeble voices. Alfred Austin, the flippant critic of the 'Poetry of the Period,'[2] and author of a recent drama, decries him as he does Tennyson and Browning. Peter Bayne, too, a Peter so dense, a friend says, that it will take more than one cock-crowing ever to wake up his slumbering faculties.

At home the rising and the risen literary lights are nearly all set against Whitman, though I know he has a large and an increasing circle of appreciative readers in this country. For my own part, I have no more doubt of his greatness than I have of the sun at noonday. He seems to me about the only American poet that a man, apart from the versifier, the scholar, the professor, the gentleman of elegant leisure, etc., would want to read, because in him alone there is a breeze, bracing and masculine, as of the mountains or the shore. I am aware that there is something for-

---

[1] Saintsbury: Review of *Leaves of Grass, Academy*, October 10, 1874.
[2] Austin: *Poetry of the Period*, 1870.

bidding about him, just as there is about the open air, and that certain delicate indoor temperaments cannot endure him; but it is so much the worse for them that they cannot. Were he less a cosmic poet, reduced in his rank, primary, human or manly qualities, with the conscious, elegant literary worker uppermost, his reception, in this country at least, would have been quite different. But he would have been so much less worthy of attention. The truth is, sweet poets, elegant poets, learned, correct, beautiful poets, are not rare in our age, but powerful poets, poets who can confront and compel the gigantic materialism of our times and land, and who by dint of native inward force can rise above the poetic and literary consciousness with which the very atmosphere is rotten, are rare, and, it seems, are misunderstood when they come. The trouble with Whitman is, he gives us something more and better than mere literature or art, and the main influence of his poems is in the direction of health, character, and manly activity, and can never be to beget a critical, sophisticated, or over-intellectual race, which is the tendency of literary culture as such. What he gives us is well oxygenated; it is red, arterial blood, and has in it the making of virile, robust men. Can the same be said of the works of our popular poets?

In highly refined and cultivated times like ours, the great mass of the poetry is written as it were out of the atmosphere, out of the general store of distilled and accumulated literary skill and refinement, and while it has its value, for any high tonic and national purposes it is absolutely worthless. You will agree with me that Whitman's poems are not so written. They are a breath from the sea and the woods, and not from the libraries, and will be valued highest by him whose spiritual lungs are strongest and cleanest.

Are we never to get beyond the point where the demand is for something elegant and scholarly, and where the analogue in art of the power and informality of elemental nature is more acceptable than any studied form and elaboration, however complete?

Maybe Whitman is not a poet or an artist in the current acceptation of those terms. He probably is not. So much the better if we have to employ new terms to describe him. Certain it is that his quality is as potent, as positive, and as deeply rooted as that of any man in literature, while the consideration of his work and methods starts a multitude of the greatest problems. Indeed, to me his poems have a political and a metaphysical background in the presence of the grandeur of which most of the mooted questions among scholars about even Shakespeare and Dante seem ingenuous or trivial.

It is a kind of disloyalty to Nature to say Whitman has no form. He has not form as a house, or a shield, or a heart, or a molder's pattern, or a sonnet of Hood's, or a dainty bit of verse by Longfellow has form; but he has form as a tree, a river, the clouds, a cataract, a flash of lightning, or any vital and progressive thing has form, and this is all the form he aims at.

In regard to the state of the case that gave rise to Mr. Buchanan's letter, I know Whitman is poor and in feeble health. I know also his life has been a singularly unselfish one; that he has bestowed himself upon others; that he has really scattered with lavish hand all that he earned or achieved. But he is a philosopher as well as a poet, and I have never yet seen him in any but the most cheerful and magnanimous frame of mind.

JOHN BURROUGHS

ESOPUS, N.Y., March 30, 1876.
[Printed April 13, 1876.]

The day of its publication, Whitman sent Burroughs a postcard as follows:

Your letter in 'Tribune' today headed 'W. W.'s Poetry' is like an artillery and bayonet charge combined — is splendid, earnest, and terribly *live* — (Wonder the T—— ever printed it) — Bad spell this forenoon — F. B. Sanborn visited me today) Am going out and will see if I can get the T —— to send you — am not sure —   W. W.

Writing to Joel Benton on April 18, Burroughs says:

My 'Tribune' letter I meant as a sort of gallant charge on behalf of dear old Walt, and I have heard of it far and near in the way of letters of thanks, etc., so I guess it was timely. Walt writes me, among other things, that it was 'terribly alive,' which I consider a big compliment.

O'Connor had a splendid article in the 'Tribune' of April 22, called, 'Walt Whitman. Is he Persecuted?' and this, be it remembered, was while he and Whitman were supposedly estranged.

The raciness of O'Connor's letter of May 4, which follows here, abundantly atones for its length:

DEAR JOHN,
I was very glad in your letter of April 31st [*sic*] as I was in your article in the 'Tribune,' which was tiptop and very effective, though you disparage it. Nothing could have been better than to display that list of believers — a constellation of celebrity which 'stuck fiery off' against the black welkin the judicious Bayard had considerately prepared for you. Then your quiet believing style, free from passion or the glitter of rhetoric, and giving one the sense of simple eyesight. Indeed, I enjoyed your article very much and it came near making me relinquish the idea of mine, enough seeming as good as a feast, until I saw by the further article of the 'Tribune' of April 12th, that this gallant Bayard was bent on making war, which made me resolve to teach him what I know about fighting! The worst is, I am afraid he has learned the lesson only too well, and that I struck too hard, for the battle has suddenly ceased in all quarters, and I

hoped to see it protracted. However, I have packed my letter over to England, and the result may make them begin again here.

I am delighted that you were pleased. You are so different from me that I count a good deal from your approbation. The letter appears to have been a success generally. I had very nice letters about it, among others one from Stedman, in which he gave me fits for remaining here at 'the drudgery of the desk's dead wood,' and not going into literature in New York, etc. Another, full of glory, was from Mrs. Whitman, the fiancée of poor Edgar Poe. Perhaps the best of all was from a lady of whom I have not heard for nearly twenty years, and whom I never saw, but corresponded with that long time ago. I knew of her through friends. She was a beautiful (*very* beautiful, I heard) young Irish lady, highly accomplished, especially in music, Miss Raymond by name. She has married, it appears, Professor Ritter, the author of a History of Music, and professor of that art at Vassar. They live at Poughkeepsie, and she writes me for her husband and herself expressing their joy in my article, and sending a pressing invitation to me for Walt to visit them at Commencement, in June, and be a guest in their 'artist home.'[1] It is a charming letter and Charles Eldridge has sent a copy of it to Walt. Her name was Fanny Malone Raymond.[2]...

You are quite right in supposing I knew Bayard Taylor wrote those editorials, and my compliments to his *Faust* work must have been honey with a fine bee-sting in it! The greatest joke is that in my first draft of the article I had him in it, as a prominent instance of the persecuting meanness complained of; and I had to take him out, which I did with a groan, it flashing upon me that he was the particular 'assassin of the great Review' in his mask and cloak, I was dealing with, and my admission into print being in sudden danger! I suppose you remember his treatment of Walt. O, but he is a peach blossom — yea, and they are all peach blossoms! They go to their scratch-my-back club, which is called 'The Century,' and their tickle-my-elbow club, which is called 'The Lotos,' and they read each other their little essays and their less verses, and they call each other gods and geniuses, and they concoct their epigrams and epithets, and arrange who shall be written up, and who down, and police Parnassus generally. Among them this gent, of whom Park Benjamin made Humboldt say that he had 'travelled more and seen less than anyone living,' is a conspicuity. He is called Bayard by way of antithesis, I suppose, because he has both reproach and fear, and Taylor because he is the ninth part of a man. How I would like to have answered, just for the fun of it, his last editorial! It was, as you say, just pitiable in its weak-

---

[1] Whitman and Burroughs visited the Ritters at Vassar a year or two later.

[2] Mrs. Fanny Raymond Ritter, wife of Professor Frederick Ritter of Vassar College, was perhaps the first musician to publish a critical account of the musical elements in Whitman's poetry. Her study was first published in a Poughkeepsie newspaper and later reprinted in part in Bucke's *Walt Whitman*, pp. 156–57. — C. J. F.

ness, and everything in it could have been turned upon him. Calling us a convex lens answers nothing — and how can we be a convex lens, exaggerating everything, when he seems to us such small potatoes! The funniest *non sequitur* was in the closing paragraph, where the ruin of the poet's venture was predicated upon the 'skillful advertising' of his 'good green friends'!!! First time mankind was told that 'skillful advertising' is a proof of greenness and the road to ruin! I always *did* like logic.

On the 'formlessness' point, I should like to talk to the 'Tribune,' but policy forbids any more at present. We shall have chance enough yet. The fact is that Walt's poetry, if they refer to its diction, which I suppose they intend, is intensely marked by its form, as any fool *might* see, and the parodists do. Its distinctiveness in this respect is its most striking characteristic. In fact, precisely the opposite of what they aver, is true. If, however, they mean to charge obscurity or incoherence, they only accuse their own intelligence and show that they have the imagination of a pint-pot. Moreover, black Chaos is a god not to be despised anyway; and in art, Turner's pictures in some instances, and some of Shakespeare's poetry, prove it.

I saw Nora's [Perry] article.[1] It was good and did good, but made me laugh to myself. The nub of her argument she got from my pamphlet — the non-levity point: but that is not what amuses me. You see I know her *so* well, and she is a perfect pussy-cat — all this *entre nous* of course. Here's the motif: Emerson left her out of his 'Parnassus' (which is not Apollo's Parnassus, by a long shot!) This, however, could be borne, but, alas! he put her detested friend, Louise Chandler Moulton, *in*, and this was unbearable. Hence she defends W. W. in order to pay off Emerson by 'displaying,' as the dry goods men say, his timidity, which she artfully sets forth with such an air of candor!! I saw the game instantly, knowing her as I do: and we have always been good friends, as you see by her tribute to 'our own' — which is partly her feline, Charles-Reade-womanly way of showing gratitude for helping her to her only serious point of argument! The remark from Carlyle was in an article in *Frank Leslie* accompanying an engraving of Walt. It is his, though not said of W. W., as it well might be, nevertheless.

Yes, I saw the article of Tittlebat Titmouse — I beg pardon: *Timothy* Titmouse — I beg pardon again: *Timothy Titcomb*[2] (knew I'd get it right) in 'Scribner's'[3]: and amazingly I'd like to show him up. What platitude,

[1] Nora Perry: 'A Few Words About Walt Whitman,' *Appleton's Journal*, April 22, 1876.

[2] The pseudonym of J. G. Holland.

[3] Editorial 'Is it Poetry?' by the editor, J. G. Holland (unsigned), in *Scribner's Monthly* (May, 1876), vol. 12, pp. 123–25. It calls Whitman's poems a 'mixture of rhapsodical passages of Carlyle's and Emerson's prose.' 'The man is capable of poetry, and always ought to have written it.' 'We believe that in his theories and performances he is radically wrong — that he is doing nothing but advertise himself as a literary eccentric, and that he ought to have, and will have, no following.' — C. J. F.

and what sophism! he forgets Coleridge's masterly remark, to the effect that the true discrimination is not between prose and metre, but prose and poetry! Why didn't he set off his fixed passages from Emerson and Carlyle against the English litanies — so sublimely poetic in their form; or the prose of our version of Isaiah? This consideration alone knocks his silly sophistries to smithereens. Meanwhile Timothy is in clover, which strikes me as a case of 'formlessness'! 'Tupper Holland,' some racy fellow in the *Sun* calls him,[1] very wittily and deservedly.

Marvin has just been in to see me and says that Mrs. Gilchrist is likely to come to this country with her son next month! There was a beautiful passage in her letter to him, in which she expressed the hope that the Buchanan testimonial will succeed for the sake of spreading *Leaves of Grass*, which she calls 'the greatest product of the time.'

I am extremely and peculiarly pleased that you liked my 'Tribune' letter. It cost me severe labor, burdened as I am with office work and fatigue. I think I covered in Buchanan pretty well. His letter was a little excessive, though the effect of the whole, as it appeared in the 'News,' was misrepresented by the 'Tribune' excerpts. Didn't I get in a good one on the 'red shirt' business! The 'Tribune' had been pushing Dana so hard for the Court of St James, that my dab at that must have made them wince. I think I served out Peter Bayne pretty well, too, though I'd like to devote an article to him.

Good bye. An awful long letter, which forgive.

Faithfully yours
W. D. O'CONNOR

Another 'awful long letter' from O'Connor to Burroughs, dated May 15, it would be a pity to miss entirely. Excerpts only are given:

Your letter was delightful. I am so self-distrustful, self-accusing, self-depreciating, that praise, if it is intelligent, often has a good tonic effect on me. I say, if it is intelligent, for I have often been terribly upset and cast down by being extolled ridiculously.

Have you seen [George William] Curtis's contribution in the last [June] 'Harper's' Easy Chair? It was formally announced in the 'Tribune,' and of course I looked for it in a palpitant condition, thinking that Cambridge had chosen its warrior, and that I was going to 'catch it.' My disappointment is ludicrous. The artificial mountain in Brooklyn park has labored and produced a toy mouse! We haven't even a living animal, when I expected at least a carnivorous, though elegant and well-conducted jabberwock! O, George William, how are the mighty fallen! Absolutely, his contribution is nothing but a dilution of Bayard Taylor's editorials — and resembles excellent mutton-broth made by boiling, without condi-

---

[1] Probably Charles A. Dana.

ment, the shadow of a sheep's trotter. We shall have no stomach for the war if this is the kind of nutriment we are to receive, and I anxiously hope for reinforcement from England.

Stedman is very friendly to Walt, and I think you'd better take him out of your article in the proofs.[1] Of course, I don't suppose he sees him as you or I do, but he is friendly, and we must encourage him. Stedman is in a position, the difficulty and delicacy of which I appreciate. You see he must, being what he is, and where he is, keep in with his tribe, and his attitude is a compromise between relative appreciation of Walt, and attachment to the men and books of the other side.

I would like to talk with you on this subject, when I could say more, and better, than I can write. I think it is policy for us, at present, to avoid attacking anyone specifically, by name, except for very grave and definite reason. The better way, I think, is to accept, to admire, to extol, all the poets as far as consistent with truth, but to discriminate between them and a poet like Walt; and to insist, in the strongest manner, that he is, with all possible respect and cordial appreciation of them and their uses, something different and greater, both in his ambition and achievement. This seems to me a position at once just, generous, and impregnable. You think of it.[2]

My own general feeling is that art is a firmament, in which there are constellations as well as stars; in which one star differs from another in glory, but all are stellar; and in which even the star-dust and nebulæ and the transient meteors, are respectable and perform their worthy offices. I hesitate to condemn anything. Let there be only comparative criticism, proper discrimination, and even the 'idle singers of an empty day,' and the empty singers of an idle day, shall not be dispraised by me, except in a sort of praise. At any rate, if we are to censure, we must be mighty careful that our points are well taken.

So far I feel that it is simply a war of out-posts. The time for attack, trenchant and tremendous, upon the main armies of Philistia, has not yet come — and never can until we get a magazine all our own. Until we have an organ, it is neither possible nor prudent to assume the offensive. If we only had some money! What a chance there is for a superb review, political, social, artistic, and literary, such as this country has never dreamed of, and in this city, of all places in the world! Go to, now! let us win the $300,000 prize in the Havana lottery and begin!

I doubt if the 'Tribune' would admit the article you propose, or if it is not rather too abstract for a newspaper, especially in these piping campaign times. However, try it.

[1] Evidently Burroughs sent O'Connor his manuscript of 'The Flight of the Eagle' on which he was then at work. Assuming the correctness of this supposition, it is also evident that Burroughs acted on his advice about Stedman, as no mention is made of him in the essay, which came out in *Birds and Poets*, in 1877.

[2] See Burroughs to O'Connor, p. 46.

But I wish you would carefully and judiciously, without alarming him, pump young [Ernest] Ingersoll and find out who are on the 'Tribune,' and all about the matter. Such information is a great guide, on occasion.

It was quite delicious in you to write that to Ingersoll about Bayard Taylor! He must have been amused. I think your idea about B. T.'s aspirations and sourness consequent upon their non-fulfilment, is probably quite correct. He aspire to be the great American poet! It is too preposterous. I could assure him, upon my honor as an oracle, that in the language of a beautiful line from one of his own poems, he will find himself, in respect to our Pantheon,

'bathed in the tenderest purple of distance' —

yea, verily, the *very* tenderest!

... Howells needs a good critical cudgelling. It would do him good. I saw the fling you mention and thought how effectively it could be turned on him! Some day I will send an arrow at him. If it misses, he will have an arrow escape! (joak!) But it will not miss.

During 1875 Burroughs had been writing much on Emerson; two of the articles came out in the 'Galaxy' in 1876 — 'A Word or Two on Emerson' in February, and 'A Final Word on Emerson' in April. Later he incorporated these with other material in his 'Emerson' in 'Birds and Poets' (1877). Evidently he had sent Whitman the first of those 'Galaxy' articles in manuscript. A letter to him from Whitman, written April 1, 1875, contains a keen, candid analysis of the manuscript, upon which Burroughs doubtless acted to some extent, though not fully:

Dear John,

I have looked over the Emerson notes—read them all over once—am precluded from anything more, or giving any very deep or elaborate analysis of them, in connection with the Emerson question (as my brain is in a state not allowing thought, argument, or study) — but still I will give you my first impressions of your pages:

In their totality they produce a not agreeable notion of being written by one who has been largely grown and ripened and gristled by Emerson, but has at last become dissatisfied and finnicky about him, and would pitch into him, but cannot — perhaps dare not — and so keeps running around in a sort of circle of praises and half praises, like a horse tied by a tether.

Your Notes also seem to me (to be plain) a good deal too diffuse, and too Emersony in themselves — I should select about one third of the MS. as *first rate* (including the opening part). My opinion is that you had perhaps better work it all over, and leave out at least half.

About the allusions to me, my off-hand thought is that my name might be brought in, in one or two places, as foil or suggestive comparison — but *my name only*, without any praises or comments (only the silently inferred ones). To my friends and circle, who know the relations and history between me and Emerson, the mere mention of the name itself, in that way, will be significant (and it might give pungency to the sentence.)

I have had a bad time the last two weeks — head and belly — and I almost wonder I stand it so well — for I *do* stand it — I go out most every day, a little. John Swinton from N.Y. has been to see me.

Love to you and 'Sula.

W. W.

Burroughs had corresponded with Benton as well as with Whitman about his Emerson essays; and in January, before the publication of the February 'Galaxy,' had told Benton how dissatisfied he was with what he had written. Later he wrote of the second essay having been written more freely, and 'less in the Emersonian style.' He said he felt delivered of the subject at last, but confessed, 'I growl considerable, but hope I give him his full meed of praise.' Then follows his real reason for his change of heart toward the idol of his youth:

I have felt pretty ugly toward Emerson because he ignored Walt Whitman in his 'Parnassus.'[1] I think Walt can afford to be overlooked, but I don't think Emerson can afford to overlook *him*, much less can Bryant and Whittier, as they have done. [In anthologies prepared by them.] It is the weakest thing I ever knew Emerson to do, and has been a great help to me in criticizing him... rather sounding him... he is not a man to be criticized, but rather to be defined and appreciated.

On June 17, 1876, Whitman comments as follows on Burroughs's 'A Final Word on Emerson':

John, I have just been reading your 'Galaxy' article, seated by the open window, front room, in my shirt sleeves, and must write a word about it.

Your late pieces show marked *vitality*, *vivacity* (struggling, almost chafing, under a continent, respectable form or exterior) and *this is the best of them* — has those peculiarities, not without one or two foibles, but the *whole* of the piece is glorious — leaves the impression now upon me (after two readings) of the noblest piece of criticism on these things yet in America — as much nobler than the superb Emersonian pages on those subjects as lines and opinions with *the blood of life* and throb of hot conviction in them, are nobler than the superbest marble statue lines.

[1] W. S. Kennedy, in his *Fight of a Book for the World*, pp. 129–30, quotes F. B. Sanborn as suggesting that Emerson's omission of Whitman from his *Parnassus* was in deference to his daughters, who scorned the *Leaves*.

It would be possible that I might be swayed into a warm feeling about the piece by the magnificent and very 'cute page about me, but as it happens by accident I had looked over and read the piece in parts, *accidentally omitting at first the entire lines in the second column* of the page, about me (which finally please me best) — and had made up my mind very decidedly as aforesaid — then when I *did* read them, you can imagine *they* didn't hurt me much — nor my estimation of the piece.

I have much to write or tell you about my own concerns — things in England, here, too, etc. etc. — have been waiting for the chance to write you fully ever since I got your kind generous note and present — but it don't seem to occur —...

WALT.

Commenting to me in 1907 on Whitman's opinion of his Emerson essay, Burroughs said: 'That is overpraise. Walt broke over his usual caution there. He never used to praise things of mine. I think he must have had a glass of whisky, or some champagne, when he wrote that.'

The passage in the Emerson essay to which Whitman evidently referred is found on page 543, of the 'Galaxy' for April, 1876, and on page 175 in 'Birds and Poets':

What one comes at last to want is power, mastery; and, whether it be mastery over the subtleties of the spirit as in Emerson himself,... or over vast masses and spaces of nature and the abysms of aboriginal man, as in Walt Whitman, what matters it? Are we not refreshed by all?...

A paragraph from 'A Word or Two on Emerson,' also used in 'Birds and Poets' (page 171), reads:

But Emerson has his difficulties with all the poets. Homer is too literal, Milton is too literary, and there is too much of the whooping savage in Whitman. He seems to think the real poet is yet to appear; a poet on new terms, the reconciler, the poet-priest, — one who shall unite the whiteness and purity of the saint with the power and unction of the sinner; one who shall bridge the chasm between Shakespeare and St John. For when our Emerson gets on his highest horse, which he does only on two or three occasions, he finds Shakespeare only a half man, and that it would take Plato and Menu and Moses and Jesus to complete him....

The part which Burroughs evidently deleted from the 'Galaxy' article, in deference to Whitman's suggestion, leaving in only the comment about the 'whooping savage in Whitman' but which he put back when reëditing the fuller essay in 'Birds and Poets,' is found on pages 170–71 of that volume immediately preceding the foregoing passage:

Much surprise has been expressed in literary circles in this country that Emerson has not followed up his first off-hand indorsement of Walt Whitman with fuller and more deliberate approval of that poet, but has rather taken the opposite tack. But the wonder is that he should have been carried off his feet at all in the manner he was; and it must have been no ordinary breeze that did it. Emerson shares with his contemporaries the vast preponderance of the critical and discerning intellect over the fervid, manly qualities and faith. His power of statement is enormous; his scope of being is not enormous. The prayer he uttered many years ago for a poet of the modern, one who could see in the gigantic materialism of the times the carnival of the same deities we so much admire in Greece and Rome, etc., seems to many to have even been explicitly answered in Whitman; but Emerson is balked by the cloud of materials, the din and dust of action, and the moving armies, in which the god comes enveloped.

When Myron Benton read Burroughs's critique on Emerson in 'Birds and Poets,' he pronounced it the most searching estimate of Emerson that had come under his eyes. However, he singled out the preceding excerpt for mild censure:

I do not quite like the way you knight errants of Walt Whitman hound Emerson about that endorsement. He ought to have the rights of a man and perfect freedom in the Republic of Letters to say what he chooses on any subject, and let it drop when he chooses; and not be kept forever in the pillory. I shall serve a writ of *habeas corpus* pretty soon if you don't stop. But you make some most excellent points.

Assuredly, when, years before, Emerson had written, 'Every opinion reacts on him who utters it,' he announced a truth of which he was to feel the full force in years to come, concerning his 1855 greeting to Whitman. But in 'Self-Reliance' the Sage had unconsciously defended himself: ' ... If you would be a man, speak what you think today in words as hard as cannon balls, and tomorrow speak what tomorrow thinks in hard words again, though it contradict everything you said today.' And who so capable of understanding Emerson's veerings as Whitman himself, who took the same stand?

> Do I contradict myself?
> Very well, then, I contradict myself.

X

WHITMAN'S NOBLEST WOMAN FRIEND
(1869–1885)

My science-friend, my noblest woman friend,
(Now buried in an English grave — and this a memory leaf for her dear sake.
WHITMAN

ANNE GILCHRIST'S essay 'A Woman's Estimate of Walt Whitman,' first published in the 'Radical,' May, 1870, was the outcome of her reading, first, William Rossetti's selections from the 'Leaves,' and, later, a copy of the complete poems. The 'deepening delight and wonder' with which she read had first found expression in grateful letters to Rossetti, letters which he regarded as so keen and comprehending that he persuaded her to work them up into an article for publication. Whitman himself called this essay 'the proudest word' that ever came to him from a woman — 'if not the proudest word of all from any source.' He also spoke of it as 'a burst of sunlight over sea.' In time letters followed between the broad-minded, courageous English woman and the poet, and later she, with one son and two daughters, followed the letters, coming to the United States in September, 1876, and remaining here three years, for the double purpose of being near Whitman and of educating her children in this country, whose democratic principles strongly appealed to her.

This is not the place to write particularly of Anne Gilchrist, except to introduce matter closely bearing on the scope of this volume. A very understanding friendship developed between her and John Burroughs, as well as between her and Whitman. From 'Anne Gilchrist: Her Life and Writings,' written and edited by her artist son, Herbert, (1887), much may be gleaned of her rare character and achievements. Her letters to Whitman were published in 1918 by Thomas B. Harned, one of the literary executors of Whitman.

Mrs. Gilchrist's first reading of 'Leaves of Grass' was in 1869.

Her fervent and ministering friendship with the poet may be said
to date from that time, ending only in her death, in November, 1885.
As has already been seen, it was she and Dowden who started 'the
blessed gales' blowing to Whitman from the British Isles (page
115). Her personal letters to Whitman began in 1871. They first
met in Philadelphia in the Centennial year.

In September, 1876, when John Burroughs visited the Centennial
Exposition, he first met Mrs. Gilchrist and her family. Writing his
wife from the hotel where they were all staying, he said:

Walt came over every evening from Camden and took supper with us,
and we had much talk. He likes Mrs. Gilchrist and her family, and they
like him. They are going to housekeeping and expect to spend several
years in this country. It will be a god-send to Walt, and he anticipates
much pleasure in visiting them.

Mrs. Gilchrist is a rosy woman without a gray hair in her head. I like
her much. The daughters are fresh and comely, like soft, light-skinned
peaches. I went house-hunting with them.

Writing Myron Benton of meeting the Gilchrists, Burroughs said
further: 'Walt Whitman was better than when I saw him before.
I have more hopes now of his recovery than ever before.'

Mrs. Gilchrist herself wrote Burroughs on December 15, from
1929 North 22d Street, Philadelphia:

DEAR MR. BURROUGHS,

If business does not bring you this way ere long, then I hope friendship
will — for we long very much for the society of a friend or two in this new
home. However, we must not definitely say, 'Will you come on such a
day?' till our landlord has fulfilled his promise of giving us a good brick
furnace to warm our rooms — for I believe an American would be fairly
perished here — the iron ones we now have are just a mere gulf for coals
to disappear in without sending out any equivalent heat in return — and
as we are on high ground, facing northwest, no houses opposite, and doors
and windows, and floors, for that matter, so ill-fitted that you see daylight
through, you may judge if it has not been pretty Arctic here of late.
Still we are not the worse in health, I am glad to say, and not having yet
been able to hear of a trustworthy servant, we have an amount of indoor
activity which is very healthful and cheerful under the circumstances.

As soon as we can get the thermometer up to a reasonable point in our
rooms, say 65 degrees, I will write again.

Meanwhile, cordial Christmas greetings.

ANNE GILCHRIST

ANNE GILCHRIST

Mrs. Gilchrist's son writes Burroughs three days later:

Since we saw you we have been slowly settling in our new home and in the main satisfactorily; not, however, without verifying a few of Mr. Marvin's predictions as to the misfortunes that would befall us if we took a perfectly new house; a furnace that wouldn't heat, range that wouldn't burn, pipes that would leak, etc. etc., but we have such a jolly lot of room, and so pleasant a situation, that we do not repent our choice.

One of our great pleasures is Mr. Whitman's society; he spends an evening with us pretty often and sometimes a day or two. Philadelphians, as far as we have an opportunity of judging, do not impress us as a very genial or hospitable race.

We often wish Esopus on Hudson were handy to Philadelphia, but, far as it is, you perhaps will manage to spend a few days with us.

Mr. Whitman has just lent us Dowden's Essays on 'Shakespeare: His Mind and Art.' It is deeply interesting; his analysis of Spenser's genius seemed to me to be profound. We presented our introductions to Dr. Furness: his son Horace is a Shakespearian scholar and possesses a pair of theatrical gloves said to have belonged to Shakespeare; they were given to Mr. Horace Furness by Fanny Kemble, who had them from Garrick, which in itself makes them sufficiently interesting.

Did you see the review of Mr. Whitman's poems in the 'Examiner'?[1] Mr. Whitman showed it us and seemed pleased with it; Justin McCarthy, jr., wrote it. Do you know him? he is about twenty, I suppose. He looks considerably younger in the face than I do! an extremely nice fellow, a friend of Rossetti. Hoping to see you soon,

Believe me to be,
Yours very truly,
HERBERT HARLAKENDEN GILCHRIST

On January 16, 1877, from the Gilchrist home, Whitman writes Burroughs:

I have been over here with the Gilchrists for a week — go back to Camden this afternoon or tomorrow — I have a nice room here with a stove and oak wood — everything very comfortable and sunny — most of all *the spirit* (which is so *entirely lacking* over there in Camden, and has been for more than three years) —

— We often speak of you — I received your letter of the 7th....

Love to you and 'Sula.
WALT WHITMAN.

Burroughs explained that Whitman was living with his brother George at that time, and that while George was kind to him, in his

---

[1] J. H. McCarthy, Jr.: 'Songs Overseas,' *Examiner*, October 21, 1876.

way, he 'hadn't much sympathy for Walt's literary life, or his unthrifty ways, George being very forehanded, as they say.'

After this, from time to time, in letters and Journal, Burroughs mentions visits to the Gilchrists to see Whitman. In early May there came to him an invitation to visit them while Edward Carpenter would be their guest:

I wish you would run over for a day or two while we have here a young Englishman whom I am sure you would like, and who would like much to make your acquaintance. The principal object of his visit to America is to see Walt Whitman, for whom his admiration and affection are deep and hearty. He was a Fellow of Trinity College, Cambridge, but threw that up because he could not stand the Orthodoxy, etc., is now one of the lecturers sent out by the University to the great towns which are desirous of higher educational advantages — has also written some poems; above all, is very genial, cordial, unaffected. So come if you can.

Friendly remembrances from us all.

ANNE GILCHRIST

It is seen from Mrs. Gilchrist's letter of May 16, that Burroughs did not go to Philadelphia to meet Edward Carpenter, but invited him to Riverby instead:

Your cordial note came to hand Saturday. I think you will find Mr. Carpenter a hearty good fellow — we have had quite a jolly time with him. I can answer for it, he will enjoy the walks and talks you promise right well. Just now he is at Washington (and Herby with him) but they return tonight — Then he goes northward, and I have no doubt you will see or hear from him in the course of a few days.

And close upon the heels of your letter came your book [1] — you may be sure, though it was morning, and dinner and bread-making on my hands, I managed before half an hour was over, to be quietly buried in it — and you know which essay I turned to first.[2] But you don't know, and you will not easily realize, the strong emotion with which I read it. I believe the hearty grasp of the hand I hope to give you at the end of the month is the only way those thoughts and feelings of mine can express themselves; that is what I felt to long for — I am quite sure the *heartiness of conviction* that breathes through it has electricity in it and will waken some out of their lethargy — with a start I trust. The selections are judiciously chosen — 'Ah! Time, you Enchantress!' your tricks shall surely be baffled while yet the beloved Poet is with us to enjoy, to bathe in the great waves of passionate sympathy and love that will sooner or later set towards him.

[1] Burroughs: *Birds and Poets*. Boston, 1877.
[2] 'The Flight of the Eagle,' *Birds and Poets*, pp. 185–235.

... Mr. Whitman is mostly at White Horse just now, spends the livelong day at his favorite creek and finds it good, soothing, refreshing. Friendly remembrance from us all.

ANNE GILCHRIST

I hope Mrs. Burroughs is well — able to enjoy outdoor life, too.

On June 5, Burroughs writes Myron Benton:

... I have just had a three days' visit from a young Englishman [Edward Carpenter] from Cambridge, who came to this country to see Whitman. I like him much — a modest, sensible man and a great admirer of W. W. He is now in Boston and has letters to Emerson and others....

From Boston, Carpenter writes Burroughs, on June 7:

Thanks for your note. I shall try to see Lathrop this evening. I have not met with a spark of appreciation (intelligent or otherwise) of Walt Whitman here yet. I had a long talk with O. W. Holmes about him. He 'whinnied' (I find they all do) at the mention of his name and then launched forth as follows: It was very curious how he [Whitman] was admired in England. Lord Napier had said that he was the one thing that interested him in the States, and then Lord Houghton came plump out about him at a dinner party, and was attacked so fiercely by Willie Everett that conversation was silenced. And he knew that Rossetti and others in England thought much of him. But—but—but—he could only say that in America no one read him. Well, their best critics, Lowell, for instance — he and Lowell and Longfellow were talking about Whitman together one day — and Lowell said, 'Why, there's *nothing* in him.' Longfellow seemed to think, 'Poor fellow, something might have been made of him if he had been trained,' and, for myself, I knew what I thought of him — O, there's *something* in him, no doubt (that thrown-in by way of a sop to me) but—but—but—' and then off he went with the usual rant about W's sexuality, etc.

I said that his nakedness was no more than the nakedness of a Greek statue, and that his flavour, which Holmes found so strong, would perhaps flavour the dishes of America for a great many centuries — but it was obvious that I might as well have argued with the wind.

So much for Holmes. Of course he isn't important, but I think he is just the kind of man who, having little or no real mind of his own, represents the literary world around him very well.

With Emerson I spent a whole day (and night), and a most enjoyable one. He was so good and gentle (by no means one of the race of 'savage old men') that I could not feel angry with him for the part he took. He did not abuse Whitman, or rant against him in any way. He spoke of him more in sorrow than in anger. Said of course that he 'thought he had some merit at one time — there was a good deal of promise in his first edition —

but he was a wayward, fanciful man.' (It appears that Whitman took Emerson to see his [Bohemian?] society at New York, and Emerson thought it very noisy and rowdy, and couldn't understand his friendliness with firemen. In fact, Whitman baffled and puzzled him.) The truth is, as it appears to me now, that Emerson is a purely 'literary' man. I never understood that before. And I believe no 'literary' mind can accept Whitman.

I saw Lowell, too, but did not say a word on that subject to *him*.[1]

Carpenter continues the following day:

I was fortunate enough to find Lathrop at home last night. I like him much. He is a sensitive, emotional sort of fellow, perhaps almost morbidly so — as unlike the hard, literary type as possible. He is very anxious to see you and Walt Whitman, and will very likely, I think, come with me to Philadelphia about Wednesday or Thursday next. I hope very much that you will manage to come, too....

In 'My Days and Dreams,' Edward Carpenter reflects some of the same disappointment concerning the Boston *literati* expressed to Burroughs; still he is unperturbed, for he adds: 'But it was Walt Whitman I came out to see, and he in interest and grandeur of personality out-towered them all.' Then, of Niagara: 'And it was the only thing I saw which seemed quite to match Whitman in spirit.' Concerning Whitman he gives this significant passage:

I was aware of a certain radiant power in him, a large benign effluence and inclusiveness, as of the sun, which filled out the place where he was — yet with something of reserve and sadness in it, too, and a sense of remoteness and inaccessibility.

Carpenter again visited the United States in 1884 and saw Whitman many times. His 'A Visit to Walt Whitman' was printed in the 'Progressive Review,' February and April, 1897, and later in 'Days with Walt Whitman,' published in London and New York (1906). This covers not only his two visits, but contains penetrating essays on 'Whitman as Prophet,' 'Poetic Form of "Leaves of Grass,"' 'Walt Whitman's Children,' and 'Whitman and Emerson.' Carpenter thus records his visit to Burroughs, in 'My Days and Dreams' (pages 89–90):

On my way down the Hudson I stopped at Esopus and stayed with

---

[1] Lowell warned Matthew Arnold, when he came with a letter of introduction from Lord Houghton to Whitman, that he should not waste time on such a boor. Arnold followed Lowell's advice. — C. J. F.

John Burroughs a night or two. We took a long walk in the primitive woods back of his house, while he talked of Whitman and bird-lore — a tough, reserved, farmer-like exterior, some old root out of the woods, one might say — obdurate to wind and weather — but a keen, quick observer, close to Nature and the human heart, and worth a good many Holmes and Lowells.

Burroughs, in his Journal, on June 1, recording Carpenter's visit, speaks of him as a 'modest, hearty, thoughtful young Englishman.' There seems nothing incompatible with the modesty attributed to him in what Carpenter says of his own book, 'Towards Democracy' (1883) in 'My Days and Dreams.' Like Whitman he believed in the potency of his own message, and in candidly expressing that belief:

If the world — it seems to me — should ever seize the central fact of such books as 'Leaves of Grass,' and 'Towards Democracy,' it must inevitably formulate new views of life on almost every conceivable subject; the aspects of all life will be changed.[1]

And in 'Days with Walt Whitman' (page 58), Carpenter says:

'Leaves of Grass' is the meeting-ground of the human race. There every nationality, every creed, every trade, every atom of humanity is represented, and all are fused in the great loving soul that overbroods them.

Carpenter had an article, 'Walt Whitman's Present Circumstances,' in 'Papers for the Times' (January, 1880), and also a chapter on Whitman in 'Angels' Wings' (1898). His poetical 'Towards Democracy' has been considered as inspired by Whitman, even imitative of him; but while freely acknowledging his absorption and admiration of the poet whose 'Leaves' 'filtered and fibred' his blood, Carpenter declared he had never tried to imitate it. In 'The Labour Prophet' (May, 1894), or elsewhere, he points out that whatever of resemblance there may be in the two books, should be set down to a deep similarity of emotional atmosphere and of intention in the two authors. He says further: 'Whitman's full-blooded, copious, rank, masculine style must always make him one of the world's great originals — a perennial fountain of health and strength, moral as well as physical.... "Towards Democracy" has a milder radiance, as of the moon compared with the sun....

[1] Carpenter: *My Days and Dreams*, p. 201. Scribner, 1916.

Tender and meditative, less resolute, and altogether less massive, it has the quality of the fluid and yielding air rather than of the solid and uncompromising earth.' Whereby it may be seen that Carpenter, as well as Whitman, had the ability to stand apart and look at himself and his work in an impartial way. I think it is in 'Towards Democracy' that the lines occur which are reminiscent of that first momentous visit to Whitman:

Grave and strong and untamed,
This is the clear-browed unconstrained tender face, with full lips and bearded chin,
   this is the regardless defiant face I love and trust;
Which I came out to see, and having seen do not forget.

Writing to Burroughs from the Gilchrist home in Philadelphia, on June 28, Whitman said:

Am here having a good time — Carpenter returns to Europe in Saturday's steamer — the Gilchrists all well — my folks in Camden doing well — Marvin comes here on the 6th of July. Shall come to visit you and 'Sula this summer.

                    W.W.

A friendship between Burroughs and Lathrop grew out of the Carpenter visit and the common love for Whitman. Lathrop's letter to Burroughs dated May 19 is given here:

I have just finished your book on 'Birds and Poets.' I like your writing always, and I have keenly enjoyed this. But you will not quarrel with me if I pass that matter over in order to speak of Walt Whitman. Ever since I first gained some fragmentary knowledge of him thro' the pruned and lopped English edition, I have not for a moment flagged in the belief that he is our greatest poet, altogether and beyond any measurement. He threw open a wide gate for me, and I passed through it gladly — thinking to be able in my separate way to make a kind of companionship with him. From the start, my intentions have been very different in some respects from those of which he has given such huge exemplification; but as I took to his poetry without any premonitory shrinking, and felt that at last here was something real, I knew that I should in some measure respond to his voice in what I should do, however far off, however fainter, and however much unlike in seeming it might be.

But my circumstances have been strangely hampering. I find myself in the midst of the camp which adheres to the old and the conventional. I am an accepted servant in it, trying to pass through my bondage patiently, working year after year in a roundabout way, slowly trying to secure my position, and hoping at last to be able to let out the accumulating thunder in my own way. I get my hands loose now and then and feel that I have done a little something. This much I thought it necessary to say because I suppose you at a distance hardly imagine a young Cambridge literary apprentice can say his soul's his own, or cherish in himself a whole revolution against the powers whom for a time he is working with. I say it also to explain why I would like now to convey through you to Walt Whitman some message expressing the fact that I have wished to speak a word of gratitude to him. To a man so wronged even this little tribute may have its value. It is also a great satisfaction to me to think of speaking the truth about him to him and through one who understands it. There are two persons hereabouts who appreciate Whitman, whom I know. Doubtless there are many more who are unknown to me. But I can believe that the scoffing narrowness which meets any avowal of their appreciation has driven them, as it has me, to preserve silence.

It is a great pity his works are not really published, and I have been wondering long how to get them. I have nothing but Rossetti's edition. Is there no way of obtaining them? I should be very glad if you would inform me as to this.

I frequently debate plans of some change of base, so as to secure something approaching independence. I was not born in New England, tho' of Puritan descent, but in the tropics. I like many things here and dislike others as much. I am a great lover of cities for their crowds, their human sublimities and horrors, yet carry always an insatiable yearning for the wilds. I don't know where to go, if I go from here, where I am now editing the 'Atlantic' with Mr. Howells, but I have before now thought of your region. I have no map showing Esopus. Is it in the Highlands — anything like Milton? Would you be willing to tell me something of your mode of life, or whether one can subsist in that vicinity on slender means?

Sincerely yours,

G. P. LATHROP

On March 29, 1878, from Camden, New Jersey, Whitman writes to Burroughs that Beatrice Gilchrist is there at his brother's for the evening, and that the Gilchrists are to break camp in three or four weeks and spend the ensuing year excursively in America.

And from Round Hill Hotel, Northampton, Massachusetts, on May 1, 1878, Anne Gilchrist writes to Burroughs:

You have my post-card long ere this, I trust, but still feel quite guilty for having put off writing it as long as I did. The truth is, I could not see my way or tell, to a day or two, when we should get off, we had planted our tent so firmly and spread our possessions around us so, at 1929. However it stands empty and forlorn now. I lent my jolly antique furniture to the loan exhibition of the Pennsylvania Museum in Memorial Hall where they will store it for me as long as I please for nothing, and glad to have it, and all my prints and pictures I lent to the New Century Club. I sold the cheap bedroom furniture I bought when I came, and packed and stored all my china and glass and blankets and carpets, etc. — all that would pack in moderate compass and cost but little to store. We were so dead tired after completing all this and rushing about to say Good-bye to many kind friends, etc., that we should have been the stupidest and dullest of guests — so it was best to come straight on here, and have the pleasure of seeing you in your beautiful home as something in store for the future.

Now about Walt. He is fairly well again — not so strong as before yet, but in a way to be so soon, now he can get out and be so constantly in the open air. Dr. Weir Mitchell's opinion was encouraging. There are no signs of malarial mischief about him, nor has the sitting in the sun done harm, nor is this attack connected with his paralytic affection which latter is progressing as favourably as could be expected; it was simply cold and rheumatism. Camden is a bad place for him; he wants mountain air, says the Dr., and I hope he will have some in the course of the summer.

How are you? If you want to set yourself up after your severe attack, and to have a pleasant time, and to give us one, too, come here for a week to this big rambling old house perched on the top of a hill amid as sweet surroundings as are to be found anywhere in the world, I venture to say. I could believe myself in dear old Haslemere — a good table, a pleasant host, terms moderate ($10. a week, if room on 3d Floor) and the place almost to ourselves.

Good-bye,
ANNE GILCHRIST

By November of that year the Gilchrists are settled in New York, Herbert working at painting and designing, and Mrs. Gilchrist drawing to her many congenial friends — the Gilders, the De Kays, the John Bigelows, Emma Lazarus, and many others. Whitman's notes to Burroughs at this time speak of seeing the Gilchrists often. One on Christmas Day gives their new address and urges Burroughs and his wife to call on them when in the city. On June 11, writing from the J. H. Johnstons' in New York about other matters, Whitman adds a pregnant sentence — 'The Gilchrists sailed last Saturday in the *Circassia*.' In 1912, Mr. J. H. Johnston told me of that June visit of Whitman in his home, when Mrs. Gilchrist and her family were also their guests before leaving for England. That last day the two friends held a long conference in the Johnston parlor; both were deeply moved on rejoining the family. It was their real farewell. What passed between them there was locked in their hearts. All their talks were ended. Whitman's noblest woman friend was going back to England; but more than the 'irresistible sea' was to separate them — she was 'Going Somewhere' beyond the bounds of time and space. Did these two divine that they would never meet again?

In August, Whitman sends Burroughs two letters from Mrs. Gilchrist, now on English soil again, probably the two quoted by Harned on pages 181 and 183 in the Gilchrist-Whitman letters. Whitman's brief reply to one of those letters is given on page 186 of the same book.

Whitman's letter to Burroughs, November 23, 1879, gives the new English address of the Gilchrists, and encloses a letter from Mrs. Gilchrist which he says need not be returned. This accounts for its never having been published, Mr. Harned not knowing of it when editing the Gilchrist-Whitman letters.

Shottermill, Haslemere,
Surrey, October 6, '79

My dearest Friend,

Your letter came to me here just when Edward Carpenter and a group of his friends, one of them a native of Ceylon of the Tamil race, and all admirers and lovers of your Poems, were with us; and greatly they enjoyed hearing it.

We look forward to the new book I need not say. We all agreed in hoping you would reconsider the title so far, that is, as to leave out the clause 'by a half paralytic.' If you ask me why, I should be puzzled to say, unless it is that one resents that mere accident of slight bodily infirmity being thrust forward as if it were a part of you — for health and vigour, dear friend, are and ever must remain synonymous with our Walt's name.

We have been spending the last six or seven weeks in this village I am so fond of where my children grew up; we came to live here after my husband's death and remained seven or eight years till the boys needed London for their studies, a wild, breezy little place lying up high amongst heath-covered hills, the walks over which, with wide views over rich green valleys below, springy turf to tread on, sweet smells around and elastic invigorating air, are delicious! And old friends have given us a very warm reception. Tennyson has been to see us, and we have been to luncheon with him, and seen his fine little grandson just the same age as mine. He made many enquiries after you, looks fairly well and is little if at all aged since we went away; is a good deal bothered just now about his new play — Irving is so shilly-shally about bringing it out on the stage, and till that is decided it cannot be published in any other way. He has lately inherited quite a large addition to his fortune from an elder brother.

Herby is busily and hopefully painting away, a small landscape on the fair days, and a piece of still life — some roses and a fragment of beautiful antique sculpture before a mirror—on the wet ones.

Bee [Beatrice] I hope by this time is at Berne. She has been successfully working away at German, boarding in a school at Wiesbaden since I last wrote, and can now speak and write it enough to enter on medical studies at Berne. Percy is, I think, in Westphalia, superintending the starting of the 'process' at some large works there.

I am going to spend a week with an invalid cousin in Essex and then we shall settle down in London or close to it for the winter.

I am trying to write a brief memoir of my Husband to prefix to the new edition of the Blake Macmillan is going to bring out.

Giddy [Grace] sends her kindest remembrances and says she would not wonder if she were to drift back again to America in a few years.

I cannot tell you, dear friend, how often and how affectionately my thoughts turn to America — the great beautiful land with its growth and its vigour and impetus and its friendly sunny welcomes.

Edward Carpenter is gone back to Sheffield to lecture there through the winter. He enjoys his work.

A friend told me an anecdote of Tennyson's two sons which will please you. One of them was going abroad and the other went to see him off at the station. They kissed one another heartily at parting. Hallam, the eldest, who is still unmarried, is such a comfort to his father and mother. He seems like son and daughter in one to them.

Write soon again, dear friend, and let us know if the book is ready that we may have some copies for ourselves and friends speedily.

Love to your brother and sister and to Hattie and Jessie.

Good bye, dearest Friend
ANNE GILCHRIST

Oct. 12th

In other letters to Whitman, Mrs. Gilchrist voices in her own generous way her love of America and its people, speaking in one letter of 'that great sunny land of hope and progress,' and of how her whole life has been enriched by the human intercourse she had here. The following year Whitman writes Burroughs of the Gilchrists being in London, except Beatrice, who is pursuing her medical studies in Switzerland.

A letter of March 9, 1880, from Herbert Gilchrist to Whitman, sent by Whitman to Burroughs, is here quoted in part for the near view it offers of Rossetti:

Last Saturday was a memorable day with me. I went to Dante Gabriel Rossetti's studio for the first time....

A pleasant housemaid opens the door to us — I and Mother — and we are shewn into a pretty little reception room; little round mirrors in black frames ornament the room; there is also a quaint sofa decorated with little medallion pictures. The door opens; a musical, friendly voice greets our ears; it is Mr. Rossetti; he leads the way to his studio. We enter a large room, a high window looking north faces us. Mr. Rossetti shows us the picture that he is at work upon — a life-size picture of a most lovely woman who has just dropped a convolvulus on the ground — the beauty of whose face 'beggars all description,' to quote Shakespeare.

Then he shews us his large picture of the 'Death of Beatrice,' a picture that is about as high and long as your kitchen. As we are seated before this glorious picture, Rossetti reads aloud to us the following:

(From Dante's Dream)

On the Day of the Death of Beatrice

9th June, 1290

> Then Love said: 'Now shall all things be made clear,
> Come and behold our lady where she lies.'
> These 'wildering fantasies
> Then carried me to see my lady dead.
> Even as I there was led,
> Her ladies with a veil were covering her
> And with her was such very humbleness
> That she appeared to say, 'I am at peace!'

I never heard such a soft, rich and full voice as that of the great artist before whose picture we sat. Rossetti said he should take the liberty of calling me Herbert, because I reminded him of my father. I told him it was the greatest compliment he could pay me. He told me also that his brother William had told him that he liked my painting, and he should like to see some of my work, but that he never went to exhibitions; so I shall go with something of mine to his studio. And, besides, he is going to shew me some more of his work.

When Burroughs was in Great Britain, in the summer of 1882, he saw much of the Gilchrists in their own home, and had some pedestrian tours with Herbert Gilchrist, in the wilds of Kent, from Rochester to Gravesend, over Gad's Hill, and from Feversham to Canterbury, on to Dover, and along the chalk cliffs to Folkestone. He did not give Mrs. Gilchrist the chance she wished, to bring him and her English friends together. He preferred scraping acquaintance with the songbirds instead of the poets, even Tennyson. She protested against his not having settled down a bit, and wrote him that, had he but done this, her national vanity made her think he would have taken back as cordial a liking for England's people as he did for her land.[1]

Some months after Burroughs returned from England, on October 22, he wrote Mrs. Gilchrist:

I am resting in the hope and expectation that before long you will give yourself up to write the article on Walt Whitman that we are all looking for. I feel sure that you will cut your way to the heart of this matter as no one has yet done....

Her reply of December 3 is given here, in part:

I have at last finished my little book — a Life of Mary Lamb — the writing of which has been a great solace to me. It was a task that came to me unsought; but I have not found it task-work; and now I am going to put my heart into an article on Walt. I don't the least know whether or where I shall get it published, but anyhow I must try once more to give a reason for the faith that is in me. There is an article in this month's ' 19th Century' [2] which I have not yet seen but Herby says it is good, and that, in spite of some carping, there is clear recognition of a new great force in Walt.

Again she writes to Burroughs on March 18, 1883, from Keats Corner, Hampstead:

Walt sent me on lately a letter of yours giving by no means a first rate account of your health. It has not clouded the inner light anyway, which is much to be thankful for. I never read anything of yours I liked better than 'Signs and Seasons' which I have just been reading in the 'Century.' Nature has vouchsafed many whispers into your listening ears, taken you into her confidence behind the scenes, or rather into her heart....

Why will not you and Walt come to England this summer? I am pondering long and writing very slowly what I would fain say about Walt....

Later, January 19, 1885, she writes Burroughs about her second article on Whitman:[3]

I could not get my Whitman article into the 'Nineteenth Century' or 'Fortnightly.' It is, I believe, coming out in the Socialist magazine, 'To-

---

[1] When the attempt was being made, in 1882, to suppress Leaves of Grass, Mrs. Gilchrist wrote Burroughs an eloquent letter about Whitman, which will be found on page 220, 221 infra.

[2] G. C. Macaulay: 'Walt Whitman,' Nineteenth Century, December, 1882.

[3] Anne Gilchrist: 'A Confession of Faith,' Today (London), June, 1885. This is incorrectly cited in Kennedy's book The Fight of a Book for the World as in 1886. Herbert Gilchrist reprints this, and also his mother's earlier essay on Whitman, in his Anne Gilchrist, and Thomas B. Harned reprints both essays in The Letters of Anne Gilchrist and Walt Whitman. Doubleday, Page and Company, 1918.

day,' which is a somewhat feeble affair, or, at any rate, with which I am but partially in sympathy, but it seemed my only chance....

Did you notice in the last volume a passage from Carlyle's Journal about America that might have been written by Walt? I have it not at hand to quote, but the substance was this: Can I honestly believe that if my Frederick were at the helm in America he would be able to do any better or so well as America is doing for herself in the vast development of material resources, the taming of the wilderness, etc. — all that must precede a great national development? No, I cannot....

Whitman writes Burroughs on June 23, of Mrs. Gilchrist's second essay, saying, 'It is a noble paper,' and offering to send on his copy if she had not sent him one. When Burroughs reread these letters with me, some years ago, he said:

Mrs. Gilchrist had asthma when I visited her over there, and could not walk much. She had had some operation when she was over in this country. She was the ablest woman I ever met. You remember Walt's poem 'Going Somewhere.' That refers to her, his noblest woman friend — 'A memory leaf for her dear sake,' as Walt calls it. I will ask Harned sometime to let you see her letters to Walt — beautiful, noble letters; They should be published — or parts of them.

In Burroughs's Journal, December 18, occurs this passage:

Read today in the 'Academy' of the death of Mrs. Gilchrist. Many sad thoughts has it caused me. Just now I can see or think of no one in England but her. She is the principal fact over there, and she is gone.... She was a rare person, a person of rare intelligence.

Whitman in 'Specimen Days,' as already noted, in an entry for November, 1881, groups Anne Gilchrist, Burroughs, Bucke, and O'Connor as 'friends of my soul — stanchest friends of my other soul, my poems.' I recall reading somewhere that he said of Anne Gilchrist's voice that it was 'the tenderest, most musical' ever to bless his ears. He is quoted by Traubel [1] as saying of her: 'Oh, she was strangely different from the average, entirely herself, as simple as nature — true, honest, beautiful as a tree is tall, leafy, rich, free.' And Kennedy in his 'Reminiscences,' page 9, quotes Whitman as saying that Mrs. Gilchrist was one with whom in conversation one did not have to abate the wing of his thought downward at all in deference to any feminine narrowness.

[1] *With Walt Whitman in Camden*, vol. 3, p. 97.

At her passing, Whitman wrote Burroughs, December 21:

The death of Mrs. Gilchrist is indeed a gloomy fact. She had cancer, and suffered much the last three months of her life with asthma — for a long time 'every breath was a struggle,' Herbert expresses it. The actual cause of death was dilatation of the heart. Seems to me mortality never enclosed a more beautiful spirit.

To O'Connor, on January 22, 1886, he said, in part:

I am not sure but she had the finest and perfectest nature I ever met.[1]

Burroughs's letter of December 15, 1885, to Herbert Gilchrist reads:

Few men have had such a mother as you. She was the only woman I have ever seen to whose strength of mind and character I humbly bowed. As I think of her death, a shadow comes over the whole of that beautiful land. Now she is gone, I see how much she stood to me for all England. I have had many misgivings about her health ever since I saw her in '82. I feared that shortness of breath proceeded from some deep-seated danger.

When the tidings had come to Whitman from Herbert Gilchrist, Whitman sent this brief poignant reply:

Nothing now remains but a sweet and rich memory — none more beautiful all time, all life, all the earth —
I cannot write anything of a letter today. I must sit alone and think.
WALT WHITMAN

A letter from Herbert Gilchrist of January 20, 1886, to Burroughs said:

I can never enjoy such sweet companionship again, every day inter changing thoughts on subjects dear to us both — and over all the wise solicitude of a perfect mother.

He wrote in the same letter of her having left a few notes of reminiscence of Carlyle and his wife, which she had contemplated using in a book on Carlyle; told Burroughs of intending to repub lish the best of her essays with a short Life; asked for the loan of letters, and enclosed notices for the 'Critic' and 'Tribune' of his contemplated Memoir. In these notices the names of her circle of English friends were mentioned, such as the Carlyles, Tennyson, George Henry Lewes, George Eliot, and the Rossettis. In a late letter Herbert Gilchrist said that he and William Rossetti had

[1] From a letter in the Perry Whitman Collection.

organized a free-will offering for Whitman amounting to about a hundred and twenty pounds. Thus was her son carrying on the warm-hearted, practical ministrations with which Anne Gilchrist had blessed the life of Walt Whitman.

True to his promise, Burroughs obtained for me the privilege from Harned of reading Anne Gilchrist's letters to Whitman. On forwarding them, Mr. Harned wrote: 'You are the only woman besides my wife that I have let read them, though others have begged to see them.' When, in 1918, after earnest deliberation, Mr. Harned brought out 'The Letters of Anne Gilchrist and Walt Whitman,' he sent me an inscribed copy and asked for my reactions, now that the letters were in print. Excerpts from my reply follow:

You tell me to go for it hammer and tongs, but I have only praise to give; your Introduction is a real one.... It was fortunate you had so fine a tribute from W. W. to A. G. to quote — a good preparation for the impassioned letters that follow.... I am glad you included her two papers on W. W. The power and penetration she shows, taken with her letters, make me regret that W. W. could not have responded to her love.... He shows such a deep appreciation of what she was that I marvel he could not go farther and accept her love and ministrations, whatever other love had been his before.

Her big soul shows in every line. A smaller nature would have withdrawn and become embittered at his lack of response, yet her tenderness and devotion breathe in the last letter as in the first. Not even a reproach for his failure to send her a word of sympathy when Beatrice dies — instead, a touching gratitude for the few post-cards and newspapers.

Whitman's few letters and remarks of appreciation, though, are wonderful. Yet, though he could say she understood him better than any one else, he could receive her impassioned letters and often make no sign! and when she planned to come over here, could try, gently but firmly, to dissuade her!

What would we not give for a real understanding of how things were between them when they did meet! That there was a beautiful and satisfying friendship, is clear enough, but the steps that led to this calm, restrained relation which Walt's firmness established!...

I am glad you did not shirk the responsibility and leave it to some one who would surely have done it some time, and perhaps with less sympathy and judgment. There are a few typographical errors which I detected.... I inclose the list.... While I'm a stickler for accuracy of quotation, I would not carry it so far as to refrain from correcting obvious slips of the pen, unless something significant is shown by the slip itself....

Thank you for letting me see the beautiful nude soul of A. G. as she poured out her love for W.W. — naked and unashamed. In her capacity to love, and in her self-abnegation, she was as great as Walt is in his poems. I find myself not so much pitying her that her love was not returned, as pitying him that he could not return it.... 'The gift is to the giver, and comes back most to him.'...

Quite different than mine were the reactions of J. W. Wallace, one of the Whitmanites in the 'College' group in Lancashire, England. Excerpts from a letter to me follow:

... I cannot read them without feeling that Mrs. Gilchrist would have been deeply shocked and pained... she would have felt they were too intimate and sacred for publication... And when I read them I feel as if guilty of an unwarrantable intrusion on her privacy of soul. Both she and Walt, however, have now passed beyond any likelihood of caring whether they are published or not. And there is nothing discreditable to either in the letters. As one reads, one can only feel an increasing respect and affection for both.

Mrs. Gilchrist's surviving daughter, Mrs. Frend (Herbert died a few years ago) is very much hurt, however. She dreads the misunderstandings to which they will give rise, and says they give a false impression of her mother's character.[1] I sympathize with her feeling, but do not share her views. I only know her by correspondence, but Carpenter is an old friend of the family, and he describes her as 'rather old fashioned.' It seems fairly obvious that she doesn't really understand either Walt or her mother.

I feel, as you do, the pathos of Mrs. Gilchrist's letters, and of her lot. But it is not to me their prevailing and final note.... The reading of the complete edition of 'L of G' was to Mrs. Gilchrist an overwhelming revelation — unprecedented and unlooked for. It opened up vistas within her own soul of unimagined glory and significance, and cast a powerful beam of light upon the whole of humanity and the universe, which transfigured them before her eyes. It included within its broad sweep the depths as well as the heights, and proclaimed them all divine. It declared the redemption of the body and the sanctity of all life. It appealed to every part of her nature — body and soul — with a voice at once individual and divine. She merits everlasting renown for her immediate and absolute response bravely and faithfully expressed — not in words alone, but with her whole soul and life.

But here crept in a danger: She found herself very much alone in the ardor and fulness of her response. Rossetti, and a very small group of

---

[1] Mrs. Grace Frend, youngest child of Mrs. Gilchrist, made a protest against the publication of these letters in an article in the London *Nation*, October 5, 1918, indicating the standpoint from which she objected.

friends, shared some of her enthusiasm, but in a colder spirit, and in a less degree. And no other *woman* shared it. What wonder, then, that she came to think that she was herself Walt's feminine counterpart, alone fully responsive to his spirit, and his predestined mate? So Walt's message became to her not only an individual one, but a *personal* one.

Looking back on it all we can see that she was mistaken, and fell into a dangerous kind of megalomania. Great of heart and great of soul as she was, she had *not* entered into Walt's full vision, and was at a lower stage of development. His message to her *was* individual and divine, but its true significance and universality was only slowly apprehended by her after long unrest and pain of heart and soul.

But how splendidly faithful she remained to the light she had seen, and to the greater soul who had revealed it to her! In every relationship of life she fulfilled it to the uttermost, nobly practical, as well as nobly ideal; on equal terms with the greatest men and women she ever met, and a human sister to the lowest. To me, therefore, the pathos of her story is merged in something far more beautiful — the resolution of all discords and unrest in an increasing harmony and peace, her soul stronger and more fully endowed after the long conflict.

Now that the book is published, questions as to its justification become out of date. And I rejoice in its story of a great and noble woman and of her soul's progress toward final peace.

Referring to conflicting opinions concerning the publication of the Gilchrist-Whitman letters, Mr. Harned wrote me:

I don't care now what they say about the Gilchrist book. It is launched, and it will take its place as an important interpretation of the great power of 'L of G.' It takes a big woman... to understand what I did, and I am willing to wait to be justified....

I have traveled the open road and tried to discharge my duty as a trustee for Walt. He must have picked me as a practical man. My dear wife catered to his comforts. He was essentially a believer in the *family* as a unit — and, of course, the *individual*, in the last analysis. His love of his kind was more than a duty, it was a living impulse, and that is the best test as to how far a man is sincere when he espouses the cause of the human race. Perhaps I have written more than I ought, and more than I would to anyone else.

Mrs. Grace Gilchrist Frend wrote me, in 1925, concerning the publication of her mother's letters:

To me, and the rest of my mother's family, it was a matter of great pain and regret that her letters to the poet were published; it was indeed a most terrible profanation; but we heard about the matter too late to be able to stay their publication.

In April, 1919, Miss Kate Buss [1] addressed to John Burroughs
some inquiries about the Gilchrist-Whitman letters, considering
him one of the few persons able to answer her. She asked because
she 'feared to be unfair to a splendid memory long cherished.' I
have her permission to quote from her letter to Burroughs:

... I have been interested to read the ardent and generous Anne Gilchrist letters to Walt Whitman. But there remains in my mind a dissatisfaction that Whitman's response was so — apparently — slight, that
he so evaded a meeting with her in the beginning, and always any personal responsibility toward her. You must know exactly Whitman's feelings toward Mrs. Gilchrist. Are you willing to write me anything about
it? His thinking, in 'Leaves of Grass,' and his action, do not parallel, and
I feel him less splendid to have found him more cautious, or should I say
only, more weary, than I had thought. It is rare to find a great poet who
has been willing to make so slight a contact with a feminine personality as
richly productive, as apparently Heaven-sent for Whitman's blessing, as
Mrs. Gilchrist's.

Do you think the collected correspondence presents Whitman as a little
inadequate to his privilege? Was he at the time of his acquaintance with
Mrs. Gilchrist a sick and disillusioned man? It almost seems that, to have
guarded the legend of Whitman, Mrs. Gilchrist's letters should not have
been published.

Although saying that he could not go very fully into the questions submitted, Burroughs replied to his correspondent on
April 25:

I know that after Whitman came to know Mrs. Gilchrist intimately his
feeling for her was very deep and tender. She was a great soul; and he saw
it. But that first letter of hers to him, and her subsequent letters, coming
as they did from a perfect stranger, must have repelled him, I think, as
they would be likely to almost any man. I do not wonder that he was reserved and unresponsive. I think she showed but little tact in writing just
as she did, and in assuming that Whitman was in need of a mate, and that
she was that mate, just because his 'Leaves of Grass' had been such an
overwhelming revelation to her. She had translated the universality of
his words into a personal message to herself, and was doomed to disappointment.

Whitman was not a marrying man. He had given himself to his work,
and to the world. He did not want the responsibility of a family, even

---

[1] Kate Buss: 'Anne Gilchrist to Walt Whitman — Some Comments on the Love Letters of a Woman to the Great American Poet whose Centenary is now Being Observed,'
Boston Evening Transcript, May 28, 1919.

when he was a younger man; and at the time she wrote him, he was too poor to assume additional responsibilities. Further than that, he was beginning to break in health; and, what is of greater importance, he had probably already lived out his life of the affections and emotions, in that particular sphere, and was contemplating the universe, and not a domestic life with any woman, much less with one he had never seen. He tried to hold her back from coming to America. He knew she would be disappointed; knew that he could never be to her what she believed they were destined to be to each other. But when she was not to be held back, he accepted the situation, and gave her a tender and loyal friendship. After Mrs. Gilchrist came to this country Whitman spent a good deal of time at her house in Philadelphia, and enjoyed her devoted ministrations, and the delightful atmosphere of her family life. I have often been there with him. His lines called 'Going Somewhere' refer to his talks with her — 'My science-friend, my noblest woman friend.' You will see in those lines that they were much to each other; and I think she came to be quietly happy, and to acquiesce in the comradeship that existed between them, since what she had dreamed and hoped for could not be.

Whitman as a correspondent was always very brief. He let himself go only in his poems. I have had a great many letters from him, and written many to him. He was fond of me, and my admiration and affection for him were unbounded, yet he never wrote me anything but brief and matter-of-fact letters.

There seems to be nothing to Whitman's discredit in the Gilchrist-Whitman letters. He was not responsible for the effect his poems had had upon her — brilliant, ardent, unhappy, and neurotic (though noble and unselfish) woman that she was. He raised no false hopes. He met her ardor with his imperturbable calm. And she learned in time to accept the comradeship he gave her, and to see that his message was not personal, but universal.

How thoroughly Burroughs divined his friend's attitude in this matter, even without the proof which came to light later, the foregoing letter shows, yet it is not probable that Whitman, in his reticence, ever discussed Mrs. Gilchrist with Burroughs in regard to these purely personal matters.

In November, 1920, Mr. Harned sent me the following letter, and, with it, a copy of one from Whitman to Mrs. Gilchrist, which throws light upon the questions raised in the immediately foregoing letters. Harned wrote:

Doubleday, Page and Co. have sent me the MS. of a proposed book to be published by Grace Gilchrist Frend. It covers the whole period from 1869 to 1885. I regard it as of great importance as it covers a wide field.

I wish you and J. B. could read this MS. It would hardly be proper for me to send it to you. It has a lot in it about J. B. and his letters. It is more than a supplement to my book. *There is a letter that I did not have.* This letter explains much.

T. B. H.

The letter he refers to was one from Whitman to Mrs. Gilchrist, dated March 20, 1872:

DEAR FRIEND,

Let me warn you about myself and yourself also. You must not construct such an unauthorized and imaginary figure and call it W. W., and so devotedly invest your loving nature in it. The actual W. W. is a very plain personage and entirely unworthy such devotion.

Mrs. Gilchrist's comments on this 'warning' are found on pages 77 and 78 of the Gilchrist-Whitman letters.

In December, 1920, John Burroughs and I read the Frend manuscript at the request of the firm contemplating its publication. Burroughs considered it a highly important contribution. To my recent inquiry as to its fate, Mrs. Frend wrote that her book failed of publication because of the high cost estimated for its production. She is now at work, she tells me, on a book which will doubtless salvage much that was contained in the earlier manuscript.

By far the finest interpretation of Anne Gilchrist that I have seen is Edith Franklin Wyatt's paper on 'Anne Gilchrist and Walt Whitman' in the 'North American Review,' September, 1919. The generosity, nobility, and dignity of Anne Gilchrist shine forth in every line. Another article in the same year, by the same writer, and printed in the same magazine, was called 'The Answerer: Walt Whitman.' Of this Burroughs said, 'No woman since Anne Gilchrist has written so penetratingly of Walt.'

Perhaps pity has been wasted upon Anne Gilchrist. With all that the 'Leaves' brought to her, rich giver that she was, she doubtless came to feel herself amply compensated in what Whitman bestowed:

For I myself am not one who bestows nothing upon man and woman,
For I bestow upon any man or woman the entrance to all the gifts of the universe.

XI

BIRDS AND POETS

(1877)

... There is the delighting of the eye and soul through that soaring and circling in the vast empyrean of 'a strong bird on pinions free' — lessons of freedom, power, grace, and spiritual suggestion — vast, unparalleled, *formless* lessons.

BURROUGHS

WHILE Burroughs was debating with himself about the title of his new book, which was to have in it much about the birds and something about the poets, and which was to contain his critique on Emerson, already discussed, and his essay on Whitman called 'The Flight of the Eagle,' he evidently appealed to Whitman for his opinion, for on January 24 he received this sanction from him:

I think 'Birds and Poets' not only much the best name for the book, but a first rate good name, appropriate, original and fresh, without being at all affected or strained. The piece you put fourth[1] should then be *first* — should lead the book, giving it its title, and having the name of the piece changed to 'Birds and Poets' — which I think would be an improvement. The whole collection would be sufficiently homogeneous (and it were a fault to be too much so) — You just want *a hint* for the name of the book — only it must be in the spirit of the book — and not too much so either. 'Nature and Genius' *is too Emersony altogether.*

I will think over the name of the piece devoted to me, and will in a couple of days write you the result. Maybe I can think of a better name.[2] I have not rec'd the MS. from Church [editor of the 'Galaxy'] — You send on anything — any MS. — which I will cheerfully read and will return with any suggestions that may occur to me....   W. W.

Accordingly, on February 13 he wrote again:

I hope you will adopt 'Birds and Poets' — and then 'The Flight of the Eagle,'[3] as, the more I think of them, the better I like both (I mean directly and indirectly, and for wear).

Come to Mrs. Gilchrist's on 16th or 17th — I will prepare them — I will be there — it is 1929 North 22d Street — ...   W. W.

[1] Burroughs: 'The Birds of the Poets,' in *Birds and Poets*. Boston, 1877.

[2] Burroughs had originally named the essay, 'The Disowned Poet,' later suggesting the 'Eagle' title.

[3] See comments on the sources of this title, page 118.

Burroughs's Journal for February 17, has this entry:

Returned yesterday from Philadelphia, where I spent the night of the 15th with Walt, at Mrs. Gilchrist's. Never saw Walt look so handsome — so new and fresh. His new, light gray clothes, his white hair and beard, and his rosy, godlike, yet infantile face, all combined to make a rare picture. After ten o'clock we went up to his room and sat and talked till near one o'clock. I wanted him to say how he liked my piece on him ['The Flight of the Eagle'] but he did not say. We talked about it — what had best go in, and what were best left out, but he was provokingly silent about the merits of the piece.

Speaking of his poems, he said it was a very audacious and risky thing he had done, and the wonder was, not that they had made their way so slowly, but that they had got any foothold at all. When the conditions were all considered, and the want of anything like matured and robust æsthetic perception in this country remembered, it was a great success to have effected a lodgment at all.[1]

It is a feast to me to look at Walt's face; it is incomparably the grandest face I ever saw — such sweetness and harmony, and such strength — strength like the Roman arches. If that is not the face of a poet, then it is the face of a god. None of his pictures do it half justice.

After Whitman had read the chapters for 'Birds and Poets' in manuscript, he wrote, February 27, a letter quoted on page 110 of this volume, in which he asked, 'Do you say the final chapter is already in print? the one about me? If so, *send me the proof*, which I will return by next mail.'

It will have been noted that when the comrades had met at Mrs. Gilchrist's, earlier in the month, they had gone over the 'Eagle' essay together. Burroughs's manuscript essay, from which the accompanying emendations in Whitman's hand are transcribed, clearly shows the parts supplied by the poet. It is possible, too, that if Burroughs also sent him the proof, he may have added other suggestions. In fact, although Whitman's hand does not show on the manuscript in the words 'talks, meals, jaunts' (at bottom of page 187 in 'Birds and Poets'), it seems to me that that is unmistakably an addition by Whitman. The manuscript is an excellent illustration of the kind of help Whitman was accustomed to giving, not only in essays about himself, but on other subjects, when Burroughs sought his critical aid. One can see here the poet's

---

[1] B. has paraphrased this quotation from Whitman in 'The Flight of the Eagle,' *Birds and Poets*, p. 187.

Much of ~~Whitman~~ his material is too near to us; it needs time. Seen through the vista of long years, or perhaps centuries, it will assume quite different hues as the statue on top the tower or tall column is not the same as when it stood here on the ground. Perhaps these long lists of trades & tools & occupations — ~~the whole mechanic~~ ~~life of America~~ — would not be so repellant if we could see them as we see Homer's catalogue of the ships through the retrospect of ages. They are justified in the poem ~~by the~~ from their historic value, because they are alive & full of action, ~~they are~~ swift moving currents, — a panorama of the whole mechanic & industrial life

*I know that Walt Whitman has written many passages of his poems with reference for more to their interpretation and scanning ages; hence thus for current reading.

A PAGE OF BURROUGHS'S MANUSCRIPT OF 'THE FLIGHT OF THE EAGLE,' WITH EMENDATIONS IN WHITMAN'S HAND

hand supplying, deleting, and altering words, phrases, sentences. The incident on pages 197–98 in 'Birds and Poets,' of Whitman on a crowded horse-car relieving a tired mother of her fretting child, was, Burroughs told me, written by Whitman at Burroughs's request. 'Walt had told me about it, and I asked him to write it out for me.' It is rather amusing that Professor Holloway in his 'Whitman,' while giving rather too much credence to the extent to which Whitman aided Burroughs in his earlier writings about the poet, cites on pages 235–37, this passage (which Burroughs said was Whitman's contribution) as a 'welcome example' of a glimpse of the poet from the 'keen eye and graphic pen' of Burroughs!

Besides the horse-car incident, and the additions which were supplied by Whitman, as shown in the facsimile page (see illustration, page 160), the following noteworthy passages are given here to show wherein Whitman contributed to the 'Eagle' essay. The page references are to 'Birds and Poets':

In fact, the main clue to Walt Whitman's life and personality, and the expression of them in his poems, is to be found in about the largest emotional element that has appeared anywhere. This, if not controlled by a potent rational balance, would either have tossed him helplessly forever, or wrecked him as disastrously as ever storm and gale drove ship to ruin. These volcanic emotional fires appear everywhere in his books; and it is really these, aroused to intense activity and unnatural strain during the four years of the War, and his persistent labors in the hospitals, that have resulted in his illness and paralysis since (page 189).

What self-knowledge, what ability to stand aside and see himself far more clearly than others could see him!

The French 'Revue des Deux Mondes' pronounces his war poems the most vivid, the most humanly passionate, and the most modern, of all the verse of the nineteenth century (page 190).

The dominant impression was of the living presence and voice (page 194).

The great lesson of nature, I take it, is that a sane sensuality must be preserved at all hazards, and this, it seems to me, is also the great lesson of his writings (page 203).

I know that Walt Whitman has written many passages with reference far more to their position, interpretation, and scanning ages hence, than for current reading (page 210).

... and puts in practical form that unprecedented and fervid comradeship which is his leading element, even more than his elaborate works.

It is printed almost *verbatim*, just as the notes were jotted down at the time and on the spot (page 230).

In the next sentence the italicized words are emendations by Whitman:

Is there not a decay — *a deliberate, strange abnegation and dread* — of sane sexuality, or maternity and paternity among us, and in our *literary ideals and social* types of men and women? (page 203).

Scattered throughout the essay are slight verbal additions by Whitman, which it would be rather difficult to indicate fully. Some of the main ones, however, are as follows:

Page 186, last paragraph, 'and its lessons.'

Page 187, first paragraph, 'printed in 1855,' and 'affectionately,' and 'and by the world.'

Page 188, top page, 'actual intimacy'; bottom page, 'special genius.'

Page 189, top page, 'after an hour's interview'; bottom page, 'and magnetisms.'

Page 190, top page, 'Before the man's,' and 'The processes are silently at work,' and 'orbic coherence'; mid page, 'suffusing' is substituted by W.W., J. B. used 'inborn'; 'modernness,' and 'advanced scientism' are also words supplied by W.W. in this paragraph.

Page 191, 'Well commenced,' 'at last,' and 'by way of those far-off, round-about,' at top page.

Page 194, top page, 'which the said critics have,' and 'conventional.'

Page 196, top page, 'I, too, love.'

Page 204, first paragraph, 'stated' was evidently substituted for 'hinted,' but J. B. held to the latter; bottom page, W. W. supplied 'sugared.'

Page 206, 'to be for every man and woman his or her Individuality.'

Page 207, 'and composite,' and 'person and,' 'lesson and' at top page, and, at bottom, 'steadily,' and 'sends out.'

Page 208, bottom page, 'ejaculatory,' 'subsequent,' and 'shoots.'

Page 210, bottom page, 'ebbing and flowing,' 'the dead water of.'

Page 216, top page, 'upon a basis and even superstructure.'

Page 217, bottom page, 'thinker,' 'æsthetic or spiritual,' and 'immeasurably.'

Page 218, top page, 'or Isaiah.'

Page 220, middle page, 'abstract,' and 'personal humanistic.'

Page 230, bottom page, 'entirely characteristic,' and 'have amazing.'

Page 231, top page, 'rolling' and 'in echelons,' and, middle page, 'like all Whitman's works,' and 'at all in the true sense,' and ('he is now, 1877, entering his fifty-ninth year').

Page 232, 'Skipping many things I would yet like to touch upon — for this paper is already too long — ' 'conclusion,' and 'or the later volume, "Two Rivulets."'

Page 233, 'just as you, and the whole spirit of our current times, have been trained to feed on and enjoy, not Nature or Man, or the aboriginal forces, or the actual, but pictures, books, art, and the selected and refined,' and 'the real landscape and the sea.'

Page 234, 'unerringly,' 'carnal,' 'the author of "Leaves of Grass,"' 'Observe that this singer and artist,' and 'the customary places.'

In the original manuscript, Whitman had deleted this significant passage; which is only briefly touched on (page 188):

... his large, perfect, dome-shaped head, his imperial ear (the only perfect ear upon the only perfect head I have ever seen), his high, imaginative brow, his glance, his heavy-lidded, absorbing eye, his sympathetic voice....

And, finally, the last paragraph, page 235, is entirely in Whitman's hand:

Finally, as those men and women respect and love Walt Whitman best who have known him longest and closest personally, the same rule will apply to 'Leaves of Grass' and the later volume, 'Two Rivulets.' It is indeed neither the first surface reading of those books, nor perhaps even the second or third, that will any more than prepare the student for the full assimilation of the poems. Like Nature, and like the Sciences, they suggest endless suites of chambers opening and expanding more and more and continually.

I should like to call the reader's attention particularly to Burroughs's description of the poet in that essay (pages 187–89), inasmuch as it gives a contemporary picture of him, yet with a background of reminiscence covering their comradeship up to that date.

On May 10 of that year, recording in his Journal the coming to hand of his new book, 'Birds and Poets,' Burroughs added:

Like the dress much, and am well pleased with all the pieces but the last — the one I set my heart on. It generally happens that the father's pride turns out the worst of all.

Whitman's verdict, which followed on the 17th, must have made Burroughs look with more favor upon his 'ugly duckling.' The poet wrote from the Staffords', at Kirkwood, New Jersey:

I am passing a good part of my time down here at the farm.... Still keep well for me, and jolly, am all tanned and sun-burnt — eat my rations every time.

I was up yesterday to Camden to get my mail and found *the book* — read it all over with appreciative and I think critical eyes, my impression of liking it, as a curiously *homogeneous* work (just enough radiations to make it *piquant*) and, in connection *liking the name*, etc., all deepened and clinched. I especially much like, and more like, the chapter about me. There has certainly been nothing yet said that so makes the points (and eloquently makes them) I most want brought out and put on record.

Are you coming to the Gilchrists, and when?

W. W.

Burroughs had now been living on the Hudson for more than three years, yet Whitman had never been to Riverby. On March 13, Whitman writes from the J. H. Johnstons', in New York City, that he would be very glad to go there, taking along his boy, Harry Stafford, 'as he is my convoy like — We occupy the same room and bed.' He tells of several receptions there, 'lots of artists, many fine ladies, and not a few ministers and journalists,' but says he can't stand such things long. He has also been sitting for a portrait which is getting on well. He does not name the artist, but John Burroughs thought this referred to a painting by Waters, owned by J. H. Johnston. He said of it: 'It gives Walt's benevolent look, but not his power—his elemental look. It makes him look rather soft, like a sort of Benjamin Franklin.'

That first visit of Whitman to Riverby is thus recorded in the Journal, March 21:

A great event! Walt came home with me from New York Friday night, the 16th, and stayed till 4 this afternoon. Harry Stafford came with him. They cut up like two boys and annoyed me sometimes. Great tribulation in the kitchen in the morning. Can't get them up to breakfast in time.

Walt takes Harry with him as a kind of foil or refuge from the intellectual bores. Walt is mending, and said he walked better the morning he left than he had for five years.

I find no record in 'Specimen Days' of that first visit to Burroughs's river home, but in an undated entry in 'Complete Prose Works' (Small, Maynard and Company, 1901, pp. 77–78) — 'Birds Migrating at Midnight' — is an entry I think very likely was written at Riverby on that early spring visit. The friend who called him up to note the migrating flocks was probably John Burroughs. It seems very improbable to me that, unaided, Whitman could detect the calls of the various species he names in that entry.

In Burroughs's Introduction to Mr. Waldo R. Browne's 'The Rolling Earth,' he wrote:

Some of the prose jottings which you have selected were made while he was visiting me in my home at West Park on the Hudson. He never seemed to tire of country sights and sounds, or country folk, or of hearing me relate experiences with bees and birds and other wild creatures. He always wanted these things in their natural setting, and in their relation to the rest of nature.

Myron Benton, commenting on Whitman being at Riverby, said: 'You have had a good visit doubtless with the genial Walt. Those were "Arabian Nights" you celebrated, were they not?' Acknowledging the gift of a copy of 'Birds and Poets,' Benton thus comments on the 'Eagle' essay:

... I suppose you have fully calculated upon some varying notes in the chorus of critics, now that you have put the chip upon your shoulder. At least I should think there would be a demurrer occasionally. But you have made by far — very far — the ablest defense of Walt Whitman's poetry that has yet been made on either side of the water. It is alive with eloquence and noble fire, as well as good hard sense. Enthusiastic as it is, there is a sanity about your criticism which not all his admirers possess. It awakens anew my old enthusiasm for some of those deep fathoming lines that we first read together when we took 'Leaves of Grass' with us and lay down to read under the shade of 'Mulberry Rock' that summer's day so long ago.

It seems to me, by the way, that it is unnecessary for you to set this poetry so much outside of artistic laws as you seem to be undertaking to do. The little technicalities are of course the accidents, and nowadays no artistic worker is judged by them; but the real artistic rules or laws which the best thinking of the race for ages has settled are not, to my apprehension, of ephemeral use — they are not mechanical laws but structural laws, and any worthy artistic work comes under them inevitably.

In the best part of Walt Whitman's poetry (though in his own very individual way) there is the same instinctive artistic process in handling his subject that the masters have always used; interpretation instead of photography is the key-note (whatever may be said of his 'inspired catalogues') and shows the inevitable distinction between poetry and science. Walt Whitman in his memorable poems chisels out complete statues, as well as Tennyson, but the block of stone is often a huge one, and the result is seldom a *statuette*. But this ground we have been all over before, have we not? and the distinctions are perhaps more verbal than anything else.

To this, on June 5, Burroughs replied:

I was greatly tickled at your hearty commendation of my essays. I sip your words slowly like some rare and costly wine that I would not miss any flavor of. Your praise is not cheap and it does a fellow good when it does come.

You say a most superb thing about W.W. — better than I have said, and I much regret that I did not have it to put in the piece. I refer to the statue and statuette comparison. I shall revolve that under my tongue as a sweet morsel. I have noted down one or two points lately touching the art question that suit me better than some of those in the essay. It is a very baffling question and I expect I shall have to have another turn at it sometime. Indeed, Walt Whitman is a baffling poet. He eludes me perpetually when I try to corner him up in an essay. I think it is one evidence of his immeasurable greatness that he refuses to be tabulated and put upon the shelf. I have had several warm letters from strangers about the essay. One from [George Parsons] Lathrop full of enthusiasm for Whitman — quite a startling letter to come from Cambridge. A gentleman on the 'Boston Herald' whose letter came with yours says I have carried my critics with me and that the press is all praising Whitman. I have seen no notices but the one in the 'Times.' I heard of a red-hot one in a Utica paper, extravagant in its praise. I expect some of the old foxes will be after me by and by, like Taylor, or the 'Nation' man, but I don't care — let them have their say — I have had mine, tho' not about them. The praise of such men as you, and of such women as Mrs. Gilchrist — what critic gall can prevail over such sweet? And then W. W. himself says it is the best thing yet about him, and puts on record many things he most wants considered. But I have myself had many misgivings about the article (not latterly). I seemed only to have faintly touched many things I at times feel about W. W.

None of the echoes from the 'Eagle' essay gave Burroughs quite the satisfaction that four words coming from Whitman on July 2, gave him:

That 'Eagle' grows, grows.

XII

'AFTER THE DAZZLE OF DAY'

(1877–1881)

After the dazzle of day is gone,
Only the dark, dark night shows to my eyes the stars;
After the clangor of organ majestic, or chorus, or perfect band,
Silent, athwart my soul, moves the symphony true.

WHITMAN

FOR Whitman the days were now taking on a mellower light, the brooding and blissful halcyon days were near at hand. New friends were coming to him, new recognition was heartening him. He was about to realize some of his long-held ambitions. He was going about more, traveling again to his 'magnetic South,' and through the 'boundless prodigality and amplitude' of the West. He had memorable sojourns in Boston and in Canada. He was, in truth, living under placid skies. Best of all, he was upborne in spirit by 'the undiminished faith — the group of loving friends.' He visited Burroughs three years in succession, and Burroughs visited him at least once a year, sometimes much oftener. Their correspondence continued. He saw Eldridge occasionally, and, as has been seen, had the rare companionship of Anne Gilchrist and her talented children.

In the summer of 1877, Dr. Richard Maurice Bucke, an Englishman from London, Canada, first visited Whitman, a visit destined to work far-reaching results. At the outset Dr. Bucke said he felt a sort of spiritual intoxication in Whitman's presence. He regarded him as a superman. The friendship increased in fervor with the years. Whitman expressed in countless ways his deep attachment and indebtedness to this ardent friend. Dr. Bucke's contributions, both written and edited, to the Whitman literature are many: A biography, 'Walt Whitman' (David Mackay, 1883), 'In Re Walt Whitman' (*ibid.*, 1893), a contribution to the 'Walt Whitman Fellowship Papers' (September, 1894), 'Calamus' (Whitman's letters of comradeship to Peter Doyle, Laurens Maynard, 1897), 'The Wound Dresser' (Whitman's letters during his ministry to the soldiers, Small, Maynard and Company, 1898), 'Notes and Fragments' (privately printed, 1899), and 'Cosmic Consciousness' (Innes and Sons, 1901, reprinted by E. P. Dutton, 1923). Speaking to me of Dr. Bucke, in the early years of our acquaintance, John Burroughs said: 'Bucke was an alienist in the asylum at London, Canada. He was tremendously taken with Walt from the start — was devoted to him — wrote his "Life," and a book on "Cosmic Consciousness" — a very fine man, very learned, but dogmatic — he tied his knots too hard.'

An excerpt from a letter to Burroughs, written by W. L. Shoemaker, with whom he used to take winter walks in Washington, is given here for the early glimpse it affords of Whitman in Camden. It was written in early July. E. J. Loomis, mentioned in the letter, Burroughs explained, had been an intimate friend of Thoreau, having boarded with Thoreau's mother, eaten at the same table with Thoreau, roamed the woods with him, and bathed with him in Walden Pond. Mr. Shoemaker wrote:

I had never spoken to Mr. Whitman but once during the whole time he lived in Washington, but when I was last in Philadelphia I resolved to go and make his acquaintance. I found him easily in Camden. He had just left his boarding-house and was some distance up the street. I overtook him and he turned back to the house with me, and we had a pleasant chat together. He gave me wine and a wood-cut portrait of himself. And shortly after, when Loomis and I arrived in the city, he and I went together to visit the genial old man. He gave Loomis also his picture with autograph. Our visit seemed to please the 'Cosmos,' and we were on our part well pleased with him. He appeared gratified to hear that we were acquaintances of yours.

This year was marked by recognition of Whitman from other Irish scholars than those already mentioned in these pages, particularly T. W. Rolleston (pen name, 'H. Rowlandson'), who had a poem on Whitman in *Kottabos* (vol. II), a publication of Trinity College, Dublin. In collaboration with H. B. Cotterell, Rolleston wrote in German a pamphlet on Wordsworth and Whitman (1883).

An August letter from Burroughs to Whitman, written on the 10th, affords glimpses of Burroughs in Boston:

I called on Guernsey of the Boston 'Herald' and found him a very likable young man, in fact, a thoroughly good fellow. He said he had written to you but had received no reply yet.... I like the looks of Boston much.

DR. RICHARD MAURICE BUCKE

We poked about Cambridge some and then went over to Concord and spent a night there. I found Mr. Sanborn and was cordially received. I had seen him the day before in Boston. I like Sanborn, all except his lofty coldness and reserve. It seems to be the style out there to affect ignorance of everything you are interested in. He showed me the home and some of the haunts of Thoreau, and then his grave, and that of Hawthorne. He took me to see Alcott, whom I like. Alcott praised my Emerson piece, but Sanborn appeared not to know anything about my writings. We were at Alcott's only a few minutes. He spoke in a friendly way about you. We passed by Emerson's house and I admired his woodpile. I did not feel like calling on him of my own motion. Alcott said he was well. I liked Concord, but I don't see how any great thing can come out of that place.

I got the 'Library Table' with Blood's sanguinary review of my book. It is very petty criticism, and I think I can stand it better than Blood can. He evidently wanted to pitch into my 'Eagle' but was afraid of the claws.

George Parsons Lathrop, writing to Burroughs on October 12, chides him for not looking him up when in Boston; tells of having left the 'Atlantic' because it seemed to be gradually killing all sense of higher things in him; but states that he will perhaps stay on in Boston, where he has gained a foothold, even though it be 'the stronghold of the small and the inimical.' He adds:

I wish I could see you and Whitman together. What is life unless we see those we admire and sympathize with?
Good bye, fortunate and happy farmer and poet!

The 'Nineteenth Century' for October had an article called 'Cosmic Emotion,' by Professor W. K. Clifford, in which the author pronounced Whitman to be more thoroughly in harmony with the spirit and letter of advanced science than any other living poet. Burroughs comments, in his 'Eagle' essay, on the use of that term 'cosmic emotion' by Clifford, as an expressive term for that 'poetic thrill and rhapsody in contemplating the earth as a whole' which is so evident in Whitman. As the Eagle essay in 'Birds and Poets' was in print several months before Clifford's article, Burroughs must have got the term 'cosmic emotion' from Clifford in conversation, or perhaps heard it from others in the literary gossip of the day.

I wish here to correct an error on my part which I made in both 'The Life and Letters of John Burroughs' and 'The Heart of

Burroughs's Journals.' In these books, quoting a journal entry for January 29, 1878 — an observation by Burroughs of eagles in the air, seen from the dock at Riverby — I stated that Burroughs's description of this observation was the germ of Whitman's poem 'The Dalliance of the Eagles.' My inference concerning that particular observation was wrong: I had remembered Burroughs having said that his own description of seeing the eagles mating in the sky had given Whitman the basis of his poem, and, coming upon that entry, had hastily inferred that it was the observation of which he had once told me. Later, I found my mistake when coming upon an early memorandum of my own. This states that Burroughs said he never saw the mating of eagles but once in his life, and that that was at Marlboro on the Hudson; that Whitman never saw it, but wrote his 'Dalliance' poem from the description he had given him. It is probable that the observation at Marlboro was in the early sixties when Burroughs lived there, before meeting Whitman. Of course he may have described the occurrence to the poet any time during their acquaintance before the publication of the poem (in 1880), but, more likely, it was brought up at one of Whitman's visits to Riverby (1877, 1878, or 1879) when, perhaps, a sight of eagles in the air brought to mind the early observation of their mating at Marlboro.

This poem, along with 'A Woman Waits for Me,' and 'To a Common Prostitute' (besides some other lines), were the parts specified by the District Attorney of Boston, at the command of Attorney-General Marston, which must be removed by the publishers (Osgood and Company) or the 'Leaves' would be forbidden the mails. (See the following chapter.) These activities against the 'Leaves' had been set going by the Boston Society for the Suppression of Vice! In 'The Fight of a Book for the World,' Kennedy quotes Dr. Foote's 'Health Monthly' (August, 1882) as suggesting, when discussing this attack on the 'Leaves,' that a law be passed forbidding babies to be born naked, and requiring our domestic animals to be petticoated and breeched!

Mention has already been made that at an early stage in his career Whitman entertained the hope of carrying his message to the American people through lecturing. Some students think that the primary impulse toward expression with Whitman was through oratory, but that, because conditions forced him to modify his plans, he cast his notes into the form of poems instead of lectures. He never relinquished his youthful aspirations as an orator. We have seen, in already quoted letters, the efforts of Burroughs, in this matter, in his comrade's behalf. The project was always there in the back of Whitman's mind. Burroughs tried to interest persons, not only in these States, but also in Great Britain, but was forced to abandon further efforts, at the time, owing to Whitman's first stroke of paralysis, in 1873. However, as will be seen, he furthered the project later, and, in 1879, the long-held hope had a semblance of fruition. Mr. Furness discusses the lecture question in 'Walt Whitman's Workshop' (pages 33–68). From him I learn of a forthcoming book by Jean Catel — 'Walt Whitman et le Style Oral.' Professors Perry and Holloway and the Reverend W. E. Barton have gone into the lecture matter to a considerable extent, the book by the last-named writer, 'Abraham Lincoln and Walt Whitman,' giving the most complete record of any extant of Whitman's lectures on Lincoln. The material which follows offers some additional information along these lines not hitherto published.

In the correspondence between Whitman and Burroughs at this period we find that it was Richard Watson Gilder who started the plans, seconded by Burroughs, which resulted in the first Lincoln lecture. On February 3, 1878, Burroughs wrote:

DEAR WALT,
    Gilder suggests that a 'benefit' be got up for you in N.Y. and that you be asked to lecture on Lincoln. He thinks it would go with a rush under proper management and that lots of money might be made. The suggestion seems to me timely and just the thing, and we will set the ball agoing if you are willing and have, or can have, the lecture ready. I saw Stedman when I passed through New York and liked him. I think he would take hold to give the project a lift. Of course Swinton and many others would, too. I think, in fact, we might have a big time and make it pay. Write me how you feel about it, and if you favor it, how soon could you be on hand?

                    As ever,
                            JOHN BURROUGHS

Whitman replied on the 24th:

DEAR J. B.

I am agreeable to the Lecture project — if it can be put through — about the middle of April (the anniversary of the eve or night of Lincoln's murder) might be a good night — Everything would depend on how it was fixed up and prepared for & put through — Let me hear more particulars —

— I could be ready to splurge April 14th or 15th.

— I am well, considering — in good flesh, appetite and trim generally

— Only returned last night from a long jaunt and absence down at my secluded creek [Timber Creek —]

— Write me immediately, and I will you —

— I am thoroughly willing and agreeable.

Yours as always
WALT WHITMAN

The next four letters deal with the arrangements for the lecture. That on March 5 is as follows:

DEAR JOHN BURROUGHS,

John Swinton lives at 134 East 34th street. (He is married lately to Mrs. Dr. Smith) — Yes, [J. H.] Johnston's taking part in the lecture enterprise would be perfectly agreeable to me — the name of the lecture should be *The death of Abraham Lincoln.*

(In my last letter among the names proposed was S. Cox, M.C. — *I wish that name cancelled.*) I should like well to have, if the letter to me is carried out, a real picture of names, representing the young blood, and all the parties, various professions (especially, as I said, journalists, artists, actors, &c, &c — perhaps some women) —

I shall be home here all the following two weeks, except next Saturday and Sunday —

WALT WHITMAN

In answer to inquiry about the name of Cox, Burroughs said, 'I don't know — he evidently had something against Cox. He was a witty member of Congress, a brilliant man. I can't remember why Walt wanted his name cancelled.'

On March 11, Whitman wrote:

Yours of 7th from N.Y. rec'd last night. I will scratch off some suggestions:

In composing the letter, let it be brief, and don't mention the subject — or, if you do, *just say indefinitely that it is about Abraham Lincoln* (which you may do, if you think proper) —

I would like Gilder's name on the letter —

The suggestion (Gilder's) *about 8 or 10 names only — good ones only —* should be carried out. About the Hall I leave to your selection (not the very biggest ones, however, would seem to me best)

I would like Whitelaw Reid's name to cap the list — Could n't the *World* man, Schuyler (if he is there yet?) come next?

Elliott F. Shepard the lawyer, might be a good name.

Take [J. H.] Johnston into your councils, in any business and pecuniary arrangements — he is very 'cute and I consider him a true friend of mine.

I am particular about the names. Let [Joel] Benton have my letters, take as much as possible my point of view, and he might write to me here.

WALT WHITMAN

.   .   .   .

Private

I care little — or rather nothing at all — about Bayard Taylor's or G. W. Curtis's names on the letter. Don't want them. If they get on, let them be, of course — but don't you make any point about getting them. I suppose you understand me.

Of course the letters I write you are for perusal by all my friends — Gilder, Swinton, Benton, etc. — but if I write *private*, it is for you alone.

Commenting on this letter, Burroughs said to me:

Whitelaw Reid was editor of the 'Tribune.' Bayard Taylor never let slip an opportunity to give Walt a stab or a slap; and Curtis held aloof and tried to check O'Connor's enthusiasm. He was a fine — superfine — kind, and that Walt wouldn't care for. I don't think they ever got on well. 'An orator that fairly leaned and languished on the bosom of the graces' — is the way I've written somewhere about Curtis. I wanted to cuff him sometimes. If there had been a little more manliness and robustness in him! He was capable only of a graceful enthusiasm. His locks would shake, but they would fall back, every one, as though trained — no disorder. Oh, dear! but he was a dear soul — a very dear soul — high-minded and very chivalrous.

It will be seen by the foregoing letters that Whitman was ready with his lecture on the Death of Lincoln; but Fate again intervened, as is seen by Whitman's letter of March 21:

For the last four days I have been and am now quite severely down again with muscular and nervous prostration, somewhat like formerly — aggravated this time by a painful and obstinate rheumatism... count on it soon passing over and leaving me about the same possession of my powers as of late — but it occurs to me to say to you that while I wish the prospecting for the N.Y. lecture to go on — I think it would be best so —

don't make any pledge about hall, or any other thing involving obligation, until further notice and advice from me.

I have just got a letter from Johnston, the jeweller, asking me to come on to his house & make it my home in N.Y. for the lecture trip. Very kind and acceptable.

Walt Whitman

That the lecture was still under consideration will be seen by Whitman's letter to Burroughs on March 29:

Dear friend,

Your card just rec'd. I am still badly under the weather — spells of prostration like those of two years ago, and now, for more than a week the restless, wretched nights of the rheumatic. Still a good heart and not only a hope, but confidence, having passed through worse spells several times, that I shall get round soon and be the same as before ill. I am up and feeling quite jolly this evening.

Instead of 15th of April *I think it would be safer to fix the lecture night anywhere between the 10th and 20th May.* If you and the rest feel to, go on that understanding, *as a settled thing.*

What is [Joel] Benton's address in N.Y.? If convenient, I should like to see the list of names and the draft of the letter before formally put out. If you think well of this, either send me the list, or *tell Benton to send it me forthwith —*

. . . .

Write me the moves. I shall be home here all the time. Everything (PO. or telegram) comes here (431 Stevens Street, Camden, N.J.) as unerringly as fate, and very promptly.

W. W.

After all, owing solely to Whitman's disability, the lecture was abandoned till April 14 of the following year.[1] I find no letters immediately after the foregoing, nor during that summer, although as Burroughs frequently gave away Whitman letters to eager friends, many gaps in their correspondence are thus accounted for.

Burroughs wrote to Myron Benton on April 18, 'Tell Joel Walt seems to be slowly regaining his health again.' Joel Benton had been especially active in arranging for the Lincoln lecture.

The poet Emma Lazarus, with whom Burroughs had become acquainted through the Gilders, writes him in early May as follows:

So far from being disappointed in the prose of 'Two Rivulets,' it exceeds

[1] See p. 182.

my most extravagant expectations. The War Memoranda are painfully vivid and have a fearful beauty of their own, and the noble chapter entitled 'Democratic Vistas' is to me the most suggestive and significant of all Walt Whitman's work. But what a giant it will take to fill in the magnificent outlines he designs!

I had heard of your plan of the lecture on Lincoln and was looking forward with great interest to hearing and seeing the poet. I trust he will soon be well enough to enable you to carry out your scheme. I was more than surprised to learn that he had ever remarked or remembered my name. I imagined that if he had ever chanced to meet with any of my work, he had classed it with the ordinary magazine writing which he so cordially despises.

And again on May 19:

I read all you say about Walt Whitman with intense interest. I cannot in any way describe the excitement, the general seething and stirring effect, produced within me by his best work, and yet I am conscious that you understand and sympathize with what I feel. In fact, I flatter myself in thinking that we start on so many subjects from the same standpoint, that the ordinary explanations and exchange of views which precede most friendships are rendered superfluous.

On June 14, Burroughs records in his Journal:

Attended the funeral of Bryant today with Walt and Gilder. Walt and Bryant used to be old friends, and had many long walks and talks together before Walt wrote poetry — after that Bryant was cold and distant.

When writing of Bryant's passing, in 'Specimen Days' ('Complete Prose Works,' pages 106–07), Whitman gives no hint of this falling off on Bryant's part. In the same volume (pages 173–74), Whitman pays superb tributes, not alone to Bryant, but to Emerson, Longfellow, and Whittier.

We now come to Whitman's account of his second visit to Burroughs at Riverby. His jaunt up the Hudson, and his visit are recorded in the 'Complete Prose Works' — 'Specimen Days' — pages 107–09, the part called 'Happiness and Raspberries' follows:

June 21 — Here I am, on the west bank of the Hudson, 80 miles north of New York, near Esopus, at the handsome, roomy, honeysuckle- and rose-embowered cottage of John Burroughs. The place, the perfect June days and nights (leaning toward crisp and cool), the hospitality of J. and Mrs. B., the air, the fruit (especially my favorite dish, currants and raspberries, mix'd, sugar'd, fresh and ripe from the bushes — I pick 'em myself) — the room I occupy at night, the perfect bed, the window giving an ample view of the Hudson and the opposite shores, so wonderful toward sunset, and the rolling music of the R.R. trains, far over there — the peaceful rest — the early Venus-heralded dawn — the noiseless splash of sunrise, the light and warmth indescribably glorious, in which (soon as the sun is well up), I have a capital rubbing and rasping with the flesh-brush — with an extra scour on the back by Al. J. [Albert Johnston, son of J. H. Johnston, of New York City] who is here with us — all inspiriting my invalid frame with new life, for the day. Then, after some whiffs of morning air, the delicious coffee of Mrs. B., with the cream, strawberries, and many substantials, for breakfast.

He writes further of his drives with Burroughs and 'Al J.,' about the country roads; of the stone fences, the brawling runs, the shrubs and wild flowers, the tramp family they encounter, the 'eloquent hemlocks — plenty of locusts and fine maples, and the balm of Gilead, giving out aroma.' His coffee-and-strawberry letter, we may say, came to 'John and 'Sula' on July 11:

I kept staying and staying in N.Y. but left yesterday in the 4 pm train; had a fine run to Phila. & here I am today in my regular den — all the better for my month's trip —
— Nothing very new — brother and sister well as usual — my two nieces, Jeff's daughters, are here and are a great comfort to me. Hot weather, awful — yet I am standing it well so far. I suppose you got the 'Tribune' of July 4 with my letter in.[1] And the box of Graham biscuits by express (of course you know they must be soaked half an hour or more in milk or water — I sweeten mine with sugar, but some don't like it)
— How are you getting along this hot weather? & how is the baby?
WALT WHITMAN

His very human postscript gives a quaint touch:

I eat my biscuits for supper only — have two or three of them in a bowl soak'd for an hour & the water pour'd off, and then a little milk & plenty of sugar — they must be fixed just right or they ain't good.

'Walt sent me a big box of those graham biscuits, a kind of hard tack,' said Burroughs, ' — very good. They came in a big tin box. We have it yet — keep sugar in it.'

In response to my request for any recollections he could furnish of that visit to Riverby with Whitman, Mr. Albert E. Johnston writes:

I was quite young when I spent a week with 'Uncle Walt' at the home

[1] 'A Poet's Recreation,' *New York Daily Tribune*, July 4, 1878 (mostly reproduced in 'Specimen Days').

of Burroughs, but two things are imprinted on my memory: the pre-breakfast dips the three of us took in the Hudson and, while drying, listening to Walt declaiming from Shakespeare, passage after passage, particularly from 'King Lear.' He was majestic in the rendering of whatever character he impersonated.

At evening, around ten o'clock, we would sit on the veranda overlooking the Hudson and watch the three Albany boats pass, which, tho' they left N.Y. at different intervals, were quite close together when they passed Esopus. The lights on the boats (and faint music) made a charming picture....

That June, Burroughs has a brief Journal entry on Whitman:

Is there another poet so impartial as Whitman? He bestows himself alike upon all; no criticism, no selection, but boundless acceptance. It may appear at first, as so many claim, that the carnal, the flesh and the appetites, are unduly exalted, but they are not; the spiritual, the æsthetic, is advancing just as far in its turn, and the integrity of the man is preserved.

From Auburndale, Massachusetts, early in July, Frederic R. Guernsey writes Burroughs:

I write to thank you for your kind gift of the 'Notes on Walt Whitman.' I like the fresh clear English of the book. It is not a bit too enthusiastic for me. I met James Parton, the biographer, the other day at his home in Newburyport, and we fell to talking of our great men. I asked his opinion of Walt Whitman, of whom he said: 'He has real Homeric touches in his poems.' But he seems to have some personal ill-feeling against Mr. Whitman.[1] However, Mr. Parton, though one of the most genial of men, has

---

[1] The matter of the loan to Walt Whitman by James Parton has been widely discussed, and the general impression created that Whitman did not settle the debt. Miss Ethel Parton, a niece of the creditor, wrote to W. S. Kennedy, February 10 and 15, 1897, giving her version of the affair, but it was based on hearsay and offered no conclusive details. The original letters are now owned by Mrs. Frank J. Sprague. The revised edition of Mr. Perry's *Walt Whitman* (1906) states in the Appendix, page 317: 'It was characteristic of Whitman that he persuaded himself that some chattels (pictures) offered in satisfaction of the Parton claim were a full equivalent for the debt. He explained his version of the transaction in a letter to W. D. O'Connor (now in the hands of Mr. Horace Traubel) and inclosed a receipt in settlement, apparently given to him by Dyer, Parton's friend and lawyer.... On the other hand, I have abundant written testimony from the Partons that the chattels offered were worthless and that the debt was never paid during Parton's lifetime. He died in 1891....'

But there is conclusive evidence that the debt was practically discharged, if not completely liquidated. Mr. Alfred Goldsmith has in his possession the following receipt:

BROOKLYN, *June* 17, 1857

Received by the undersigned (as attorney for James Parton) the sum of One Hundred and eighty-one dollars in part payment and settlement of a judgment and Execution at

vehement likes and dislikes. He is very busy on a life of Voltaire, and his library, in the sitting-room of one of our square New England houses, has a corner devoted to innumerable books on the French philosopher. 'It is to Voltaire,' said Mr. Parton, 'that we owe the privilege of talking freely on all subjects.'

Apropos of the Partons, it is stated with Mrs. O'Connor as authority, in a letter in the Perry Whitman Collection, that Mrs. Parton ('Fanny Fern') by no means shared her husband's ill-feeling toward Whitman, but on the contrary, had a warm admiration for him. I am indebted to Mr. Clifton Furness for the information that 'Fern Leaves' probably furnished Whitman with suggestions for the make-up of the cover of the 1855 edition of 'Leaves of Grass,' as well as for its title.

Mr. Guernsey's letter, interrupted by the foregoing paragraph, comments further on Whitman:

By yesterday's 'Tribune,' in which is a letter from Mr. Whitman, I see that you have had the delight of a visit from that splendid man. I do so envy you such an entertaining of angels *not* unawares.

... Before closing, let me say that Mr. Whitman seems to me to be destined to a sort of resurrection from the half-death of invalidism. How affectionately this great poet is already regarded....

In 'Complete Prose Works,' 'Specimen Days' (pages 101–02), under the heading, 'Three Young Men's Deaths,' Whitman copies a letter of September 29 of that year, received from John Burroughs — a description of a Catskill youth which had strongly impressed him. Burroughs's letter, which Whitman gives verbatim, is condensed here:

Smith [Smith Caswell, Burroughs's hired man] was away when your picture came, attending his sick brother, Charles — who has since died.... Charlie... was about the best specimen of a young country farm-hand I ever knew. You would have loved him. He was like one of your poems. With his great strength, his blond hair, his cheerfulness and contentment, his

suit of James Parton against Walt Whitman — Leaving thirty-five dollars due, which, when paid, is hereby declared to be a full settlement of said judgment, Note, &c. And all demands connected with the same.

OLIVER DYER.

On the back of this document Whitman wrote: 'Mem. Mr. Dyer also took Jefferson's works and Carlyle's Cromwell at $9 (if he keeps them) — which would then leave $26 due on the judgment and claim.' W. W. June 17, '57.

See also Traubel's *With Walt Whitman in Camden*, vol. 3, pp. 235–39. — C. J. F.

universal good will, and his silent manly ways, he was a youth hard to match.... In the morning Charlie put up his arms around Smith's neck and pulled his face down and kissed him. Smith said he knew then the end was near.... When I was home in August, Charlie was cradling on the hill, and it was a picture to see him walk through the grain. All work seemed play to him. He had no vices, any more than Nature has, and was beloved by all who knew him.

I have written thus to you about him, for such young men belong to you; he was of your kind. I wish you could have known him. He had the sweetness of a child, and the strength and courage and readiness of a young Viking....

In Burroughs's Journal for September 22, he writes further of this youth:

Today is the funeral day of Charley Caswell. Today they put his body in the ground, the ground that but a few weeks ago I saw him turning with the plow. Death has seldom despoiled the race of a nobler specimen of a young man. He was a young giant in strength and robustness. With his blond hair and fair skin he was like a Norse Viking.... He was the ideal farmhand — worthy the muse of a Virgil or Theocritus. He had the virtue and quality of all sweet rural things.... But yesterday, it seems, Aaron and I saw him cradling on the hill, and remarked his fine manly form, and power. How he walked up to the grain and through it! It was a delight to see him pitch hay, but no fun to the one who had to mow it away. But perhaps his great mastery was best seen when he had hold of the ax. It was better than a play to see him make the white chips fly, and the big logs vanish before him....

My heart is full of unshed tears for the lost youth. I will go walk over the hill and consecrate this day to the memory of him.

The following June (1879), on the 11th, Whitman wrote Burroughs:

I send you the 'Tobacco Plant' with a piece of mine [which] will interest you. (You'll see I have used one of your letters of last winter) — How nicely those English get up their print things....

The piece of which he wrote, in 'Cope's Tobacco Plant,' quotes Burroughs's foregoing letter about Charles Caswell. Speaking of this, Burroughs said to me, 'I had told Walt that Charley was his offspring, and it pleased him.'

Recently I ran across a sample of contemporary criticism in an old 'Scribner's' (October, 1878), in 'Topics of the Time,' presumably by J. G. Holland. It is called 'Our Garnered Names.' After commendatory comments on Bryant, Hawthorne, Longfellow, and Whittier, there follow condemnatory comments concerning Poe, Thoreau, and Whitman: 'When these [the first-named] have become classic, our people will have ceased to discuss Poe, Thoreau, and Whitman.' He speaks further of Poe's poems — the 'crazy products of a crazy mind' — as 'studies in mental pathology.' His only other reference to Thoreau is possibly in his comments on the 'morbid love of the eccentric'; but he dilates on 'the abominable dissonances of Whitman.'

In a brief November note, Whitman tells Burroughs that his book is slowly getting into form, and says, 'Your suggestion about Roberts or Osgood agreeable to me.' Just what there was to Burroughs's suggestion as to the possible publishers for Whitman's new edition, one can only guess, but I have seen statements from two or more sources that it was due to the efforts of James Boyle O'Reilly that James R. Osgood and Company proposed to Whitman to handle the seventh edition (1881–82) of the 'Leaves.' [1]

On December 12, Whitman writes enclosing a recent letter from Tennyson, and a 'muddled sort of criticism' from a late English magazine; he asks after J. B., wife, and baby, and wishes he were with them for a few weeks, but will probably stay in Camden the winter; he tells of a recent order from London for six sets of his books; speaks of the Gilchrists in Brooklyn, and says Jeannette Gilder is asking for items to write his life.

By December 23 plans are again on foot for the Lincoln lecture to be given in the spring. Whitman writes Burroughs about it:

... The lecture is a *fixed fact* (to come), but I shall wait till I get good and ready.

He adds:

Write me more fully about your proposed book of next spring (it is in the gestation of a book — the melting of the fluid metal, before the casting — that it receives that something to make its idiosyncrasy, identity — its 'excuse for being,' if it is to have any). I have written to Jenny Gilder and sent her a small budget of printed slips etc. (I would like best to be *told about* in strings of continuous anecdotes, incidents, *mots*, thumbnail personal sketches, characteristic and true — such, for instance, as are in the second edition of your old Wash'n *Notes*.

[1] See *The Conservator*, December, 1895, January, 1896.

Yours of 17th Dec. rec'd, Tennyson and the criticism safely rec'd back. I suppose you rec'd the hat photo you spoke of. (I sent it to you Oct. 1st) I mailed you also a pair of buck gloves, and Smith a pair, too — four days since — I shall send this to Delaware County, as you say you are going home for a few days. Write me if you get it all right.

W. W.

Happy New Year to you and all [written in red ink]

Referring to the comments about Miss Gilder's sketch, Burroughs said to me, in 1907:

I don't remember what Jeannette Gilder wrote about Walt — probably an obituary. She wrote *my* obituary long ago for the 'Herald.' They have it tucked away and add to it from time to time to bring it up to date. Walt used to send Smith Caswell, our hired man, and me, a pair of warm gloves for Christmas, and he used to give gloves to his friends among the street-car drivers.

Whitman was interested in the name Burroughs was to give to his new book, and in late January, 1879, wrote him saying that he could think of no better name than the one Burroughs had suggested, 'Locusts and Wild Honey.' But he mentioned 'Speckled Trout' as a book title to be considered later — a title of one of the essays in the book in question. Burroughs said the title of his new book had occurred to him after his soldier comrade, Aaron Johns, had written asking when he could come and eat locusts and wild honey with him in the wilderness: 'Walt set the seal of his approval on it, you see, which settled it.' Whitman had himself appropriated the title of Burroughs's second nature book, 'Winter Sunshine' (1875), for a newspaper article of his own in the 'Philadelphia Times' for January 26, 1879 — 'Winter Sunshine — A Trip from Camden to the Coast.' As a rule, both the comrades were felicitous in their titles.

The increased clouding of Emerson's faculties was now becoming sadly apparent. To Benton, with whom he had seen Emerson in his prime, Burroughs wrote on February 9:

Mrs. Gilchrist told me she visited Emerson last fall in Concord, twice. He is very serene and cheerful, remembers earlier things and events, but is fast losing his hold upon later. He saw Walt Whitman's photograph in her album, and on being told who it was asked her if he was one of her English friends.

'What was the name of my best friend?' he will inquire of his wife.

'Henry Thoreau,' she will answer.

'Oh, yes, Henry Thoreau.'

Concerning the revival of the lecture project, Whitman writes on March 20 to Burroughs:

How are you getting along? Haven't heard from you in a long time — My splurge on the *Death of Lincoln* is all ready to be splurged — I should like to deliver it on Monday evening, April 14 in N.Y. — (or Tuesday evening — if for any reason preferable) How about making the arrangements — some respectable second or third class hall? Is Gilder off for Europe? Would not Chas. De Kay be a good man to help? I should have written you before but I have been waiting a little to see if this March-April attack I had last spring wasn't going to give me another hitch — but I believe not. If the arrangements could be conveniently made, I shall *positively be on hand* for April 14 (or 15).

Write forthwith — Love to 'Sula — How is the young one? How Smith, and his?

Nothing very new with me — I keep well for me — have had a good winter — Got a letter from one Riley, from Sheffield, Eng. day before yesterday — he is a friend and young chum of Ruskin — the latter accepts me and goes it strong — he adjectives the word 'glorious' for L of G.

W. W.

Commenting on this letter, Burroughs said:

Charlie De Kay, a brother-in-law of Gilder, has written several volumes of poems, some of them pretty good — a very likable man.

And of Ruskin:

I remember that Ruskin said somewhere in print that Whitman's words were like rifle bullets.

Ruskin's sentence, to which Burroughs doubtless referred, is 'They [Emerson and Whitman] are deadly true — in the sense of rifles — against all our deadly sins.' Kennedy quotes this in 'Reminiscences of Walt Whitman' (page 84), in a letter from Ruskin of January 28, 1880, to Mr. Herbert J. Bathgate, of Chester, England.

This time the Lincoln lecture came off as planned. It was held in Steck Hall, Fourteenth Street, New York, on April 14, 1879. Whitman remained seated and read from his notes. The 'New York Daily Tribune' reported the lecture, and stated that Whitman wished for other engagements. I find nothing in the correspondence to tell how it was received, but we have Whitman's facetious statement afterwards, printed in 'The Complete Works' (page 506):

And now, since it has come off, and since neither my hearers nor I myself really collapsed at the aforesaid lecture, I intend to go up and down the land (in moderation) seeking whom I may devour, with lectures and readings of my own poems....

Whitman gives a rather full account of his third and last visit to Burroughs, April, 1879, in 'Specimen Days,' [1] with his ride up the Hudson, the scenes on the river, an especially graphic description being 'Hudson River Sights,' also with descriptions of bird songs, and unusual neighborhood characters. A brief note by Whitman on April 29 enables one to see the comrades on that April twilight so long ago — almost to hear what they heard:

As we drove lingering along the road we heard, just after sundown, the song of the wood thrush. We stopp'd without a word, and listen'd long. The delicious notes — a sweet, artless, voluntary, simple anthem, as from the flute-stops of some organ, wafted through the twilight — echoing well to us from the perpendicular high rock, where, in some thick young trees' recesses at the base, sat the bird — fill'd our senses, our souls.

He also gives a precious bit of description of a waterfall which he and Burroughs visited. It is in the region which Burroughs later named 'the Whitman land,' and about which he comments on the first page of 'Whitman: A Study.' Forever after it was associated with his great friend. Many a time, in later years, he has pointed out to his visitors the fallen hemlock upon which the poet sat as he made the note here transcribed:

'An Ulster County Waterfall'

I jot this mem. in a wild scene of woods and hills, where we have come to visit a waterfall. I never saw finer or more copious hemlocks, many of them large, some old and hoary. Such a sentiment to them, secretive, shaggy — what I call weather-beaten and let-alone — a rich underlay of ferns, yew sprouts and mosses, beginning to be spotted with the early summer wild flowers. Enveloping all, the monotone and liquid gurgle from the hoarse, impetuous copious fall — the greenish-tawny, darkly transparent waters, plunging with velocity down the rocks, with patches of milk-white foam — a stream of hurrying amber, thirty feet wide, risen far back in the hills and woods, now rushing with volume — every hundred rods a fall, and sometimes three or four in that distance. A primitive

---

[1] See *Complete Prose Works*, pp. 122–26.

forest, druidical, solitary and savage — not ten visitors a year — broken rocks everywhere — shade overhead, thick underfoot with leaves — a just palpable wild and delicate aroma.

To the many who have visited that scene in later years will be borne in upon afresh Whitman's 'divine power to use words,' so perfectly does he re-create the scene. 'Not ten visitors a year' was, of course, true when Whitman wrote those words, but a few years after the poet's death John Burroughs chose a site for his rustic cabin not far from this place, and ever after it was the scene of countless pilgrims who found their way to Slabsides. In that cabin, in late 1895, and in 1896, Burroughs wrote the preliminary chapter, and made his final revision, of his second book on Whitman.

In Burroughs's Journal, April 26, is preserved his account of this same visit from Whitman:

These days I am happy. The days are perfection — sweet, bright, un-cloying April days — and then Walt Whitman is here. He sits in the open bay window, reading, writing, musing, and looking down upon Smith and me grafting the trees or ploughing among the currants, or upon me alone wheeling baby Julian about the grounds. His white beard and ruddy face make a picture there I delight to see. Occasionally he comes out and strolls about, or sits on the wall on the brink of the hill, and looks out upon the scene. Presently I join him and we have much talk.

And on April 30:

A most delicious April day — the flower of the whole month. Walt and I drove over in the Russell woods and visited the falls. Walt was much impressed with the scene and made some notes.[1]

And then the brief entry of May 3:

Walt left today. The weather has been nearly perfect, and his visit has been a great treat to me — April days with Homer and Socrates for company.

A reader of Burroughs coming upon a certain paragraph descriptive of bird songs in Whitman's 'Complete Prose' will be struck by its resemblance to a familiar passage in Burroughs's 'Wake-Robin.' On comparing the passages he will conclude that Whitman was quite as susceptible of catching from Burroughs as Burroughs had been formerly of catching from Whitman. 'Look at this picture, and then on that!'

[1] See p. 183.

Burroughs wrote in an essay in 1863, and published in book form in 1871:

Yet the coming and the going of the birds is more or less of a mystery and a surprise. We go out in the morning and no thrush or vireo is to be heard; we go out again, and every tree and grove is musical; yet again, and all is silent. Who saw them come? who saw them depart?

This pert little winter wren... does he travel by easy stages from bush to bush and from wood to wood?...[1]

Whitman wrote in 1879:

The birds are plenty; of any sort, or of two or three sorts, curiously, not a sign, till suddenly some warm, gushing, sunny April (or even March) day — lo! there they are, from twig to twig, or fence to fence, flirting, singing, some mating, preparing to build. But most of them *en passant* — a fortnight, a month in these parts, and then away.[2]

Farther on in the paragraph just quoted from Whitman his comments about the song of the meadowlark make one feel that he has been less impressed by the bird's song itself, and more by Burroughs's description of the same, which he has confused a little in the writing. He does not then seem to have heard the song sufficiently himself to have used very felicitous words in translating it — 'the meadow lark's, so sweet, so alert, and remonstrating (as if the bird said, "don't you see?" or "can't you understand?")' Now this bird's song is sweet, and alert, piercingly sweet, but there is nothing the least 'remonstrating' about it. It is challenging, not to say, taunting — seeming oftenest to say, 'You can't *see* me — see me.' And somewhere Burroughs has similarly described it. But I can't imagine any note of this bird ending on a sound which by the widest stretch of the imagination could be translated by 'understand.'[3] What Whitman says in this same entry about the various tones of the robin reminds me of a reply of Burroughs's, when I once remarked that a certain sundown note of the robin affected me in a way I could find no word to describe — 'Why,' said he, 'that's the way Walt felt about it — he said he had tried for years to find a word to describe exactly that evening call and the feeling it aroused in him.'

It was on this same visit, I think, that Burroughs drove Whitman

[1] *Wake-Robin*, page 2.   [2] *Complete Prose Works*, p. 123.

[3] In *Complete Prose Works*, page 103, Whitman gives a very felicitous description of the meadowlark's song.

over to Poughkeepsie and visited the Ritters at Vassar College,
Dr. Ritter [1] then seeming to be the only one on the faculty who
knew anything about Whitman. On this, or a later occasion,
Dr. Ritter told Whitman that when he wanted to get into the free,
exalted mood necessary to compose music, he read aloud from
'Leaves of Grass.'

From 1309 Fifth Avenue, New York, on June 11, Whitman wrote
Burroughs of being at the Johnstons', and how the visit had been
good for him — 'It sort of *rehabilitates* me for speaking and literary handling, writing, off-hand, more than I anticipated — half-
paralytic as I am. Henceforth I feel more at ease, more self-
confidence, which is always half the battle —' This would seem
to indicate that he might have been doing some speaking in public,
though no other allusion looking that way is made.

An August letter tells of his summer in Camden and encloses letters from Mrs. Gilchrist in England, and one from Mrs. Botta in
New York, who, Burroughs explained, was a well-known lady
there, the wife of an Italian professor, in whose home Walt sometimes attended literary receptions.[2] Burroughs replies from the
Catskills on August 24:

Since I have been here I have written an article on Nature and the
Poets,[3] showing where our poets trip in their wood lore and natural
history, and where they hit the mark. I catch them all napping — Emerson, Bryant, Whittier, Longfellow. I shall have something to say about
you, with extracts, but I cannot catch you in any mistake, as I wish I
could, for that is my game. I wish I could also find a slip in Shakespeare
or Tennyson, but I cannot — according to my knowledge, except where
Shakespeare follows the unscientific thought of his times, as in his treatment of the honey-bee.... I will send you the proof of the article on the
poets before it goes to the magazine.

There are two articles in the August 'Appleton's Journal' that are
worth glancing over — Arnold on Wordsworth, and Earl D. on moose-
hunting. What simple good hearty fellows those English earls must be;
not a false or conventional note in this one.

The baby is doing well and completely fills my heart. Wife is about as
usual.

[1] Frederic Louis Ritter, composer of 'The Dirge of Two Veterans.' See also pp. 129,
190, 359.
[2] Anne Charlotte Lynch Botta (1820–91), author of a *Handbook of Universal Literature* (1860).
[3] 'Nature and the Poets,' *Scribner's Monthly*, December, 1879; also *Pepacton*, 1881.

I find I cannot read Whittier and Longfellow and Lowell with any satisfaction. Your poems spoil me for any but the greatest. Coming from them
to you is like coming from a hothouse to the shore or the mountain.   I
know this is so, and is no pre-determined partiality of mine.

> Faithfully
> JOHN BURROUGHS

In 1888, when Whitman gave this letter to Traubel, he called it
'One of John's come-out letters,' remarking that his later ones
were less so — that he seemed to have lost color a little — was not
'quite so definitely, quarrelsomely virile' as he used to be. Judging
from Traubel's reporting of Whitman's talk to him (though ample
allowance must be made for the reporter's personal bias as to the
things stressed), it looks as though Whitman's appetite, in those
last years, was so insatiable for expressed praise, that if praise was
not forthcoming on every occasion, his doubts crept in as to whether
his staunch friends were falling off a bit. But Whitman knew in his
heart that they were not; his words to Traubel, from time to time,
testify to this. Of course Burroughs did not maintain a militant
attitude all down the years, but whenever there was need for action
he was as strong as ever in defense — a defense all the more
effective because of its sane reasonableness. In connection with
Whitman's expression of transitory doubts, one recalls other
comments quoted by Traubel:

John's letter appeals to me because of its undemonstrative personal
affection — that, first of all; then because of its uncompromising, red-
blooded espousal of the book — of my code. I respond to John; I feel the
eminent kindliness, love, of his declaration. John never slushes, but he is
always on the spot.

Following is a copy of one of the few letters in which Whitman
addresses Burroughs as 'Jack.' It is dated August 29, 1879:

DEAR JACK,
As I sit here the weather is now perfect, day and night — I have jotted
off the enclosed I send you (of course use it or not).
Your letter arrived with the enclosures. I keep well, go out most every
day.... I sell a book now and then.
No, I have not been to any watering-place — they are no company for
me — the cities, magnificent for their complex play and oceans of eager
human faces — but the country or sea for me, in some sparse place, old
barn and farm house, or bleak seashore, nobody round — meanwhile I get
along very well here.   WALT

The enclosed passage which he mentions is found on page 111.

In the fall of 1879, Whitman traveled as far west as the Rocky Mountains, tarrying for some time with his brother Jeff in St. Louis, Missouri, whence he writes Burroughs on November 23:

I am still here — 'not yet' (as an old Long Island aunt used to say) 'not yet out of my misery,' but I go out on the streets, or to the Public Library most every day, and have no doubt I shall be as well as usual before long. I believe I told you I was in nice quarters and very comfortable here.

I send you Mrs. Gilchrist's letter which you needn't return, Gilder's, which I also enclose, I wish you to send back sometime. Upon receiving this, post me a card — tell me how the mother is, and 'Sula, also the baby, also Smith.

Just got a postal from Mrs. Gilchrist giving her address....

The rough map enclosed gives you some idea of my present jaunt, on the red line (the blue lines are old travels of mine).

I have seen the December 'Scribners' — what you say of me in 'Nature and the Poets' thoroughly delights, satisfies, and *prides* me.[1] I saw in the Library a late London 'Fortnightly' in which J. A. Symonds, touching briefly but very commendingly and mentioning my name, makes quite an extract from 'Dem. Vistas' (summing up the general spirit of British literature as being markedly sombre and bilious).[2]

A. B. Alcott is expected here to talk — I may see him — This is quite a place for the most toploftical Hegelian transcendentalists, a small knot but smart — the principal of them, W. T. Harris, editor of 'Speculative Philosophy,' has been often to see me, has been very kind, and I like him much. Probably ten days more will end my stay here (but I am not fixed)....

WALT WHITMAN

Burroughs said, in commenting on this letter, that W. T. Harris was Commissioner of Public Education in Washington, a very able man, a metaphysician. The map which Whitman mentions having sent, Burroughs thought had got chewed up by the mice, but it was found later among old mementoes which he had given me, and is here reproduced as of unique value in tracing all of Whitman's Southern and Western journeyings. A map in which he outlined his second journey only is given by Herbert Gilchrist in 'Anne Gilchrist.' The map reproduced here was one of the items lent from

[1] 'Nature and the Poets' (*Pepacton*, pp. 107–09). See also this volume, p. 111.

[2] Symonds's article, 'Matthew Arnold's Selections from Wordsworth,' *Fortnightly Review* (November, 1879), vol. 32, pp. 686–701, quotes a long passage from *Specimen Days* and comments favorably upon it (pp. 699–700). — C. J. F.

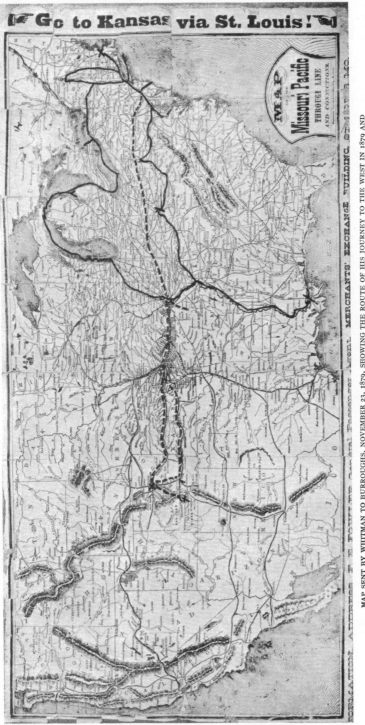

MAP SENT BY WHITMAN TO BURROUGHS, NOVEMBER 23, 1879, SHOWING THE ROUTE OF HIS JOURNEY TO THE WEST IN 1879 AND ALSO HIS EARLIER TRAVELS NORTH AND SOUTH

For the red and blue lines Whitman drew on the original, heavy broken and solid lines have been substituted in the reproduction

the Burroughs Whitman Collection to the Exhibition of Whitmaniana, held in the New York Public Library in 1925.

It was while Whitman was still tarrying in St. Louis that James T. Fields wrote Burroughs as follows concerning him, December 22:

It is a real grief to me that I was obliged to go off and not see you at my house, as I hoped to do, during the Holmes week.[1] Among other matters I wished to speak about was this:

WALT WHITMAN. How is he getting on as to his daily bread? I know that you keep the run of him, and will know if he is comfortably off in these days. Is there a fund at his disposal? or does he depend on what chance greenbacks float into his exchequer from his writings? The noble old veteran ought to be placed beyond discomfort, and if he is not, it is a disgrace to his companions in letters who are accidentally a little better off in a pecuniary way.

I would like to send him a small Christmas remembrance in money, if such an act w'd not be distasteful to him. You will know, and will please tell me by return mail if I may send to you for him a check for $100. There is no occasion for his being told who sends it, you know.

Concerning this Burroughs said:

That was while Walt was stranded in St Louis. I used to give him a windfall occasionally. When Fields gave me this one hundred dollars to send him it struck him at just the right time. Fields gave Aldrich $10,000, and other authors $10,000. But every one enlarges on the help given Walt. They gave Aldrich and Howells and Sarah Orne Jewett purses of $5000, and more, and *they* didn't need it. 'Mark Twain' was helped tremendously by his wealthy friends. Walt had Eddie, his imbecile brother, to provide for, and was always fearing Eddie would be neglected after his death.... It is ridiculous — the hullabaloo they make about the money that was given Walt.

From St. Louis, January 2, 1880, Whitman writes Burroughs:

DEAR FRIEND

Yours of 29th Dec. with *the present* came safe today. Believe me I feel the gift, and it comes just right, too. John, please forward the enclosed slip to unknown friend —

The above [engraving on letter-head] is a fair picture of the great Mississippi Bridge, East St Louis, where I have loafed many hours — only it sets up *much higher* than the print gives. I don't believe there can be a grander thing of the kind on earth.

I leave here Sunday morning Jan 4 at 8, on my return east, and shall be

[1] The celebration in Boston of Oliver Wendell Holmes's seventieth birthday.

due in Philadelphia Monday evening before 8. The last two or three weeks I have been well for me, and am so now.

Your letter was deeply interesting to me, made me see Emerson no doubt just as he is, the good pure soul —

John, I sympathize with you in the arm, and the treatment too.

A great thaw and dense fog here as I write

WALT WHITMAN

The bridge to which Whitman refers, the Eads Bridge — the first long bridge in the United States — ranked at that time as one of the engineering wonders of the world.

On February 21, from Camden, Whitman writes:

Yours of 20th with enclosure came safely — Best thanks.... Nothing very new with me since return — I have not written out for print any notes of my jaunt yet. I am well, considering —

Addington Symonds has sent me a copy of the American edition of his 'Greek Poets' — Ruskin has sent to me for five sets of my books.

Does Mrs. Gilchrist write to you? They are well — are all in London, except Beatrice, who is in Switzerland —

Dr. Bucke of London, Canada, is writing *my life* [1] — I suppose he has sent you his printed circular, asking information, &c. What do you think of the project?

Rec'd a letter from Mrs. Ritter — she speaks of a musical composition of her husband's to go with my 'Two Veterans,' and asks if I am willing it should be published — I answered, expressing my consent.

Burroughs said of the foregoing letter:

Dr. Ritter was Musical Doctor at Vassar, a German whom I liked much. His wife, Fannie Raymond, was a singer, had a tremendous voice.

Bucke's book collected some things of value, but it is not a biography that will stand — a kind of hodge-podge. Bucke tied his knots too hard — was dogmatic and disputatious, and that isn't the best temper for literature. He was an able man, very learned — a cripple — he nearly lost his life when a young man — froze his feet in an overland journey to California. That affliction may have had something to do with his irritability and vehement tendencies. He was English, you know, and an alienist, as I've told you before.

In 'Edward Dowden's Letters' is one quoted on March 21, 1880, to his brother John, telling of Dr. John Brown having told Dowden that he was 'too indulgent to that strange, wild savage, Whitman.' Dowden thus comments on this: 'As to Walt, if I stay away from

[1] R. M. Bucke: *Walt Whitman*, David Mackay, 1883.

him I can agree with those who think him harmful, but the moment I come near him I know he is bracing and wholesome.' This recalls what Sidney Lanier, in 1878, wrote Bayard Taylor — that Whitman was refreshing, 'like rude salt spray in your face.' That same year Dowden's friend Dr. John Todhunter had a fine passage about Whitman as a democrat in his 'Study of Shelley.' Thus, abroad and at home, Whitman was gaining a little ground. His letter of May 9 to Burroughs contains much of interest:

I have just returned from a two weeks' visit down in the Jersey pine woods and had a good time in the simple, savage way I like. Am well for me, sunburnt and fat. (Some twitchings, but I don't dwell on them.) Nothing very new in my affairs, sell a couple of books occasionally.

I suppose you saw my Riddle Song in the first number of Sunnyside Press — if not, I can send you the 'Progress' with it in.

I delivered my Lincoln lecture last April 15 in Philadelphia — the same as the N.Y. version. I took it very coolly and enjoyed it (No great audience — $90, after paying expenses).

Mr. Abbott of Boston wrote to me for a poem for his May 22d 'Emerson Number' of the 'Literary World.' I could not write him a poem, but I sent him a little prose criticism which I believe he is to print in said number.

Dr. Bucke is coming here to Philadelphia about May 22. Eldridge passed through here day before yesterday, returning to Washington....

I had the May 'Scribner' and read it leisurely down in the woods — Stedman's Poe, and your 'Notes.' (Scratched off my Emerson screed down there, as it was there I rec'd Abbott's letter.)

I hear from the Gilchrists; they are in London; the daughter Beatrice has suddenly abandoned her medical pursuits and intentions. Herbert thrives....

I hear at second remove, and vaguely, that Symonds is writing a book, or something, about me.

... When you write, send me Smith Caswell's exact post office address, so I can send him papers. Don't forget.

Is it *you* who says so emphatically the blackbirds don't sing? — What they call here the Virginia blackbird, with red dabbed shoulders — Harry Stafford says they do, at times, and very finely (and I say so, too) How are you? How the arm? how the babe? Love to 'Sula —

In Perry's 'Whitman' (opposite page 224) he gives a facsimile of the ticket of admission to Whitman's lecture on the Death of Lincoln, in Philadelphia, April 15. The ticket is printed in heavily inked letters and bordered in black and silver. It was lent Professor Perry from the Burroughs Whitman Collection.

Of course the ups and downs continue, but the fact that 'Scribner's Monthly' was now to give room to an article on Whitman was highly significant. The correspondence to follow furnishes some inside information on the much-discussed article by Stedman. From New York City, October 7, E. C. Stedman wrote Burroughs:

I made up my mind to write you and O'Connor (he is an old and dear friend of mine) after completing my article on Walt. But as I am not very well I send you a copy of a letter to O'Connor, so that you may consider it as addressed to you 'justly,' as Captain Cuttle might say.

Mr. Johnson has promised to see that the two photos you loaned me reach you again in safety.

I trust you had a fine summer and are hard at work with your pen. Last August I enjoyed greatly boating, swimming, loafing, writing on W. W., and occasionally visiting the Concord Academe (which is worth visiting).

With compliments to Mrs. Burroughs, the baby, the snakes, and other tenants on the Esopus-on-Hudson estate, etc. etc.

Here follows his letter to O'Connor, which he inclosed:

My dear O'Connor,

I think as often and as kindly of you as ever, but it is an unusual occasion that brings me to indulge myself with the luxury of writing a friendly letter to anyone. We slaves of the pen, men like you and myself, don't handle for pleasure the implements with which they have toiled all day for a living.

What I want to tell you is that I have written, during my vacation, a very long and yet condensed paper on Walt Whitman, which will appear in the next number of 'Scribner's.' Mr. Burroughs loaned me a strong photograph of our old Hesiod, which has been well engraved for an illustration. I made it a positive condition of my contributing a new series of articles to 'Scribner' that Walt should be the subject of one of them, and that I should say what I chose.

For years I have been a close observer of his writings, and have read almost everything written upon him. The mass of the latter is immense, but among it all there has not appeared what seems to me a *judicial* estimate of his works and career. This I have honestly attempted to make. In sincerely trying to discover both his strength and his weakness, I have said many things which doubtless you will dissent from, but not a few, I hope, with which you will agree.

Mr. Burroughs has written upon him delightfully, in pure and glowing English, and with fine insight and sympathy, but my article is more critical than his, and in much of its criticism you and he possibly will not concur. But at least you will give me the credit for openly declaring my perception of Whitman's genius, and of his masterly qualities as a part of nature and an artist. For I differ from many of my brother-poets as to the last-named point. If I know what constitutes broad and high art in the matter of rhythm, Whitman is an artist. In deprecating what I consider his foibles and errors, I have avoided personalities, of course: and if you knew how I have resisted the temptation to be epigrammatic, and the number of my 'bright things' which I have cut out, you probably would take those I have retained with good unction.

However, I only write to assure you of my conscientious effort to measure your friend as I would wish to be measured myself — if anything of the little work done by me were worth anybody's measurement. I shall send Burroughs a copy of this letter.

Remember me always to your dear wife, and believe me, as ever

Your old friend

E. C. STEDMAN

To Stedman's letter to him, Burroughs replied, October 9:

I have been looking for your article on Whitman with a good deal of interest. You told me when you were here that it would make all of Whitman's friends mad, and I have felt justified in getting mad a little in advance. In fact my wrath has been slowly fermenting and rising for the past month, and had you not sent me this letter I do not know what might have happened on the appearance of your article.

... But really I do not expect to be mad, but rather to be glad. It is not fair and honest criticism that W. W.'s friends resent, but insult, like that which Whipple [1] and Holland [2] and many others have dealt in. I know you will be respectful and appreciative, whatever flaws you may find in his work.

The tone and style in which you have treated Taylor and Poe are eminently judicial, and such as any poet could wish to receive at the hands of another — the treatment is affectionate, though impartial. No doubt you have approached dear old Walt in the same spirit, and I am half disposed to resent the insinuation that you expect his friends to be mad. I am sure that neither O'Connor nor myself would ever have taken up the cudgels in behalf of Whitman in the way we have, had not his treatment at the hands of the literary men of this country been simply outrageous. Your article, I trust, and hope, marks the beginning of a

---

[1] This may refer to an original paper by Whipple which was published later as a book, *American Literature, and Other Papers* (Ticknor and Company, 1887), pp. 112–14.

[2] Kennedy cites Holland's hostile editorial as being in *Scribner's* in April, 1876. This is an error. There is, however, one in that monthly for October, 1878 (see p. 183); and the second series of 'Every Day Topics,' *Scribner's*, 1882, by Holland, under the heading 'Is it Poetry?' contains references to Whitman, the matter being culled from *Scribner's* editorials of five preceding years.

different state of affairs — that of honest and respectful criticism, and I for one expect to cry Bravo!

I myself have never felt like criticising Whitman any more than I have Nature herself; his very defects, if they are such, are vital, and such as belong only to the first order of minds. Much of his poetry is what may be called negative poetry, just as so much of the beauty of Nature is negative. ... In his most arid stretches and catalogues I feel the same poetic throb, the same tremendous spirit that knows well enough what it is doing....

I must give Holland credit for more liberality than I thought he possessed in allowing you your own way in the matter, portrait and all. You must have made a spirited fight.

After Burroughs had read Stedman's paper in the November 'Scribner's,' he wrote Joel Benton:

Stedman's article on Walt Whitman will do its subject good — help sell his books, I think. Some parts of it are very fine, but it does not settle the case. It will not do to compare the sexual passion and procreation to the mud and slime that Nature covers up. Nature covers up mud when she can, but she does not cover up procreation. This part of the article is weak.

Burroughs said elsewhere of Stedman's article:

Of Whitman's prophetic character, of his modernity, of his relation to science, to democracy, of his political, national, racial, and religious significance, we hear very little. It is a sort of literary class-room drill the critic [Stedman] puts him through, and the wonder is that he finds so much to approve, and so little to condemn.

In August, before receiving Stedman's letter in defense of his Whitman article, O'Connor had written Dr. Bucke that he was wondering how much mischief the excellent Stedman would feel compelled to do Whitman in his 'Scribner' article, in order to maintain his credit with Stoddard, Macdonough, Bill Winter, et id. (Macdonough had once derisively called Whitman the 'swan of the sewers,' perhaps in allusion to the characterization of Burns as 'the Swan of the Nith.') On November 8, to Burroughs, he thus comments on the Stedman-Whitman matter:

Just returned from a month's absence. I find a curious letter from E. C. S. anent his article on WW, a copy of which (the letter) he tells me he has sent to you. Before I answer I would like to hear what you think about the letter, its *motif*, etc. and how the article impresses you. Drop me a few words if you can. I desire to reply to him *prudently*, but he richly deserves a hetchelling. His mere blunders of fact are cardinal and really invalidate the whole paper, *I* think.

O'Connor wrote Dr. Bucke that Stedman's critique was what he expected, only better. Told him that Stedman had written him 'in a decidedly tremulous tone, evidently anticipating the wrath of Achilles,' and added: 'How he could be chawed up! and his points of censure and objection turned on him — still I think on the whole his article will help Whitman's cause.'

Months later O'Connor wrote Dr. Bucke further:

I never answered Stedman's letter to me, for which I expect he will feel vengeful. The fact is I could not. When I first got his letter, and then read his article, the letter I meant to write him ran sketching out like loops of lightning through my mind, but to get it all down on paper was a task I never executed for the reasons herein given — lack of time and eyes. After all, it is as well. He would have been very sore to read what I should have written him, however kindly phrased, for to exterminate all his positions would be the easiest thing in the world, and I am surprised that he should have laid himself so open. On matters of fact alone he is preposterous, and his article simply shows he has not mastered the subject. But what's the use of bothering about what such snips write in regard to the mighty imaginations of Walt Whitman! Do you remember in Hugo's *Legend of the Ages* the magnificent poem Eviradnus? It has a blistering line which I should like to apply to such as Stedman when they venture to handle Walt Whitman. The princess Mahand utters it to the dwarf Zeno in the hall of the ancestors, when he lays hands on the great mail:

> *Laissez-donc... dit Mahand, qui murmure:*
> *Vous êtes trop petit pour toucher cette armure.*

O'Connor then mentioned the 'New York Star' having disposed of Stedman's paper in ten words:

Stedman on Walt Whitman — a man milliner writing about Samson!

Whitman's brief comment on Stedman's article is found in a letter of November 26 to Burroughs: 'I thought Stedman's article full as good as could be expected.' And years later he is reported by Traubel as saying of it:

I regarded the piece as thoroughly friendly, thoroughly courteous, thoroughly fair — if not more.... It had been free criticism, and I never resented free criticism... no man has held himself so open to it — and I may add that I have got some of my best points from it. I am only too glad to be read and examined as Stedman has read and examined me. After a long experience with men who neither hoped for truth, nor would see it, it was like daylight to meet with such treatment as Stedman accorded me.

This accords with a letter Stedman wrote to Professor Perry, January 2, 1905, in which he states that Whitman, on his death-bed, told him that he had understood him aright and that he was satisfied with his article about him, as was Cromwell with his 'Paint me as I am, warts and all.'

However, at the time, something of far more concern to Whitman than Stedman's essay about him was engrossing him, and in the letter of November 26, he wrote about it at length:

DEAR JOHN

What could you do toward helping me in the matter stated by these two pages? — badly copied, but I can't write them out — I have sent duplicates of the two pp to Watson Gilder and said I requested you to see him as soon as convenient.

The two pages enclosed are dated November 26, 1880:

R. Worthington 770 Broadway, New York about a year ago bo't at auction the electrotype plates (456 pages) of the 1860–61 edition of my book *Leaves of Grass* — plates originally made by a young firm, Thayer and Eldridge, under my supervision there and then, in Boston (in the spring of 1860, on an agreement running five years). A small edition was printed and issued at the time, but in six months, or thereabout, Thayer and Eldridge failed, and these plates were stored away and nothing further done till about a year ago (latter part of 1879) they were put up in New York City by Leavitt, auctioneer and bought in by said Worthington. Leavitt before putting them up wrote to me offering the plates for sale. I wrote back that said plates were worthless, being superseded by a larger and different edition — that I could not use them — the 1860 ones — myself, nor would I allow them to be used by anyone else, I being the sole owner of the copyright.

However, it seems Leavitt did auction them, and Worthington bo't them (I suppose for a mere song). Worthington then wrote to me offering $250 if I would add something to the text and authenticate the plates to be published in a book by him. I wrote back (I was in St Louis at the time, helpless, sick) thanking him for the offer, regretting he had purchased the plates, refusing the proposal, and forbidding any use of the plates. Then and since I thought the matter had drop't. But I have to add that about September 1880 (I was in London, Canada at the time) I wrote to Worthington referring to his previous offer then declined by me, and asking whether he still had the plates and was disposed to make the same offer, to which I rec'd no answer. I wrote a second time, and again no answer.

I had supposed the whole thing drop't and nothing done, but within a week past, I learn that Worthington has been slyly printing and selling the Volume of *Leaves of Grass* from those plates (must have commenced early in 1880) and is now printing and selling it. On Nov. 22, 1880, I found the book (from those plates) at Porter and Coates' store, cor. 9th and Chestnut Str., Philadelphia. P and C told me they procured it from Worthington and had been procuring it off and on, for nearly a year.

First, I want Worthington effectually stopt from issuing the books. Second I want my royalty for all he has sold (though I have no idea of ever getting a cent) Third, I want W. taken hold of, if possible, on criminal proceeding.

I am the sole owner of the copyright, and I think my copyright papers are all complete — I publish and sell the book myself — it is my sole means of living. What Worthington has done has already been a serious detriment to me. Mr. Eldridge (of the Boston firm alluded to) is accessible in Washington, D.C., will corroborate first parts of the foregoing (is my friend)

WALT WHITMAN, 431 Stevens St Camden, New Jersey

On December 7, he wrote further:

In the letter I sent you yesterday ab't the Worthington matter, I spoke of W. probably buying with the plates a lot of the old Boston edition in sheets — Dr. Bucke yesterday stopt at Leavitt's (the auctioneer's) in N.Y., and today I receive from B. the following postal:

'Leavitt sold the plates to a Mr. Williams (for Wentworth of Boston) in Sept. '79 for $200. Leavitt never saw or heard of any *sheets* Worthington must have bo't the plates from Williams. He must have printed from them. R. M. B.'

I thought I might as well let you know every new discovery, etc, and I shall continue to do so.

W. W.

Evidently Dr. Bucke had got wind of this matter some time before he had told Whitman about it, as his letter of August 20, 1880, to Charles W. Eldridge shows:

MY DEAR MR. ELDRIDGE

Some months ago a bookseller in Boston named W. B. Clarke (340 Washington Street) with whom I have some dealings wrote me that some 300 copies of the '60, '61 ed. of 'Leaves of Grass' (Thayer and Eldridge) had turned up amongst the old stock that used to belong to that firm; he said they could be had for $3.00 a copy. Subsequently in New York City, I found copies of same edition and bought one for $2.25. Some years ago I bought a copy of this ed. in London, England for 24 s ($6.) and had thought I was lucky to get it for that. There is something a little curious to me about this batch 'turning up,' and I do not feel altogether satisfied that some tricky individual has not got hold of the old plates and been striking off some copies on *spec'n*. I have been talking to Walt

about it, and he consentèd that I should write you and ask you whether
you knew for certain about these 300 copies, or whether it was possible
they could be in existence without your knowing anything about them....
  I am faithfully yours,

R. M. BUCKE

Eldridge has written on the above letter, 'Answered Aug. 24,
1880, C. W. E.' But I lack his reply to Bucke, and other letters to
supply the gaps. However, the note I made from Burroughs's
comments, in 1907, says:

Worthington stopped the publication, but whether he paid Walt anything, I can't tell. I think he paid him something. I had a few copies
which Walt gave me, which I used to cut up when I wanted extracts.
When Walt died there were many copies among his effects.

Burroughs used to speak of it as 'the pirated edition.'
  For those interested, the matter may be followed up in several
references to Worthington in Traubel's first volume of 'With Walt
Whitman in Camden' (pages 195, 196, 250, 251, 255, 256, 424).
Whitman is there quoted as saying, in 1888, that Worthington was
continuing to print editions and sell them. But by that time he had
evidently lost all desire to bring the sanctimonious, unscrupulous
Richard Worthington to terms, although his publisher, McKay,
and other friends, had strongly urged him to do so. Traubel says
that Whitman was sometimes indignant about it, and sometimes
only laughed it all away, saying that 'holy Dick' would 'have a
lot of *débris* to unload before he could enter the Kingdom.' He
was 'a sour mess' to Whitman, who was not inclined to have 'any
sort of encounter with him.'
  On February 1, 1881, Whitman wrote Burroughs as follows:

Yours rec'd and very opportunely — all today has been the dismalest
of this grim winter here, furious snow and wind howling, and I have not
stirred out — the roads and rivers here all block'd with snow and ice —
the last week my physical system block'd, too, with a chill and depression
— right in the middle of the smoothest sailing I have had for years — but
I feel that it will be a passing cloud (such indeed as comes to me every
two or three months) —
  Yes I am quite tickled and favorable to coming there and am about sure
I shall come, accepting your good invitation right out — Will write again
this week — I have one or two newspaper bits about the *Review* article [1]

  [1] Probably refers to 'The Poetry of the Future,' by him, in the *North American Review*,
February, 1881.

which I will send you; it has been extracted from considerable — the best thing is a letter from the *Review* editor, Allen Thorndike Rice, to me about a week after the piece appeared, one of the most eulogistic, solid accept-ances of my theories possible — he paid me $100 for the piece and supplied me with a hundred pamphlet copies of it. I have rec'd five or six letters from one and another, none of any acc't. I saw Marvin some weeks ago. Eldridge is in Boston, in U.S. office. Dr. Bucke is writing his book.

W. W.

After Carlyle's death (February, 1881), from his river home, on March 14, 1881, John Burroughs writes:

DEAR WALT: I send you a little remembrance — enough to pay your expenses up here when you get ready to come, which I hope will be before long. I have rec'd reminders from you, from time to time, in the shape of papers, etc., which I have been glad to get. I see about all that is in the 'Tribune' as I take the semi-weekly. The sketch of Carlyle in the London paper was the best I have seen. Your own words upon his death were very noble and touching.[1] It was a proper thing for you to do and it be-came you well. The more one reads and knows of Carlyle the more one loves and reverences him. He was worth all other Britons put together to me. What have we to do with his opinions? He was a towering and god-like man and that was enough. He is to be judged as a poet and prophet, and not as a molder of opinion. He was better and greater than any opinion he could have. His style too I would not have different. To me it was not the 'Mary-had-a-little-lamb' style of most of his critics, any more than your own prose style is, but grand and manly and full of thunder and lightning.

The robins are just here, and the ice on the river is moving this after-noon, bag and baggage. Ursula is still in N.Y., but is doing pretty well and hopes to be home soon. Julian and I have all sorts of ups and downs. I am correcting the proof of 'Pepacton' and writing an article for 'Scrib.' on Thoreau. I first wrote them a notice of his Journal just published, which they were pleased to say was too good for a book notice and that I must make a body article out of, etc. 'Scrib.' has displayed some re-markable journalistic enterprise lately. They have got from Emerson his article on Carlyle for their May No. This is *sub rosa* and is not for the public yet. I enclose you a slip of the article or lecture which you may have seen. I do not think his trip hammer with the æolian attachment figure conceived in the highest spirit. It is so preposterous and impossible that it spoils it for me, but it raps soundly upon the attention for a mo-ment, and I suppose that is enough for his purpose.

I hope your clouds lift as spring comes and that you are better. If you

---

[1] Whitman: 'The Dead Carlyle,' *The Critic*, February 12, 1881; also 'Death of Thomas Carlyle,' *Complete Prose Works* (Small, Maynard and Company, 1901), pp. 160–63.

see young Kennedy tell him I will write to him again by and by. I guess he is a good fellow, but he needs hetchelling to get the tow out of the flax. How do you like him? I shall want a set of your books by and by. Let me hear from you.

Whitman's brief comment on Carlyle in the following letter of March 29 to Burroughs should be taken with much else that he wrote about him, both in 'Specimen Days' and 'Democratic Vistas,' in order to reach an understanding of what he really thought of Carlyle.

DEAR FRIEND,

Yours rec'd with the good 10 — God bless you — I half-moped along, all through February, but am coming round, same as before. I go down three or four days at a time to my friends, the Staffords and get out in the woods a great deal.... It is only half an hour's journey. Should have come up there with you a month ago but was hardly able. I got a bad chill six weeks ago, struck in (was quite well up to that time)

Your letter *don't contain* the slip about the Emerson business you allude to — the just-published Carlyle Reminiscences, so well and strongly praised in the 'Herald,' the 'Critic,' and everywhere, don't confirm or add to my estimation of C — *much the contrary* —

Kennedy comes here quite often and is disposed to be friendly — I guess he is a pretty good man, but has *the fever called literature*, and I shouldn't wonder if he was in for it for life. Lathrop has visited me — very pleasant. Shall be glad to supply you with a set of books of course. I have plenty yet

WALT WHITMAN

[His poem, ' Patrolling Barnegat,' enclosed — proof from ' Harper's,' April, '81 — this last written in his hand above the poem.]

'William Sloane Kennedy wrote his " Reminiscences of Whitman "[1] some years later,' explained Burroughs. He added that George Parsons Lathrop was then assistant editor of 'The Atlantic.' Kennedy's latest book, 'The Fight of a Book for the World,'[2] published in his last years, shows that Whitman was right in thinking he was 'in it for life.'

The early letters that passed between Burroughs and William Sloane Kennedy concerning Whitman merit a place in this chronicle, but I have only a few excerpts from Burroughs's replies from

[1] Kennedy: *Reminiscences of Walt Whitman*, Alexander Gardner, Paisley, Scotland, and London, 1896.

[2] This book is published by the Stoneycroft Press, West Yarmouth, Massachusetts, 1926.

which to quote. Kennedy was attached to a Philadelphia literary weekly in 1880–81, when his friendship with Whitman began. Burroughs admonished him, February 20, 1881, to take a good look at Whitman, since he would not see his like again, and urged him to keep notes of conversations with him, even though Whitman talked less well than before his illness. Of Whitman's paper on the death of Carlyle, Burroughs wrote Kennedy: 'There is no other voice in America that could have sounded that strain.... Give my love to Walt, and tell him I wish for him daily and nightly.' I have not been able to find what critique of Kennedy's on Whitman is referred to in the following letter from him to Burroughs, of date, February 26, 1881:

I am glad to get your letter of criticism, and am not at all offended by it. I really hope that I shall hereafter accomplish so many good things that you and I shall perforce retain a mutual esteem in spite of the fact of our limitations and faults. It is hard for a lover to see faults in his mistress; it is not his business to do so. I do not wonder that [you] have not been able to detect them in Whitman. I see now, since I have known him, that the magnetism of his personal presence serves as a powerful enchantment to wholly en-net the hearts of his friends, and I also see that if I had known him before writing my really wholly unimportant critique I sh'd not have been able to view him so impartially. But, my good friend, are you not going further than W. himself goes in claiming for him almost perfection? Twenty times he admits his great faults, sins, limitations, crudeness, tentative character....

I admit cheerfully *my* faults. I confess to the pertness, tendency to priggishness in my essay; it is one of those cursed imperfections we inherit. I am doing my best to root it out of my nature. I regret it as much as anyone, and regard it as a vice of the blood, and as 'unmanly' (to use your phrase as applied to my criticism of W's animality) as I regard your killing of birds as unmanly, and unnecessary.... My essay has value in this that it is the opinion of an intense admirer of W, viewing him in the cold light of intellect as a thinker and poet purely, and not as a man. *As a man and friend I think W as near perfect as it is possible to be.* I think him the equal, and in many respects the superior of the much misunderstood Jesus, and I have said so in a note to my revised article. I have erased all those 'beastlies' from the article, and have added a good many notes in an appendix. I fully feel the audacity in a young man like myself criticizing at all such a God as W. It was only desperate financial straits that induced me to write my critique so soon. I am only thirty and have had a good many hindrances to the development of my nature.... I shall always be fearless in proclaiming what I have matured as truth. I hope to grow out of my limitations.... These gymnastics that we take in analyzing great men's thoughts are good for us. You must not refuse to be good humored at analysis of your favorites when you launch out yourself at Emerson so boldly. I know 'worshippers' of Emerson who are deeply offended by your criticism of him. I was not. I consider it the most subtle estimate of him that has been made, y'r finest essay, one that puts you in the front rank of essay writers of any age.... You are as keen-scented as a sleuth-hound in tracking Emerson, but you can't see Whitman's limitations. I don't ask you to pardon this freedom of expression, because I mean to be as impartial, critical, and kindly-implacable towards you as you are towards others.... Whitman, *e.g.* is stern and hard in his strictures on his brother poets, the d[ii] *minores* of song. Damn a white liver who is afraid to give and take hearty sword strokes, I say. As to our noble master's few, very few, limitations (I hate to dwell on them), I say that coarseness is not manliness. No one else could have done his pioneer work. He is one of the prophets and saviors of the world. But he is no more perfect than was Jesus. What Jesus gained in the spirituelle violet quality of nature he lost in breadth and rich universality of nature. What W. gains in breadth and rich univ'ty of nat. he loses in the delicate quality, though he has a deep infusion of that in his nature, too. But this is distasteful business to me, this carping, but it is a duty. I conceive that W's treatment of the body will do much good, clear the air, etc.; but that it w'd have done 40 times as much good if it had been less realistic. The work needed to be done, but we may have to try a good many times before we learn how to do it. On the whole I think it is better that he spoke; anything was preferable to the contemptible prudery and lascivious prurient dandyism of the hot-house school of dabblers in that weak sentiment and comical rhyme-jingling which has hitherto passed under the name of poetry. The more I read W, the more unendurable become the minor poets. When Nature palls upon the taste, then will his writings, and not before. They are like invisible writings: as you warm them by sympathy and new power of your own, continually new thoughts start out of the pages. *E.g.* I never saw the *full* depth of beauty in those magnificent lines you quote (about music). But you mistook my meaning. I surely tried to make it clear that I only compared Cranch's lines to W's to illustrate the superior musical quality in Cranch. In *essence*, of course, W's lines are as great poetry as C's. And, in fact, in the first letter I wrote to W, I expressed the opinion that Cranch had stolen the idea of his Overture from this very passage of W's, and another very much like it in 'Proud Music of the Storm.'

Cranch told me that he had read W., but did not like him! I fully agree with you that Cranch is a small man, a mere mouse, compared with W. W. has in him the stuff of a thousand Cranches. Oh, that W. had more leisure and wealth! This is a cursed world that does more honor to quacks than Gods. In ancient Greece, W. w'd have rec'd ovations and pensions from the state.

You say W. speaks not as a conventional man, but as the eternal abysmic man, in his Adamitic poems. I say that if he is anything he is by avowal and unquestionably a lover of men and a writer for the great body of men, and not an esoteric philosopher or physiological writer. And he does not reach his own ideal if he fails to be popular.

Now he has written a few things that are anachronistic; things that it is enough to refute you to say that you w'd not write yourself. These few lines, like the fly in the ointment, diffuse a bad odor over all the rest. I abide by my first impressions. I welcome with acclamation the grand and healthful praise of fatherhood and motherhood, athletic offspring, etc., That is superb, just what we need, manly. But I do object to [realistic lines quoted] as indelicate.... In these things W. is animalistic and not poetical. These few blemishes he ought to remove — these twenty or thirty lines. As long as we are social beings, and male and female, we shall need to be careful of our language; at any rate, in this age. You noticed that I am careful to state in my article that *for this age* W. has made a mistake. Of course there is no essential impurity in the bodily functions, viewed from a universal stand-point. But we are not cosmoses, only little fractions of one. But even the cosmos does not fail to discriminate. It is an amelioration, a steady selection and refinement. We are passing (as humanity) from the lower naïve to the higher. I conceive that the time will come when the relation of the sexes will be different from what it is now. Marriage will not be done away with. That is (I think) the most necessary and noble of institutions. But I can conceive of a time when the laws of conception shall be so well-known that there will be no immorality (because no danger of conception) in the cohabitation of unmarried persons under certain conditions and limitations and decencies. There is, of course, no more essential harm in the act (if conception is avoided) than there is in eating a peach. Society is, however, too crude and superstitious now to make it safe to teach openly such doctrines. As things go we have to take every precaution (at the risk of our health even) to be chaste. And it is just because of this condition of things that I maintain that such descriptions as one or two or three passages in *Enfans d'Adam* are anachronistic, and calculated to do harm to the great mass of men and children who have but weak wills, slight control of their passions. We must proceed slowly in these things as Nature does in her work. Furthermore, certainly as long as we are limited human beings, that do not take as much pleasure in ordure as we do in bread and flowers, any realistic descriptions of the odor and color, etc. of the excrements and secretions of the body will not be considered by us as even agreeable, much less as poetry. We may sometime be able to talk freely and refinedly about the sexual act with women, but we shall never talk grossly about gross things.   ·

But granting that even as society is now constituted, Whitman's Adamitic descriptions will do but little harm to young people, I still, for all the reasons I have given, object to them on artistic grounds, even on universal and abysmic grounds. Stedman's remarks on Nature's processes are just the truth. I admit the superiority of Stedman's article in modesty and delicacy of expression. I have done so before to all my friends.... As to W's prose style, you mistake me if you think I do not admire it hugely. I call it, however (as seen in Demo. Vistas) exasperating.... It is hard reading, but I like it. I like with all my soul anything I have to wrestle with. His prose is splendid, but tough.... As a lover of W. I c'd wish that he w'd consent to drop those few realistic descriptions I have mentioned. I yearn for it. I wish he c'd read this letter. He knows how much I love him. He knows that my poor little-great heart beats nobly and high when I think of him. Why will he not remove these few blemishes.

But — cordially yours

W. S. KENNEDY

I met W. strolling along the sunny side of Market St. recently. I gave him y'r message. He looked a bit discouraged, poor man! I fear this winter, so severe, and the excitements of it, have not been good for him. He tries to be cheerful, though said the reason he had not come up to see you was because of his depressed mood. He tho't it better to stay in his room till it was over. He expects these moods regularly, he says. Still he is cheery and hearty.

Of course he is too grand to mind my little mosquito bites; even if he has read my critique, which I doubt. I have suffered more over it than he ever will, if he ever thinks of it. He told me, since it appeared, that he is thick-skinned. I suspect or fear he has read it. But he likes me just as well....

One would like much to see Burroughs's rejoinder to this letter of Kennedy's. On November 18, 1881, Kennedy wrote Burroughs briefly from Cambridge, Massachusetts, where he was lecturing and working for the publishers. His mouth watered, he said, for such an article on Thoreau as he knew Burroughs could write, and tells of his longing to see him. Mentioning a recent article of his own, he said that he had stated therein that Whitman and Burroughs alone of the American *literati* give forth to his ear a perfectly healthy and cheery tone. He added exultantly, 'I too have at last reached perfect and glad at-one-ment with the universe.... I think that the universe hinges on joy, and that the test of the right of a thing to live is its power to give joy.'

Mr. Clifton J. Furness furnishes me with the following information concerning Whitman's lecture on Lincoln in Boston — his third (or fourth?) delivery of the lecture:

G. P. Lathrop secured an engagement for Whitman to give his Lincoln lecture at the Hawthorne Rooms in Boston, April 15, 1881. In a letter he wrote from Concord, Mass., April 11, 1881, he says: 'O'Reilly has arranged matters at the Revere House and you are to be a guest there during your stay.... Mrs. John T. Sargent (at whose house the Radical or Chestnut Street Club meets) has, I learn, issued cards for an informal reception to you on Friday at 3 pm. This you would best go to unless it will annoy you or in any way interfere with your comfort in lecturing that evening. And bear in mind that we expect you around at the St Botolph [Club] after the lecture, and nothing must be done which will tire you too much for that. We have sold a fine lot of tickets.' *The Boston Evening Traveler*, April 16, 1881, has a long eulogistic account of the lecture, stating: 'In the audience before him were many eminent in art and letters, who had come to pay homage to one who is already fast being regarded as the typical citizen of the Republic. There was something of poetic justice, too, in thinking of the reception of this man who had been scorned as a barbarian rhymester, whose burning lines, surcharged with the future, had long fallen unheeded upon the indifferent ears of his countrymen, and whose very presence was now felt almost as a benediction.' The *Boston Herald*, April 18, 1881, commenting upon Whitman's visit, gives further details: 'Many of the leading *literati* were at his lecture, and among them Mr. Howells was most cordial in his greeting. On Friday afternoon Mr. Whitman called on Mr. Longfellow, and Saturday morning he breakfasted with Mr. James T. Fields, where Mrs. Celia Thaxter was also a guest.' The *Boston Evening Transcript*, April 18, 1881, published a sonnet to Walt Whitman by Linn B. Porter, and the Boston *Index* published a sonnet to him by Walter R. Thomas, December 20, 1883. Surely Boston is exonerated from the charge of ignoring Whitman during his lifetime. —

From Camden, on June 17, Whitman writes Burroughs:

... I have just concluded a contract with J. R. Osgood and Co of Boston for the publishing of my poems complete in one volume, under the title of 'Walt Whitman's Poems' (the old name of 'Leaves of Grass' running through the same as ever) — to be either a $2. book or a $2.50 one — if the former, I to have 25 cts royalty, if the latter, 30 cts) The proposition for publication came from them. The bulk of the pieces will be the same as hitherto — only I shall secure now the consecutiveness and *ensemble* I am always thinking of — Book will probably be out before winter.

Nothing very new otherwise — you must have kept posted about my Boston jaunt, for I sent you papers — it was altogether a curious success — not so much in quantity as quality —

Last January, I think it was, I took a bad chill — bothered me for over two months, lingering along — but I believe the Boston jaunt drove the last of it away....

My forthcoming summer movements are not exactly decided — probably go on to Boston for two or three weeks, as I like to keep a sharp eye on my proofs and typography — then I must go a month in Canada — I will keep you posted, and will try to pay you a visit, too....

Burroughs explained:

This was, of course, before the row with Osgood. Walt and Dr. Bucke made the trip up the Saguenay. They urged me to go with them. I have often regretted it — guess I was too poor to go. Oh, to have been with Walt in Canada!

Writing from Concord, Massachusetts, September 19, 1881, Whitman says:

DEAR JOHN,
I keep on fairly in health and strength — have been out here a few days the guest of Mr. and Mrs. Sanborn, and everything most affectionate and hospitable from them both — and from others — Have had a curiously full and satisfactory time with Emerson — he came to see me Saturday evening early, Mrs. E also, and staid two hours — Yesterday I went there (by pressing invitation) to dinner, and staid two hours — a wonderfully good two hours — the whole family were very cordial, including Mrs. E and the son, Edward, a doctor, a fine, handsome, 'cute, glowing young man, with a beautiful wife and child. I took to them all. I cannot tell you how sweet and good (and all as it should be) Emerson look'd and behaved — he did not talk in the way of joining in any animated conversation, but pleasantly and hesitatingly, and sparsely — fully enough — To me it seemed just as it should be.
The book is about through — will appear last of October — everything satisfactory. I go from here in about a week to Johnston's, Cor. Mott Ave. and 149th Street, N.Y. — then to Camden. Shall go to Canada this winter.
                                        WALT WHITMAN

And from Boston, on the twenty-fourth of the same month, he gives a further glimpse of Emerson:

... I am now back here finishing up, only staid a few days in Concord, but they were marked days.... For my part I thought the old man in his smiling and alert quietude and withdrawnness (he has a good color in his face and ate just as much dinner as anybody) more eloquent, grand, appropriate and impressive than ever, more indeed than could be described. Isn't it comforting that I have had, in the sunset, as it were, so many significant, affectionate hours with him, under such quiet, beautiful, appropriate circumstances?...

Besides this general death-gloom of the nation,[1] have you heard of the sudden and dreadful death of our young friend, Beatrice Gilchrist, in performing some chemical experiment with ether?

Joaquin Miller is here, is with me every day. Longfellow has been to see me. I have met O. W. Holmes, and old Mr. James.

With love
WALT WHITMAN

The James to whom he referred, Burroughs explained, was Henry James, Senior, father of the novelist. 'He wrote a splendid, slashing article on Carlyle after his death, for the " Atlantic " — rather unfair to Carlyle, but very picturesque.'

During 1881 and 1882 a voluminous correspondence, relating chiefly to Whitman and to Bucke's forthcoming book about him, passed between Dr. Bucke and O'Connor. O'Connor contributed his 'Good Gray Poet,' and some supplementary matter. On December 11, he writes Bucke in part as follows:

Did you see the atrocious notice of Walt's book in the 'New York Tribune' of November 12, I think? [November 11]... I shall leave my mark upon this obscene reviewer — concise as one blow of the knout, brief as a brand, if I can make it so. The miserable cur! What surprises me is the 'Tribune,' so friendly to us lately, printing this effervescence of the cesspool.

O'Connor had demurred against the inclusion of his 'Good Gray' in Dr. Bucke's book, but finally yielded to the Doctor's insistence, writing, when consenting (December 13), that he would have liked to strike out some parts, such as the last two pages, but thought it would be unfair to the reviewers who, sixteen years previously, had selected just those pages for flagellation. 'So I let them stand,' he wrote, 'with all their flamboyant declamation.'[2] Aware as he then was of 'the volcanic crudity' of passages in his early pamphlet, he commands respect for his fairness in refraining from obliterating some of its early faults. He was, however, just to himself in saying that, under the circumstances, those faults could not have been avoided at the time. They were needed then. In fact, as early as 1868, in a letter to Freiligrath, now in the Perry Whitman Collec-

---

[1] This refers to the death of President Garfield.

[2] From typed copies of the Bucke-O'Connor correspondence, given me by Charles N. Elliot, from his Whitman Collection.

tion, O'Connor wrote that he had written the last two pages of his pamphlet deliberately 'for effect' — had thrown in his pamphlet 'as one throws in a bomb.' The revisions which he made in 1882, but did not use, are in his hand in a copy of the pamphlet now owned by Professor Perry.

XIII

THE SUPPRESSION OF 'LEAVES OF GRASS'

(1882)

Shut not your doors to me, proud libraries,
For that which was lacking on all your well-fill'd shelves, yet needed most, I bring.

. . . .

The words of my book nothing, the drift of it everything....

WHITMAN

A STRANGE coincidence concerning 'Leaves of Grass'! In the month which marked the passing of the Sage of Concord, who, in 1855, had hailed its advent as 'the most extraordinary piece of wit and wisdom that America has yet contributed,' there came out of Boston the edict which threatened for a time the very existence of the book which had buffeted the waves of prejudice and opposition for twenty-seven years, and which had at last seemed successfully launched on friendly seas with favoring winds. To John Burroughs, on April 28, 1882, Whitman makes the two significant announcements contained in the following paragraph from his letter, both of which filled Burroughs with dismay:

So Emerson is dead — the leading man in all Israel. If I feel able I shall go to his funeral — improbable though. A new deal in the fortunes of 'Leaves of Grass' — the District Attorney at Boston has threatened Osgood with indictment 'under the statutes against obscene literature, — specifies a long list of pieces, lines, &c — Osgood is frightened, asks me to change and expurgate — I refuse peremptorily — *he throws up the book and will not publish it any more* — wants me to take the plates, wh. I shall try to do and publish it as before (in some respects shall like it just as well). Can you help me? Can you loan me $100?

Whitman continues with other topics:

The next 'N. A. Review' (June number)[1] will have a piece, 'A Memorandum at a Venture,' signed by my name, in which I ventilate my theory of sexual matter, treatment and allusion in *Children of Adam* — I shall have some slips and will send you some to England.

— Am writing this in great haste, angry with myself for not having

---

[1] *North American Review* (June, 1882), vol. 134, pp. 546–50.

responded before to your good letter of April 10. Love to 'Sula and the kid.

Walt did not go to the funeral [1] [said Burroughs]. Myron Benton and I talked of going, but Myron hung back, and I didn't go. I wrote something about Emerson — 'Emerson's Burial Day' — which appeared in the 'Critic.' I was getting ready to go abroad, and I hadn't very much money, so had to be economical.

Yes, I lent Walt the $100. I think he got the plates and published the book himself.[2] William O'Connor wrote some particularly vicious attacks in the 'N.Y. Tribune,'[3] incidentally giving Osgood a slash, but directed especially against the District Attorney and Anthony Comstock, who was back of it, I think.[4] William was always eloquent and stimulating. If Walt was ever inclined to weaken, O'Connor would rush to the rescue and brace him up. A young Englishman,[5] Binns, told me he had seen a letter in which Walt weakened a little, on that or some other occasion, and was willing to strike out a few lines.

The instant O'Connor heard of this attempt to suppress Whitman's book, from the Life Saving Service in Washington, on April 28, he wrote Burroughs:

DEAR JOHN:

I have just been thunderstruck by a letter from Bucke telling me that Osgood, under a threat from the District Attorney from Boston, Sanger,[6] has stopped the publication of Walt's book. I don't let the grass grow under my feet when an outrage of that kind is committed — one which makes Harlan's insignificant — and I am going to make the District Attorney regret that he was ever born, if I can compass it. As soon as I read Bucke's letter I flew down stairs with 'Leaves of Grass' to the Solicitor of the Treasury, Kenneth Raynor, and for two hours to him and Robinson (the Assistant Solicitor) and Barton (the Law Clerk) I gave the District Attorney *unlimited volcano*. They all agree with me, especially after hearing me read and expound the accused poem,[7] that it is the great-

[1] Whitman's brief tribute, called 'By Emerson's Grave' (see *Complete Prose Works*, Small, Maynard and Company, pp. 189–90), is no more proof that he attended Emerson's funeral than is his account of Lincoln's assassination proof that he witnessed it. Nor did he so intend to imply. He could always place himself bodily, as it were, wherever he was 'roaming in spirit.'

[2] He published it as the author's edition. Fifty copies only were published, says Mr. Goldsmith.

[3] The dates of O'Connor's *Tribune* letters were May 25, June 18, and August 27, 1882

[4] Kennedy, in *The Fight of a Book for the World*, p. 248, says that the Reverend Frederick Baylies Allen admitted to him that he instigated the movement.

[5] H. R. Binns: *Life of Walt Whitman* (1905), pp. 284–85.

[6] As appeared later, it was not United States District Attorney Sanger, but Oliver Stevens, the District Attorney for Suffolk County, Massachusetts, that made the threat

[7] 'To a Common Prostitute.' I have often felt that this poem was unfortunately

est outrage of the century. I am next going straight to Brewster, the Attorney General, who of course controls the District Attorneys, and will see if I can't get him to crush Sanger and annul his action. I have only been stopped by Brewster's absence at Newport. He returns on Monday, and then I will see him, taking, if possible, Bob Ingersoll along with me — Ingersoll being a warm admirer of Walt's book. If we don't raise the biggest row Sanger ever dreamed of, I'm mistaken. He doesn't know the kind of man on his track when I start after him.

Now, pending the arrival of Monday and Brewster's return, I want to know all the facts. Tell me *everything* you know, and speedily. To be posted is to be armed.

Of course if we annul the District Attorney's action by a fulmen from headquarters, perhaps we can next shore up that cowardly fool, Osgood, and get him to go on with the publication. The infernal idiot should have defied the District Attorney, published his official warning as an advertisement, stood a suit, defended it with Evarts or Charles O'Connor, won it, and sold a million copies of Walt's book on the strength of it. The jackass!

... I am trembling with fury, and with the fervor of my oration down stairs in the Department of Justice.

After a few words more and his signature come these words from O'Connor: 'Emerson gone! The world grows darker.'

It will have been seen in a preceding chapter that it was at this time that the estrangement between Whitman and O'Connor was forever wiped out.

On May 1, Burroughs wrote of the affair to Gilder:

Whitman writes me that the District Attorney of Boston has threatened to prosecute Osgood and Co. for publishing obscene literature in 'Leaves of Grass,' and Osgood has dropped the book. So far as this is the wish of the city of Boston, I pray for the wrath of Sodom and Gomorrah to descend upon her. We shall try to head off the miserable idiot of a District Atty by reaching the Atty General in Washington.

To Whitman's initial letter on the Osgood matter, Burroughs also replied on May 1:

With your letter came one from O'Connor bursting with wrath. No doubt he will be a host there in W[ashington], and will reach that miserable Dis't Att'y yet. 'Tis a pity Osgood has not got some pluck and so make a fight. No doubt we could beat them to tatters and make a big strike for

named. Rossetti's 'Jenny,' overflowing with a like charity, though far more criticizable from the Pharisee's point of view, met no such ignominious fate. Whitman's poem has been willfully misread. 'It is nothing but the beautiful little idyl of the New Testament — about the woman taken in adultery,' Whitman himself said of it.

the book. Write and ask him if he will fight, if he is well backed up. It is the last thing I ever dreamed of. If this is the wish of Boston, then I pray for her purification by a fire ten times bigger than the fire of a few years ago.

I enclose my check for the amount you ask for, $100.

What a blank there in New England! To me Emerson filled nearly the whole horizon in that direction. But I suppose it is better so, though the very sunlight seems darkened....

If our passage was not paid to England, I should not go. I am ashamed to go off at such a time. I have had no heart for the trip from the first, and now the death of Emerson (how those few words penetrate me!) and your troubles, make me want to stay at home more than ever.

If you have Mrs. Gilchrist's address, send it to me; also that of Mr. Carpenter....

O'Connor's rage over this affair knew no bounds. On April 29 he let himself out to Dr. Bucke even more freely than he had to Burroughs:

To think that after twenty years — after the continental fame, after the tributes from Emerson and Ruskin, from Concord and London — to think that this satyr of the law should dare to let the Brocken shadow of his buboed and chancred carnality project upon these sane hallowed pages; that he should dare to protrude his dirty interpretation upon that book, and that he should dare to begin persecution! But he will rue the day. Wait!

Now is the time your book ought to be out, with this thing in it.

Osgood and Company, who were to have published Dr. Bucke's book on Whitman, declined doing so after giving up the publication of the 'Leaves.' In March of that same year, O'Connor had already been much exercised in Whitman's behalf, and had written Dr. Bucke of an infamous article about Whitman that had appeared in the New York 'Nation,' December 15. The vilest thing about it, he said, was concerning Whitman's hospital services. He wished he knew the name of the indescribable scoundrel who wrote it, and added astutely, 'The worst thing about such publications is that they poison the public mind with prejudices.' A remark which may well apply to much that has been written about Whitman in recent years, even by some who pose as admirers, but who fall into the category of those of whom Whitman said, 'I charge you forever reject those who would expound me.'

Conversing with Traubel, in 1888, about these foregoing letters from O'Connor and Burroughs, Whitman is reported as saying of O'Connor:[1]

... When aroused — when there was occasion for it — he... was a human avalanche; nothing could defy him, stand up before him — nothing. Stedman said to me once: 'O'Connor is the finest fighter of us all, with the noblest sense of right and justice.'... John Hay... said: 'You are lucky, Whitman, in the adhesion of a man like O'Connor; he is a giant influence; he is the sort of man who lasts out the battle.'... William... had the arm to sling an axe and the soul to sling it justly... you notice how even John was mad and said so beautifully; but how tame John's anger (which was not tame) seems when coming up against the intenser vehemence of William!... John had his own way of getting mad; a sort of Quaker anger; whereas William storms and blows and rains and snows and freezes and roasts you all at once; goes for you tooth and nail, hammer and tongs — leaves nothing of you for the dogs — not a bone.

Further word from O'Connor shows how he was rallying to the fray. Witness this of May 3 to Burroughs:

I just have yours of the first instant and reply at once so that you may hear from me before you sail.

I hope you will have a good time abroad, although I can understand readily why you should not much want to go at present. If you will give me your foreign address, I will see that you are advised of the progress of the war I mean to make to the death upon this scoundrel lawyer. I wonder whether Stedman has yet made up his mind whether Walt is persecuted. Mark now whether any member of our *literati* takes up this infamous outrage — this revival of sixteenth century methods — the rehabilitation of Montfaucon and the Place de Grève — this suppression of a grand and honest book by an improvised and illegal censorship, the tool of private spite, and bigotry, and club-house lust, anxious about its figleaves.

As yet I have nothing to report. Brewster has been away and Ingersoll (who was, I see, at Emerson's funeral, and who I am anxious to take with me, to assist success) returns this evening. Tomorrow, therefore, will probably be the field-day. I am all ready to talk to Brewster, and if I don't move him, it will be because he is not made of penetrable stuff. I have never been so roused by anything as this. Harlan's action was a trifle — a mere bagatelle — in comparison. When I think of it — when I think of its significance and consequences — my blood seems to turn to lightning, and I feel my brain flashing.

What complicates the matter is the damnable stupidity and cowardice of Osgood. *Under the law*, the District Attorney has no right to threaten

[1] Traubel: *With Walt Whitman in Camden*, vol. 3, pp. 352–53.

prosecution unless the book *was sent through the mails.*[1] He couldn't threaten 'Fanny Hill,' or 'The Lustful Turk,' under the law, *unless mailed.* Osgood could, therefore, have sold all he pleased, sent by express, never troubled the Post Office, and told the District Attorney to go to hell. This, even if the book was obscene, which is a position utterly untenable and ridiculous. The District Attorney, therefore, exceeded his authority under the United States statute, as I hope I can make plain even to his comprehension.

We shall see. I wait for tomorrow. If I fail with Brewster, the only thing is war through the press, which all we fellows, at home and abroad, must make, without mercy, upon Sanger. May Jesus help me to a hammer and nails that I may crucify this new savior of society between that thief Harlan and that thief Osgood! These miserable peddlars called publishers, creatures without hearts, without honor, without even sense, rouse my gorge. It is to the lasting honor of Napoleon that he hanged one of them. To think of Osgood cowering under such a fool threat as Sanger's! I wish I could find out who is at the bottom of the matter.

Now is the time Bucke's book ought to be out. I wrote a long article for it — dreadfully hurried, I was so busy, and he drove me so, but he thinks it good — intended as a preface to his republication of my old pamphlet in the appendix.

In any case, whether we get anything from the Attorney General or not, we must make war upon Sanger, and I want you to inspire everyone you meet abroad on this point — Swinburne, Rossetti, everybody. No matter how wrongly or foolishly or weakly anyone may write in reprehension of this action. *All we want is moral matter in motion.* That is the condition of success for Walt's book — for any man's book. We have nothing to fear but apathy.

No use to attempt to brace up Osgood unless we can give him assurance that prosecution will not be countenanced at headquarters. This we must get if possible, both to endeavor to persuade Osgood to go on, and to flax Sanger with afterwards — for in no case must he be allowed to go scot free. The one only duty of every thinking man is to make this scoundrel attorney stink in the nostrils of the generations.

As for Walt's publishing his own book in the face of this menace, it will be simply ruin. He will be crushed, and easily, unless we can take down this sword of Damocles.

Yes, Emerson's death darkens. I felt as if Monadnock had sunk from the old horizon. There never was another place like Concord, and now it melts away.

It lends a pang to this outrage to remember Emerson's estimate of the book — his *unretracted* estimate — whatever they may say, *unretracted.*

In what I wrote for Bucke I made a scoring point of this, which no one

[1] This was written under the erroneous impression that the United States District Attorney was concerned.

can ever answer. To think that in the very hour of his death, the book he so glorified should be proscribed! This thought will do to conjure with, and I hope I can get a chance to use it.

I must retain the letter you send me as it may help my pleading, but I will return it to you in England, if you will send me your address abroad.

I wish I had another copy of your 'Walt Whitman as Poet and Person,' and if there were time I would get you to send me one, but perhaps can find one myself.

This is an abominable answer to your letter, hurried, peevish, dispersed, but I am thoroughly upset by this occurrence, and shall not regain composure until I am in Brewster's presence.

Good bye. A good voyage and a good time!

I could almost wish you were not going, but you can greatly help Walt's book abroad, and fire the British heart on this new infamy.

To Burroughs in England, O'Connor sends, on June 4, the following account of the progress in Whitman's affairs:

I got your letter of the 16th ultimo, and at once mailed to you, to Henderson Brothers, a 'Tribune' of May 25th, containing my opening. I hope you will get the paper, for I want you to be posted, and to fire up the *literati* abroad. My 'Tribune' letter contains the case.

Its success has been immense. The enemy so far has not opened mouth, and the press generally has warmly taken up for me, and given Oliver Stevens and Osgood the very devil. I write you a few lines in a great hurry, being quite overwhelmed by the letters of congratulation and sympathy which have poured in upon me, and many of which I feel I must answer.

You will see how the case really is: Bucke misled me, and I supposed it was the U.S. District Attorney, when, in fact, it was the State (Mass.) District Attorney, Oliver Stevens. Behind him (but I haven't got this on evidence, so couldn't use it) was the State Attorney General, Marston, who, so Ben Ticknor told Walt, instructed Stevens — peremptorily instructed him — to threaten, and indict if the book was not suppressed!

Consequently I give Oliver Stevens the first application. If he stands such a blistering without incriminating Marston, it will be funny; and the moment, he or any one else, brings Marston forward, then Vesuvius will be in full eruption, and Marston will catch all the hell I can give him, which will be less than he deserves. I want to smoke out those behind him — the buboed and chancred old saints who have instigated this raid — the rotten hypocrites who hunt 'Leaves of Grass' because they dote on 'Fanny Hill.' It is they, not these miserable dogs of elected attorneys, who are my true quarry. I'll teach them what it costs to oppress and prosecute genius.

I hope you will be in a position to see some of the boys abroad and set them afire in the matter of this damnable outrage. Do all you can. Moral matter in motion is all we need.

The 'Tribune' of Sunday, May 28th, had a rejoinder to me from the Rev. John W. Chadwick, bringing out Walt's reminiscence of his talk with Emerson in 1860 in contradiction of my construction of Emerson's letter, and *formally calling me a liar*. His effort is, of course, to break the force of my use of the Emerson letter of 1855. I have just (yesterday) sent an answer to the 'Tribune,' which I think you will pronounce simply *blasting*. Chadwick will wish he had never been born. It is quite composed in tone, notwithstanding the personal insult dealt by this clerical blackguard — but it cost me severe labor, and I am greatly mistaken if it will not prove fire in the marrow of his bones, and cover him with dismay and confusion. I am thoroughly roused on this matter, and feel that the time has come to defend Walt at every hazard, and to the last extremity. Woe, therefore, to any Chadwick who attempts to shield these dogs of Rhadamanthus, directly or indirectly.[1]

[1] June 18, 1882, the *New York Tribune* published a reply to Chadwick's attempt to prove that Emerson had recanted his 1855 approval of *Leaves of Grass*. The letter was signed by O'Connor, but a part of it was contributed by Whitman himself to O'Connor, who embodied Whitman's material in his own letter. The original manuscript of Whitman's draft is now in the collection of Mr. Bliss Perry, together with the following letter which Whitman sent with it to O'Connor:

'Camden, Sunday, May 28, 1882.

'Dear William O'Connor: I like the big letter of May 25 the more I read it. I think it will never die. I am glad the Rev. Mr. Chadwick appears with his *Tribune* letter to you today (as enclosed), for the fine chance it affords to ventilate the real account and true inwardness of that Emerson talk on the Common in 1860. And I at once send you the best synopsis of it I can recall — quite certainly the same in amount as I told you while it was fresh in my memory — to which, with hasty scribblings on my relations with Emerson — I hope (working it in as from yourself) you will incorporate in your answer to *Tribune*.'

The defense, as finally published in the *Tribune*, follows substantially the elaborate scheme outlined by Whitman to O'Connor in his letter of May 28, supplemented by another letter May 30, in which Whitman submits still further manuscripts to O'Connor with the admonition: 'Seems to me would be good to bring in quite verbatim — it is certainly true.' O'Connor did not use all of Whitman's contributory matter in his *Tribune* letter, however, but elaborated his diatribe *suo genere*. Whitman succinctly summed up his relations with Emerson as follows: 'Emerson had much more of a personal friendship for W. W. than has been generally known; making a determined visit to Brooklyn in 1857, soon after the appearance of *Leaves of Grass*, twenty-five years ago, walking out to the little cottage in the suburbs, several miles from the ferry, where W. W. then lived. From that time regularly for years afterwards whenever he came to New York he appointed a meeting, and they two generally dined together and spent some hours. When Mr. Whitman was in Boston in 1860 Emerson was his frequent and cordial visitor. As time elapsed, though officious persons intervened, and there was a lull of some years, I doubt if it could be said that Mr. Ralph Waldo Emerson's love and affection (and few knew how deeply he could love!) ever went out more warmly to anyone and remained more fixed under the circumstances than toward Walt Whitman.' The remainder of Whitman's unpublished manuscripts concerning Emerson will appear in a forthcoming series of articles on Whitman and the New England Poets, in the *New England Quarterly*.

C. J. F.

Burroughs wrote Whitman, on June 16, from London:

DEAR WALT:

I have delayed writing to you longer than I intended to. We had a pleasant passage over, and have been as happy as sight-seers can expect to be. We keep pretty well and take things easy. My first taste of the country was at Alloway, Burns' birthplace. We spent a week here in a cosey little inn on the banks of the Doon, surrounded by one of the sweetest and finest farming countries I ever beheld. From there we went up into the Highlands, where I did some mountain climbing; thence around to Edinburgh. From there we went down to Carlyle's country and spent a week at Ecclefechan, arriving there the first day of June just as the first red clover was beginning to bloom. I walked a great deal about Ecclefechan and shall write something about it and weave in certain things I want to say of Carlyle. I enclose a daisy and a spray of speedwell that I gathered from Carlyle's grave. There is no stone yet marking his grave. I saw the graves of eight 'Thomas Carlyles.'

The 'Carls,' as the Scotch call them, were a numerous race in this section. They were a stern savage set, not to be trifled with. One old Scotchman said they were 'bullies.' Then we went down into the Lake region for a few days, and thence to London.

Mr. [Edward] Carpenter has been up and spent a day and a night with me. He has recently lost his father. He is well. We have been out to Mrs. Gilchrist's twice to tea. She and Grace are alone, Herbert being off in Wales, painting. They chided me for not bringing you, and entertain hopes of seeing you yet. They are well and have a pleasant cheery home. You would have a good time if you were to come. I have seen no one else in London and do not expect to. Rossetti, I hear, is not well. We shall leave here tomorrow, or I shall, for Haslemere, and thence through some of the southern counties for a week; wife and Julian will stay with an old acquaintance of ours at Brentford, near London. I presume we shall be home in August. June has been cold and wet here; no heat, no warmth.

Conway has an article on Emerson in the June 'Fortnightly Review,' but it is hasty and of not much account. I hope to hear yet that Osgood has not thrown up 'Leaves of Grass.' I expect a letter from O'Connor every day. Drop me a line....

> Ever your friend
> JOHN BURROUGHS

Of this letter Whitman told Traubel: 'It gives a little look into the Carlyle country — yes, and a big look into John's soul.' Then his oft-recurring contrast of Burroughs and O'Connor: 'John and William are very different men. John is a placid landscape — William is a landscape in a storm.... The only critical doubt I ever have about John is that sometimes I feel as if I would like to poke him up with a stick or something to get him mad; his writing sometimes seems to go to sleep. It is always attractive to me, but always leaves me in a slow mood. William is quite different; he whips me with cords — he makes all my flesh tingle — he is like a soldier who stirs me for war.' A little later he himself voices what the reader often feels on seeing his comparisons of these two friends — 'William and John stand for such unlike temperaments, they can hardly be talked of together.'

O'Connor's further account of the fight for the 'Leaves' goes to Burroughs, still overseas, on July 12:

MY DEAR JOHN,

I have just received yours of the 30th ultimo.... It is too bad the papers miscarried; however, I enclose Chadwick's letter and my answer,[1] which has had the desired effect of shutting Chadwick up for good.

I think the truth about Emerson is simply that he was frightfully bull-dozed by the *literati* and clergy and that he tubbed the whale by a few flings, etc., but that *privately* he was true to his first convictions, and never really qualified or retracted his utterances of '55. Prof. Loomis, the astronomer, a distinguished man, recently told me that he was at Concord just after the publication of that letter, and talked with Emerson about 'Leaves of Grass.' He says Emerson's tone utterly precludes the possibility of his having had any reservations about the book. He spoke of it with great enthusiasm, descanting chiefly upon its utter newness. He said it was an absolutely new manifestation in literature and history — a fresh revelation, etc. Thoreau, and the other Concordians, all held the same tone. Then, too, the last time Lord Houghton was in this country he came to see Walt at Camden, after a long conversation with Emerson at Concord, and upon leaving, shaking his finger playfully at him, he said, 'Don't you ever believe, no matter who tells you so, that Emerson ever went back on that letter.'[2] All this is pretty strong, added to the *a priori* impossibility of reservations accompanying an utterance so absolute as that of '55.

The worst thing about Emerson's mind was that canniness. He often became a box-turtle. It is impossible that he, with such perceptions, could have failed to see Walt's sane and noble import. But yet, he could be silent, he could even utter some trifling disparagements — in pious deference to the storm of tongues. It is almost his superstition.[3]

---

[1] *New York Tribune,* June 18, 1882.

[2] See Kennedy: *Fight of a Book for the World,* p. 58, note.

[3] *Per contra,* Conway says in his *Autobiography* (vol. 1, pp. 216–17) that Emerson told him that had he known his letter would be published, he might have qualified his praise.

You will see a letter signed 'Sigma' [1] — maybe Stoddard's. It is miserable gollawash, but I mean to answer it presently, not because it is worth an answer, but because I can score a point with it. I have been waiting for developments.

My letter fell like a thunderbolt upon the enemy, and unluckily they won't fight. At least, so far that is the story. The only rejoinder has been Chadwick's and 'Sigma's' — little enough, God knows. *Per contra*, the press generally, and especially the Boston and Massachusetts press, has taken sides with me and flaxed Stevens, which is as bad for me in one way as for him in another. I really want a picador that can make the bull fight. However, a change may come, for one result of the muss has been that a Philadelphia firm, Welsh and Co., has bidden for the publication of 'L of G,' and are now rushing the new edition through the press. When it appears, we may expect all the row there ever will be, and can rough grind our sabres for the onset.

Meanwhile, I have given the enemy a bad black eye on a side matter as follows: George Chainey, formerly a clergyman, now a liberal lecturer, lectured in Boston on 'L of G,' eulogizing Walt to the skies, quoting liberally from my letter, and berating Oliver Stevens. This lecture upon its publication in Mr. Chainey's weekly paper, entitled 'This World,' E. S. Tobey, the Boston Post Master, acting under the advice of Oliver Stevens, prevented from going through the mails, stopping the whole edition, 2000 copies, on the ground that a poem quoted from Walt's book — 'To a Common Prostitute' — was obscene!

I knew of the matter first by an item in a Boston newspaper, and instantly telegraphed to Mr. Chainey, who was a stranger to me, for the facts, which he sent me by telegraph. Then I went to see Bob Ingersoll and told him the story. After an indignation meeting of two, we arranged to go together to the Postmaster General, before whom we argued the matter. The result, after several days' consideration and pressure, was that we got the Boston Post Master's decision reversed; had the embargo taken off Chainey's paper; and got moreover the private assurance that 'Leaves of Grass' would not be interfered with in the mails, in spite of Anthony Comstock.[2] This was telegraphed all over the country, day before yesterday, exultingly commented on by a number of papers (those of Boston and Philadelphia being warmly on our side), and you can fancy

He apparently did qualify it to Conway, who reports him as saying, 'There are parts of the book where I hold my nose as I read...'

It was these veerings of Emerson, doubtless, that led R. G. Ingersoll into saying, inelegantly, 'After all, there was a baked-bean side to Emerson.'

[1] *New York Tribune*, June 18, 'Sigma' (R. H. Stoddard), 1882. O'Connor, that summer, characteristically styled 'Sigma' an 'anonymunculus.'

[2] In Holloway: *Whitman*, p. 302, credit for the revocation of the order to exclude *Leaves of Grass* from the mails is given to the Philadelphia journalist, Whitman's loyal friend, Talcott Williams, although no authority is stated, nor is mention made there of the lion's share of credit, which seems clearly to belong to O'Connor and Ingersoll.

the delightful little Waterloo the transaction has been for the foe! Now, on top of it, I propose to give the Boston Post Master particular damnation in another 'Tribune' letter, taking care that Stevens comes in for his well-earned share in this new piece of vile business.

If we only had a good weekly literary paper of our own, we would have a battle on this matter that the centuries would remember.

I am glad you think my 'Tribune' letter telling. It made a stir, I can tell you. Walt was greatly pleased with it. They shall never hurt his book while I live, if I can help it, come what may.

What you tell me of Rossetti is horrible. How can a man fall back that way! I wish I had been there when he talked that way. He would have been startled from his Della Cruscan dream. I would have daubed him with Rabelais and Dante. He, the translator of the *Inferno*, to prate of Walt's book as 'nasty,' in the name of art and taste! How could Signor Alighieri stand his dainty tests? How I would like to have flung some of those savory lines, dripping with the cloaca, right into his teeth, when he dared, by implication, to set 'Leaves of Grass' below the *Divina Commedia*! O, these dilettanti![1]

As for Swinburne, he hasn't it in his moral make-up to understand 'Leaves of Grass,' and his praise of it, like his praise of Victor Hugo, always seemed to me affectation and paradox. He is no more *en rapport* with Hugo, despite his pyrotechnics of eulogy, than he is with Walt.

I am glad you have had a good time in England. Your account of the country is delightful. How I should like to go with you on a tramp through that beautiful and finished land! If I could only make some money I would exchange my life of dull and fettered fag for a good free rampage.

Let me hear when you return. There will be lots of news. Didn't things look dark and sad for W. W. when you left! I felt as though ruin was impending. Now we have changed all that, and the innings are ours at present, whatever we may have in the future....

From Hampstead, where Burroughs had previously visited her, Anne Gilchrist wrote him on July 28:

I am glad you sent me the newspaper slip before sailing. I agree with you in wishing Mr. O'Connor would not lay so much stress on the Emerson affair; but not perhaps quite for the same reason as you. I think (though I admire and reverence Emerson as much as you do, or any American) that its importance is immensely overrated. No man, however eminent, can make or mar another's fame. If Emerson recognized greatness in Walt Whitman, so much the better for Emerson; to himself the chief benefit. Walt Whitman has to abide longer and severer tests. Time

[1] From England, Burroughs had written O'Connor a vigorous denunciation of Rossetti, declaring that his mind had 'gone fallow' since his earlier appreciation of Whitman. (Letter in the Perry Whitman Collection.)

is the arbiter. Time — in other words, successive generations of men, with fresh wants, fresh aspirations, born to new points of view, set down on a fresh-turned plot in the seed-garden of Time. If these continue to find, as some of us do now (and it would not be the first nor the second time in the world's history that 'babes and sucklings' have been in advance of venerable authorities in welcoming a new light — they are looking about and longing for it, while the others are preoccupied with their own aims, ideals, standards, and are filled and satisfied with the Past) — if these successive generations find Walt Whitman's poems a source of wisdom, joy, elevation, impetus, strength, purity, then the question of his claims will be answered. It can be authoritatively answered, and his bold enterprise finally justified, in no other way. In regard to the letter signed 'Sigma' which followed Wm. O'Connor's, all the while I was reading there ran in my head our famous motto, *Honte y soit qui mal y pense* — The shame be to him who finds evil in this. He has certainly read in between the lines something that you and I do not find there. But one sweeping misstatement of his should be corrected. It is not true that 'Leaves of Grass' is solely or mainly a 'glorification' or 'celebration,' as the Poet himself calls it, of the body. That theme occupies perhaps some thirty pages out of more than three hundred.

> 'I am the Poet of the Body
> And I am the Poet of the Soul,'

and the last is as true and is fulfilled, as befits, with far more amplitude than the first. Who, casting aside the support of dogmas that will no longer bear the daylight, has risen into such a high, serene region of Faith? Who has written of Death as Walt Whitman has done? transformed the grinning skeleton that pitilessly mows men down into the beautiful veiled figure that takes them in her arms and dips them into the Dark Sea only to renovate their growth and launch them on a free plane of existence? Who by his faith in humanity, his ardent love for it, has discerned a soul in the great clumsy young Giant, Democracy, that will make him bye and bye a divine Conqueror?

But it is plain 'Sigma's' volume has only opened in one place (and that misread). He can never have looked into the 'Whispers of Heavenly Death,' or 'Drum Taps,' or 'Calamus.' The 'Voice out of the Sea' has never sounded in his ears!

O, I do wish Mr. O'Connor with his eloquent pen, instead of dwelling on what Emerson said, or the Classics did, would convict these men out of Walt's own mouth. I should like to try myself were I not, just now, pledged to other work; but I hope to one day.

Remembrances, etc., follow, after which she adds:

If you think it would be of any use to print this letter in the 'Tribune,' or elsewhere, you are welcome to do so.

In his letter of August 13, welcoming Burroughs and family
home, Whitman carries further the story of the fortunes of the
'Leaves'; he tells Burroughs that he and O'Connor are corresponding quite often now and on just the same terms as of yore:

> I commenced publishing 'L of G' in June on my own hook, but found it
> vexatious from the start, and having quite vehement proposals from Rees
> Welsh (2d hand book dealer and law book publisher, 23 South 9th St.
> Phila.) I passed the use of the plates into his hands — he printed it (the
> plates are here in Phila.) an exact copy of the Osgood edition — Welsh's
> first edition (a cautious 1000) was ready about three weeks ago and was
> exhausted in a day — the second came in ab't five days ago, and is now
> nearly gone — a third is ordered — I am very glad I let him have it —
> I am throwing together a prose jumble, 'Specimen Days' — (see slips
> enclosed) — nearly 200 pages already cast —
> ... When you have a leisure hour reel me off a letter — put in about
> Mrs. Gilchrist and Herbert. Dr. Bucke is keeping back his book till
> 'Specimen Days' comes out — will come out by winter likely.
>
> WALT WHITMAN

Burroughs, commenting on things suggested by the foregoing,
said:

> That was after my second trip to Europe. Yes, I dined many times at
> Mrs. Gilchrist's; saw Rossetti there, but didn't like his foppishness. He
> was severe and cantankerous about Whitman. He had been so cordial to
> me when I was there in '71, and I had dined at his house with his mother
> and sisters. He seemed 'put out' about something. I have thought later
> it might have been something I had said about Dante Gabriel Rossetti —
> he had probably got hold of it and resented it. I couldn't account for his
> change of manner in any other way.

When welcoming Burroughs home, O'Connor wrote that he
wished they were where they could confer readily, as they were
going to have a bitter fight yet; and on October 6, he wrote:

> Have you a spare copy of my reply to Chadwick? If so, please send it to
> me.... Did you get the Sunday 'Tribune' I sent with my warning to Com-
> stock? He has lain down under it like a beaten cur, and never dared to
> carry out his threat.
> I sent the 'Tribune' on Sept. 16th, a perfect dressing down of Tobey, the
> Boston Post Master, which has not yet been published, and I am querying
> whether Whitelaw [Reid] has shut down on me or not. I hope not, for
> I have at least two more letters on the subject before I close.
> I want memoranda about Professor Tyrrell's lectures on Walt before

Dublin University, years ago. Can you furnish me with any? I had a
letter from him at the time, which I cannot, in the packed-up condition
of my papers, lay hold of.... I want all I can get on this point, with a view
of doing justice to Mr. Joseph Potiphar Galbraith [J. P. Galbraith] who
has distinguished himself by getting 'Leaves of Grass' tabooed from the
College Library, and who shall be rewarded by an ebony immortality for
his virtue, as also shall Mr. Attorney General Marston for publishing his
letter.

I have just had a copy of Walt's new book,[1] which looks splendidly rich
within, judging by a hasty glance inside the covers. I hope this adventure
may prove the turning-point in the adverse fortunes of his book, as I think
it will.

O'Connor and Bucke were the only ones of the Whitman circle
(and later, Kennedy), who made any attempt to be scholarly. To
O'Connor, Whitman's acceptance by such men as Dowden and
Tyrrell was especially significant; hence the attempt to exclude
Whitman from the Library of Trinity College roused him again
to white heat. On October 19 he writes Burroughs:

If you feel you can spare the copy of your 'Notes,' please send it. I
want it for Chainey, who is lecturing around the country on 'Leaves of
Grass,' and it seems to me a way of helping Walt — to indoctrinate one
of his most zealous propagandists. Of course if you feel like saving it for
what may seem a better use, don't send it.

My Tobey letter will not appear in the 'Tribune,' which has shut down.
I had a very nice note from Whitelaw Reid, returning the MS, with the
remarks that 'it has even more strength and sparkle than your other com-
munications,' but he thinks the game not worth the candle, and decides to
close. I am sorry, for I certainly gave Brother Tobey the devil, and the
letter would have made a prodigious uproar in Boston, where our Christian
friend is thoroughly disliked; but I have no reason to complain, for Reid
has given me a pretty good show, and the advertising for Walt has been
extensive. So I am honestly grateful to Whitelaw, who, considering his
limitations and, well — handicapped condition, has done well by us.

I shall now gather into a pamphlet (just as soon as my cursed burden
of work lifts a little) all that have appeared in the 'Tribune,' the Tobey
letter, and two or three others I have sketched out already (one on Marston and his Joseph Surface Galbraith, and one on 'Sigma,' of the catawam-
pous claw variety) and let the fur fly. I mean to make this Comstock
crowd memorable, if I can compass it, and they need not imagine that the
matter has ended with some stray articles in the newspapers.

I am surprised that you have not heard of the Galbraith episode. In

[1] *Specimen Days and Collect.* Rees Welsh and Company, 1882-83. (Later incorporated
in the *Prose Works.*)

brief: In the very University where Tyrrell gave a course of lectures on Walt, extolling him to the uttermost, this academic Devil's dung (*Teufelsdröch*) Galbraith, succeeds in getting the book excluded from the library; then writes a vainglorious letter on this feat to Marston, assuming that the latter is the author of the movement against 'Leaves of Grass' in Massachusetts; and Marston, who has always privately denied that he had anything to do with it, *prints the letter in the public journals*, which is confession. Some of the papers dressed him down for this, notably the 'Boston Post,' and I mean to give him a dose of strappado for eternity, if I can....

Could you lend me Mrs. Gilchrist's letter, or the passage you mention? I will return it faithfully. I should like very much to see it.

Poor Blood became quite insane a year ago, and has been since then in an asylum. So he is not 'Sigma,' who is more probably [R. H.] Stoddard.

As you say, the 'Tribune' is without courage or independence, but what American press has? They are all in the pay of the devil — mortgaged to stock-jobbers, monopolists and wealthy churches. When you see the 'Tribune' humbly reporting Comstock's lecture on Evil Literature (perfect rot, as Comstock is a mass of moral putrefaction) don't you wonder that I was ever allowed to say what I did in May on Stevens?

I, too, have got Walt's new book, which to a cursory glance or dip appears very rich. I really have not yet been able to examine it — I am so driven. The 'Boston Herald' of Sunday had a two-column notice of it, extremely eulogistic and satisfactory. The 'Tribune' had a short review — probably Winter's — quite contemptible, of course.[1] The critics friendly to Walt are called 'feather-brained' and 'howling dervishes,' which is quite in Winter's elegant and accurate style. Emerson, Thoreau, Ruskin, Freiligrath, Clifford, Tyrrell, Charles Sumner, Henry J. Raymond, etc., 'feather-brained' and 'howling dervishes'! And this from the chair in which once sat George Ripley! *O tempora, O holy Moses!* as the Latin poet has it.

Good bye. Apropos, why don't you make your publisher reissue the 'Notes'? Now is the time when the W. W. literature is booming.

Mr. Clifton J. Furness supplies me with the following information which supplements the account of O'Connor's valiant defense of the 'Leaves':

[1] O'Connor had an amusing way, when writing of this critic, of decapitalizing and condensing him — 'littlewilliewinter' — which reminds one of Kennedy's comments on a spiteful piece of Winter's writing about Whitman — as to his having 'delivered some Lilliputian kicks at the giant's shins.' Writing Bucke of Winter's having commended Marston for suppressing the *Leaves*, O'Connor said that Winter did it in 'his usual style of eunuch maliciousness'; and he spoke of 'Sigma's' [R. H. Stoddard] 'savage dive' at Whitman as 'full of mush and malignity.' Evidently these 'good green friends' of the 'good gray poet' had some fun among themselves at the expense of the hostile critics.

I find in the Bucke Collection the original MS. of O'Connor's letter to the New York *Tribune* editor, which was published in part in that paper, August 27, 1882. The following paragraph in the original MS. was deleted from the published version:

'Sir: Mr. Anthony Comstock's hostility to the nude, of which an illustrious example was his famous prosecution of three unfortunate women whom he had hired to dance before him for over an hour, without clothing, in a New York brothel, appears to extend even to the naked truth.'

Later, in the same controversy, November 10, 1882, Ezra H. Heywood, editor of the Boston *Word*, writes to W. W. in regard to Anthony Comstock's being the concealed instigator of the Boston suppression of *Leaves of Grass*: 'Knowing of your illness... I do not like to intrude anything upon you, but think perhaps... you would like to know the latest raid on *Leaves of Grass* — or rather on printed extracts from it — for which offense I was arrested by Anthony Comstock, October 26.... Nov. 2, 1872, Comstock came as "Edgewell," a Free Lover; this time he is a Labor Reformer, masked under three different aliases, and telling a dozen lies to get what he calls evidence. As March 18, 1873, he wrote from Washington *on Treasury letter paper which he must have dishonestly obtained*, to New York doctors, signing himself, "*Miss* Anna E. Ray," a Treasury clerk three months on with child, wanting to procure abortion; as May 9, 1878, signing himself "Mrs. Farnsworth," he got a vaginal syringe of Dr. Sara B. Chase, and then arrested her for selling him one; as when, June 14, 1878 (see N.Y. *Tribune* report), he with other men went to an ill-famed house on Green St., hired young girls to go into a closed room with them, disrobe and show their nude persons to him and the men, and then seized them for "indecent exposure" — so now, Comstock is the same lying, rude, lascivious decoy he has always been. Twenty-one years ago when I was acting general agent of the Anti-Slavery Society in Boston, and occasional "preacher" for the 28th Congregational Society in Music Hall, I bought your book and read extracts from it from Theodore Parker's pulpit! No one then thought of obscenity in connection with it. ... In order to assert, in the most direct way possible, citizen right to acquire and impart knowledge, denied by "obscenists," we reprinted in the *Word*, without note or comment, the two condemned poems.' (From MS. letter now in Bliss Perry Collection.)

April 14, 1883, Whitman writes to O'Connor (letter in Mr. Perry's collection): — 'In the Heywood trial, the judges peremptorily ruled out the *Leaves of Grass* part of the indictment (which "ruling out" was received with applause) and H. was afterward acquitted. So Anthony Comstock retires with his tail intensely curved inwards.'

Whitman evidently did not care to be identified with Heywood, if we may judge from what he wrote to Dr. Bucke, March 19, 1888: 'Heywood, the Massachusetts free lover, here today, very cordial, &c. I treat him politely but that is all.'

O'Connor's 'dressing down' of Tobey, the Boston postmaster, written September 16, 1882, which Whitelaw Reid declined to print, though admitting its strength and sparkle, was entitled 'Tobey or not Tobey? — That is the Question.' Since O'Connor did not carry out his intention of collecting all his philippics into a pamphlet, this one about Tobey, which is in his best vein, and introduces much important evidence and details of the suppression of the 'Leaves,' is liberally extracted from here, from a manuscript in O'Connor's handwriting in the Bucke Collection. It is dated September 16, 1882. Quotations from it are afforded me through the kindess of Mr. Furness:

TOBEY OR NOT TOBEY? — THAT IS THE QUESTION

To the Editor of the Tribune

Sir: In August Mr. Anthony Comstock told your reporter that if he found 'Leaves of Grass' on sale in New York, he would certainly take steps to suppress it. August has melted into September, five large editions of 'Leaves of Grass' have been sold under his very nose — his ubiquitous and omni-present nose — and he has taken no steps whatever. This adds another to the group of bold and beautiful works of the imagination he exposed to the public through the agency of your reporter. It is a small but precious gallery. In old days, one of the Boston wits called a fine but highly fastidious art critic, Mr. Franklin Dexter, a man of the most exquisite distastes. Only a connoisseur of this description would be fit to inspect the mendacious masterpieces of Mr. Comstock. The eye trained to repugnance by severe regard for truth, finds in these compositions an infinity of details for objection, while admiringly aware of the audacious chaos of fact and dream which makes them miracles of artistic lying. No one of them vies better with Turner's latest pictures, in which imagination splendidly drowned out veracity, than the brilliant portrayal of the action of Mr. Tobey, the Boston postmaster, in respect to Mr. Chainey's lecture. Upon this, I promised you in my last letter, a separate communication....

The cold, hard, prosaic reality which gave basis to this particular art-gem of Mr. Comstock's, is as follows:

In May last, I unmasked the impudent and sinister attempt made by Mr. Oliver Stevens, the Boston District Attorney, and the gang of which he made himself the tool, to establish, in the instance of 'Leaves of Grass,' a censorship of the press in America. The subsequent conduct of Mr. Stevens freshly lights the dark import of that deed without a name. As Coke said at Raleigh's trial — 'See the reach of this man!' Except that he has a 'reach,' I know of no resemblance Mr. Stevens bears to Sir Walter, unless indeed, as his conduct would seem to suggest, that he has lost his head. How worthless and how wicked the head he had to lose, is shown in the story of his base and silly coalition with Mr. Tobey to continue his original act of iniquity.

In Boston there is a brilliant lay-preacher,... named George Chainey.... He was formerly a clergyman, but is now, as Colonel Ingersoll wittily says of him, 'reformed.' He is settled over a large and respectable congregation, privileged to hear his weekly discourses, and in his capacity as a guardian of public morals, and with a paladin spirit worthy of the man, and too sadly infrequent in our scholars and men of letters, he took occasion on Sunday, June 11th, following the suggestion of my May letter in the *Tribune*, to address his audience upon the scope and purpose of 'Leaves of Grass,' and upon the recent wrong done its author. The discourse was a gallant vindication of the work of our Homer of the heart, as one of our scholars has, with apt beauty, called Walt Whitman, and its incidental censure of the shameful abuse of power which had been practiced upon the book by Mr. Oliver Stevens, was marked by manly temperance and dignity. Mr. Chainey's discourses are published regularly in a debonair weekly journal which he edits,[1] and this one of June 11th went duly into type. It was illustrated by several citations from the poem: among others, the noble verses I also had defended, entitled *To a Common Prostitute*; and it appears that the printer, although he saw nothing objectionable in the piece, shrank from setting it up, lest under the peculiarities of the law in Massachusetts, his business should become subject to the prosecutions of the Boston District Attorney. To relieve his apprehensions, Mr. Chainey had the verses printed upon a separate leaf, and included in his paper as a supplement. Then, with perhaps undue conscientiousness... anxious that his journal should not infract postal law, he went to lay the question that had been raised before the Boston postmaster, Mr. Tobey.

Mr. Tobey is a pious elderly gentleman, well known in Boston, prior to his appointment as postmaster, for his prominent connection with several business enterprises, all of which, I believe, he successfully conducted to failure. Hafiz tells us, in one of his most charming poems, that the earth of which Allah made him, was kneaded up with wine. The most unquestionable oil might have been used in mixing up the clay of Mr. Tobey. He exudes it like an exhalation. Words, tones, looks, demeanor, are all sleek, sanctimonious and oleaginous.... Early in life, he avoided the vulgar error that Church and State are separated in this country, and resolved to make piety grease the ways of trade and politics. He lost no opportunity to make known his religious professions, and, inching along, became president of the Boston Young Men's Christian Association. A sniffling speech he made last January at the Bethel to the poor little children of the First Baptist Mariners' Sunday School, parades the avowal that he indirectly obtained his present official position by means of this

[1] *The Word.* Boston.

agency. It is now his pious wont to sit, like an anchorite, in the cavernous recess of his private room in the Boston Post Office, and meditate, as he says, 'on the comfort of Jesus' — keeping, meanwhile, as will be seen, a sharp lookout for any official chance to tamper with the mails of the free religionists. This is the unctuous gentleman called upon by Mr. Chainey.

If, superimposing one miracle upon another, the prophet Jonah could have absorbed the whale that had previously swallowed him, he would not have been a completer interfusion of sanctity and oil than was embodied in the suave saint of the Boston mail-bags on that holy Thursday. He blandly assured Mr. Chainey that no objection had ever been taken to the passage of Walt Whitman's book through the mails, and, moreover, that no such objection could possibly be taken without putting an embargo upon literature, inasmuch as such action would exclude the Decameron of Boccaccio, the works of Rabelais and Shakespeare, and many other illustrious volumes. The postal laws touching obscene matter were, therefore, clearly inapplicable in this instance; the only doubt, slyly suggested Mr. Tobey, was whether Mr. Chainey's interleaf was properly in the form of a supplement, and this question he proposed to submit to the Post Office Department at Washington. This being the conclusion, Mr. Chainey meekly assented, and left Mr. Tobey to the little task he was to slip in between his post-office meditations on the 'comfort of Jesus.'

The next day, Friday, Mr. Tobey wrote to Washington. The paper, issuable on Saturday, the 17th, had to wait unpublished. On the Thursday following, the 22nd, the answer came from the Post Office Department that the supplement did not come within the definition of the law, and hence that the paper containing it was not mailable at pound rates, but must go as third-class matter. And why was the interleaf not a supplement? Marry, come up, now! Are not reasons plenty as blackberries? Perhaps, because it was supplementary. There is one reason already! Moreover, Mr. Chainey, bowing to official wisdom, paid the extra twenty dollars to have his paper mailed as third-class matter, and the next day, Friday, the 23rd. — twelve days after the delivery of the discourse — the mail-bags containing the noble lay-preacher's vindication of the poet, went rejoicing to the Boston post-office, and Mr. Chainey rested happy in the assurance that his light was sown in the minds of his subscribers.

The seed-time of his rays was, however, still deferred. It is characteristic of the dulciferous benevolence of Mr. Postmaster Tobey that he spared this misguided man the shock of knowing that his mail-bags had never left the post-office. Kindly, sweetly, silently, with never-ceasing exudation of oil, he detained every bag, but forbore to break the news to Mr. Chainey. Why vex the heart of the citizen with sorrow, the knowledge of which cometh sooner or later in slow leakage? Mum be every post-office clerk, while we sit upon the mail-bags of the Man of Sin, and meditate upon 'the comfort of Jesus.' It was late on the following Monday, the

26th — three days afterward — that Mr. Chainey learned by the merest accident — a chance meeting with a subscriber on the street — that his discourse on Walt Whitman's book was not yet in circulation; and hastening to the post-office he found that not a copy had been suffered to leave the building. Thunderstruck, he sought the presence of Mr. Tobey and demanded the reason. The good and faithful servant of the people instantly became a gushing geyser of holy oil. He had stopped the paper, he declared with unctuous and saintly fervor, because he considered the quoted poem, 'To a Common Prostitute,' obscene. Upon Mr. Chainey's fiery demand why he had not thought so at their first interview, ten days before, Mr. Tobey suavely responded that he had not then read the poem. As a mere matter of fact, he had read it three or four times, with Mr. Chainey looking at him and seeing him do it; but a good father of the church, Eusebius, I think, says it is allowable to lie for the glory of God, and Mr. Tobey is too faithful a disciple to fail in any precept. Continuing the bland explanation and defence of his action, he presently let the cat out of the bag — in this instance, unhappily, a mail bag. He had consulted the District Attorney, Mr. Oliver Stevens, who had assured him — As Sterne says, 'Shall I go on? — No!' All this was on the 26th of June. Two days before I had seen an item in the Boston *Advertiser*, announcing the stoppage of Mr. Chainey's address in the mails. It bore reference to the first detention on mere postal technique. But a man's nose is placed between his eyes that he may smell out what he cannot see into, and knowing 'the ways of such people' (Boccaccio's phrase in speaking of the pranksome devils depicted by Dante in the *Inferno*, and quite apropos of Messrs Stevens, Tobey, Comstock, and the rest), and suspecting the true mischief, I at once wrote to Mr. Chainey, personally a stranger to me, asking the particulars. In due time I got them. They included the fact that Mr. Tobey had again referred the supplement (on June 26th) to the Postmaster General, this time for decision upon the question of obscenity. He had promised Mr. Chainey that he would simply submit the case without any attempt to bias the judgment of the Postmaster General, but in making this promise he had remembered his Eusebius, for in his letter of transmission he distinctly expressed the conviction that the supplement lay within the intent of the postal law against obscene matter; cited in confirmation of this view Oliver Stevens' original action; brought up as additional proof Osgood's sneaking desertion of the book; and, in a word, said all he could to artfully prejudice the question.

I thought the cause, under the circumstances, possibly a desperate one, and seeking a comrade fit for a forlorn hope, I went at once to the good, the gallant Colonel Ingersoll....

We agreed that the fate of the book was at stake — the book Emerson told Professor Loomis was an absolutely fresh revelation in literature and in history — the great book which is the seed-corn of all the future of America; we agreed that the interests of free discussion, in the instance of

George Chainey's lecture, were at stake also; and we went to plead the issue to the Postmaster General. I need not state the result which the telegraph of the 10th of July carried, with essential truth, to all the public journals. Mr. Howe deserved the cordial thanks of every true American. The Man of Letters sustained the men of letters, and Mr. Chainey's lecture went free. Yet even after this decision reached him by telegraph, the good and faithful public servant, Mr. Tobey, neglected to give the order for the transmission of the mail-bags he had contrived to detain for three weeks, and they were despatched, without orders, by the honorable audacity of a subordinate. Furthermore, his spiritual oil heated to boiling at the news wired to the journals that the Postmaster General had ruled that 'Leaves of Grass' could not be excluded from the mails, he took pains to furnish items to the Boston papers, stating that the report was false, and that the ruling only covered a quotation. If Mr. Tobey thinks this true, let him try to stop the flying editions of 'Leaves of Grass' as they pass through the Boston Post Office. The general principle which animated the Postmaster General's decision in the special instance, is known to no one better than to Mr. Tobey, despite his contributions to literature in the Boston journals.

I do not propose to dwell upon the part played by Mr. Oliver Stevens in this precious transaction. Yet his reappearance upon the stage is both significant and memorable. Writhing, smarting, gasping with the dose of bamboo he got from the public journals in May — my letter in the Tribune only the first stroke of the gantlet — he totters in, like the cudgelled attorney of a farce, and wreaks his spite and fury in putting up the postmaster to a war upon the rights and interests of citizens. May the scene be remembered to him forever, and may the remembrance begin when Suffolk County next seeks to elect a decent District Attorney! My present concern is not with him, but with that extension of him constituted by Mr. Postmaster Tobey — the servile catspaw of a malignant chimpanzee. We have been favored of late years with several varieties of the terra cotta Christian — far other than the image whose marble beauty looms across the ages from the low hills of Palestine, and stirs the pulses of every thoughtful as well as every adoring heart. We have had the Christian statesman, with his Bible interleaved with Credit Mobilier bonds; we have had the Christian banker receiving deposits up to the very hour of dishonest failure; and we have had the Christian cashier absquatulating with the funds. We are now treated to a view of the Christian Postmaster. Appointed to send the mails, but surcharged with mean moralism and *odium theologicum*, he occupies himself with revising them. As in the transformation scene of a pantomime, the postman changes into the inquisitor. He stops a public journal for three weeks, injuring the business of the publisher and trampling on the rights of the subscribers. While several thousand people wait for their paper, he dips with Oliver Stevens into a low intrigue against the freedom of the press, holding in leash the discussion of his partner's original act of infamy, while he endeavors by artful sophistries to commit the Government at once against the issue of the periodical which had touched his *confrère* with the whip of Juvenal, and the immortal book from which it had quoted half a page. He coos, he smiles, he dissembles, he lies, to gain time for the secret correspondence by which he hopes to effect his dirty double end. Mr. Tobey knew his duty perfectly. He knew perfectly well that Walt Whitman's book, and every part of it, was mailable matter, as he admitted when, in his first cajoling conversation with Mr. Chainey, he classed it with Rabelais and Shakespeare (to either of which it is as snow to scarlet) avowing that it could not be banned from the mails without laying an embargo upon literature. Knowing and having admitted this, he had but one official duty in regard to the page Mr. Chainey had reprinted from the volume, namely, to mail it, to mail it without note or comment; and his subsequent attempt to bar its transmission on the charge of obscenity was, in all its details, no less a ridiculous inconsistency, than a piece of low chicanery, and a culpable breach of public duty. And who is he anyway? Who is this little old pigmy of a postman that occupies himself with the moral questions of the mails — that takes upon himself the tremendous office of public censor, and endeavors to arrest the armed march of free letters, and stop the roaring looms of free discussion, in America? It stirs the blood even at the distance of three centuries, to read as a preface to *Don Quixote* the inquisitor's printed certificate that the book contains nothing prejudicial to religion and good morals, and is therefore licensed to pass into circulation; and to reflect that there has been a time on earth, which some would like to evoke again from hell, when the radiant and noble wisdom of Cervantes was dependent for its liberty to enter the mind and soul of the human race, upon the arbitrary will of a man. Still, we might endure, if only for the tragic dignity of it, that our poems and our lectures, our journals and our literature, should take their imprimatur or their doom from the dark hand of Torquemada — but who is Tobey?...

O'Connor closes this diatribe with another long paragraph, the gist of which is that, considering the proof Mr. Tobey has given of his menace to liberty, his blindness to his civic duties, and his poverty of the higher qualifications of his office, he feels justified in remarking that a petition for the appointment of Mr. Tobey's successor would at this time be in perfect order.

Just before going to England, Burroughs had built him a little one-room bark study on the river-bank, a few rods below his stone dwelling at Riverby, and on his return he longed to see Whitman sitting there in the big chair in front of the open fire. The letter which follows, dated October 29, is one of many futile attempts to get Whitman to come again to Riverby. Burroughs's rustic cabin, Slabsides, a retreat in the wooded hills a mile and more from his river home, where he often hied himself during the summer months, was not built till 1895, so, of course, Whitman never saw or heard of it, although Miss Elizabeth Corbett, in her book called 'Walt,' in which the fiction about Whitman and his friends is far stranger than the truth, anachronistically 'quotes' Whitman as telling Traubel, in 1888, of Burroughs then living in his woodland cabin — the cabin which was not built till three years after Whitman died!

DEAR WALT,

I was much disturbed by your card. I have been thinking of you as probably enjoying these superb autumn days down in the country at Kirkwood, and here you are wretched and sick at home. I trust you are better now. You need a change. I dearly wish that as soon as you are well enough you would come up here and spend a few weeks with us. We could have a good time here in my bark-covered shanty, and in knocking about the country. Let me know that you will come.

The 'Specimen Days and Collect' came all right. I do not like the last part of the title; it brings me up with a short turn. I have read most of the new matter and like it, of course. I have not seen any notices of the book yet. I have just received an English book — 'Familiar Studies of Men and Books' — by Stevenson, with an essay upon you in it. But it does not amount to much. He has the American vice of smartness and flippancy. I do not think you would care for the piece.

I am bank-examining nowadays, but shall be free again pretty soon.

O'Connor writes me that he is going to publish his 'Tribune' letters in a pamphlet with some other matter. I am glad to hear it. He draws blood every time.[1]

I fear poor old Alcott will not rally; indeed, he may be dead now. I had a pleasant letter from him the other day. I had sent him a crate of Concord grapes.[2]

---

[1] In volume I, *With Walt Whitman in Camden* (p. 334), Traubel reports Whitman as regretting that O'Connor never carried out his plan: 'A half dozen of O'Connor's pieces bound in one book would have seemed like a battery of guns.... He was past-master in controversy.... John is a milder type — not the fighting sort — rather more contemplative. John goes a little more for usual, accepted, respectable things, than we do — rather more; just a bit, maybe — though God knows he is not respectable enough to hurt — not usual[ly?] enough to get out of our company.' Again: 'The best of John is not in the cities — the best of him is in the woods; he gets to be wholly himself only when he is let loose with himself away from the towns.'

[2] Bronson Alcott's letter is quoted in Barrus: *The Life and Letters of John Burroughs,* vol. I, p. 248.

... Drop me a card when you receive this; also write me when you will come up.

With much love
JOHN BURROUGHS

The correspondence between Burroughs and Dowden, which had lapsed for some years, was resumed by Dowden in a letter, dated November 27, and by Burroughs in his reply of December 14:

MY DEAR BURROUGHS,

Walt Whitman tells me he has sent to you a letter of mine to him, so I need not recite what was in it. It has grieved me to hear of his recent prostration, but I did not hear of it until I also heard of his recovery.

I post a copy of the 'Academy' to you containing a review of his 'Specimen Days.'...

We jog on. I told W. W. that I had allowed myself to be swallowed up by Goethe — I do not wholly rejoice — but I cannot help it now, and go on resolutely to try and see all that is to be seen in the belly of that whale.

Sometimes a longing comes to cross to New York — hold hands with Whitman — and see you and your wife and your house by the Hudson. But it is only a delightful dream — ties strong as iron, though silken ties, keep me at home, and doubtless it is best, so.

Believe me, always most sincerely yours

EDWARD DOWDEN

The reply of Burroughs is condensed here:

... Time, the broker, has discounted my locks at a usurious rate since I last saw your handwriting, but I manage to keep him away from my heart yet.... But he has touched Whitman much more lightly than his friends had any reason to hope. When I last saw him, now many months past, he looked better and moved better than he had for years. There appears to be a freshness and youthfulness in his very physiology that is proof against the years.

You have touched off his book with delightful grace and ease. It is just the kind of notice that will please him. Indeed, who would it not please? ... It is quite an easy thing to do now, to cross the Atlantic, and I sincerely hope you may yet see your way to do it. I will agree to meet your steamer in New York any time you will name, and will take you to Whitman and show you the country in one man — the country as it is to be. If you can't leave home, do as I did, bring your home with you....

I see you speak of Robert Stevenson in your notice of Whitman's book. I recently ordered a book of his — 'Familiar Studies,' etc. and regretted to see that in his essay on Whitman he so far underbids his own true estimate and appreciation of the poet as revealed by his preface. Still, he is a bright writer....

It is curious to see how Stevenson jumps back and forth in his 'Familiar Studies.' Earlier he had written an article, 'The Gospel According to Walt Whitman,' in the 'New Quarterly Magazine' (October, 1878), and later also said much in Whitman's favor in 'Books Which Have Influenced Me.' ('Pall Mall Budget,' January 27, and May 12, 1887.) Quite candidly he had said that 'Leaves of Grass' had tumbled the world upside down for him, blown a thousand ethical illusions into space, shaken his tabernacle of lies, and had then set him upon a firm foundation of the original and manly virtues; and yet, in his 'Familiar Studies,' he virtually admits that he is deliberately understating his admiration, and overstating his adverse criticism in order to curry favor with the public! The Tabernacle of Lies evidently had merely been shaken, not razed to the ground. Such trimming of his sails would seem to entitle the dear R. L. S. to the so-called 'coarse epithet' which Professor Perry in his 'Walt Whitman' (page 260), says Whitman dismissed Stevenson with. Professor Perry evidently refers to Whitman telling Traubel [1] that Stevenson was 'lacking in guts.' This expression, used so commonly in Great Britain by refined persons, surely was not meant to be coarse as used by Whitman. To have 'guts,' is to have a generous supply of homely, hearty, human qualities, such as go with a sound, robust body. Would it not have been better to have quoted the epithet, and let the reader be the judge as to its coarseness?

Another brilliant man of letters, with something of the same charm as R. L. S., and perhaps something of the same visceral deficiency, was Lafcadio Hearn. When, in 1883, Dr. Bucke's 'Walt Whitman' came out (in which O'Connor's contributions were conspicuous, and which, 'for reasons,' came out in the United States as copyrighted by O'Connor), Hearn wrote O'Connor, August 9, 1883,[2] that he had always secretly admired Whitman, and had longed to say so, but that he really did not dare to, being in journalism, lest the proprietors of the papers for which he wrote accuse him of loving obscene literature. His further comments show that he admires as with a difference, preferring his gold wrought into fantastic shapes, and the gems much cut and polished, instead of,

[1] Traubel: *With Walt Whitman in Camden*, vol. 1, p. 145.
[2] Perry: *Walt Whitman*, pp. 239–44.

as with Whitman, being left in the ore. He compared Whitman's titanic voice to a giant beneath a volcano, half-stifled, then roaring betimes, since articulation is impossible. Again, his songs are like a savage skald, or a forest Druid — immense in thought, mighty in words — wild, harsh, rude, primeval. On the whole, he considers him only the Precursor of a greater Singer yet to come.

Many Europeans were continuing to come to America, from time to time, to see Whitman and our other natural wonders.

After Oscar Wilde had called on the poet, he is said to have declared that the most impressive room he had entered in America was that little room of Whitman's in Camden.[1] In a clever satirical skit in the 'Century Magazine,' November, 1882, Helen Gray Cone gives an imaginary conversation in verse between Paumanokides (Whitman) and Narcissus (Oscar Wilde). The title is 'Narcissus in Camden.' The skit is so ingenious, and so like, in its caricature, as to provoke many an involuntary smile even from one who hates to see a hero parodied.

Wilde visited Burroughs at Riverby during his tour of these States. I quote from a letter to me from John Burroughs, dated December 28, 1906. Commenting on Wilde's 'De Profundis,' he said:

> It is impressive. What a genius was destroyed or perverted in that man! He is in many ways a paradox. He seems to think of all things in terms of art. Christ is to him the great Artist. Did I ever tell you that he came here once to see me? Henry Abbey brought him — a splendid talker, and a handsome man, but a voluptuary. As he walked from you, there was something in the motion of his hips and back that was disagreeable.

At the time, in 1882, when the Authors' Club in New York was in process of organization, and Burroughs had signified his willingness to become a member, when he learned that at one of the preliminary meetings they had been unwilling to include Whitman, Burroughs wrote Stedman in high dudgeon to strike his name from

---

[1] The Library of Congress has the following letter written on office stationery of J. M. Stoddart and Company, Philadelphia, January 11, 1882, to Whitman: 'Oscar Wilde has expressed his great desire to meet you socially. He will dine with me Saturday afternoon when I shall be most happy to have you join us. The bearer, Mr. Wanier, will explain at greater length any details which you may wish to know, and will be happy to bring me your acquiescence.'
The signature has been torn off. One is curious to know who wrote the letter, and whether Whitman went or not. — C. J. F.

the list. At least this is my recollection, gathered from hearing it mentioned by Burroughs on several occasions. Stedman's reply to that letter of Burroughs, dated September 30, 1882, follows. I have tried in vain to obtain Burroughs's letter, of which no record seems to have been kept either in Stedman's files, or in those of the Authors' Club.

MY DEAR BURROUGHS,

I thought we agreed to drop the Mister. Your note is rec'd, and I have had your name taken off. For one, I shall always be glad to advocate your reëlection, whenever you see fit to give the sign. If I remember rightly, you were unanimously included in the first lot named for organization — Mr. Gilder and Mr. De Kay both thinking you would like to join.

I envy you your country retreat at this season, when we are overrun with people and 'things.'... A good new year to you and yours,

Ever cordially yours

E. C. STEDMAN

Clearly Burroughs never saw fit to 'give the sign,' and although he held certain members of the club in high regard, and on a few occasions dined at the club, he never became a member, and never could overlook their 'shameful treatment of Walt.'

Of late years some controversy has arisen as to the question of Whitman and the Authors' Club, and I have tried diligently to get at the facts, without very definite results. I can only give whatever of evidence I can obtain and leave each interested person to judge for himself. Aside from my own recollection, and that of others with whom I have talked, who have similar recollections of hearing Burroughs give his reasons for not becoming a member of the Authors' Club, there is a passage in 'Visits to Walt Whitman in 1890-91,' by Dr. J. Johnston (page 83) which quotes Burroughs thus:

In New York there is a society of authors of which I was a member; but some two or three years ago they actually blackballed Whitman! I've never been inside the doors since that. They would have done themselves infinite honor had they elected him — *I* didn't propose him — but they showed themselves contemptible little fools by refusing him....

Now it is very possible that, unwittingly, Dr. Johnston may have misquoted Burroughs to some extent, but Burroughs certainly said something of the sort to him. The facts are that Burroughs did not become a member of the club, although originally intending to join it, and that on several occasions he did express indignation toward the club for its attitude toward Whitman. However, indignant as he was, he did, on a few occasions, years later, attend a dinner at the club. An entry in his Journal, February 13, 1886, runs thus:

Home from N.Y. after five days' visit.... Stayed two nights with Gilder and went with him to the Authors Club — a slim turn-out, a pretty slim set of authors at the best, when all are there. They black-balled Whitman not long since. Think what the hope of American letters is in the hands of such men! I sincerely pity them. They are mostly the mere mice of literature. Such men as Gilder, Stedman, and De Kay recognize Whitman, but probably the least one of the remainder believes himself a greater man.

And again, in his article 'Walt Whitman,' in 'The Critic' (April 2, 1892, page 199), Burroughs says distinctly that when Whitman's name was proposed for honorary membership at the Authors' Club, 'the great poetic luminaries of that august body said "No" emphatically.'

On the other hand, Professor Holloway, in his 'Whitman' (page 294), states, but gives no dates or authority, that Whitman was invited to join the Authors' Club, but, though declining, was grateful for the honor. It seems strange, if this statement is correct, that neither Burroughs nor Kennedy, both of whom were in close touch with Whitman through those years, had no hint of it; also that Traubel makes no mention of it in any of his three volumes. One would like to get at the facts in the case, but efforts in several directions yield only conflicting statements. Mrs. Laura Stedman Gould thinks it probable that her father turned Burroughs's letter, declining membership in the club, over to the club, even though it was a personal letter. Mr. Robert Underwood Johnson, to my inquiry in 1922, wrote, 'I don't remember that Whitman was ever blackballed, and never heard of the Burroughs letter.' He added that it was inconceivable that Mrs. Gould would overlook such an incident in writing her 'Life' of Stedman. He suggested that I write Mr. Ernest Ingersoll, then secretary of the Authors' Club. Mr. Ingersoll writes me, April 10, 1930, that, being no longer connected with the Authors' Club, he cannot get at its records, but that his memory is clear that Burroughs did not join 'because of the late hours and too much tobacco,' and that he never heard him mention any other reason. He adds: 'If there ever was any controversy over Whitman's proposed entrance, I never heard of it that I can remember; nor can I remember that he was ever proposed. Mr. Charles De Kay writes me, May 9, 1930:

> There was never any trouble on the part of the Authors' Club with Walt Whitman and John Burroughs. These ideas were brought out by people who wanted something piquant to write about. Walt Whitman did not join because he could not come to New York to the club meetings, and for much the same reason John Burroughs decided not to join, although at first he expected to.... These are the actual facts which I am sure of, because it was I who suggested the club to Stedman and R. W. Gilder, and I was also the first secretary. Apropos of a suggestion to make Walt Whitman an honorary member, there were no such members made at that period....

My appeal to Mr. Daniel Henderson, present secretary of the Authors' Club, brings this reply on May 9, 1930:

> I referred your letter of May 1st to Prof. Emory Holloway and he gives me this answer:
> '... It was Mr. Charles De Kay, the founder of the Club, who made the statement [1] at a meeting in Carnegie Hall when he was giving reminiscences of the Club History. Afterwards I asked him about it to make sure I had his meaning aright. I did not feel free to write him in his sickness (it is not important enough) to ask for any of the sort of corroboration which Dr. Barrus seems to be seeking. As to any Club records about it, I am quite ignorant....'

Although Mr. Henderson's letter told me of Mr. De Kay's illness, and suggested that it would be unwise to write him about the matter, I had already written and received Mr. De Kay's reply before learning of his illness. To my inquiries of the present club secretary as to whether the club records showed that Whitman had ever been refused membership, or had had it offered him, and had declined, Mr. Henderson replied:

> As for the Club's archives, they are on file at the clubhouse, 48 West 76th Street, New York, and you are at liberty to search such as we have, on personal application to Steward Hutchinson.

[1] This refers to the statement that Whitman had been invited to join the Authors' Club, and had declined.

The matter was certainly not important enough to me to pursue further, but from all that I can gather I 'hae ma ain doots' as to the Authors' Club ever having cast 'the hospitable glance' in Whitman's direction.

XIV

'*AS I EBB'D WITH THE OCEAN OF LIFE*'

(1883–1888)

As the ocean so mysterious rolls toward me closer and closer
I too but signify at the utmost a little wash'd-up drift,
A few sands and dead leaves to gather,
Gather, and merge myself as part of the sands and drift.

WHITMAN

THE mysterious ocean was in truth rolling closer and closer to the old poet, but among the sands and drift still to be gathered was much to cheer his days. Dr. Bucke's book about him came out in 1883, the renewed visits and letters from O'Connor were a deep joy, even though O'Connor's bark, too, was in the ebbing tide. A happy holiday with Burroughs at Ocean Grove was probably the most joyous experience of this period. A heart-warming gift came to him from noted poets and authors of the day. Sir Edwin Arnold, Edmund Gosse, and Ernest Rhys were among later Europeans who sought him out. His Lincoln lecture of '87 was probably the one of all he gave that yielded him the greatest satisfaction. There were irreparable losses for him, too — the passing of Mrs. Gilchrist and of O'Connor — and he knew his own voyage was nearing its end; still he sang on exultantly:

... Steer forth...
I will not call it our concluding voyage,
But outset and sure entrance to the truest, best, maturest;...
Spurning all yet tried ports, seas, ...
Sail out for good, eidólon yacht of me!

On February 9, 1883, from Camden, Whitman wrote Burroughs of having had some rather bad spells of late, and of not being busy at anything in particular: 'Seem to be like a skipper who has come into port at last and discharged cargo & don't know what to do next.' He also wrote Kennedy that he was 'hawsered by a pretty short rope' — so naturally did he fall into use of terms suggested by his early familiarity with the sea. We find him on March 12 rendering Burroughs advice, always so valued by his comrade. He writes that he will read the 'Century' proof carefully when it comes, and return it with any suggestions he may have to make. He adds:

Chew on what I said in my last — the position you occupy in your printed books is just what it should be *to last* — the paragraph or two of let-up or disclaimer in 'Signs and Seasons' is right, too, 'for reasons' — let it stand — but *nothing further of apology* — not a word.

The month before he had also cautioned Burroughs, 'Don't go back on any position taken,' referring to Burroughs's contention in earlier essays — that the poets should keep close to the truths in Nature. Whitman had evidently read Burroughs's essay named 'Signs and Seasons' in manuscript, and here proposes to read it again in the proof from the 'Century' (25:672). When Burroughs incorporated this essay in the book called 'Signs and Seasons,' he renamed the essay 'A Sharp Lookout.' Commenting on this letter Burroughs said: 'In the essay I had overhauled the poets. When I came to put it in book form I modified and excised a little.' The modified passages are found on pages 27–30 of the book.

When Dr. Bucke's 'Walt Whitman' was about going to press, O'Connor, writing Bucke on February 23 concerning his own contributions in it, spoke gloatingly of his expression, 'the ass reviewers blattering bray': 'Shouldn't wonder if that would stick, as my name for Walt — "the Good Gray Poet" [1] — has stuck, even his enemies being forced to use it. I once wrote gaily to one of the fellows in New York that I was a *Hugolater* and *Whitmaniac*. Soon after I saw in some of the ring papers sneers at us as Whitmaniacs! You see if hereafter they won't fling that word at us. They are indebted to us for even their epithets of abuse.'

Referring to Mrs. Gilchrist's letter, quoted on pages 220–21, O'Connor writes Burroughs on March 21, 1883, that he is enclosing it, and adds:

In a few days Bucke's book will be out of the press, and as it contains a long critique of mine, which, though hasty and fragmentary in treatment, may have passages which will meet Mrs. Gilchrist's views better than my 'Tribune' letters would seem to have done, I mean to send her the volume, and with them write to her and 'define my position.'

Of course I quite agree with her that it makes no difference in the long run what Emerson thought of Walt's book, but that was not the point.

[1] See also pages 311–12.

The thing to do, when I wrote my 'Tribune' letter, was to cross swords with the Puritan, and what blade could I have chosen for the duel like that sword *Excalibur* — the Emerson letter of '55? The result proved it — the weapon of the persecution shivered to the hilt in the encounter attested the wisdom of the choice. I say it without the least vaingloriousness or immodesty, just as a matter of cold record, that never, in public estimation, was there a more crushing rejoinder than I made with that letter of Emerson's at that time. This Mrs. Gilchrist fails to see, but I think Mr. Oliver Stevens does not fail to see it, as Shakespeare says, 'feelingly.'

I am really much obliged to you for letting me see the letter. It is the lovely voice of a lovely soul, and the 'Tribune' did itself little honor in declining to become its audiphone.

My cares and griefs [the death of his daughter] prevented the publication in a pamphlet of those *'Tribune' letters*, as I meant, but I hope to soon get them together, *and seal up the record for the next ages*, which will not forget what some of us say or do about *this book with the strong aureola*.

As readers of Traubel's 'With Walt Whitman in Camden' will have noted, Whitman was curiously given to repeated comparisons between Burroughs and O'Connor. Referring to an August letter from Burroughs in 1883, he said to Traubel:

Burroughs takes exception to O'Connor's vehemence — he often does. It seems to be too strong for John's nerves; but what's the use of kicking? It is very like making a fuss because the wind blows too hard — because the waters raise the devil when the storm comes in. Well, there's a law for noise as well as for quiet.

And, a little later:

John is always calm — I think his calm helps me. I find myself comforted in his good will. I suppose it would help both if William would exchange some of his surplus stir for some of John's surplus calm.

A little-known sonnet on Whitman by George Mereditn, first published in 1883, deserves chronicling as a contemporary deliverance:

AN ORSON OF THE MUSE

WALT WHITMAN

Her son, albeit the Muse's livery
And measured courtly paces rouse his taunts,
Naked and hairy in his savage haunts,
To Nature only will he bend the knee;
Spouting the founts of her distillery

Like rough rock-sources; and his woes and wants
Being Nature's, civil limitation daunts
His utterance never; the nymphs blush; not he.
Him, when he blows of Earth, and Man, and Fate,
The Muse will hearken to with graver ear
Than many of her train can waken; him
Would fain have taught what fruitful things and dear
Must sink beneath the tidewaves, of their weight,
If in no vessel built for sea they swim.
Poetical Works of George Meredith (London, 1912), pp. 187–88.

From a correspondent, W. G. B., in Salem, Massachusetts, came this letter to Burroughs in the summer of 1883. The man had written three years before about Whitman, saying then, 'I respect him, and would respect him more if he were not such an unveiler....' His second letter (July 26) says, in part:

I suppose I am one of those who strain at a gnat and swallow camels. I am willing, glad, to count myself as an admirer of Walt Whitman. The sight of him in Boston two years ago, which I wrote you something about, certainly helped confirm me in my suspicion that he was sincere and pure in intent. My own marriage more than a year ago has perhaps helped clear away what there may possibly have been in me of old maid prudery. His 'Memorandum' is a sturdy and strong apology with evidences of firm and high purpose in it. His 'Specimen Days' are meaty, and they have a cheerfulness which brighten them all through.

I have just read for the first time O'Connor's first letter — a remarkable piece of writing, but the second, though a marvel of trenchant, incisive, scathing literary work, does not help matters. There is a superabundance of luxuriant denunciation in it, too much damning. I read the other day about Newman Hall, the author of a tract I have never seen, called 'Come to Jesus,' which had a great sale, but which in some quarters was fiercely attacked. Dr. Hall wrote a scathing reply which he took to read aloud to a venerable clerical friend of his. 'What shall you call it?' the latter asks.

'I haven't decided.'

'Well, I thought as you read some of the most forcible passages that this would be a good title — "Go to the Devil," by the Author of "Come to Jesus."'... Things may be overdone....

Burroughs replies, in part, as follows (July 30, 1883):

Remember that Whitman assumes and maintains a certain typical character throughout his poems, a character whose chief traits are love. charity, acceptance, and the largest and most intense democratic comradeship towards all persons and things.

The poem that so troubles you ('To a Common Prostitute') seems to me perfectly consistent with this character, and one of his most significant. I can conceive such a character as he portrays in his poems — one embracing not only the divine, the spiritual, but in equal measure the human, the emotional, the sexual, meeting a prostitute and being kind and affectionate with her, pitying her, loving her, and buoying her up by his tremendous sympathy and brotherly love. She is not unclean to him, she is a woman, a betrayed and soiled angel; he understands her, and he at least will not 'exclude' her. If he had pitched his poem in the key of high conventional and ecclesiastical morality, or in any other key than the one of absolute acceptance, it would have been false and out of keeping with the rest of his book. It is just that tone of unworldly equality and comradeship in him, backed up as it is by his enormous spiritual and redeeming power, that so delights me in the poem.

Perhaps no other poet of modern times dare place himself alongside of a woman of the street in that way. But when Walt Whitman says he is 'no stander apart from men,' he means it. All his poems are to be read in the light of that fact. He touches the lowest, and has an actual feeling of kinship with them. Only so can he reach and lift them. This poem is the seal of his love for woman, and gives meaning to all his eloquent boasting on behalf of the sex.

Hungering for a sight of his friend, Burroughs wrote on August 17:

DEAR WALT: Drop me a line where and how you are and what your plans are for the fall.

We are just back from Roxbury, where we went in July. We are all pretty well. I rec'd Dr. Bucke's book and thank you for it. I had already purchased and read it. I cannot say that I care much for what Dr. Bucke has to say; he gives me no new hint or idea. Wm. O'Connor's letter is a treat, with a little too much seasoning. If Wm. would only practice a little more self-denial, he would be much more effective. He *could* write so that his critics could not laugh at him....

The latter part of June, Gilder and I went to Concord and spent a couple of days there. Called on Mrs. Emerson, liked her much, supped and breakfasted with Sanborn and had a pleasant time. Young Dr. Emerson seems a worthy son of his father. I liked him much.

If we ever get another girl in this house and the kitchen machinery running smoothly again, I shall come for you and take no denial. I think it would lengthen my days to see you once more.

With love
JOHN BURROUGHS

We find from the Journals that his hunger was fed, if not appeased, the following month. He writes from Ocean Grove, New Jersey:

Sept. 27. Walt Whitman came yesterday and his presence and companionship act like a cordial upon me that nearly turns my head. The great bard on my right hand, and the sea upon my left — the thoughts of the one equally grand with the suggestions and elemental heave of the other. From any point of view W. W. is impressive. The slope of the back of his head and shoulders and back — how suggestive! You would know that he was an extraordinary man.

Sept. 29. Long autumn days by the sea with Whitman. Much and copious talk. His presence loosens my tongue, that has been so tied since I came here. I feel as if under the effects of some rare tonic or cordial all the time. There is something grainy and saline in him, as in the voice of the sea. Sometimes his talk is choppy and confused, or elliptical and unfinished; again there comes a long splendid roll of thought that bathes one from head to foot, or swings you quite free from your moorings. I leave him and make long loops off down the coast, or back inland, while he moves slowly along the beach, or sits, often with bare head, in some nook sheltered from the wind and sun....

September 30. Perfect days by the sea with W. W. A sort of realization of Homer to me. No man I have ever seen cuts such a figure on the beach as W. W. He looks at home there; is ample for such a setting.

Oct. 1. A last look at the sea with W. W. In the early gray light we stood upon the windy verge and saw the 'foamy wreck of the stranded waves cover the shore.' Looking down the beach, the scene recalled November frosts and snows — the waves churned into foam and spume blown by the winds — the rime of the sea. Great fluffy masses of sea-foam blew like wool far up the sands. The swells not large, but grand and full of fury. ... Return home at 2 pm. The crinkling and dimpling river looks tame enough. The sea is the place for large types....

Whitman spoke of those days by the sea with Burroughs as 'a rare experience,' and said, 'John himself was in extra good feather.' It is probable that the comrades had few meetings after their Washington days which were more truly satisfying than those joyous September days by the sea. Out of the experience Burroughs wrote 'A Salt Breeze' ('Signs and Seasons') [1] and Whitman, the poem 'With husky-haughty lips, O Sea!' [2]

[1] See Burroughs: *Signs and Seasons*, page 176 (early trade edition), where Burroughs states that Whitman's poem was written, as stated above, in 1883. It was printed in *Harper's Monthly*, March, 1884. In *The Fight of a Book for the World* (page 268) Kennedy gives incorrect dates for the Ocean Grove visit, and quotes Burroughs incorrectly as placing that visit in 1884. Whitman's conversation with Traubel also says his poem was written when with J. B. at Ocean Grove. (Traubel, vol. 1, p. 406.)

[2] As a parallel to Burroughs's entries in his Journals, these passages from notebooks of Whitman, made at the time of his visit to Ocean Grove, with Burroughs, September 26 to October 1, 1883, throw light upon how the two comrades worked and played together.

Stedman comments on this companionship by the sea in a letter to Burroughs in early October, in which he discusses an anthology of sea poetry:

I would have given much to be out of all this coil, and with you and Whitman on the sea-beach. You made a grand two—and we should have made a good three — a kind of Athos, Porthos, and Aramis, of natural life. You see I am modest enough to assign to you and Whitman the first and nobler two of the countertypes....

'Starting from Paumanok' as he did, I wonder he did not write more and earlier of the ocean, even, than he has. Can anything outside of Walt's unsurpassed 'Sea-shore Memories' equal his 'Man-of-War-Bird' for suggestions of boundlessness, spiritual unfetterment, the breadth, the sweep, the dawn-and-eve, gloom and glory of the elemental world? Thoreau in the prose of 'Cape Cod' should be bound side by side with Whitman — both have Homeric traits.

Late in October, Whitman wrote Burroughs of having derived much good from their sojourn at Ocean Grove. He calls attention to the September 'Scottish Review,' and to the 'Academy' of September 8, having 'long and friendly notices,' the latter by Dowden. About this time Burroughs learns from Charles Eldridge of the serious break in O'Connor's health. Deeply concerned, he thinks the 'night is not far off for some of us,' including himself, yet he outlived O'Connor, Whitman, and Eldridge by many years.

The original manuscript is now owned by Mr. Oscar Lion. 'September 26, 1883, New Jersey Sea Coast, Ocean Grove. I write this on the beach, the husky surf rolling and beating a little way from my feet — the sun, half an hour after rising, a round red ball up in the heavens right before me east — the long line of sand and beach and beating surf as far as I can see on either hand north or south. I have come down here to be with my friend John Burroughs and for a sea change. Everything is soothing, monotonous, refreshing, a slight saline smell, the music of the rolling surf, the gold-shine of the sun on the water starting in brightness near me and gradually broadening the track leading away out to sea, and expanding there. Several sails in the distance. A fishing boat with three men just comes in and lands close by.

'October 1, Still here. J. B. just left for New York. I walk long on the beach. A partial tempest of wind, from north, following a heavy rain storm last night. The waves rolling and dashing and combing. An unusual show of foam and white froth, not only on shore, but out everywhere as far as you can see; not a sail in sight.... The sea-beach and surf — its myriad ranks like furious white-maned racers, urged by demoniac emulation to the goal, the shore, breaking there ever and dissolving in other myriads pressing beyond and driving in the same, with husky guttural utterance of the sea, and ever its muffled distant lion roars.'

There is a rough draft of the poem 'With Husky, Haughty Lips, O Sea,' composed on Ocean Grove Hotel stationery, in possession of Mr. Milton Einstein. It is unmistakably an adaptation and elaboration of material contained in the notebook above described. This is one more instance of one of Whitman's best poetic inspirations growing out of contact with John Burroughs. — C. J. F.

The next letter, from Burroughs to Whitman, was characterized by the poet as 'better than a good apple.' It was written from West Park on the Hudson, January 8, 1884:

DEAR WALT: That piece of writing of yours in the last 'Critic'[1] is to me very impressive. It is seldom you have fallen into such a noble and lofty strain. As I am myself trying to write a little these days, it makes me sad. It is like a great ship that comes to windward of me and takes the breeze out of the sail of my little shallop. I shall have to lay by today and let the impression wear off. I think you have hit it exactly with that word 'physiological.' It lets in a flood of light. The whole essay is one to be long conned over.

I went down to New York to hear Arnold on Emerson, Friday night. Curtis — the pensive Curtis — introduced the lecturer. I wonder if you have heard Curtis speak. 'Tis a pity he is not a little more robust and manly. He fairly leans and languishes on the bosom of the Graces, one after another. Arnold looked hearty and strong and spoke in a foggy, misty English voice that left the outlines of his sentences pretty obscure, but which had a certain charm after all. The lecture contained nothing new. The 'Tribune' report you sent me is an admirable summary — the pith of the whole lecture. He did not do full justice to Emerson as I hope to show in my essay. At least Emerson can be shorn of these things, and left a more impressive figure than Arnold leaves him. He had much to say about Carlyle, too, but would not place him with the great writers! Because he was more than a literary man he denied him literary honors.

Drop me a line when you feel like it. Winter is in full blast up here and the river snores and groans like a weary sleeper.

With much love
JOHN BURROUGHS

On March 27, 1884, Whitman wrote Burroughs from the new address, 328 Mickle Street, Camden, where henceforth he had his

---

[1] Whitman: 'A Backward Glance on my Own Road,' *The Critic* (January 5, 1884), vol. 4, pp. 1–2.

'The intellect of today is stupendous and keen, backed by stores of accumulated erudition — but in a most important phase the antique seems to have had the advantage of us. Unconsciously, it possessed and exploited that something there was and is in Nature immeasurably beyond... what we call the artistic, the beautiful, the literary, and even the moral, the good. Not easy to put one's fingers on, or name in a word, this something, invisibly permeating the old poems, religion-sources and art. If I were asked to suggest it in such single word, I should write (at the risk of being quite misunderstood at first, at any rate) the word physiological.... The physiological point of view will almost always have to dominate in the reader as it does in the book [i.e., *Leaves of Grass*] — only now and then the psychological or intellectual, and very seldom indeed the merely artistic.'

It is noteworthy that this significant passage was deleted from Whitman's later adaptation of the same material in his 'A Backward Glance O'er Travel'd Roads,' so it is here reprinted in its original form. — C. J. F.

home, cared for by the kind-hearted Mrs. Mary Davis with the help, later, when his condition demanded it, of two young men who, in turn, nursed him. He tells of a recent set-back in health, a 'chilly, stagnant lonesome three weeks'; the death of a young fellow, a near neighbor, to whom he was much attached; of moving the day before into the new place which, he says, is half way nearer the ferry.

That spring Whitman was much exercised by a false report which came out in a fairly friendly notice of the 'Leaves,' in the 'Saturday Union,' May 24 — so much exercised that he did what he almost never did, contradicted it in print. It was a statement by James Berry Bensel to the effect that Longfellow had once told him that Whitman had asked to dedicate the 'Leaves' to him but that he had declined the honor. In 'The Critic,' May 31, Whitman flatly denied ever having asked this of Longfellow, adding that, consequently, of course, Longfellow had not refused what had not been asked, and that he was very sure that Longfellow had never made such a statement. Kennedy, commenting on this, charitably absolves Mr. Bensel from conscious fabrication, pointing out that, on his own admission, he was a mere lad when the alleged conversation took place — many years before writing about it — and that the imperfectly remembered conversation, mingled with confused recollections of other reports heard since, accounted for the myth.[1]

One Walker Kennedy, a Southerner, no kin of the doughty William Sloane Kennedy, came out in the June number of the 'North American Review' with a weak, abusive article about 'Leaves of Grass,' which he declared was neither prose nor poetry. He styled it 'a literary mermaid.'

That Burroughs, with all his love for Whitman, did not blind himself to his faults is shown by a letter (Perry Collection) which he wrote to O'Connor, June 12 of that year, in which he complained: 'Walt is very often lacking in the merest rudiments of common courtesy.' He said further that he wished Whitman would stop writing himself up in the papers; and told O'Connor of having heard that Whitman pocketed an Iowa man's two dollars sent for an autograph, but never sent the autograph! O'Connor's reply ad-

---

[1] Kennedy: *The Fight of a Book for the World*, pp. 69–70.

mitted that he too had reluctantly observed similar flaws in their hero, but neither of them could dwell long on such flaws.

From O'Connor's letter of August 8, one can gather something of Burroughs's which had called it forth:

DEAR JOHN,

Your charming letter of June 31 [*sic*] but I have not been able to answer it till now....

I took your admonitions graciously, I assure you, and if I thought only half as much of my powers as you do, I would certainly abandon the road to the Presidency and turn my face toward Parnassus for good and all. Alas! I do not!

I have never, I believe, gone on the war-path except in my Oliver Stevens letter, and the letter in Bucke's book, and the tone I took in both cases was on considerations of policy, and intended to help Walt's cause. If I had thought a different tone would have helped better, I would have chosen it. But I judged this would prove most effectual, though I was perfectly well aware that it would personally injure me in many quarters. Controversy is war, and if you make your artillery so terrible as to win the battle, you will certainly incur the enmity of the Stoddards and Winters, *et id*.

Now apart from such as they, have I been too belligerent? I should really like to know. Who are the people you tell me I repel and offend? Of course you have a better opportunity than I to know the effect of my writings on the public mind. All that ever reached me on the Oliver Stevens letter was highly favorable, and I have some splendid letters. Of the Bucke contribution I have heard much less, but it was all sympathetic and commendatory, except in one instance, which was decidedly the other way, alleging that I was 'too meat-axey.'

To please every body, especially in a case of a philippic, is out of the question. There is always a class of people — and our literary class is a marked instance — who recoil from the literature of attack, and in direct proportion to its unction. Long, in his Life of Cicero, even after two thousand years, reprobates the great censor for his style on Catiline, Verres, etc., calls him 'scurrilous,' simply on account of the just severity of his flagellation of those villains. A notable instance is Wendell Phillips: those beautiful and noble speeches, beautiful and noble as lightning, and as blasting, make many people talk of him even now as a 'common scold.' You cannot please certain people with satire; they feel repugnance to this form of mental activity; 'an agreeable man is a man that agrees'; yet satire performs its great function even on those who are repelled by it. To be salutary, criticism must be truthful and severe. It will not be liked, but it will be efficacious.

Don't think I am arguing against you, or defending myself. I am only presenting a view which may commend itself to you as one side of the

matter. Meanwhile, I seriously cogitate on all you say, and examine myself. Still, when I think of the twenty years of raucous abuse and slander
to which Walt has been subjected, I cannot feel regret that at last I gave
those scoundrels a broadside which they are likely to remember. The only
mistake in doing this would be to lose the sympathy of the public by
doing it.

As for winning the favor of the magazines, or writing down to their
level, that I fear is not for me. Just in proportion as literature aims high,
can it find no entrance at those gates. Anything bold, original, earnest,
sincere, grand, must not expect publication in popular monthlies. The
'Atlantic' prints Longfellow's 'Michael Angelo,' but what month of
what year would it print 'Timon of Athens'? Do you think the 'Century'
would publish the 'Letters of Junius'? Our magazines are simply summer
picnics. They are immensely entertaining, and I really have nothing to
say against them; only, would to Heaven we had at least one that aimed
at something higher than amusing people! You can depend that no real
literary man — no man of the type of Voltaire — the sower of new ideas,
new ways of thinking, new light — will ever make his fame in our magazines. They are not for such as he, but for those who can please and
charm. The 'Song of Myself' cannot be considered 'available' for
'Harper's Magazine.'

But I won't bore you further on these topics. You surprised me much
by your high estimate of my abilities, which I never suspected you entertained; and it was impossible not to feel flattered at praise so ardent, even
though self-inspection had to sadly deny the tribute....

O'Connor writes again, September 16:

I don't share your rosy faith in the receptivity of magazines, and you
made me laugh deeply when you wrote that the 'Century' would be open
to the Letters of Junius, after the row with Mrs. Burnett, and her com-
pulsory softening of the *dénouement* of one of her stories, which has led her
to break off the connection.... Still, it is a very nice summer picnic, and,
as you say, it is going to serve up Walt on Father Taylor, etc., as a *pièce de
résistance* at the feast; but 'A Woman Waits for Me' — wouldn't that be
a dainty dish to set before a king!...

Some day I'll talk with you about those 'Tribune' letters and show you
that they were effectual, and that I was not laughed at by anyone that
I ever heard of. Ask Anthony Comstock whether he laughed.

In Burroughs's Journal, December 4, is a significant entry about
Whitman. One can but note the assured tone of Burroughs now.
It is no longer as disciple to master that he speaks, but as one can-
did friend to another:

To Philadelphia to see Whitman. Found him and Dr. Bucke at Green's

Hotel. Walt looks as well as usual, and seems to be so. The grain of him yet seems sound and good; though perhaps a little more inclined to a purplish tint, at times, than I had noticed before. Dr. Bucke a large man, with a broad, long head; of choleric temperament mainly; voice rather hard and harsh; brow with a nervous pucker; whole look rather harsh and intense. Pass the night, all of us, at the Smiths' [Pearsall Smith], a Quaker family in Germantown; a fine hospitable family.

A long drive next morning in the park; then to Philadelphia; dine together, and part at 4 pm.

Walt says his opinion about our poets fluctuates a good deal. He used to place Emerson first, then Bryant, and Longfellow. Now he puts them in this order: Bryant, Emerson, Whittier, Longfellow. He has much to say in praise of Bryant, though does not like his poem on Death; but praised the 'Winds,' and such poems.

Walt is writing a long Preface for his poems. Has many ups and downs about it. One day thinks it a good idea, and the next thinks it too much like a concession — that his poems should be taken as they are, without any argument or explanation, like the works of Nature. He seemed anxious to hear what I had to say about it. I told him it was a secondary matter; that the poems would have to stand or fall on their own merits; as time went on, his Preface would be dropped if it had nothing important in it; but, if necessary to the poems, it would be retained. I said, 'Write it, if you feel you have something valuable to say, and let it take its chances; it can neither make nor break.'

Mr. Furness gives me the following information concerning Gosse's visit to Whitman. The Camden 'Post,' January 7, 1885, quotes Mr. Megargee in the Philadelphia 'News': 'Mr. Gosse had many pleasant things to tell of Alfred Tennyson. His friendship and deep appreciation of the good gray poet is not of recent growth, and but for Walt's indifferent health he would have accepted Alfred Tennyson's earnest invitation long since received to spend a month in summer at Tennyson's country home in England. Mr. Gosse described an evening's entertainment in London recently at which the author of "Locksley Hall" delighted a considerable audience with recitations for half an hour from Whitman's "Leaves of Grass."' [1]

Mention is made by Charles Eldridge in a letter to O'Connor, written in 1885 (now in the Perry Whitman Collection), of an association of cultured Englishmen in London of whom Miss Mary

---

[1] Whitman says of Gosse in a letter to Bucke, October 31, 1889: 'Gosse I should call one of the amiable conventional wall-flowers of literature. (See Thackeray's "Yellow-plush," I think.)' — C. J. F.

Smith, of Philadelphia, had recently written Whitman. They met at Toynbee Hall, had organized a sort of priesthood, with self-imposed vows, and had taken Whitman as their exemplar and Master.

From his Mickle Street home on June 23, 1885, Whitman writes Burroughs:

Yours just received (with the 10 — many thanks), the kind invitation reiterated, etc.

I am in pretty fair condition generally, but unable to walk or get around, except very small stretches, and with effort — somehow feel averse to leaving this shanty of mine, where I am probably getting along better than you think —

Mrs. Gilchrist's essay has appeared in the *To-Day* — probably she will send it to you — if not, I will send you mine. It is a noble paper.

I have a little poem to appear in the *Outing*, perhaps in the forthcoming number. Mary Smith and all the family (our Germantown friends) start for Europe tomorrow to be gone over a year.

As I write it is a delightful day — temperature perfect — I take the car to the ferry and get out on the river every pleasant day.

WALT WHITMAN

On one corner of the sheet J. B. has written — probably in sending the letter to some friend:

Just rec'd this. Looks as if W. was not going to move. I shall try him again by and by.

J. B.

Commenting on the foregoing, Burroughs said:

Walt was then talking of building a little house in the country. I had also proposed building him one at West Park — I had a little plan — what a joy it would have been to have him near! But probably he would not have been content there — so few people. Mrs. Gilchrist's son prints that second paper by his mother in his 'Life.' The Pearsall Smith family were good friends of Walt — wealthy Germantown people. Mary, the daughter,[1] was a beautiful girl, very fond of Walt and he of her. The mother was quite religious; she didn't quite take to Walt, I think. She was the author of a religious book or two that had some vogue — I've forgotten their names.

In August, O'Connor writes Dr. Bucke of his own rapidly declin-

---

[1] Mary D. Smith (later Mrs. Costello; still later, Mrs. Berenson) wrote 'Whitman for the Drawing-Room' (*Papers for the Times*, 1886 or 1887), and a paper, 'Walt Whitman in Camden' (*Pall Mall Gazette*, December 23, 1886).

ing health, his loss of strength, especially in the legs, but of his contemplated trip to Canada. He adds:

How glad I shall be to see you, and how much we have to talk about! In your letter of the 10th you told me about the English edition of your book. Its day will come yet. As you say, there is a remarkable lull in our matters, and we can't force them. But something will make a boom before long.

There was a contemptible review of John Burroughs's latest volume in the 'Nation'[1] — that icicle in the caves of darkness, dripping its cold drip. The book was praised, it is true — at any rate, patronized; but there were slurs and sneers at W. W., and at John for championing him, all in the Cambridge and Boston persifleuring style, to which for flavor I prefer an ipecac julep. I like John extremely. In his own true vein he is quite inimitable.

In 1885, a little coterie of Whitman readers in Lancashire, England, formed a society which they facetiously called 'The College,' which in 1931 is still carrying on, although most of the original members are gone. Dr. J. Johnston and J. W. Wallace were the chief movers, the joint authors of 'Visits to Walt Whitman in 1890–1891.'[2] For many years, through my association with John Burroughs, I corresponded with J. W. Wallace and Dr. Johnston, and in 1926, shortly after Wallace's death, met, in Lancashire, Dr. Johnston (then in very feeble health), W. A. Ferguson, and some of their later associates, notably John Ormrod, of Bolton. In 1929, I also met another member, Fred Wild. A strong bond of fellowship held these diverse personalities together throughout the years, and still holds the newer men, despite the incalculable loss of Wallace and Johnston. Dr. Johnston's fine collection of Whitmaniana was given by him to the Bolton Public Library, where it is well housed and treasured. Mrs. Johnston sent over by me, for preservation in the Whitman House at Camden, some souvenirs which

---

[1] *The Nation*, July 9, 1885, reviewing *Fresh Fields*, said that Burroughs presented the curious spectacle of a man actually engaged in annihilating his own literary theories. It gives him several back-handed compliments, but hits at Whitman and Carlyle over Burroughs's head, and at Burroughs directly for championing them — a curious review which admits that Burroughs is writing better and better, in fact is 'in danger of joining the despicable army of good writers.'

[2] Johnston and Wallace: *Visits to Walt Whitman in 1890–1891*. London, Allen and Unwin Ltd., 1917. This book was an expansion of Johnston's pamphlet *Notes of Visit to Walt Whitman* (July, 1890), printed for private circulation in Bolton, 1890, and of a book, *Diary Notes of a Visit to Walt Whitman and Some of his Friends* (1890), printed in London and Manchester, 1898.

had been given her husband by Whitman. At the Wallace home, so long the shrine of British Whitman enthusiasts, through the hospitality of Mrs. Minnie Whiteside, the adopted daughter of Wallace, I drank tea from the large cup which years before had belonged to Whitman — a gift from him to Wallace.

Edward Carpenter, in 'My Days and Dreams' (page 250), tells of

the ardent little coterie at Bolton, where for many years Whitman's birthday was celebrated with songs, and speeches and decorations of lilac blossoms, and the passing of loving cups to his memory.... It helped largely to spread the study and appreciation of Whitman's work in the North of England; it welcomed Dr. Bucke on his arrival from Canada... some of its members crossed the Atlantic on a pilgrimage to the good grey poet; and Dr. Johnston wrote quite an excellent little book, 'A Visit to Walt Whitman,' descriptive of Whitman's personality and surroundings, which I believe is now being reissued... in conjunction with some Notes on the same subject by Wallace.

In a letter to Burroughs in the spring of 1885, Whitman speaks of going to Moorestown to see his brother Ed. This was the feebleminded and crippled brother of whom Whitman was always so solicitous. Walt contributed largely, if not wholly, to his support for years. Burroughs once told me that he understood Walt's father had at one time been addicted to alcohol, and that Walt thought this habit might have been responsible for Ed's condition. He instanced a line in 'Faces' as referring to this — 'I knew the agents that emptied and broke my brother.' Burroughs characterized the mother of the poet as 'a large handsome woman, a strong character.' On inquiry of Miss Jessie Whitman, a daughter of Whitman's brother Jefferson, I received a letter stating that she had never known of Walter Whitman, the father of Walt Whitman, being intemperate, and doubted the statement. 'He was a fine-looking man,' she said, 'and temperance in all things was a strong family trait.' [1] She said further that Ed's condition could hardly be charged to the father's habits, as he was born a normal baby; his childishness, and the dragging of one foot, had followed an attack of scarlet fever at the age of three, and infantile paralysis later. He was able, she said, to get about and do errands, and was a steady church-goer for many years; boarding him out, after his

[1] See *Poet and Person*, p. 79.

mother's death, was necessitated by the illness of the wife of George Whitman.

It was in the summer of 1885 that Thomas Donaldson set going the plan (said to have been conceived by Whitman's friend and housekeeper Mary Davis) of getting up a subscription, limited to ten dollars a person, for the purchase of a horse and phaëton for Whitman, whose increasing difficulty in locomotion was keeping him almost house-bound. The gift contributed greatly to his pleasure and comfort for the next few years. Letters were sent to thirty-five men and one woman, thirty-three of whom responded cheerfully, sending ten dollars each (two of those addressed were away at the time). In his book on Whitman, Mr. Donaldson gives the entire list of subscribers. Among the many well-known names are those of Oliver Wendell Holmes, 'Mark Twain,' Charles Dudley Warner, Talcott Williams, William J. Florence, Edwin Booth, John Boyle O'Reilly, R. W. Gilder, Horace Howard Furness, Mrs. S. A. Bigelow, Lawrence Barrett, William D. O'Connor, Wayne Mac-Veagh, and George W. Childs. From the many interesting letters which Mr. Donaldson received, and from which he quotes, the following from the Quaker poet is selected for use here:

DEAR FRIEND:

I am sorry to hear of the physical disabilities of the man who tenderly nursed the wounded Union soldiers, and as tenderly sung the dirge of their great captain. I have no doubt, in his lameness, that a kind, sober-paced roadster would be more serviceable to him than the untamed, rough-jolting Pegasus he has been accustomed to ride — without check or snaffle. I inclose my mite for the object named in thy note, with all good wishes.

I need not say perhaps that I have been pained by some portions of W. W.'s writings, which for his own sake, and that of his readers, I wish could be omitted.

Thy Friend
JOHN G. WHITTIER

It has often been stated, but not, so far as I know, authenticated, that Whittier threw the complimentary copy of the 1855 edition of 'Leaves of Grass' which Whitman had sent him into the fire. Whether that story be true or not, one delights in the dear old Quaker's fling at the poet's 'rough-jolting Pegasus.' It must have tickled greatly the rider of that Pegasus.

Although so many years had passed since Burroughs had put forth his 'Poet and Person,' it was long before there was another appreciation of Whitman in book form to keep it company. In 1885, we find Dowden writing to Bertram Dobell:

I think Thomson's essay [1] on Whitman would be worth reprinting, both for Thomson's and for Whitman's sake. The best introduction, however, to Whitman, as far as I know, is John Burroughs's 'Notes on Walt Whitman as Poet and Person,' New York [2d ed.], 1871. This little book must have become scarce, for Professor Corson of Cornell University, who is now in England, tells me that he was unable to procure a copy in America. It would be well worth reprinting, with a supplementary note on Whitman's writings since 1871.

Burroughs's Journal for October 1, 1885, records:

Go down to Camden to see Walt,... find him stretched upon his back. 'Come in, sir,' he says cheerily, hearing my voice in the doorway of his room, and taking me for a stranger. He put up his hand as I approached him and then recognized me. 'Oh, John, it is you, is it? how glad I am to see you!' His eyes are running from the effects of some drops just applied to them, and he can hardly see. He looks the same as usual, but he moves with much more difficulty than when I last saw him, and his eyes are very bad for a week now. He had resigned himself to being blind, he said, but now his eyes are improving, right eye pretty good, left much congested and nearly useless. I took his hand and he arose from the sofa and walked to his big chair by the window, and I sat opposite. Here we spent the most of the day engaged in talk. Walt talked as well as usual, and was just as cheery and buoyant as ever. Told me about O'Connor, who left him but yesterday; is much disturbed about him; fears he is breaking up. O'Connor, it seems, can hardly walk.... He talks as brilliantly as ever.

I got 100 oysters of a street-vender and we have an oyster dinner together. Walt eats very heartily — too heartily, I think, and tell him so.

How delightful to be with him again! It does me immense good. I feel like a new person. It satisfies a kind of soul and body thirst. I grow like corn in July for the next two or three days. Leave at 3.30 pm. Walt drives me to the station with his new horse and buggy — the first time I ever saw him drive. He is very proud of his present.

Burroughs's concern for Whitman's health often led him to write suggestions looking to its betterment, as this of October 7 shows:

[1] In Cope's *Tobacco Plant* (London), May to December, 1874 (says W. S. Kennedy), and in the *National Reformer*, James Thomson published a series of papers on Whitman. And in 1910 the same writer published two essays, *Walt Whitman, the Man and the Poet*, with an introduction by Dobell, and published by Dobell.

DEAR WALT:

We left Ocean Grove the next day after I was with you, and are now all home again, safe and snug. I gave up the Kentucky trip for the present. Gilder said next spring would do, so I expect to go next May, and see the season open down there.

I hope you are still mending, Walt. I am almost certain you eat too heartily and make too much blood and fat; at least that you eat too hearty food. As I told you, I was profoundly impressed by a couple of articles in the 'Fortnightly Review,' by Sir William Thompson, on Diet with relation to Age and Activity. He shows very convincingly that as our activities fail by the advance of age, we must cut down in our food. If not, the engine makes too much steam, things become clogged and congested and the whole economy of the system deranged. He says a little meat once a day is enough, and recommends the cereals and fruits. I think you make too much blood. This congested condition of your organs at times shows it. Then you looked to me too fat; and fat at your age clogs and hinders the circulation. I shall talk to my Dr. about you when I see him again, but if I were you I would adopt such a diet as would make my blood as thin as possible, and so lessen the arterial strain. This is common sense and I believe good science. In the best health we grow lean, Sir William Thompson says, like a man training for the ring. I gained much flesh this summer, and am dull and spiritless this fall, as a consequence. I must work it off some way. Drop me a card, if you can, how you are.

With much love
JOHN BURROUGHS

Horace Traubel reports Whitman, in 1888, as saying of the foregoing letter:

He talks to me like a Dutch uncle about my health. I really believe John thinks I am mostly or mainly the cause of my own ill health....

John is always calm — I think his calm helps me. I find myself comforted in his good will. I suppose it would help both if William [O'Connor] would exchange some of his surplus stir for some of John's surplus calm.

Referring again to the letter, Whitman said:

Yes, John about hit the truth. But I have been very abstemious the past three years — very conservative, as you know, and still here I am thrown down. Well, my time has come, that's all. You see I am somewhat of a fatalist.

Whitman writes Burroughs on December 21, with a Merry Christmas to him, the wife, and boy written in red ink across the top. His letter refers to a sorrow recorded in a preceding chapter:

MY DEAR FRIEND,

Real glad to hear from you once more.... The death of Mrs. Gilchrist is indeed a gloomy fact. She had cancer and suffered much the last three months of her life with asthma — for a long time 'every breath was a struggle,' Herbert expresses it. The actual cause of death was dilatation of the heart. Seems to me mortality never enclosed a more beautiful spirit.

The trouble ab't my eyesight passed over, and I use both eyes now same as before.

I am living here, rather monotonously, but get along. As I write, feel ab't the same as of late years — only the walking power seems quite gone from me. I can hardly get from one room to another — sometimes quite force myself to get out a few yards, but difficult and risky —

O'Connor seems to be holding on at Washington. I think he is middling well, except the leg power — his 'gelatine legs' he calls them — will pass over, I rather think.

I drove down yesterday (Sunday) to my friends, the Staffords, 10 miles from here, and staid three hours, had dinner, etc. I go there every Sunday. So I get stirred up some, but not half enough — three reasons, my natural sluggishness and the paralysis of late years, the weather and my old, stiff, slow horse, with a lurking propensity to stumble down —

The 'free-will offering' of the English, through Rossetti, has amounted in the past year to over 400 — [1] I am living on it — I get a miserable return of royalties from McKay, my Philad. publisher — not $50 for both books, *L of G* and *S.D* for the past year.

John, I like *both the names* in your note — I cannot choose — if I lean at all it is in favor of 'Spring Relish' [2] — either would be first rate — Did you get W. S. Kennedy's pamphlet, 'the Poet as a Craftsman'?

I hear from Dr. Bucke quite often, he was, the past season, somewhat broken in physical stamina and health but is better — he gives up for the present his European tour, but is coming here soon for a week.

As I close my bird is singing like a house afire, and the sun is shining out — I wish you were here to spend the day with me.

W. W.

On the last day of the year Burroughs sent the following letter to Whitman:

A happy new year to you, and many returns of the same! I was right glad to get your letter and to know your eyes were so much better. I feel certain that if you eat little or no meat you will be greatly the gainer. It

---

[1] Charles Aldrich, State Librarian of Des Moines, Iowa, in a letter to *The Critic* (April 23, 1892), states that after visiting Whitman in 1885 he wrote to William Rossetti, and thus started the movement of that second fund contributed by British friends. It amounted to about $750. For further details of the raising of this fund, see *Walt Whitman's Workshop*, by Mr. Furness, p. 248.

[2] 'A Spring Relish' is one of the chapters in Burroughs's *Signs and Seasons*, 1886.

will not do to take in sail in one's activities etc., unless he takes in sail in his food also.

We are pretty well here this winter so far. I have just sent off the copy for my new volume. I think I shall stick to 'Signs and Seasons' for the title, as this covers all the articles.

Kennedy sent me his article on 'The Poet as Craftsman.' I liked it pretty well. What he has to say about you is excellent. He wanted my opinion about the argument of the essay, so I told him that I never felt like quarreling with a real poet about his form; let him take the form he can use best; any form is good if it holds good poetry, and any form is bad if it holds bad poetry. I would not have Tennyson or Longfellow or Burns use other forms than they do. If a man excels in prose, he is pretty sure to use prose. Coleridge is greater in prose than in poetry. Poe is greater in poetry than in prose. Carlyle tried the poetic form and gave it up.

I hope you will keep well and that I see you before long. How much I wish you were here to eat a New Year's dinner with us. I wrote Herbert Gilchrist the other day. These must be dark days for him and Grace. To me a black shadow seems to have settled on all England since I read the death of Mrs. Gilchrist.

I wish you would send me by mail or express those books of Emerson, the Essays and the Miscellanies. I want to use them. I am going to re-read Emerson and see how he strikes me now.

With much love.

A few days previously he had entered this passage in his Journal:

It is no doubt inevitable that Whitman's poems, launched as they are in the midst of modern literature, should be judged and tried by the standards of such literature; but how different, how vastly different, they are from it! How sacred books of a race, or a people, rise above the familiar songs and poems of that people! Whitman's poems are much nearer akin to the sacred books than any other modern poems. It will take ages to assign them to their true rank.

I suppose there are times when every cultivated person turns to literature for consolation, for strength, for spiritual refreshment, the same as our fathers turned to the Bible. What poets does he read then? Not the more literary poets — the third-and-fourth-rate singers — but the real bards. I can read Wordsworth, Emerson, Whitman, but not Byron, or Shakespeare. I can read Tennyson and Arnold, though not when in my most serious moods. I cannot say that these poets help me, as certain others do. Swinburne and Rossetti I cannot read in any mood.

Whitman replies to Burroughs, March 18, 1886:

I send today by mail the three vols. of your Emerson so long detained — deepest apologies for not returning them before.

I don't know that I have anything to tell you on my account. I have not written anything. Have a small screed of three or four pages to appear in A. T. Rice's forthcoming Reminiscences of Lincoln, but I consider it unworthy the theme. James Redpath who manages things for A. T. R. has been very good to me, persistently so, and it is to his urgency I have responded. Have not yet finished the Army Hospital article for the 'Century,' but intend to do so forthwith.

Had a violent spell of illness ab't a week ago — remained in bed all last Friday — am up since and go out a little, but don't feel even as half-well as usual — Beautiful here today and I am enjoying the sunshine, sitting here by the window, looking out —

Have read my Death of Abraham Lincoln paper twice this spring,[1] on application ($25 and 30) — got along with it rather slowly, but didn't break down, and seems to have given a sort of satisfaction — Want to scoop up what I have (poems and prose) of the last MSS since 1881–2 and put in probably 200 page book (or somewhat less) to be called 'November Boughs.'

I am getting along comfortably enough here — spirits generally good — my old horse has given out — we have a canary bird, dog, and parrot — all great friends of mine (and teachers) —

Best love to you and 'Sula, not forgetting the little boy.

Burroughs explained, concerning the Emerson Essays: 'Walt had wanted to look through Emerson and sort of estimate him afresh. I think I let him take the books in Washington.' Traubel reports Whitman as saying in 1888, that he had borrowed the Emerson books of Burroughs, who had told him to keep them as long as he liked — that he had more books than he knew what to do with. He explained to Traubel that when he left Washington suddenly in 1873, he had packed hurriedly, leaving most of his belongings behind, but that three years since, sending for them, on unpacking, the five volumes of Emerson came to light. On receiving the books, Burroughs wrote of their arrival and added:

I am just back from Roxbury, where I went a week ago to make sugar

[1] There seems to be some confusion in the data concerning Whitman's Lincoln lectures this year. The Reverend W. E. Barton gives one of the lectures as taking place March 1, in Morton Hall, Camden. The Camden *Coast Pilot* of March 6, records a Lincoln lecture by Whitman in Camden in Morgan Hall, and the Philadelphia *Press* for March 2, also reports the same event. It is not probable that Camden had both a Morton and a Morgan Hall where Whitman lectured early in March, and yet, on March 18, Whitman had written of having already given his lecture twice that spring. We know that he gave one later, April 15 of that year, in Philadelphia. It is probably owing to insufficient and confusing data that Whitman and other authorities differ in stating the number of Whitman's Lincoln lectures as anywhere from nine to a baker's dozen, although Whitman has been charged with magnifying the number of his lectures by one who has found himself unable to ferret out the full number claimed.

in the old woods of my boyhood; had a pretty good time, though too much storm. Only my brother is now upon the old farm. I have to go back there at least twice a year to ease my pain. Oh, the pathos of the old place where my youth was passed, where father and mother lived and died, and where my heart has always been!

I have been pretty well since I saw you, except that I have been off my sleep a good deal. Just now I am having a streak of sleeplessness. I do not quite know what to make of it. Today is my birthday, too; I am forty-nine today. I hope spring finds you better. I lately heard from you through J. W. Alexander, the artist. I think he will make a good picture of you. He is a fine fellow. I am glad to hear of the projected new book. I hope it is to be a reality. Your title is good. My book ['Signs and Seasons'], will be out this month. I do not think much of it — the poorest of my books, I think. No news with me. I hope to see you in May as I go to Kentucky. I hope you will not try to face the summer again in Camden. It is very imprudent. A bright afternoon here with remains of last night's snow still lingering.

With much love.

The Alexander portrait of Whitman never really pleased Burroughs; he used to speak of it as a Bostonese Whitman — an emasculated Whitman — failing to show his power and ruggedness.

Although regarding his 'Signs and Seasons' so slightingly, Burroughs must have felt somewhat encouraged on receiving the following from Whitman, dated April 20:

Your book has come so nice and fresh like a new pot-cheese in a clean napkin — I have read the first piece — 'Look Out' [1] — all through and thought it fully equal to anything in the past, and looked over the rest of the pages — doesn't seem to me to deserve the depreciatory tone in which you speak of it.

Dr. Bucke went to England April 14 — I rec'd a letter from Wm. O'C, and his little book.

Written in red ink between the lines is the following:

I am much the same as of late — made out very handsomely with my lecture April 15th — $674 — have seen Gilder — Early summer here — — I have a new horse — very good —

Burroughs said he thought the little book of O'Connor's must have been 'The Carpenter,' adding:

It first appeared in 'Putnam's Magazine' in '66 or '67; it was a long, powerful story, a Christmas story, in which Whitman appeared as the

[1] Burroughs: 'A Sharp Lookout,' *Signs and Seasons*, 1886.

Christ; it had O'Connor's faults of excess. He wrote it in the attic of our house in Washington, on Capitol Hill, keeping up on tea and tobacco. He wrote like a house a-fire — like Balzac. His wife was away at the time. 'The Ghost' was another of his stories.

It is more probable that Whitman refers, in the foregoing letter, to 'Hamlet's Notebook,' by O'Connor, which was published by Houghton, Mifflin and Company in 1886. 'Three Tales,' by O'Connor, consisting of 'The Ghost,' 'The Brazen Android,' and 'The Carpenter,' were published in a little book by the same firm in 1892. O'Connor's 'Harrington' had been written at a much earlier period.

W. S. Kennedy says that it was in either 1883 or 1886 that Sir Edwin Arnold visited America,[1] his chief object being to see Whitman, of whom he says, in 'Seas and Lands' (Longmans, 1891), that no living singer has composed more divinely musical lines than those beginning, 'Come, lovely and soothing Death.' Sir Edwin's account of his visit is a bit saccharine. One wonders how much of it actually occurred. He writes of sitting beside the most beautiful old man he ever beheld, Whitman's shapely hand resting on his, as together they read from the 'Leaves,' while sweet-voiced Mary Davis, sitting near, joined 'in the lyrical and amiable chat,' her handsome boy lounging in the doorway, and a big setter resting his muzzle on Whitman's arm. Perhaps!

A glimpse of Whitman is offered in Burroughs's Journal, May 5, 1886:

On Wednesday I saw Walt Whitman; spent two or three hours at his house in Camden. He was not very well, and I was myself dull. He looked as fine as usual, sitting there by the window.

Whitman sends the following letter, from Eldridge about O'Connor, on to Burroughs. It was written from Pasadena, California, February 11, 1887:

DEAR WALT,

William and I are here at Dr. Channing's home.[2] I brought William out here from Washington in the hope that the climate might arrest the progress of his disease. It was a serious undertaking to bring so sick a man

---

[1] It would seem that Kennedy is wrong in his dates, as Whitman wrote to Bucke, September 14, 1889: 'Sir Edwin Arnold here yesterday afternoon about an hour — a tann'd English traveler — I liked him.' (Bucke Whitman Collection.)

[2] Mrs. Channing and Mrs. O'Connor were sisters.

three thousand miles on a railroad train, and he was much exhausted when he arrived. He has hardly recovered from the effect of the journey as yet. In fact, he is worse than he has ever been. Can walk very little without the assistance of a friendly arm. If any improvement is to be achieved, it must come hereafter.

This is a garden of fruit and flowers....

William and I received here (forwarded from Washington) letters from Mr. Lovering, M.C., relative to your hospital services. William was unable to answer, much to his regret, but I did the best I could on my own account. Hope for a favorable result....

He [O'Connor] has received an indefinite leave of absence from the Treasury Department with pay. He says he will write you as soon as he can. He sends much love, and so do I. Sorry to hear from the newspapers that your health is so feeble. Wish you could come out here and get strong.

As ever, faithfully yours
CHARLES W. ELDRIDGE

Burroughs explained that this probably referred to an effort being made at the time to get a pension for Whitman. Mr. Furness tells me that he has seen records among Dr. Bucke's Whitman papers proving that Whitman opposed these efforts to secure him a pension. In his book on Whitman, Thomas Donaldson states that the bill for Whitman's pension had been favorably reported in the House, but that further proceedings were stayed because Whitman himself objected, not then actually needing the aid.

A letter of February 25 is one of many which Whitman sent out to Burroughs with the request to send on to Bucke and Kennedy:

Walt Whitman to his friends:
Am sitting here by the window in the little front room down stairs, well wrapt up — for though bright and sunny it is a cold freezing day — have had my dinner (of rare, stewed oysters, some toasted graham bread, and a cup of tea — relished all) — am about as usual — ups and downs — had rather a bad day yesterday — lay on the lounge most of the day — now better; the worst is my enforced house-imprisonment, sometimes two weeks at a time — Spirits and heart though mainly gay, which is the best half of the battle. Love and comfort to you, my friends, your wives, and all. Write often as you can. Monotony is now the word of my life.

WALT WHITMAN

Another glimpse of the old poet is found in Burroughs's Journal, March 9:

Found Walt sitting in a chair with a long, gray-bearded goat-skin behind him, a shawl pinned about him, and a chaos of papers, letters, MSS., books, and so on at his feet and reaching far out into the room. Never saw such confusion and litter; bundles of letters, bundles of newspapers, slips, cuttings, magazines, a cushion or two, foot-rests, books opened and turned downward, dust, etc. etc., and, above all, the grand, serene face of the old poet. He is, or seems, more alert and vivacious than when I saw him in May; inquires anxiously about William O'Connor. Has a little too much blood, I think, and tell him so. Walks out to supper without help, and tells the story of the old woman who, when commiserated for her blindness, said, 'But I have so many things to be thankful for!'

We have much talk, and it does me good to be with him again. He talks affectionately about Beecher, just dead, and says many things in his praise. The word 'miscellaneous,' he says, describes him. Beecher was very cordial to him and pressed him to visit him in Brooklyn. We sit by the firelight till 9 p.m., when I go back to Philadelphia.

The Journal for April 14 tells of going to New York to see Whitman, and to be at his Lincoln lecture:

Found Walt at the Westminster Hotel, fresh and rosy and sweet as ever. The lecture went off finely. A distinguished audience and much sympathy with, and appreciation of, him. At the reception in the evening saw many new people. Walt looked grand and distinguished as he sat in his chair and received the callers. His is easily the grandest face and form in America. He stood it well; the little excitement was just what he needed — a wholesome human breeze that quickened his circulation and made his face brighter.

At 12 P.M. John Fiske, and some one else, came in and began to discuss the immortality of the soul. Walt said he would have given anything to get away to his room and to bed, and as some one else caught on the discussion, he did so. In the morning at eight I found him dressed and resting after his bath, and fresh as a pink. At ten he went to the photographer's with Jennie Gilder, and then to the studio of Miss Dora Wheeler for a sitting. Think Miss Wheeler will make a strong picture of him. I left him at 2.30 P.M. on his way to the ferry, brighter and stronger than I had ever expected to see him again.

This was at least the seventh time that Whitman gave the Lincoln lecture. It was held in the Madison Square Theatre, on April 15. Commenting on all this, Burroughs said, many years later:

Charles Eliot Norton, Lowell, Stedman, etc. were there. When I went into the Century office that day, Gilder introduced me to Lowell and Norton; we had some talk. In the evening we all sat together in a box. The last thing I did for Lowell was to hand him his hat. Stedman's daughter, looking like a little fairy, ran on the stage with a big bouquet of lilacs for Walt. He took her up in his arms and kissed her. It was a great occasion. They realized several hundred dollars for Walt.

Apropos of Miss Wheeler's portrait of Whitman, made at that time, I have lately learned from the artist, now Mrs. Keith, that the portrait is now permanently placed in the Whitman house in Camden.

Whitman had already given his Lincoln lecture once before in that year, earlier in April, at the Unitarian Church in Camden; and he gave it at least twice more — in New York in 1889, and in Philadelphia in 1890.

Although Lowell paid Whitman the tribute of attending this lecture on Lincoln, in 1887, when asked to submit a list of names for inscription on the Boston Public Library, he omitted the name of Whitman! [1]

News of the now widely scattered group of Whitmanites goes to Burroughs from Whitman on July 22:

Your letter to H. G. [Herbert Gilchrist] is rec'd and he has shown it to me. He is here yet painting the portrait. William O'Connor has got back to Washington — he is very poorly — nearly utterly disabled in leg power (walking or even standing) — Eldridge is at Los Angeles to stay. Three or four weeks of fearful heat here, but I have stood it — am fairly today. Sidney Morse the sculptor is here — I hear from Dr. B[ucke] and Kennedy.

Burroughs said of Gilchrist's work:

Herbert tried to paint Walt, but it was a failure. It gave none of Walt's power. Morse made a big, shaggy sort of Homeric bust of him that had power, but he overdid it. He didn't show the womanliness there was in Walt — there was something fine, delicate, womanly in him.

That summer the friends of Whitman were astonished and incensed to read the attack made upon him by Swinburne in the 'Fortnightly Review,' August 8. Swinburne had been one of the earliest British men of letters to express appreciation of Whitman.

---

[1] December 13, 1888, W. S. Kennedy writes to Whitman that he has discovered a poem in Harvard Library attributed to W. W., and given to Harvard by James R. Lowell, September 26, 1860. It was called 'Solitude,' sixteen pages in length, divided into two sections with running titles, 'Chamber' and 'Street,' and beginning,

'O! this everlasting contact with man;
This agony of a continual presence.'

Whitman has written on the back of this letter (now in Bucke MSS.): 'The "Solitude" MS. is of course a fraud entire.... I have never had relations with Lowell.' — C. J. F.

In 1862 he had written to Lord Houghton [Richard Monckton Milnes], rhapsodizing about 'A Voice out of the Sea'; he had called the Lilac requiem 'the most sonorous nocturn ever chanted in the church of the world'; and, in 1868, in his critique of William Blake [1] had commented upon the spiritual kinship between Blake and Whitman — their splendor of stars and of storms, their flights across vast spaces of air and upon shoreless seas, their passionate love of liberty, and their oceanic quality — showing, even in their shortcomings, the faults of elemental and eternal things. And in 1871, in 'Songs Before Sunrise,' [2] he had written a fervent poem 'To Walt Whitman.' A year later, in a critical attitude, in 'Under the Microscope,' he declared that when Whitman begins taking himself too seriously as a 'representative poet,' and an 'official democrat,' 'the strength forsakes his hand and the music ceases at his lips.' To this dignified expression of his opinion, no one could take exception, but when, in the August 'Fortnightly' he published his venomous insult, the amazing apostasy struck the Whitmanites dumb. He said Whitman's Eve was a drunken apple woman, and his Venus a Hottentot wench, befuddled with rum and cantharides. Over all this abuse Whitman refused to get excited, his terse summary of Swinburne being, 'Ain't he the damnedest *simulacrum*!' We shall see, from the journal entry describing his midsummer visit to the poet, how Burroughs had always regarded Swinburne's espousal of Whitman.

... He came slowly down the stairs... looking better than last year. With his light gray suit and white hair, and fresh, florid face he made a fine picture.

Among other things we talked of Swinburne's attack. Walt did not show the least feeling on the subject — was absolutely undisturbed by the article. I think he looks upon Swinburne, as I do, as a sort of abnormal creature, full of wind and gas, but not worth attending to. I abhor his poetry, and I know that Walt has no stomach for it. He is a mere puff of mephitic gas. I told Walt I had always been more disturbed by Swinburne's admiration for him than I was now disturbed by his condemnation — I was heartily glad that his true character had come out at last. [3]

[1] Swinburne: *William Blake: A Critical Study* (London, 1868), p. 303, *et seq.*

[2] Conway, in his *Autobiography*, styles these rather as 'songs of an afterglow.'

[3] Burroughs quotes from this journal entry, in an article 'Walt Whitman,' in *The Critic* (April 2, 1892), vol. 20, pp. 199–200, making slight verbal changes from his diary entry; e.g., 'a sort of abnormal creature of the bloodless fungus sort....' — C. J. F.

By and by Walt had his horse hitched up, and we drove down to Glendale to see young Gilchrist — a fine drive through a level farming and gardening country. Walt drives briskly, and salutes every person he meets ... he said as he grew older the old Long Island custom of speaking to everyone on the road was strong upon him....

We talked of many things. I recall this remark of Walt's: that it was difficult to see what the feudal world would have come to without Christianity to check and curb it. Walt gave a history of the inhabitants in many of the houses they passed.... The cherry-lipped young Englishman was well and brisk, and apparently enjoying himself in a very flat, uninteresting country, and an uninteresting household. Walt drove back before dark, was apparently not fatigued by the drive.

In 'Whitman: A Study' Burroughs thus comments on the poet at this period:

The spectacle of this man sitting there by the window of his little house in Camden, poor and partly paralyzed, and looking out upon the commonplace scenes and people, or looking athwart the years and seeing only detraction and denial, yet always serene, cheerful, charitable, his wisdom and tolerance ripening and mellowing with time, is something to treasure and profit by.

Whitman did express himself about Swinburne later, but never with any bitterness. In 1888, he said to Traubel:

It's funny to me how you fellows all get so hot over Swinburne's recantation — all but John. John was hot over the original position of Swinburne — said he couldn't understand it — wondered if I had been misbehaving.... When Swinburne took it all back, John said: 'Now things look about right again; now I see the trouble was not with you, but with him.' It's not necessary to believe Swinburne's original notion was dishonest, nor that the new view is; they stand for two Swinburnes: you can take your choice; one is as honest as the other.... Maurice said, 'Swinburne's gone crazy.' But Swinburne's friends originally thought he had gone crazy for exactly the opposite reason.

And again:

Swinburne has his own bigness; he is not to be drummed out of all camps because he does not find himself comfortable in our camp.

Such ability to take a disinterested view, such superiority to bitterness for the personal affront, show not only the bigness, but the charity of the man — Not till the sun excludes Swinburne will he exclude him, any more than he would a 'drunken apple woman' or other outcasts. On this subject Traubel quotes him further:

And if Swinburne had a few grains of thought with all his music, wouldn't he be the greatest charmer of all? I never liked him from the first, from the very first; could not take him in — adapt myself to him. I know of nothing I think of so little account as pretty words, pretty thoughts, pretty china, pretty arrangements. I have a friend, a woman, — a 'cute one, too; one of the very 'cutest — who takes most to 'Bothwell.' ... My taste is alien — on other currents: I do not seem to belong to the Swinburne drift. I find it difficult to account for my dear woman's taste. Did you not hear it said somewhere that Schiller was very fond of rotten apples — the rottener the better? Maybe that... explains her taste.

Swinburne's disgraceful abuse of Carlyle, George Eliot, Emerson, and Whitman may well deprive him of a place in the bin with sound apples. While his shocking controversy with F. J. Furnival, which he waged in 1879 in the 'Gentleman's [*sic*] Magazine' — and Furnival in the 'Spectator' — shows to what depths he could descend in offensive and brutal personalities. And, indeed, what can one expect of him who could call Emerson 'an impudent and foulmouthed Yankee philosophaster'?

In the spring of 1887 some of the benevolently inclined in New England, at the suggestion of Sylvester Baxter and W. S. Kennedy, contributed to a cottage fund for Whitman, hoping he would carry out his dream of a shanty at Timber Creek, New Jersey. They raised a purse of $800. The reverend Cyrus Bartol said on contributing, 'In comforting his old age, let us pay him a part of our debt to him.' 'Mark Twain' declared, 'What we want to do is to make the splendid old soul comfortable.' (Boston *Herald*, May 24, 1887.) Kennedy, in his 'Reminiscences,' page 11, says of the project, 'But Walt never got around to building, and used the money, by cheerful permission of the contributors, for other purposes.' [1]

References are so frequently made to the hostility shown Whitman by New England literary folk that it behooves us to remember how much of friendliness toward him really came out of New England. Emerson had visited him shortly after his first edition of the 'Leaves,' and had sent many another person to see him. Thoreau

[1] On October 7, 1887, Whitman wrote to Baxter acknowledging the receipt of $800 in all. Among the subscribers to the fund were Mrs. Ole Bull, John Boyle O'Reilly, W. D. Howells, Edwin Booth, James R. Osgood, Frank B. Sanborn, Cyrus Bartol, W. S. Kennedy, Sylvester Baxter, Charles Eliot Norton, 'Mark Twain,' C. S. Sargent, T. B. Aldrich, and J. T. Trowbridge. (Records in Boston Public Library.) The whole history of this is included in a series of articles on the relations of Whitman and the New England authors, now in preparation by myself for the *New England Quarterly*. — C. J. F.

and Alcott had visited him in 1856. Longfellow called on him in 1878, and in 1881 Whitman returned the call. Frank B. Sanborn visited him in 1877, and remained a stanch friend. Trowbridge and Kennedy, also New-Englanders, were eminently friendly. Lowell, Holmes, and Whittier, while never 'accepting' him, contributed cheerfully to a benefit fund for him, and Lowell gave the support of his presence to Whitman's lecture on Lincoln in 1887. Sylvester Baxter, another New-Englander, was a warm and helpful friend, and Charles Dudley Warner and 'Mark Twain' showed their good will by contributing to a beneficiary fund for the poet. Whitman wrote O'Connor, March 4, 1889, that T. B. Aldrich had sent $25 for the 'big book' with a kind letter, and on March 18 of the same year he wrote him again saying he had just had a call from a Boston lady and adding, 'Some few of my most determined friends and understanders appear to be in Boston.' [1]

O'Connor's visit to Whitman, after his return from California, is reported by the latter to Eldridge. He tells of O'Connor going with crutch and cane, but being as fine as ever in conversation, with mentality entirely unaffected; he is still hopeful about him. He writes of Herbert Gilchrist's portrait of himself, just taken to London, as 'meaty and sensuous' — quite a different estimate from Burroughs's, although, since Gilchrist painted two or three of Whitman, these diverse comments may not have been about the same portrait.

Burroughs said of the following letter of October 26, "It was a little kink of Walt's to give in letters to his friends a concrete picture of his daily life."

Early P.M. Have just had my dinner (Plain boiled beef, potatoes, and a roast apple — all relished well), and am now sitting here in my big chair in the little front room — cold and cloudy out — looks like winter.

O'C was here eight days ago, spent an afternoon and evening with me, and is now in Washington and at the office — He is in a pretty bad way — paralysis, the Dr. now calls it — (I will get Kennedy to send you on a letter giving full details)

The 'Pall Mall Gazette' letter you spoke of appears to have erased a sentence or two (showing my gratitude and appreciation of home-helpers), but even as it is, I hope it doesn't bear the construction you speak of —

I enclose my last two bits tho' you may have seen them before — I have

[1] In the Perry Whitman Collection.

just rec'd letters from Dr. B. and Kennedy — Herbert G. went back five weeks ago with his picture, and I have heard from him and it in London — they like the portrait. The Smiths are back in Phila. I am much as usual — but the peg-letting-down goes on with accelerated pace —

Burroughs said, on rereading the letter:

What construction could that have been? I can't imagine now. I think I got an idea that he had implied that he got no help here — was neglected and unappreciated here.

That Whitman did, as he wrote Burroughs, give credit to his American helpers is seen by an undated clipping (manifestly in 1887, and later than May) in the Bucke-Whitman papers, apparently from an American newspaper:

Walt Whitman writes thus to the editor of the 'Pall Mall Gazette':
'First thank you again for the handsome money present of some months ago, which did me more good than you perhaps think for — it has helped me in meals, clothing, debts, &c ever since. My best help however has come in my old age and paralysis from the British Islands. The piece in your paper (was it early in May last?) from "a distinguished American man of letters" about me was a very large inflation into fiction of a very little amount of fact — in spirit it is altogether, and in letter mainly untrue about my affairs, &c. My income from my books (royalties &c) does not realize $100 a year. I am now in my 69th year, living plainly, but very comfortably, in a little wooden cottage of my own, good spirits invariably, but physically a sad wreck, and failing more and more each successive season, unable even to get about the house without help — most of the time, though, without serious pain or suffering, except extreme weakness which I have a good deal — the paralysis that prostrated me after the Secession War (several shocks) never lifting entirely since, but leaving me mentally unimpaired absolutely (thank God!) I have a few, very few, staunch and loving friends and upholders here in America. I am gathering a lot of pieces — verse and prose — uttered within the last six years, and shall send them out under the name of " November Boughs " before long — a little book (200 pages or less), some new pieces — a sort of continuation or supplement. Then I think of printing a revised edition of complete writings ("Leaves of Grass," " Specimen Days and Collect," and " November Boughs " all in one volume) soon. Please accept personal thanks from me (never mind the literary) and I know you will accept this impromptu note in the same spirit in which it is written. Best thanks and love to all my British helpers, readers, and defenders.'

On January 7, 1888, Whitman sent the following letter to Burroughs; misdirected to West Farms, instead of West Park:

Your sister Abigail and Mrs. Dart have just been here to see me and have given me the latest news I have had ab't you for a long time — Glad to get the visit and glad to hear — I am getting along in much the same fashion as before — do not get out or around at all, but keep fair spirits and am comfortable enough.... Am sitting here by the fire — a parrot and canary in the room — Ernest Rhys has been here some time — ... Morse, the sculptor, has gone temporarily to Indiana — Kennedy's W. W. book is to be published by Wilson in London I believe[1] — I hear frequently from Dr. Bucke, he is all right. I got a letter from O'Connor three days since — he is pretty ill yet, but I believe gets to the office — I write a little — short bits, to order, mostly — spend the time seated in my big chair here, quite aimlessly....

Burroughs said concerning Morse, the sculptor:

He made two busts of Walt. We all paid $5.00 a piece toward one. I broke mine up. It made Walt look smart, and American, and wide awake, but had nothing of his repose and grandeur. I think the 'Herald' did it as an act of charity. Some of them he preserved.

From Philadelphia, May 30, 1888, W. S. Kennedy, after visiting Burroughs at Riverby, wrote him of Whitman and Camden friends:

I struck it rich today in lighting on the little lawyer Thomas B. Harned and Horace Traubel — both good fellows. We have just drunk a bottle of champagne with Walt. Harned has invited me to be present at a supper and reception at his house with Walt tomorrow.... Walt walks with great difficulty, and with weakened leg-power. Head power all good, except occasionally slight deafness.... Jeff, his brother, was there yesterday. I like him much. He brought W. a day rose in a pot, and was very affectionate and brotherly....

I gave all your messages to Walt and he received them with beaming face and grunts of satisfaction.

Donnelly's book (with the previous long talks of O'Connor) has finally won him over to belief that Wm Shakespeare, the actor of Stratford, cannot be the writer of the plays. But he will not admit that Bacon *was*....

On June 5, from Belmont, Massachusetts, Kennedy wrote again:

The N.Y. Graphic for June 2 had its first page completely occupied with Whitman illustrations....

We had a divine and sweet time of it the birthday night at Harned's. I sat next to WW. at a preliminary private supper... later came a company of twenty odd.... Walt *is visibly* losing his *magnetic power*. I did not feel that powerful, sleep-disquieting, magnetic pull that I did even two

[1] Kennedy: *Reminiscences of Walt Whitman*. Gardner (London), 1896.

years ago. Still he is worth three or twenty other men *yet*. He said he needed cheering; but most visitors come with their own burdens.

During the eve, at H's, came young H. Traubel with the first roll of 'November Boughs' proof-sheets. Walt has not yet decided on a pub'r. McKay told me he had Walt's receipts for $2000, copyright payments, and evidently wants the new job.

... I think Walt, in days of his mighty strength, w'd have laughed (and did) the *Bakespeares* to scorn.

... Be sure to let me serve you in all comradely kindness, in looking up of references (no matter how many) in the libraries here.

I wish I c'd entirely approve as of universal value and application Walt's free and easy way of taking good and evil — messing them all up together. But I think that while an occasional poet with such universal charity is good, for a rarity, yet that he is nevertheless by so much weaker than the greatest souls of the world who have always distinguished sharply between right and wrong, and have never suffered their faculty of intense indignation to be chilled. I know W. W. possesses this faculty deep down in his profound and composite-terrible soul; but has he, think you, suppressed it a little too much in his books? I noticed that he has gradually cut out of his books the severest and bitterest things. Well, I feel somehow that in writing the above I have only exhibited my own limitations (Calvinism) and I have an uneasy feeling that Walt is towering up above me all the while, and that love, charity, is the divine solvent of all, the *vis medicatrix*.

Whitman writes on February 11 — a joint letter to Burroughs and Kennedy, writing on the back of a letter from Dr. Bucke. He tells them that Dr. Bucke's view of the gravity of O'Connor's case is 'about as dark and severe as the case will stand.'

... Nothing very new or special with me — I am jogging along much the same — down hill, no doubt even if slowly. This is the most nipping winter I have ever had — At present am sitting here by the fire in my little front room — have had my late breakfast (I rise late these cold days) of chocolate and buckwheat cakes with quince jelly — feel so-so fine —

Ernest Rhys is here — was here last evening; his lecture, debate about and advocacy of 'L of G' last Tuesday evn'g in N.Y. seems to have been quite an affair — a success — the leaning of the full-dress audience (many ladies) was palpably certainly on our side — quite remarkable — Tho' little Fawcett and Rev. Lloyd had their say against 'L of G.' Rhys delivers lecture again here in Phila. next Tuesday evn'g. I still have little bits in 'N.Y. Herald.'

Explaining about the foregoing, Burroughs said:

Rhys was an English author, poet, and lecturer. His lecture about Whit-

WILLIAM SLOANE KENNEDY

man was before the Nineteenth Century Club. Edgar Fawcett,[1] an English-man, lived in America for some time.[2] I don't remember who that Rev. Lloyd was.

Rhys edited a Prose Selection from Whitman for the Walter Scott Library (London). He lectured several times on Whitman both in England and in America, in 1885 and 1888. An article by him in the 'Scottish Art Review,' of Glasgow, June, 1889, was called 'Portraits of Walt Whitman.' [3]

If Swinburne had turned his coat concerning Whitman, evidently others in Great Britain were becoming stronger in allegiance to the poet. Kennedy, in his 'Reminiscences,' page 96, quotes a letter to Whitman from Sheridan Ford of New York, written April, 1888, asking him if he would entertain a proposition to lecture in Great Britain:

> From facts in my possession I am quite sure that you would be very successful, for the cultured class of Great Britain have an abiding interest in you and everything which concerns you. I should be willing to guarantee to you a stated sum, or, if you would prefer it, star you on a percentage. My friend and yours — R. Macaulay Stevenson of Glasgow, perhaps better known to you as 'Calamus' — thinks that your reception throughout Scotland would partake of the character of an ovation.

To Whitman, with his long-held ambition as a lecturer, this invitation, coming when he was beyond entertaining it, must have tasted like Dead Sea apples.

From his armchair Whitman seemed to be doing the biggest part in keeping the circle of friends in touch with one another — his own letters, and letters from the friends — Bucke, Burroughs, Kennedy, and O'Connor — going the rounds, either sent out by him, or he

[1] Burroughs paper, 'Walt Whitman Again,' *Conservator* (October, 1895), was in reply to one by Edgar Fawcett in a preceding number.

[2] Fawcett was an American, born in New York, where he always lived except for occasional visits to Europe.

[3] From the St. Botolph Club, Boston, February 20, 1888, Ernest Rhys writes to Whitman. He describes in detail how he has just given a lecture at Concord on 'The New Poetry' at Emerson's house, and had discussed Whitman at length. Among other things he says: 'Old Mrs. Emerson and Ellen Emerson formed part of the audience, which though small was perhaps as remarkable as any I am ever likely to have. The discussion after my paper was full of interest and there was a general agreement with my position, and that part based on *Leaves of Grass* in especial. Mrs. Talcott Williams gave me two pictures of your house, inside and out, one shewing you seated by the window, and, on Sanborn's suggestion, I took these to shew to the people at the lecture, who were quite delighted with the glimpse of you thus given.' (From the Bucke MSS.) — C. J. F.

giving digests of them and reporting his condition to one, with the request that the messages be relaid to the others. On April 27 he writes Burroughs that although O'Connor's letters show the old fire and fervor, his physical decline increases. Of himself he adds: ' A little feebler every successive season and deeper inertia; brain power evidently very little affected, and emotional power not at all — I yet write a little for the "Herald."'

He tells of a recent visit from Mrs. Louise Chandler Moulton, of a recent letter from Mr. Hamlin Garland, who had found his poems 'nearly irresistible in effect'; and speaks of getting out in his 'rig.' A May letter tells of having turned his ankle, which will prevent him from visiting Burroughs that spring, as planned. Burroughs, commenting on this, said: 'He was never there after 79, though he planned to come many times. He would get to New York and stay there. And then, he didn't want to be a burden to Ursula.... Nothing was said, but I understood.'

In view of the many times Burroughs tried to arrange for Whitman to visit him, it seems a little puzzling that Whitman is quoted by Traubel as reverting to 'John's aloofness.' The same month that a visit had been planned to Riverby, Traubel reports Whitman saying of Burroughs:

I rarely hear from him. I don't know about John — he stands aloof so much of the time. I have asked myself whether this betokens any change of feeling. I suppose it don't. When John writes things — has occasion to mention me — he seems to be of the old spirit — I can see no retreat or compromise. But he don't come round so much — he seems to avoid visiting me — which must have its good reasons, too. On the simply convivial, social side — at the table, face to face, in the jolly hours when all the fences are down, John is not our sort; anyhow, I miss him a lot.

Burroughs's letter of June 11 must have entirely dispelled any fleeting doubts of his loyalty. Whitman said of it, to Traubel: 'It is a June letter — worthy of June; written in John's best out-of-door mood. Why, it gets into your blood and makes you feel worth while. I sit here, helpless as I am, and breathe it in like fresh air.'

DEAR WALT:

I hear through Kennedy that you are ill, or were so last Monday. I do hope you are well again. Drop me a card if you are able and tell me how you are. I want to find time soon to come down and see you if company does not bore you. I shall think of you as able to be out occasionally enjoying these June days. The world has not been so beautiful to me for a long time as this spring; probably because I have been at work like an honest man. I had, in my years of loafing, forgotten how sweet toil was. I suppose those generations of farmers back of me have had something to do with it. They all seem to have come to life again in me and are happy since I have taken to the hoe and crowbar. I had quite lost my interest in literature and was fast losing my interest in life itself, but these two months of work have sharpened my appetite for all things. I write you amid the fragrance of clover and the hum of bees. The air is full these days of all sweet meadow and woodland smells. The earth seems good enough to eat.

I propose for a few years to come to devote myself to fruit-growing. I have seventeen acres of land now, nearly all of it out in grapes and currants and raspberries. I think I can make some money and maybe renew my grip upon life.

I was glad to see Kennedy. I like him much.

How I wish you were here, or somewhere else in the country where all these sweet influences of the season could minister to you. Your reluctance to move is just what ought to be overcome. It is like the lethargy of a man beginning to freeze.

We are all well. Julian goes to school in Po'keepsie and is a fine boy. He goes and returns daily on the little steamer. I hope O'Connor is no worse. Do drop me a line. With much love

JOHN BURROUGHS

XV

NOVEMBER BOUGHS

(1888–1891)

You lingering sparse leaves of me on winter-nearing boughs,
And I some well-shorn tree of field or orchard row;
You tokens diminute and lorn (not now the flush of May, or July
    clover-bloom — no grain of August now);

. . . .

Yet my soul-dearest leaves confirming all the rest,
The faithfullest, hardiest, last.

WHITMAN

IN the spring of 1888, Whitman began to collect his later poems, under the heading 'Sands at Seventy,' his prose essay, first called 'My Book and I' — and later, 'A Backward Glance o'er Traveled Roads' — and some miscellaneous prose, the book to be called 'November Boughs.' He said to Horace Traubel, '"November Boughs" will be my good bye.[1] Any day the slender thread may be cut — any day. Horace, we will take the book up and see it through — eh?'[2]

He also told him: 'Of all the people I have known or know you are the most fitted to help me just now.'[3] And Traubel did help him, devotedly, persistently, and Whitman failed not, time and again, to acknowledge that help with affectionate gratitude. One brief sentence which he wrote in a letter of September 1, 1888, to Kennedy, will suffice as illustration: 'Traubel is unspeakably faithful and kind.'[4]

Whitman told Traubel that he had the dread of leaving something unfinished, side-tracked; and, knowing the precarious state of his health, his dearest wish was to see this work brought to completion. His friends, as well as himself, realized by what a slender thread his life hung. The dauntless O'Connor, whose state was even more pitiable and precarious, wrote to Dr. Bucke in June, feelingly: 'Poor Walt! I wish he could be better. It makes me heavy-hearted to think of him, so sick, so shackled, so infirm, in the Druid grandeur of his age.'

---

[1] Traubel: *With Walt Whitman in Camden*, vol. 1, p. 209.   [2] *Ibid.*, p. 186.
[3] *Ibid.*, p. 187.   [4] Kennedy: *Reminiscences of Walt Whitman*, p. 58.

The following letter from Horace Traubel to Burroughs came on June 18, the first of many reporting on Whitman's condition:

DEAR JOHN BURROUGHS:

Walt Whitman has thought it would be well for me to write you a word in his behalf, or about him, and has assured me there was no danger that you would consider my entrance upon your courtesy as an unwelcome interruption. And, indeed, I intend no full word with which you might be disturbed.

I am honored in being upon free and close personal relations with our mutual friend and father: am daily near him, aiding in the production of the new book, playing willing courier in this hour of his necessity, conferring with him upon matters of mutual duty [?] or interest. This, perhaps, is ample introduction. I hope it is. My purpose in writing now is wholly in reference to him and to you — wholly apart from any desire to thrust my personality into your view — and that, therefore, you will understand and appreciate.

Walt has been very seriously ill — is still physically astray to a degree that excites our regret and fear. But he is full of the thought of his friends — of you among them as a chief figure; and of that I have wished to tell you.

He lies down, sits up, reads by piecemeal, dozes (this, alas! too freely!) — and the invariable days give him no great release. Sunday week we thought he was dying — but radical treatment brought him about again, at least to such an extent as relieved the immediate situation. Some of the paper accounts of him have been too rosy, some of them too despondent. It is my impression that the whole matter is one of but a short time. I may be mistaken; and hope I am.

Now, my dear John Burroughs (for I, too, have my own spiritual reasons for knowing and loving you) — if there is aught I may do for you here, any word I could from time to time transmit, any thought you could value out of the solicitude we all feel for the great and good man now not far from his departure — summon me and I shall be yours. I may say again, Walt has himself indicated his pleasure in my addressing you. And yet you must be free to close me out if that may be deemed the just thing to do.

Ever cordially

HORACE TRAUBEL

On June 27 came a second letter from Traubel in which he said Whitman had been much touched and pleased by the tone of gentle concern in which Burroughs had written; he sent messages of goodwill and expressed the strong hope of again rallying, and said:

Tell him also I am quite sure Dr. Bucke this time saved my life; that if he had not been here to roll up his sleeves and stay and work and watch, it would have been a final call....

Traubel adds:

This puts the brightest phase on the trouble. Even yesterday he had an experience of feebleness almost to the death.... You may be easily aware that his state is critical. He seems to gain no strength. His mind is not to be depended upon for any applied labor. My experience with him, which is always on closest terms, indicates many mental changes from the period of thirty or sixty days back. We hope, but we fear, too, but we love through all.

I am advised, too, but not by W. W., to tell you one thing more: I believe it is his desire — expressed to Dr. Bucke — in case of a fatal issue to this or another attack, that John Burroughs should stand by and say the last wise word over his body.

Traubel closes with trusting that the suggestion does not seem precipitate, since the inevitable event may best be met by being anticipated.

Again, from Traubel, comes this of July 3:

Until your note came yesterday, I had supposed you realized the gravity of Walt Whitman's condition. I don't wonder that the tone of my communication alarmed you.

But things are indeed as bad as the worst. His progressive paralysis is going over a sure course. We watch it helplessly — not without hope, as I have said, but with the knowledge of its one possible issue, some day soon or remote.

I read W. W. such passages from your message as I thought he would delight to hear. He listened and was pleased and touched. But beyond signifying that he wished his love conveyed, he attempted no greeting. Last night was a bad one for him. His mind refuses all exertion — is in some degree shattered — as he puts it, has 'lost all grip — utterly refuses to act or be strong.'

He has been confined to his room now for weeks, and sees nobody except doctor, nurse, and two or three others of us. He becomes feebler by slow stages, but with a perceptible sureness. How grievously this moves us you can well imagine. I have been thus plain because you seem to have been somewhat in the dark.

I write you at once today to ask if you cannot be prevailed upon to reconsider the decision rendered in the recent note. I am in daily communication with Dr. Bucke, but in the message just written a few minutes ago withheld reference to your judgment in the matter until I may have heard again. You know well enough, I am not likely to be one from whom you would need to fear friction or discourteous insistence. But the case is likely to be so extraordinary in itself — so truly historical — that one is constrained to look upon it with an eye studious of W's desires, and that his expressed desire for your presence — your word — is his heart's hope, his heart's affection, you, who know him well, may easily comprehend. We therefore dare not wholly give up the hope. No word of this, of course, goes to W. W. himself. And you may rely upon my instant respect for all you have said or may say to meet the hour. If you can find it in your courage, your appreciation of the occasion, your mind's capacity, to yield a consent, you may be sure the world would come to know, as the few of us know now, the eminent harmony of place and man.

O'Connor, you know, is as sick as Walt — or, at least, as I understand it, too sick to promise an acquiescence. And that is aside from the fitter personality you could bring to the duty, noble as I admit the other to be.

Address me always at Camden. I shall delight to keep you informed.

Ever cordially
HORACE L. TRAUBEL

The shore seems impossible. Walt appreciates but objects. His doctor, whom I saw today, says there's nothing to be gained by it. If you were here, you doubtless would comprehend, but the proposition was worthy of you.

In his book, Traubel quotes Whitman's comments on July 2, concerning Burroughs's letter about wanting to take him to the sea-shore:

John is fine, fine, about all that, but he does not quite take in the situation here. All my good friends suggest different cures, places, diets — changes of geography; one sort and all sorts of revolutions; but I am bound after all to keep to my own path. The best place for me is just where I am — here, retired, in quiet, alone, to wait and see what results. For the present everything must be held in abeyance. I am touched with John's solicitude — I do not want to seem ungrateful — I push his idea aside, but gently, gently.

Whitman is reported by Traubel as saying further of Burroughs on July 6:

You must never write him without sending him my love. And, Horace, do not forget the wife, Mrs. Burroughs, for she, too, has been kind and noble to me and I want her to know that I think of her. [pause] John is one of the true hearts — one of the true hearts — warm, sure, firm — I feel that he has never wavered in his friendship for me; never doubted or gone off — that I can count on him in all exigencies; and I think affection plays a great part in John's regard for me as it does in mine for him....

The day following Traubel quotes Whitman as saying: 'You would like John — he makes a great companion, but one you must understand.'

On being told that Burroughs had written about coming to see him, Whitman replied:

Tell him to postpone it — to put it off — for the present; feeling as I do these days I could not stand the visit; my head can stand no unusual experiences. Tell him I no doubt will rally — rally enough for that, anyhow — and then we can have it out... my mind is now such a jelly — such a seething mass — always in such strange agitation — I dare not consent to see anybody except the few who are in effect in this household.

Burroughs writes in his Journal, July 12:

Full of sad thoughts about Walt Whitman; expect each day to hear of his death, and trying to taste the bitter cup in advance, so as to be used to it when it really comes. How life will seem to me with Whitman gone, I cannot imagine. He is my larger, greater, earlier self. No man alive seems quite so near to me....

But on July 14, this brief entry:

A letter from Walt. He is better and my spirits revive.

The letter was a pathetic one, with erasures and occasional omissions of words, and other signs of the progress of his malady, which signs recur from now on with more frequency. His chirography, however, continues firm, bold, and picturesque, his punctuation, as usual, a law unto itself — seldom a comma or a period, mostly dashes:

CAMDEN *July* 12 '88
Thursday night after 9

As if it gets very tedious here) (I have now been in my room and bed now five weeks here I am sitting up in a rocker and get along better than you would think — I think upon the whole I am getting mending — slowly and faintly enough yet sort o' perceptibly — the trouble is sore and broken brain — the old nag gives out and it hurts to even go or draw at all — but there are some signs the last two days that slight ambles will justify themselves — even for old habit, if nothing else —

It was probably the sixth or seventh whack of my war paralysis, and a pretty severe one — the doctors looked glum — Bucke I think saved my life as he happened to be here — Shimmering, fluctuating since, probably gathering, recruiting, but as I now write I shall rally or partially rally — only every time lets me down a peg — I hear from you by Horace Traubel — I have an idea that O'Connor is a little better.

A rainy evening here, not at all hot, quiet —

Friday July 13   Just after noon — Ab't the same. I am sitting up, had a fair night — rose late, have eaten my breakfast have rec'd a good letter from O'C — nothing very special or new — fine, clear, cool. Today my head *thicks* somewhat today. Love to you dear friend. Love and remembrance to 'Sula to July, too. I am on to 90th page Nov. Boughs — it will only make 20 more.

WALT WHITMAN

It made fifty more, but, even so, that seems a surprisingly close estimate. Whitman was almost gleeful as he told Traubel of having written Burroughs the letter. He said it was quite a good-sized note, in pencil, saying nothing in particular, 'rather aiming to give him something right from my own hand — that's all. Dear John!' And he wrote him still another on the 31st:

DEAR J. B. Just a line sending Mrs. O'C's letter to me, as the best last news of Wm. Quite certainly I am weathering — to all appearances — this ab't sixth whack of my war paralysis — (thanks mainly I opine to a sound strong body heredity from my dear father and mother) — I am still keeping my room, shall attempt a mild raid soon — take no medicines — have finished (sent in all copy) my little 'Nov. Boughs' — Horace Traubel is a noble faithful fellow —...

WALT WHITMAN

I wish I had gone oftener to see him [said Burroughs]. It was a busy year for me — the year I extended my farm, bought ten additional acres, planted a vineyard, and went at it in earnest — the year of the triple eights — it won't come again in a thousand years.

In the correspondence between Dr. Bucke and O'Connor at this time, Dr. Bucke implies a criticism that Burroughs would not consent to do the last office for his friend, urged so forcibly in two of the foregoing letters from Traubel. But O'Connor's reply to Dr. Bucke (July 19) shows how perfectly he understood the refusal:

Poor John Burroughs! I can sympathize with him in his declination. He *could* not speak. It would split his heart in two. I feel now as if the effort would break mine; but, if I can, I must make it.

Dauntless O'Connor! But this effort was not required of him; he died early in the succeeding year, while Whitman lived more than three years after Bucke and Traubel had been so intent upon getting his funeral services arranged.

Burroughs records in his Journal of July 25 that Whitman is still improving, and that a great load is lifted from his spirits.

When, on August 16, Whitman is looking forward to a September visit from Burroughs — evidently the first since Traubel's daily attendance on the poet had begun — Whitman said to Traubel:

I expect you and John to take a shine to each other.... John is never a gamble — he is always a sure risk.

Pending his visit, Burroughs sent on a basket of pears. He often sent Whitman pears, peaches, and grapes from his fruit-farm. When, in mid-September, Traubel came in, laden with a basket of grapes, Whitman said fervently:

Ah! John Burroughs again! Still thinks of us here in our prison. John is good to us — good — good! The mere sight of it makes my mouth water. And the odor — deliciously fragrant! You'll write to John. Give him my love; tell him they came, and that I knew why they came.[1]

After reading an essay by Burroughs on Matthew Arnold, in the June 'Century,' Whitman said to Traubel that he could never bring himself to applaud Arnold; he thought Burroughs, in spite of himself, had been touched with the frost of the literary clique in New York. Continuing:

John's preëminent features are good nature, good humor, eligibility for friendship; he proposes to include everybody — to accept the meanest creature in the tribe; to draw no lines; he is, in fact, for the *ensemble*. John's world would have no outcasts.

Strange talk from one who wrote of an outcast, 'Not till the sun excludes you do I exclude you!' It would really seem that Whitman was here outlining his own portrait rather than that of Burroughs — his comments being much more applicable to himself. On being reminded by Traubel of his own all-inclusiveness, he replied:

True, true, but I am not good natured, no, no, not at all as good and kind as John. I get riled — a fellow like Arnold stirs me up. I accept the world, most of the world — but somehow draw the line somewhere on some of those fellows. John detects in me primarily the lesson of comradeship, the comrade spirit — is drawn to that — sees that as the vitalizing, spinal force.[2]

[1] Traubel: *With Walt Whitman in Camden*, vol. 2, p. 312.
[2] Traubel: *With Walt Whitman in Camden*, vol. 2, pp. 203–04.

On the day before Burroughs came, Whitman said to Traubel:

John's faithfulness and affection are beyond question. Our relations with each other have always been comradely — largely and directly personal.

He then dwelt on their years together in Washington. He thus described Burroughs to Traubel:

He is plain, large, not heavy — a farmer in appearance, a little hesitating in speech — a little more and it would be a stammer; cordial; just such a man as you like — contented with what comes; fare frugal as a Jersey ploughman's, or a country innkeeper's. John wins you by just such qualities. They say of him — I know it of him — when there's a particularly hard job of work to be done on the farm, he does it himself — reserves it; he has hands there to help him, yet he chooses his own place, and that generally the most difficult one.[1]

To his wife, on September 13, Burroughs wrote:

I must go to Camden next week. Horace Traubel writes me there is no chance of Walt's being any better than he is now, and that if I want to see him I better come at once.

His Journal for the 19th records:

To Camden. Walt is lying on his bed when I enter the room. I stand by his bedside a few moments, his hand in mine, and then help him up to his chair, where he sits amid a chaos of books, letters, and papers. He talks and looks almost the same as usual. Is alert and curious when I speak. I note his hearing is poorer than when we met a year ago. I stay an hour, then, for fear of tiring him, go over to Philadelphia. Came back at night and found him bright and ready to talk. But we soon tire him, and so leave.

Sept. 20 This was one of Walt's poor days and I do not see him, though I call twice.... In the evening see Walt for a moment. He presses my hand long and tenderly; we kiss and part, probably for the last time. I think he has in his own mind given up the fight, and awaits the end.

Burroughs spoke of Mrs. Mary Davis, Whitman's housekeeper, as 'a motherly soul, a home body, who took good care of Walt.'

Two days later Traubel noted an exceptionally large and beautiful apple, which Burroughs had brought to Whitman, still in his room, and asked why he had not eaten it. 'It's too grand. I hate the idea of not having it just where I can look at it.' When, on that visit, Burroughs had asked if he should send him more pears, or

[1] Traubel: *With Walt Whitman in Camden*, vol. 2, p. 343.

grapes, Whitman had said no, but when he queried, 'Cider?' Whitman succumbed. One finds something significant in John Burroughs carrying Whitman a beautiful apple. Whitman felt it, too, and said: 'John is sweet — equable, breathes out the life of pears, cherries, grapes — odors of wildwood.'

Of Burroughs's visit Whitman was able on September 22 to write Dr. Bucke:

John Burroughs has been to see me, the good, hearty affectionate nature-scented fellow, very welcome. J. B. is not so hardy & brown & stout as formerly — that bad friend, insomnia, haunts him as of old — he thinks himself it affects his literary power (style, even matter) — Horace told him of my half-suspicion that his association with the superciliousness and sort of vitriolic veneering of the New York *literati* had eat into him, but he denied and pooh-poohed it — attributed it to his bad health, insomnia, &c — said he knew himself he could not, or did not, write with the vim of his better days (probably makes more account of that by far than really *is*).

That year, in September, talking reminiscently of the old Washington days, Whitman said to Traubel:

The mornings — shall I ever forget them? And John's wife — and the unmatchable griddle cakes — the best in the world — no one's could equal hers (and at that time I set more store by such facts than I do now).... Mrs. Burroughs managed things then — kept some of the department clerks — and there was always a rub with the precious coffee — that, too, the best on earth; and then the hour's talk after the meal — the sweet talk. They were precious days; I can never forget them — precious, sacred days.

To Burroughs himself, on October 6, Whitman writes:

I send you O'Connor's just rec'd as I know you want to hear — Pretty much 'the same subject continued' yet with me. I am still imprisoned in my sick room — good spirits and about the same mentality as ever — great blessings and remains and privileges — but after that is said pretty much everything wrecked else — But I must not get into complaining — nor do I fail there. Will send you a Nov. Boughs for it is done. In a month the big book — Best love. Send O'C's letter to Dr. Bucke.

Whitman inscribed a copy of 'November Boughs' for Burroughs, 'With love and Memories.' Soon Burroughs was cheered by a note in which Whitman said, 'My food nourishes me better,' to which he replied that he felt he should surely see him again, and that he was consequently working with better heart. But it was only a lull. A letter of October 25 by Whitman to Kennedy, sent on to Burroughs, showed signs of further breaking; especially in its first paragraph:

First thank you for your good affectionate letter, inspiriting me more than you knew — That seems to me too long, condensed dwelling a pull proof reading work-pressing work too on the *delication* of the brain — I had a friend a woman of 30 a counter in the Redemption Bureau in the Treasury — told me she was 'going to the devil fast and steady' (her own description) from her dense brain-exhausting-dulling labors, till she adopted the plan of getting a 10 or 12 minutes nap (sleep or even doze) at noon or one o'clock every day — just leaning down on her desk — fortunately she could fall in her nap — wh. is the great part of it — at any rate it cured.

I heard from Bucke today, he sends me the enclosed little slip from O'C — the condition is bad, and I feel pretty gloomy ab't my best friend — yet he has great vitality and may tide over it —

Nothing very different with me. Dr. Osler (very 'cute, a natural physician, rather optimistic, but best so) thinks I am either on a very good way, or substantially cured, of this last attack — I only wish I could feel so, or even approximate it. But, anyhow, thank God, so far my thoughts and mental power are entirely within my control.

I have written a short letter to 'Critic' (by their request) on the 'poet' question (which they may print) My sister [George's wife] has just paid me a good cheery visit (with some nice home-made graham biscuits) So I get along well, am comfortable, have a fair appetite, and keep a good oak fire. Love.

WALT WHITMAN

From Belmont, Massachusetts, Kennedy wrote to Burroughs, in part as follows:

What a good nice letter from the dear old fellow this is. How cheery he is — keeps up heart most of the time.

O'Connor's letter, of October 20, enclosed, which had gone the rounds from Bucke to Whitman, Kennedy, and now Burroughs, reads:

I enclose letter had yesterday from Walt through John Burroughs.

I will answer your two letters soon, I hope. A month ago my right eye closed, and the lid has not yet lifted, spite of battery, so I am practically blind, seeing only a little with the left eye. Too bad. Paralysis of the eyelid.

Long ago Whitman had envied the live-oaks of the South that, standing alone, with no companion near, could utter their joyous leaves of green. He had said candidly, 'I know very well I could not.' And now, though hearing from, and seeing, his friends frequently, he hungered for their companionship. He felt himself much alone. On November 2 he asked wistfully of Traubel if no letters had come from Burroughs or Morse, adding pathetically:

Oh, I need the fellows — they feed me; lying here, cribbed here, they are a sustenance — life — to me. I am sorry for myself when I think how little John writes me nowadays.

But there came a letter from Burroughs to Traubel on that very date:

DEAR HORACE:
I received the book 'November Boughs' all right, and wrote so to WW in a few days. Many, many thanks. I shall find time to read it by and by. I see there are new things in it. I am busy with the farm these fine days.... I hardly need to tell you how much joy your letters have of late given me. With love to W. W. and yourself,

J. B.

At this Whitman said:

I guess John wrote if he says so, but the letter never reached me. If you write, tell him this. Make it plain to him always that he is eminently present to me always here — no matter what happens — remains vitally with me, sharing my life.

The letters dwindle in 1889 to bulletins of his own and O'Connor's failing conditions. The following, of February 8, written in pencil, reads:

DEAR JB
Nothing very special with me — bad enough yet and imprison'd in the room and chair, but easier and freer of the intestinal and bladder troubles and fearful weakness of ten weeks ago — At present I am sitting by the oak fire in my big chair, well protected — as it is bitter cold the last two days and now here
— The news from O'Connor is bad, and worse — he is confined to the house and seems to be failing.... Most probably I shall continue ab't the stage I am at present — maybe some time, but the future will eventuate itself, and it will of course be all right. I continue almost totally disabled from getting around, can hardly get across the room — have a good stout nurse, Ed Wilkins f'm Canada — no serious pain in particular — good

heart yet — eat and sleep fairly — so you see it is not so bad as might be
— (and perhaps will be yet)

I enclose a piece you might like to see — Dr. B is expected here in a week
or ten days — I suppose you hear f'm Horace Traubel and that keeps you
posted. H. T. has been and is invaluable to me — my books are all
printed etc. (I have a big book, complete poems and prose for you)

Love to you and 'Sula and Julian

WALT WHITMAN

Commenting on Horace Traubel, Burroughs said:

Yes, he was Walt's right hand during those last years — did his errands,
read his proof, performed a thousand services, and always disinterestedly.
He is entitled to a great deal of credit and gratitude from us all. If he only
hadn't gone on with his miserable imitations of Walt! That would have
sickened Walt himself.

I have always been puzzled by a letter in which Whitman wrote
to Kennedy, March 20, 1889, 'I count on Burroughs coming out of
his hole yet.' Nothing in the context explains this. Perhaps he
meant he looked for him to review 'November Boughs'; but, even
if that particular service was lacking, the sturdy adherence of
Burroughs surely proved that he never holed up where Whitman
was concerned.

After the publication of Traubel's first volume of 'With Walt
Whitman in Camden,' Burroughs pronounced it a remarkable piece
of reporting, adding, 'If Traubel could only have discriminated, he
would have made a wonderful contribution.' In some places, he
said, he could almost hear Walt breathe. He did not doubt that
Traubel usually got the spirit of what Walt said, but by no means
always his exact words.

Of course he couldn't help coloring it all with his own mannerisms. His
own talk was saturated with 'hells' and 'damns,' but Walt's was not.
Walt could bring out a good honest 'damn' if the circumstances called for
one; but in all the twenty-nine years I knew him, I never heard him say
'damn' as many times as Traubel makes him say on a few pages. He
sprinkles them all through Walt's talk. I can't credit that Walt himself
used them so freely, much less that he urged Traubel to 'put in all the hells
and damns.' That is Traubel's contribution.

Thomas B. Harned said practically the same thing to me about
the Horatian additions to Whitman's talk; and Mr. W. S. Monroe,

a friend and correspondent of Kennedy's, says that Kennedy also took exception to Whitman being thus misquoted. Professor Perry writes of Traubel's reporting Whitman with 'pitiless accuracy'; but who shall vouch for the accuracy, since most of Traubel's notes were not made in Whitman's presence, and usually late at night, after his busy day's work, and from memory? That he caught and reported many of Whitman's mannerisms of speech, and much of his talk, is not to be gainsaid; but that he unconsciously Traubelized much of what was said, is doubtless equally true. Probably he was as generous with his own ready supply of 'hells' and 'damns,' as with his own time and service, given so unstintedly to Whitman in his declining years.

During the early spring of 1889 bulletins from Whitman about O'Connor came frequently, and at last, May 10, came the terse tidings, misdirected in his confusion to West Plains, instead of West Park: 'Our dear friend O'Connor died peacefully at 2 am yesterday.'

Thomas Donaldson says he was with the poet when he received this news; that he sat in silence for some time, a far-away look in his eyes, then, in a deep voice, said, 'And *such* a friend!' again lapsing into silence.

On May 11, Burroughs writes in his Journal:

While waiting for the train in Kingston, saw in the 'Tribune' the notice of the death of William O'Connor, my old Washington friend, and co-defender of Walt Whitman. A man of extraordinary parts, but lacking the sanity or moderation of the greatest men. I cannot write about him now — it is too great a subject.

A week later, from Whitman:

As I write (noon) I have not heard a word from Wash'n — but of course our dear friend is buried — All has gone like tracks on the shore by sea waves washed away passing —...

Stedman, a friend of O'Connor's from the early eighteen-sixties, paid a fine tribute to O'Connor, in 1905, in a letter preserved in the Perry Collection. Describing him as 'a man of full and rich attainments and a genius, needing only a brake on his prodigal and opulent expression,' he added, 'He gave up the better part of his career to Whitman, whom he excelled in humanity, aspiration, self-surrender, and to whose fame he was loyal, even after he had parted from him under the sense of a grievous wrong.'

A graphic bit of testimony as to the ineradicable impression made by Whitman upon Burroughs's inmost self is found in the following tribute which Burroughs sent for Whitman's seventieth birthday. Barring some slight omissions, it was printed in the 'Critic,' June 8, 1889, and later included in its entirety in 'Camden's Compliment to Walt Whitman,' edited by Horace Traubel:

It is now twenty-five years since I first made the personal acquaintance of our poet, and over twenty years since I first used my pen in his behalf. The memory of those years in Washington during the latter half of the War and later, I think will be the last to leave me. My life since has been poor and thin in comparison. Those walks and talks, the great events that filled the air, Whitman in the pride and power of his manhood, the eloquent and chivalrous spirit of William D. O'Connor, so lately passed away, and whose presence among you today, as I knew him then, would be like music and banners, my own eager youth and enthusiasm — all combine to make those years the most memorable of my life. But they are gone; a quarter of a century has passed; O'Connor is no more; our Good Gray Poet, whom he so gallantly defended, has reached his seventieth year, and I am sequestered here on the banks of the Hudson, delving in the soil and trying to give the roots of my life a fresh start; looking wistfully to the past, hungering for the old days, and regretting many things — among others, regretting that I am not with you and sharing the festivities on this occasion.

The following July, Whitman writes Burroughs that Horace Traubel's dinner book, with all the speeches and letters, will soon be out, and that he will send him a copy. He sends on a morocco-bound copy of 'Leaves of Grass' in August, and in September, as Burroughs's Journal records on September 28, he received another visit from Burroughs:

Up early and off to Camden to see Walt.... Find him eating his breakfast of toast and tea, and looking remarkably well, much better than a year ago. He stands a fair chance of out-living us all yet. Sit three hours with him and have much talk. He sits amid the chaos of books, papers, etc., so serene and clean and calm, and such wild confusion about him! Even the window papers [shades?] were partly torn from their places and hung down, as if to heighten the effect.

A few days later, from Whitman comes the following note:

So you didn't come back. I expected you, & Tom Harned & Horace Traubel too were here looking for you and were disappointed. The 9th vol. of the big American Literature from Stedman came this morning — I see you appear in it with a good portrait and ten pages of text well selected.... I see you are extracted from and biographized in 'Harpers Fifth Reader.'...

'Lucas Malet,' from Clovelly Rectory, Bideford, North Devon, England, writes Burroughs appreciatively in the midsummer of 1889 of his essay on Whitman in 'Birds and Poets,' which she has been rereading, and asks him to order for her Whitman's collected prose and verse:

I trust you will not think me very presuming in asking you to do me this kindness. Life is pretty short — especially for those who work with their pens, like myself — and I feel there would be hope of my spending the rest of my particular life more usefully and happily if I was in possession of all Walt Whitman has to tell me about it — in print....
Trusting that... some day — though my name will mean nothing to him — if an opportunity should arise, you will offer Walt Whitman my reverent and loving homage.

After receiving the books which Burroughs sent, 'Lucas Malet' again wrote saying she had often thought in reading both Burroughs and Whitman, how warmly and truly her father, Charles Kingsley, would have appreciated parts of them: 'His love and knowledge of nature was so profound and intimate, while his attitude toward science was wholly fearless and hopeful.' Of the 'Song of the Open Road' she wrote, 'It made me very glad.' This author quotes Whitman in her novel 'The Wages of Sin,' picturing one of her characters as becoming suddenly illuminated on reading the passage beginning, 'There will never be any more perfection than there is now.'

A letter from John Addington Symonds to Whitman, of July 29, 1889, now in the Bucke Whitman Collection, bears eloquent testimony to the fact that Symonds regarded Whitman as his 'master.' Excerpts only are copied here:

Your 'November Boughs' has been my companion during the last week. I have read it with the deepest interest, finding the autobiographical passages regarding your early life and the development of your great scheme particularly valuable. Rejoicing also in the delightful vigor of your critical notes.... I have long wished to write about your views regard-

ing the literature of the future. Each time I have attempted to do so, I
have quailed before my own inadequacy to grapple with the theme. But
I have in preparation a collection of essays on speculative and critical
problems, one of which will be called 'Democratic Art,' and will be based
upon your 'Democratic Vistas,' and 'Leaves of Grass.' This I have been
working at during the last month; and however imperfect it may be,
I have contrived to state in it a portion of what I think the world owes to
you both for your suggestions and for the illustrations you have given in
your poems — not only by asserting the necessity of a new literature adequate to the people and pregnant with the modern scientific spirit, but
also projecting it and to a large extent realizing that literature in your own
work.... Meanwhile I am able to congratulate you in the autumn of your
life upon the achievement of a monument more enduring than brass or
marble. Believe me, dear Master, to be, though a silent and uncom-
municative friend, your true, respectful and loving disciple.

I am indebted to Mr. Furness for the following letter copied from
the Bucke Whitman Collection. Burroughs writes reminiscently, in
late February, 1890:

DEAR WALT,
Here I am back from Poughkeepsie in my little study tonight with
a maple and hickory fire burning in the open fireplace and thinking of you.
How many times have I planted you there in my big chair by the window,
or here in front of the open fire, and talked the old talks with you. Alas,
alas, that I should never see you there in the body as well as in the spirit!
... How sacred is memory. As one grows old, how much he lives in the
past, how trivial and cheap seems the present. A tender and beautiful
light fills my mind when I think of those years in Washington when we
were all there; a light I know that never was on sea or land. How solemn
and pathetic, as well as beautiful, it must seem to you, considering all you
passed through there!

With the old love
J. BURROUGHS

Whitman's answer came on Sunday afternoon, March 2:

Yours came yesterday and welcomed. I am here yet and allowing for
the wear and decay-change, the situation continues much the same. You
know I am well on my 71st year — lame and almost helpless in locomotion
— inertia like a heavy swathing ample dropping pall over me most of the
time, but my thoughts and to some extent mental action ab't the same as
ever (queer ain't it?)
   — I have had my daily mid-day massage (another just as I go to bed)
Tho't of going out a little in my wheel chair but it is bitter cold today here
and I shall not. I have just sent a half-page poem to Gilder, they have ac-

cepted, paid, proofed it, and I believe it will be out in May number. ['Century'] . . .

I have just had a drink of milk punch — am sitting at present in my two-story den in Mickle St, alone as usual, more buoyant than you might suppose

WALT WHITMAN

Burroughs commented on the foregoing:

During Walt's last illness Traubel used to send me cards after Walt could no longer write. I've given away many of Walt's letters and cards. This seems to be the last I have from him.

In his Journal, July 24, 1890, Burroughs notes:

A visit from Dr. John Johnston, of Bolton, England, a modest, quiet, interesting man, 36 years old, born at Annan; went to school in the Academy where Carlyle once taught. A canny young Scot. Like him first rate. . . . A great lover of Whitman, whom he had just visited.

Some months later, acknowledging Dr. Johnston's pamphlet with an account of his visit to Whitman, Burroughs wrote:

You certainly have a wonderful gift to catch the flying moment. Whitman has never been so vividly and realistically sketched. . . . If you lived near him, or if you had my opportunity, you would make a book better than Boswell's. Do come again and complete your sketch. . . .[1]

In Whitman's Mickle Street home, on May 31, 1891, the Camden group of friends, and a few others, celebrated Whitman's seventy-second birthday, a celebration which is given with regrettable detail in 'In Re Walt Whitman.' Reading it, one is sure that Burroughs chose the better part by honoring his friend in his own way. He writes Whitman on *the Day*:

Walt, I keep your birthday pruning my vineyard and in reading an hour from your poems under my fig tree. Will let you eat your dinner in peace, as I shall want to do if I ever reach my seventy-second.

Whitman, on that occasion, elated with the love and homage of his friends, and the flowing bowl as well, is reported as leaning toward Traubel, when Burroughs's absence was mentioned, and saying (*in vino veritas*):

The only trouble with John is he has a bit of suspicion of us all — thinks I must have fallen in bad company [laughing] — the Colonel, and you and Bucke — and yet John, of all men, ought to be right here tonight. . . . Well, well, *here's love to John forever!* [sipping his champagne].

[1] See page 253, note 2.

XVI

'THIS IS THY HOUR, O SOUL'

(1891–1892)

This is thy hour, O Soul!
Thy free flight into the wordless!
Away from books — away from Art —
The Day is closed — the lesson done,
For thee freely forth emerging, silently gazing
Pondering the themes thou lovest best —
Night, sleep, death & the stars.

WHITMAN

THE thought of the soul emerging into a peaceful, fully conscious freedom, we are told by Mr. Furness, was Whitman's conception of death.[1] The poem here quoted was intended, at the time of its composition, to be the final poem in 'Leaves of Grass,' although the intention was not carried out. It serves well for the closing chapter of the poet's life.

In late December, 1891, at Traubel's word that Whitman was sick unto death, Burroughs hastened to Camden. His Journal records the scene:

Walt on the bed with eyes closed, but he knows me and speaks my name as of old, and kisses me. He asks me to sit beside him awhile. I do so, holding his hand. He coughs feebly.... Asks about my family and sends his best love to Wife and Julian. Gives me two copies of his complete poems just out. He tells me where to find them. After a while I go out for fear of fatiguing him. He says, 'It is all right, John,' evidently referring to his approaching end. He said his brother George had just been in and it had unnerved him for the first time.

Xmas.... Walt... rallied considerable during the day.... He speaks of Mrs. O'Connor, of Eldridge and his wife, his voice natural and strong.... I dined at Harned's and spent the evening there....

Dec. 26. Walt had a bad night. Doctors think he may live a day or two yet, or may go any hour. I go up and look at him long and long, but do not speak. His face has steadily refined; no decrepitude or breaking down; never saw the nose so beautiful. He looks pathetic, but how beautiful! At eleven I take a silent farewell.

[1] Furness: *Walt Whitman's Workshop*, pp. 174, 258–59.

Even after this, Whitman rallied, and the shadow was lifted for a time from the heart of his friend. Miss Jessie Whitman wrote me of meeting Mr. Burroughs at her uncle's house at the time of this visit, adding: 'And although a host of others were there, I felt he was the only one truly grieving. To all the others, it was the glamour of Walt Whitman, the Poet.'

To Bucke, Burroughs, Kennedy, and the British friends, Whitman wrote a last message, February 6 and 7, 1892, which was lithographed and sent out by Harned and Traubel, who remained in close touch with him to the end:

Well, I must send you all, dear fellows, a word from my own hand, propped up in bed, deadly weak, but the spark seems to glimmer yet —
The doctors and nurses and New York friends are faithful as ever — Here is the advertisement of the '92 edition. Dr. Bucke is well and hard at work.
Col. Ingersoll has been here — sent a basket of champagne. All are good. Physical conditions are not so bad as you might suppose, only sufferings much of the time are fearful. Again I repeat, my thanks to you, and cheery British friends, maybe for the last time. My right arm gives out.

WALT WHITMAN

Feb. 7. Same cond'n cont'd — More and more it comes to the fore that the only theory worthy our modern times (for grt literature politics & sociology must combine all the [best?] people of all lands, the women not forgetting — But the mustard plaster on my side is stinging and I must stop — Good bye to all — W. W.

Replying to Burroughs's anxious inquiries, Traubel wrote on March 15 that Whitman's condition was again critical, and that Dr. Longaker thought the struggle could not continue much longer. And on March 26 the 'Dark Mother,' gliding near, came and wrapped the poet in her 'sure-enwinding arms.' He who had welcomed the 'Strong Deliveress' was now cradled in her cool embrace, and the robust soul of Whitman went forth to laugh at what we call dissolution, to know in reality — if it might — the amplitude of time.

> Dearest comrade, all is over and long gone,
> But love is not over — and what love, O'Comrades!

For a time Burroughs was benumbed. One must read between

the lines, for the journal entries but feebly express his real feelings:

March 29. Black crêpe on Walt's door-bell, shutters closed. I find Bucke, Harned, and Traubel there. Look upon Walt's face long and long. Cannot be satisfied — it is not Walt — a beautiful, serene old man, but not Walt. After a while I have to accept it as him — his 'excrementitious body,' as he called it. Pass the night with Traubel.

On the funeral day, March 30, Burroughs again went to the house and watched vaguely the crowds drifting in and out. His Journal speaks of going out with Conway and others to eat oysters. What memories that must have revived! The oyster man showed them a book of Whitman's poems, a gift from Walt, autographed. Burroughs continues:

At the cemetery.... A great crowd. The scene very impressive; the great tent perfumed with flowers.... [Robert G.] Ingersoll speaks — an eloquent, impressive oration. Shall always love him for it. Some passages in it will last. As he was speaking, I heard a bluebird warble over the tent most joyously. The tomb is grand, and will endure as long as time. At night twelve of us go to Philadelphia and have dinner and much talk.
March 31. Warry [Whitman's nurse] and I, and Horace Traubel go out to Walt's tomb. Very glad to be there again with the crowd gone....

At the burial, an uncounted multitude thronged the great tent, the hillslopes, and all about as far as eye could see. The common people, his own, to whom he had come, but who had received him not, came now to look their last upon the Poet of Democracy. There were readings and remarks by Francis Howard Williams, Thomas B. Harned, Dr. Daniel G. Brinton, Dr. R. M. Bucke, and Robert G. Ingersoll. Messages came from Tennyson, Symonds, William Rossetti, H. Buxton Forman, Edward Carpenter, T. W. Rolleston, Rudolf Schmidt, J. W. Wallace, Dr. J. Johnston, Ellen O'Connor, Elizabeth Fairchild, Herbert Gilchrist, Sidney Morse, John Herbert Clifford, Hamlin Garland, Sylvester Baxter, I. Newton Baker, Percival Chubb, Harry L. Bonsall, Dr. Daniel Longaker, and Harry D. Bush.

Thomas Bailey Aldrich, Richard Watson Gilder and Helena Gilder, and Edmund Clarence Stedman sent wreaths of ivy and laurel; Harrison Morris wrote a sonnet, 'He was in love with the truth,' and Stedman sent the following tender lines:

Good bye, Walt!
Good bye from all you loved on earth —
Rock, tree, dumb creature, man and woman —
 To you their comrade human.
 The last assault
Ends now, and now in some great world has birth
A minstrel, whose strong soul finds broader wings,
 More brave imaginings.
Stars crown the hill-top where your dust shall lie,
 Even as we say good bye,
 Good bye, old Walt!

Among the honorary pallbearers were Dr. Bucke, H. L. Bonsall, Dr. D. G. Brinton, John Burroughs, Julius Chambers, George W. Childs, M. D. Conway, Thomas Eakins, Dr. Horace H. Furness, Herbert Gilchrist, Thomas B. Harned, Julian Hawthorne, R. G. Ingersoll, J. H. Johnston, W. S. Kennedy, Harrison S. Morris, Horace Traubel, Francis Howard Williams, and Talcott Williams.

A memorial pamphlet, containing the readings and addresses at the burial, was edited and issued by Horace Traubel. So desirous was Traubel of having John Burroughs represented in this pamphlet, he included a critical fragment on Whitman by Burroughs which assuredly was not written for the occasion, consequently was not in key with what took place at the time. It seems probable that Traubel persuaded Burroughs to affix an opening paragraph to something already written, in order to adapt it for use in the pamphlet. Since it is not an utterance from out the heart of Burroughs for that occasion, its inclusion is regrettable. Could he have written anything at the time, how different would have been its tone! But he could not write then with his sorrow fresh upon him, neither could he speak at the services. As O'Connor had well said, 'It would split his heart in two.' His silent presence was his tribute. But a tribute of another kind he could and did pay when roused by the anonymous attack on Whitman, launched by Higginson in the 'New York Evening Post' of March 28, before the poet's body had been laid away. Stirred by its unfair, insinuating charges, Burroughs wrote a reply to Higginson on March 30, called 'Walt Whitman After Death,' which the 'Post' refused to print, but which the 'Critic' printed on April 9. The Higginson article was reprinted by the 'Nation,' April 7. (Shortly before Whitman's death Burroughs had written two articles about him — 'Mr. Howells's Agreement with Walt Whitman,' published in the 'Critic,' February 6, and 'Walt Whitman,' which came out in the 'Critic,' April 2, of that year.) In his attack on Whitman, Higginson had accused him of a drench of passions which at the age of 55 had resulted in paralysis and premature old age.

A few paragraphs from Burroughs's rejoinder follow. After explaining that Whitman identifies himself with all types and conditions of men, speaking now in this character, now in that, Burroughs says:

That Whitman's life was entirely blameless in this respect [sexual irregularities] I am not prepared to say, because I do not know, I think it highly probable that it was not, but that his partial paralysis was in any way traceable to any such cause, I am very sure is not the case. His paralysis resulted from the bursting of a very small blood vessel at the base of the brain — an accident to which all robust full-blooded men are peculiarly liable, especially if they have been subject to great emotional strain, as Whitman was during the war....

I have known Whitman for nearly thirty years, and a cleaner, saner, more wholesome man, in word and deed, I have never known. If my life depended upon it, I could not convict him of one unclean word, or one immoral act.

He was always the picture of sweetness, sanity, and health, even after his partial paralysis up to within a few months of his death. No man who had led a debauched life in any way could have made the impression of purity and nobility, upon old and young, male and female, that he made....

[Journal, April 1:] Get proof from 'Forum' and 'N. A. Review.' Lunch with Gilder at Players' Club; meet [George] Woodberry, the poet; have a two hours' talk with him and rub Whitman into him with a vengeance. But I am sure he is really lost — nothing in him but 'art' and 'art' and 'art.'... Pass the night again with [Ernest] Ingersoll.

To Hamilton W. Mabie, on April 3, goes this fervent letter:

I seem to be a good deal broken up since I came home last night, and can hardly hold my pen, but I cannot wait longer to thank you for your magnificent editorial on Whitman. From the depths of my heart I thank you. I shall love you always for these brave manly words....

There is great hope for literature when the younger men like you show such a spirit. More and more I see that the 'Christian Union' is rising into the great currents that are to shape the future. I never want to see you take in sail, but to throw yourselves more and more to the free winds of God's open sea.

In two April letters to Miss Ludella Peck, Burroughs shows more of his real feelings than the Journal has yet revealed:

I am just back from the funeral of my great friend and am a good deal broken up. And, too, I am under a strange excitement which I do not clearly comprehend. My heart beats so loud and strong it disturbs me when I try to sleep. I have had but little sleep during the week, and, strangely enough, do not feel the need of more....

This is my birthday, my 55th, and I walk about, listening to the happy birds, and looking out upon the placid river, in a curious kind of dream. But one thought fills me — the thought of the 'large sweet soul that has gone.'...

I have written much this winter about Whitman. In December the 'Critic' asked me to write about him; this set me going and I kept on. I shall have an article in the May 'Forum' [1] and in the May 'North American Review.' The past week's 'Critic' and 'Christian Union' each had articles by me. [2] I have one more paper to write on Whitman the Man.

Again, to the same:

The April days have a pathos to me they never had before. I have been in such close communion with Whitman's spirit during the last few months in writing these articles, that his loss takes deeper hold on me than it otherwise would.

I have not his faith in immortality and cannot have. Some people are born with faith, some achieve faith, and some have faith thrust upon them. What faith I have I must earn by the sweat of my brow, and that is very little. In some moods I lean strongly upon my great friend, and find comfort in his unconquerable belief in immortality. In other moods death seems a great blank. We are simply sponged off the blackboard of existence, and the great Demonstrator goes on with new figures and new problems. We exist in his thought — is that enough?

In Burroughs's Journal, April 6, his awareness of his loss is more apparent:

Again, dear Master, I have bitten into this great apple of an earth with my plow and find it sweet and appetizing as ever — the same old delicious smell; the same old fresh look; yet the new furrow is more eloquent and pathetic to me than ever before. Again the swelling buds and the sprouting grass; again the robin-racket in the twilight; again the long-drawn *tr-r-r-r-r-r-r-r-r* of the toad in the gloaming; again the tender ditty of the sparrow; again the water-fowl streaming northward; again the 'fields all busy with labor' — but thou, thou in thy tomb!

[1] The Forum article did not appear, see page 301.

[2] Burroughs: 'The Poet of Democracy,' *North American Review*, May, 1892. Burroughs: 'Walt Whitman, Poet of Democracy,' *Christian Union*, April 2, 1892.

And in other entries, rehearsing the spring tokens, he sighs:

The world so sweet, so benignant these days, yet my thoughts are away in that Camden cemetery where the great one lies.

And in the exaltation born of sorrow, he adds:

W. W. is the Christ of the modern world — he alone redeems it, justifies it; shows it divine; floods and saturates it with human-divine love.

Something of the same exaltation that Burroughs felt, Kennedy also experienced. When speaking of the burial he said, 'I felt as if I had been at the entombment of Christ.' Surely something sacred emanates from a personality when those in closest touch discern so clearly the divine in the human.

With a brooding nature like Burroughs's, sorrows deepen with time; the more he dwelt on Whitman's passing, the greater was his stress of emotion. On April 15 he writes in the Journal:

I am fairly well these days but sad, sad. Walt constantly in mind. I think I see more plainly how Jesus came to be deified — his followers loved him; love transforms everything. I must still continue my writing about him till I have fully expressed myself.

Writing to Myron Benton at this time, Burroughs says:

I liked your O'Connor letter very much.[1] ... It was the only adequate word that has yet been spoken on that eloquent and chivalrous soul. I heard it highly spoken of in Camden and in N.Y. The critics seem to pass O'Connor by on the other side, as if they were still afraid of him....

He writes of his recent articles on Whitman, and of one or two more on the stocks, and of Higginson's 'dastardly attack on Whitman in the "Nation."'

Among Burroughs's papers I found the accompanying undated fragment by him which is evidently a tentative rough draft of what he contemplated saying at some Whitman dinner, or other gathering where close friends of Whitman met:

This ought to be a kind of experience meeting. We all ought to tell our experiences — what the Lord has done for us. For one, I think the Lord has been very good to me to open my eyes to the grandeur of Whitman. We may look upon ourselves as upon the elect, the blessed few. It is not given to the great mass to see Whitman; this is a felicity denied them. The great army of the Philistines know him not. Do we not pity them? Think

[1] Benton: 'W. D. O'Connor,' *The Critic*, March 26, 1892.

what a privation it is. Think how different your own outlook into the universe would be if Whitman — all that he stands for, all that he has made dear — were cut off! It would not be the same world to me. America, my country — I fear I should utterly despair of. He justifies it, redeems it, gives it dignity and grandeur, bears it all on his shoulders, as Atlas the Earth.

When a great race or people comes to a head in a single man, and that man touched with the divine, the god-like, why, that settles it. The thing has proved itself. The race and land that can produce such a man as Whitman is in favor with the powers that rule this world.

His is not the voice of the people so much as it is the voice of that which lies back of the people, and gives them sanity and health and perpetuity. The very virtue and sanity of the globe is in him. What types he has planted, what largeness, what breadth, what freedom!

'I charge you,' he says, 'leave all as free as I have left all free.'

One great service of his is to free: he takes down the bars....

What problems he has started for us! What problems he has solved! I see that his work will be a perfect mine of suggestion to the critic, the artist, the poet of the future. There are divine things well wrapped up in these poems.

The future, I think, will do wonders for Whitman. Tennyson has had his day, etc. But Whitman's day is to come. He has committed himself absolutely to the gods of the future and they will not desert him. Such faith fulfills itself.

'Thus I pass,' he says, 'a little while visible, vocal, contrary,' etc.

How largely his work is planned with reference to the future. How did he know his words would 'itch at our ears'? His help is an entire help. He does not help to make you a scholar, or an artist, or a poet, he helps you to be a man, to be yourself, and to fill your own place in life.

Mr. Johnson Brigham, State Librarian in Iowa, writing in the Des Moines 'Sunday Register,' April 10, 1921, tells of a midnight talk with Burroughs on Whitman, in 1889, when they were guests at the Gilders, in New York City, and how Burroughs's explanation of Whitman's philosophy on the sex relation, which proclaimed that passion as sacred as the intellect, made him see a light in a dark place. Accordingly, in 1892, on seeing an article by Burroughs in the 'Critic,' he renewed the acquaintance by letter and received the reply, dated April 16, which is in part quoted here:

... I am more than glad if my rather hasty 'Critic' article and letter put Whitman in a different light to you. He was a great, noble, loving and lovable soul... a man whom all his friends loved and clung to. His charity was like the sunlight, his benignity like the rain and the dew; his wisdom like Time's. His poems do not please at first; they repel; he must be wrestled with like Nature herself, but what riches are in store for him who can win them....

In July of the same year, replying to another letter from Mr. Brigham, he wrote:

I see you are right about the Whitman articles — the one in the 'N.A. Review' is the least valuable — too much dead wood of criticism. The 'Forum' article never appeared: When the editor learned I had one on the same subject in 'NAR,' he took it out — he would not share WW and myself with his rival. A part of the same paper will soon appear in 'Lippincott's Magazine.' I shall also have an answer to a criticism of WW in June 'Atlantic,' in 'Poet-Lore' for September. I shall probably have a little book on Whitman one of these days. He was a man of the centuries. If we build upon him in this country, we are sure to build large and broad enough. I see plenty of evidence every day that his soul is marching on. In time such a man creates the taste and the type of character that appreciates him....

Seven years later, when Mr. Brigham had written some articles in the 'Midland Monthly' (St. Louis), showing how Whitman's Western visit had filled his imagination with the grandeur of the prairies and mountains out there, making him the 'best interpreter and prophet of the prairie states,' he sent on the articles to Burroughs, and received in acknowledgment, a letter of April 9, 1899, which says in part:

I rejoice to see that you are growing in grace and that you really feel W[hitman] to be a 'great soul.' That is enough. It is the great souls that save the world....

XVII

THE OLD GUARD AND NEW RECRUITS

(1892–1897)

Afterward a melodious echo, passionately bent for (death making me really undying),
The best of me then when no longer visible, for toward that I have been incessantly
preparing.

NOW that their leader was gone, the band of Whitmanites drew closer to one another. Eldridge and Burroughs were the only ones left of the Old Guard, but Kennedy, Bucke, and many younger recruits who had rallied around Whitman and his 'Leaves,' now felt the ties of fellowship drawing them all together; and henceforth every year more and more recruits were added. Colonel Higginson's unsoldierly attack upon their fallen hero outraged them all. Eldridge wrote Burroughs feelingly on April 21:

I want to thank you for your reply to Higginson's malignant article in the N.Y. 'Nation,' on Walt. It was well done. Frank Sanborn also, in the 'Boston Advertiser' of the 14th instant has a quiet but very effective rejoinder in which he turns his literary points on him in a very satisfactory manner. Besides, he brings out the fact that the article is the offspring of deep-seated prejudice against Walt and his work. I have personal knowledge that this is true. When we were about publishing the 1860 edition of 'Leaves of Grass,' in Boston, Higginson occasionally came into our place. On one occasion he saw a copy of 'L of G' on my desk and said that the book always made him seasick, having first become acquainted with it on a voyage to the West Indies when he was just recovering from *mal-de-mer.* He further showed his disgust by saying that if Walt's book represented health then he (Hig.) was diseased. Since that time, he has not failed, when opportunity offered, to say spiteful things about Walt and his book; notably in an article in the 'Woman's Journal,' called 'Unmanly Manhood,' February 4, 1882, in which he twitted Walt with the fact that, being of lawful age when the War broke out, he did not enlist, and to which William O'Connor made a stinging retort in his letter to Dr. Bucke.[1]

Now that our great friend has departed to other spheres I have thought that it would be advisable for some one to organize a Walt Whitman

[1] Other acrimonious articles on Whitman by Higginson were in *Harper's Bazaar*, March 5 and 26, 1887, and in his *Cheerful Yesterdays.*

Society of America, to promote the circulation and study of his work, and protect his fame and memory. I wrote to Dr. Bucke on the subject, but he thinks it is a little premature, and I don't know but he is right. Such a society would be useful in letting us know who our friends are, and promoting the intercourse of congenial spirits. The Press on the Coast has always been friendly to Walt, but I have never met anyone (outside the Channing family) who was especially interested in him or his works. No doubt there are many such.

I see that Traubel proposes to buy the Camden house for preservation. That might well furnish a home for the Society, and from what I hear of Traubel, I should think he would make an excellent secretary. If I were East, I would try to organize such a society....

I am preparing my Recollections of Walt Whitman, and hope to publish them sometime. There are some reminiscences which I am doubtful as to the expediency of putting in, and would like to see you about later on. Do you know anything about the provisions of Walt's will, and whether that deficient brother, Eddy, is still alive?...

Again, in May, Eldridge writes to Burroughs:

Your welcome letter of the 27th ult. was duly received. I am glad to see that you are doing such valiant service in the Press in behalf of Walt and all that he represents. Your 'N. American article' was eagerly read. I found it excellent in the main, but I am not quite sure that you are right in what you say about William's defence of Walt by covering him with the shield of the great poets who used like freedom in treatment of sexual functions. I have never understood Walt to deny the 'jurisdiction' of the Bible authors, or the great Greeks, in matters of morals or taste, which are the main points related to this question. It has nothing to do with Democracy, *per se*. However, I will think the matter over and not argue it further here, but reserve the point, mayhap, for future discussion. It seems a pity that William is not alive to give Theodore Watts [1] the treatment he deserves; only the knout wielded by his hand could make such a shameless blackguard as that wince.

If we may not have a society, I wish we could have an organ in which the Whitmanites might have their say, and full liberty to slay and 'lambaste' the Philistines right and left. Perhaps you remember that it was the dream of William's life to start such a paper. He wanted to call it 'The Open Road.' He was always hoping to make his 'pile' in some fortunate patent or speculation through which the necessary funds might be secured. But he died without the sight. I am afraid we shall have to

---

[1] See *Athenæum*, April 2, 1892, an article of which the *Pall Mall Gazette* said was one of foul abuse, 'the most outrageous in the whole, sad, foolish, bitter history of criticism,' and which 'Argus' in a letter to the *Critic*, May 7, 1892, said contained the most offensive phrase he had ever seen in print. 'Argus' calls Whitman 'the only American poet.' He has another letter about Whitman in the *Critic* for June 11 of that year.

wait till some 'Whitmaniac' inherits or is endowed with Rothschild's fortune before his dream is realized.

We have a right, I think, to congratulate ourselves on a great change in public sentiment in the 30 years since I published the Third edition of 'Leaves of Grass.' Then the tone of the Press was universally contemptuous, when not abusive. When he died, the leading American newspapers agreed that a great and good man had passed away; and the two representative periodicals of England, the 'London Times'[1] and 'London Punch,'[2] paid tributes to his memory seldom equalled in the case of an American. Such cowardly attacks as appeared in the 'Nation' and the 'Athenæum' are now the exception. Formerly they were the rule.

I hunted up and read Conway's tribute in 'The Open Court.'[3] I suppose he is also the author of that short reply to Higginson which the 'Nation' admitted April 21st.[4] There are fine things in both pieces, but it seems to me highly inaccurate to say that Walt never could criticize his country any more than a child could criticize its mother. There never was sterner or more relentless criticism of America than is contained in 'Democratic Vistas.' Perhaps Conway never read those pieces, but more likely he has forgotten them. Yet it is true that in many ways Walt was as a little child; and of such are the kingdom of heaven.

I shall look for Traubel's volumes with much interest. I have not been favorably impressed with what I have heretofore seen of his relating to Walt, because of his seeming imperfect command of English idiom. I had thought that he was foreign born, but am informed that he is a native. Dr. Bucke says that we all owe him a debt for his services to Walt in the last years of his life, and I am willing to acknowledge and pay my share. His book is another matter.

Other writers than Higginson took the occasion of Whitman's death to disparage him. A journal entry in late April shows Burroughs again incensed on this account:

There is no hate or bitterness toward Whitman like that of many of our minor poets. They fly at him like a whiffet dog at a mastiff. The same set, if they happen to be story-writers, like the Crawfordsville poet,[5] also

---

[1] 'Walt Whitman,' an obituary notice, London *Times*, March 28, 1892. (Reprinted in *Eminent Persons: Biographies*, Macmillan, London, 1896, vol. 5, 1891–92.)

[2] 'The Good Grey Poet, gone!' (poem) *Punch*, April 9, 1892. (Reprinted in *In Re Walt Whitman*, p. 56.)

In addition to these, there was an article on Whitman's death in the *Daily Chronicle* (London) of March 28, 1892, by his warm friend H. Buxton Forman, who also wrote of Whitman in *Celebrities* (Cassell and Company, 1890); and an article in the London *Literary Opinion*, May, 1892, by Elizabeth Robins Pennell.

[3] Conway: 'My Little Wreath of Thoughts and Memories,' *Open Court*, May 26, 1892.

[4] That article is signed 'C,' and dated from Garrison, New York, April 13, 1892.

[5] Maurice Thompson, in *The Independent*, March 5, 1888, had a reply to Howells in *Harper's Monthly*, February, 1888, but of what later article by Thompson Burroughs wrote, I do not know.

snap and snarl at the heels of Tolstoy, one of the most heroic and powerful characters of history. How I ache to lift them with my boot!

Burroughs wrote to Dr. Johnston, and the Lancashire group of Whitmanites, April 22:

The opinion of Whitman held by your countrymen is much more interesting to me than the opinion held by my own, because it shows so much more insight and appreciation. There have been a few good notices here, some flippant ones, and many atrocious ones. One has just been sent me from a Maryland paper that makes me ashamed of my kind....

I am still writing on him. Indeed, I am only just beginning to see his real greatness. I don't think any of us fully realized how great he really was.... I don't suppose any of us knew how much we loved him till since his death....

Buchanan's poem [1] is very beautiful. It made me weep. Indeed, it does

[1] The poem by Buchanan is copied here from the *Complete Poetical Works of Robert Buchanan* (London, 1901), vol. 2, p. 398:

WALT WHITMAN

One handshake, Walt, while we, thy little band
    Of lovers, take our last long look at thee —
One handshake, and one kiss upon the hand
    Thou didst outreach to bless humanity.

The dear, kind hand is cold, the grave sweet eyes
    Are closed in slumber, as thou liest there.
We shed no tears, but watch in sad surmise
    The face still smiling through the good grey hair.

No tears for thee! Tears, rather tears of shame
    For those who saw that face yet turned away;
Yet even these, too, didst thou love and claim
    As brethren, tho' they frowned and would not stay.

And so, dear Walt, thine Elder Brother passed,
    Unknown, unblest, with open hand like thine —
Till lo! the open Sepulchre at last,
    The watching angels, and the Voice Divine!

God bless thee, Walt! Even Death may never seize
    Thy gifts of goodness in no market priced —
The wisdom and the charm of Socrates
    Touch'd with some gentle glory of the Christ!

So long! we seem to hear thy voice again,
    Tender and low, and yet so deep and strong.
Yes, we will wait, in gladness, not in pain
    The coming of thy Prophecy. (So long!)

not take a great deal to make me weep when Walt Whitman's name is mentioned. I trust you keep well, and that your band of Whitman brothers has lost none of your love for him or for one another....

The following letter which Burroughs wrote Gilder, April 18, is self-explanatory:

I have a question which I wish to put to you as an editor, and I want your exact view.

I wrote an article on Whitman of about 8000 words, cut it in two and offered half to the 'Forum,' and half to the 'N.A. Review.' Each part discussed a different phase of Whitman's work and personality. I said nothing to either magazine that I had written for the other. The papers were differently named. Now am I to blame?

The 'Forum,' hearing I have an article on Whitman in the May 'N.A. Review,' stops the make-up of the magazine and withdraws my article. Maybe, in my zeal for the Whitman cause, I have overstepped the line; have I? Neither article was ordered or asked for, but offered and accepted. Let me hear briefly what you think?

I do not find Gilder's reply to this, but, as before stated, the 'Forum' article never appeared. Among some old papers I find one page of proof on which J. B. has written 'In "Forum" — never published.' The running title is 'An Estimate of Walt Whitman.' As this matter is not found in 'Whitman: A Study,' its one complete paragraph is given here. The paragraphs at top and bottom of page are incomplete:

Yet in the same breath we must direct attention to what a recent critic has called the 'waves of profound thought' that surge through the poems and buoy up their huge masses of materials like ocean currents.

Some of the ideas which come from these thought-waves I may briefly indicate. The curious physiological strain that runs through the poems, of which I shall have more to say; the glorification of the body and the identifying it with the soul — an idea which, as it is followed out in 'Children of Adam,' in the begetting of offspring, has given much offence; the idea of identity through materials — through sight, hearing, touch, taste, smell — the soul vibrated back from outward objects; the idea of the spirituality of all things, which crops out again and again in the poems, and which is fully expressed in such a sentence as this, 'Sure as the earth swims through the heavens, does every one of its objects pass into spiritual results'; from which it follows that whatever a man or woman thinks or does is attended by consequences that follow him or her through life and after death. 'No specification is necessary — all that a male or female does that is vigorous, benevolent, clean, is so much profit to him or her in the unshakable order of the universe, and through the whole scope of it forever.' The idea of the absolute equality of the sexes, and that what the man requires for his health and development is equally required by the woman; the idea of creation as womanhood, or as symbolized by womanhood; the idea of religion as independent of all Bibles and creeds, as no more bound up with ecclesiasticism than the air we breathe or the water we drink; the idea of the 'vast similitude which interlocks all,' and makes the least fact significant; and the high moral conception of life as a perpetual journey, an endless field of action and effort — finally illustrated in that magnificent 'Poem of the Open Road'; the idea that is riveted and clinched in poem after poem, that everything is for the individual, that 'underneath the lesson of things — spirits, nature, governments, ownership,' is the lesson of personality — that the 'whole theory of the universe is directed to one single individual — namely, to You.' These and many others run through the poems, and make them stimulating and suggestive to the moral and intellectual nature no less than to the poetic.

To Miss Harriet Monroe, April 20, 1892, Burroughs wrote appreciatively as follows:

Your 'Word about Walt Whitman' in the 'Critic' of April 16 shows unusual penetration and appreciation. I want to thank you for it. You have put your finger upon many of his strong points. His French critic and admirer Gabriel Sarrazin says he is *not* an artist, that he is above art. Your conclusion is nearly the same. Most critics say he is below art, certain it is that he did not aim to make the impression of art, but of life, and nature at first hand. He aims to build a man and not to carve a statue. He was far greater and more significant than any of us have yet dared to say. The more I study him, the more his greatness of mind and soul loom up before me. Some day I hope to be able to express more fully than I have yet done all that he means to me.

A journal entry of Burroughs, May 14, 1892, commenting on Mr. Havelock Ellis's 'The New Spirit,' says he finds it very suggestive, yet lacking in something, 'perhaps in coördination and singleness of purpose.' Two quotations from Mr. Ellis's book are transcribed below.

Whitman represents, for the first time since Christianity swept over the world, the re-integration, in a sane and whole-hearted form, of the instincts of the entire man, and therefore he has a significance which we can scarcely over-estimate. Goethe had done something of this in a more artistic and intellectual shape; it is from no lack of love or reverence for Goethe that I have chosen the American, a democrat rather than an aristocrat, the very roughness of whose grasp of life serves but to reveal the genuine instinct of the modern Greek.[1]

[1] Ellis: *The New Spirit*, Houghton Mifflin Company (Boston and New York), 4th ed., p. 32.

Whitman has achieved the rarest of all distinctions: he has been placed while yet alive by the side of the world's greatest moral teachers, beside Jesus and Socrates —

'the latter Socrates,
Greek to the core, yet Yankee too.' [1]

In his Journal, May 1, Burroughs records a visit from Dr. Bucke. A pensive tone prevails this year in Journal and letters — spring, with all its recurring tokens, and his Comrade gone from the 'rich, apple-blossomed earth.' He welcomes every one who brings him in closer touch with Whitman:

Dr. Bucke came this morning.... Very glad to see him. He reminds me strongly of Walt — large, long, gray beard, and walks with a cane.

We have a day full of talk and communion. How true it is that you must love a man ere he seem worthy of your love! I did not use to like Dr. Bucke, but since the death of W. my heart has softened toward him, and I begin to feel a strong attachment towards him. I see more and more in him to love and admire. A little inclined to run off with a single idea and make too much of it. His idea now is that there is such a thing as Cosmic Consciousness; [2] that it is a new sense or power developing in the race; and that Walt had it in a preëminent degree — Paul had it, Buddha, and Mahomet. I fear he will ride the idea too hard. In afternoon we drive to the woods and get arbutus.

Another link with Whitman was the artist Herbert Gilchrist, who was then tarrying at an obscure place on Long Island. After an autumn visit to him Burroughs writes in his Journal:

... An old farm house in a little trough on the shore, shut in by low woods, a picturesque spot, but secluded and lonely. Here this young Englishman lives all alone, year in and year out, and works at his picture (Cleopatra).... We sat up till midnight by the open fire and talked.... In the morning we made clam fritters for breakfast.

We talked much of Tennyson, whose death is near. G. knew him well. Said he was much less gentle and guarded in speech than Walt Whitman; would say rather blunt, rude things before ladies. G. said such men as Whitman and Tennyson strike us as poets and artists all through — they are born such, while such men as Browning strike us as only poets at times, or in part. The lives of T. and W. were the lives of poets, pure and simple — the lives of children — unworldly and unconventional. They were not men of current society, or of current affairs at all. G. feels that Whitman

---

[1] Ellis: *The New Spirit*, p. 99.
[2] Bucke: *Cosmic Consciousness*, Innes and Sons, 1901.

was a great artist from the start, but regrets a crude, uncultured streak in him at times.

[Journal, *October* 10:] Golden October days. I spend the days looking into Tennyson and musing on various matters — a mellow, poetic spirit, like that of the dead poet, seems to pervade the air. All the woods and groves stand in their richest autumn livery.

Is there more reverie than contemplation in Tennyson, and is he, to that extent, weakening and dissipating? Does he sap the will? Longing, retrospection, regret — these largely make the atmosphere of his poems....

He was the poet of the old world, not of the new — of a rich, deep, refined civilization — not of a new, fermenting, democratic era and land, like America. We enjoy him, but he is not of us. He is not always manly. He is much less, as a personality, than Whitman — much more of a polished, conventional, orthodox poet. It is rarely that he gives one the impression of mass, of power, or makes you a partaker in the universal brotherhood of man. Ripe and mellow always, but tonic and uplifting rarely.

Writing from Anderton, near Chorley, in Lancashire, J. W. Wallace acknowledges to Burroughs the receipt of inscribed copies of 'Poet-Lore'[1] for him and Dr. J. Johnston, and adds:

It is another evidence, added to so many, of how Walt's influence tends to make all his friends, of every grade, helpful and kind to each other, true comrades and equals. I am amazed as I look back over the past few years, at the wonderful good fortune which has attended the whole relation of my friends and myself with Walt, and with the circle of his friends. It is deeply touching and inspiring to note how his example — all-accepting and loving, gracious and tolerant — is followed by *them*, and how the humblest of his friends may find himself in warm, human relations with the highest and best — a democracy of love where no one is excluded, and where the best is eligible to each on the due terms.

I thank you from my heart for the additional proof that *you*... have given me of this. And I venture to rank myself henceforward as one of your friends — affectionate and reverent, however unworthy....

I read your article aloud at the last meeting of our 'College' friends. We all concurred in hearty appreciation of the article, and in the emphatic verdict of one of the boys: 'He is Walt's "explication," as no one else is!'

I envy Horace Traubel his visit to you at the beginning of this week, and wish that I could have been with him.

Shortly after Whitman's death, Arthur Stedman, the son of E. C. Stedman, edited 'Autobiographia, or the Story of a Life,'

[1] Burroughs: 'A Boston Criticism of Whitman,' *Poet-Lore*, August–September, 1892.

from Whitman's prose writings,[1] and 'Selected Poems from Whitman.'[2] Commending this, the 'Critic' said that Mr. Stedman knew the tufts of grass from the bales of hay.

For the four years following Whitman's passing, Burroughs was writing and rewriting his second book about the poet, attempting, as he said in that book, to compass and define Whitman, who would not be compassed and defined. He was also writing much about the poet for the magazines, as a glance at the Bibliography will show. And he was associating more and more with those who were thinking and talking of Whitman — such men as Dr. Bucke, W. S. Kennedy, and Oscar Lovell Triggs. He even attended some of the Whitman reunions, and occasionally visited the Harneds in Germantown, where Whitman had so often been an honored guest. In the spring of 1893, writing Miss Ludella Peck about Professor Triggs's book on Whitman and Browning,[3] he said that if it was not a very wonderful book, it at least showed that Whitman's soul was marching on. Concerning Symonds's book [4] on the poet he expressed himself quite differently, in his Journal, May 12:

This day Symonds's book on Whitman came to me, and I nearly finished it at odd intervals, sitting in the summer house and looking out into the lovely world. It is a strong book and will play its part in settling Walt's fame. I see in it little to except to. The hearty endorsement of the sexual poems quite surprised me. Symonds acknowledges his own debt to Whitman in strong, eloquent words. I suppose the very first order of men never owe so great a debt as this to a book. They get it at first hand from God, from Nature, from the soul. Men of the stamp of Symonds, and of myself, get it from our masters. I could have wept over the book, thinking of Symonds just dead, and his words ringing so clear and eloquent; and of Walt, whom my soul so loved.

The following letter from Eldridge, in California, came in late March:

[1] Charles L. Webster and Company, 1892.

[2] David McKay, 1892.

[3] Triggs: *Study of Browning and Whitman*, Swan Sonnenschein and Company, London; Macmillan, New York, 1893.

In view of the fact that Whitman had small appreciation for Browning, this juxtaposition of their names is rather incongruous. When Browning died, Whitman wrote Dr. Bucke, December 13, 1889: 'So Browning is dead. As it happened I never read him much. (Does he not exercise and rather worry the intellect — something like a sum in arithmetic?)' — C. J. F.

[4] Symonds: *Walt Whitman: A Study*, Geo. Routledge and Sons, 1893.

It was a year ago that Walt passed over to what the Frenchman calls 'the Great Perhaps.' There is no 'perhaps' with me, however. I have no more doubt that I shall see him again in the 'land of the departed' than that I shall die. The world gets lonelier to me every year as one by one our cherished friends pass into the silent land. It has seemed lonelier than ever since Walt has gone. Once in a while it has seemed also as though the world had forgotten him, and then again there will be an outburst, showing that his influence is working silently and sometimes in unexpected quarters.

I send you today the 'Californian,' a little magazine published here, which has two articles on Walt. The one under the specific title is by John Vance Cheney, Librarian of the San Francisco Public Library. It is a curious medley of sense and nonsense. The other article on The Good Gray Poet is by Dewitt C. Lockwood, of whom I know nothing. I could not forbear enlightening him on the origin of the phrase, Good Gray Poet, in a letter to the care of the publishers. I send you a copy of my letter as it may interest you. I think William [O'Connor] is entitled to the full credit of inventing that name, and he is otherwise inseparably identified with Walt's fame; although I see that some of Walt's later critics are inclined to deprecate the style of his pamphlet. Perhaps you noticed that Clarke did so in his book which I have.[1] A little heat and blood does no harm when you are in a fight, and I have no doubt that William's pamphlet was quite as effective as though it had been cold and bloodless.

I have not seen Professor Triggs's book on Browning and Whitman, but hope to. I saw a notice of it in the 'Nation.' Symonds's book ought to be interesting and valuable. Your own, I know, will be so. I saw your speech at the Authors' Club dinner. You always manage to say something good about Walt. The tendency among the other American literary men seems to be to ignore him. I see that Marion Crawford in a recent interview thinks that Hawthorne is the only great writer we have produced, and, inferentially, places him above Emerson, whom he mentions.

I have made no progress with my proposed Reminiscences of Walt — a few written notes is all. I have plenty in my head, however, and when the circumstances are favorable, it will not take me long to put them in shape....

Eldridge's letter to Dewitt C. Lockwood settles the question of how the name 'The Good Gray Poet' came about:

I have read with interest your biographical sketch of Walt Whitman in the April 'Californian.' In the opening paragraph you say that it is a matter of conjecture how the name of the 'Good Gray Poet' was first applied to him. I am able to give you definite information on that point: The

[1] William Clarke: *Walt Whitman*, Swan Sonnenschein and Company, London; Macmillan, New York, 1892.

epithet was first applied by William O'Connor in his pamphlet with that title, published in 1865, as a vindication of the poet, and an excoriation of Harlan, the Secretary, who had dismissed him for his book.

This pamphlet is undoubtedly the most brilliant monograph in American Literature.

I am a lifelong friend of Walt Whitman and [of] his champion, William D. O'Connor.

I was considerably surprised that you were able to give a somewhat extended sketch of the former without mentioning the latter person, who was Walt's earliest defender. I was in Washington when that remarkable pamphlet was written, and held frequent conferences with O'Connor about it. The title was also a subject of conference, and O'Connor has the sole honor of inventing it. It was suggested to him, he told me, by a line in Tennyson's Ode on the Death of the Duke of Wellington — 'The good grey head which all men knew.' [1]

In his own copy of William Clarke's 'Walt Whitman,' Burroughs made these two annotations:

All notions that W. was an unlettered, uncultivated person must be dismissed. He had all the enlargement and liberation of spirit that books can give.

Whitman's work is not literary — the supreme works never are — it does not reflect the cultivated, academic spirit, but the spirit of a regnant, masterful personality.

Burroughs spoke at the Whitman dinner in New York in May, 1893, but not at all to his satisfaction. He said in his Journal that he did not say the best things he had in mind.

Eldridge wrote further on Whitman matters, February 26, 1894. He told Burroughs he should soon get together his 'Reminiscences' of Whitman, but did not intend to publish until there should be a demand for such a book. He felt that the 'literary fellers' had returned to their old trick of ignoring Walt. He would wait for a revival of interest. He is pleased with the get-up of Traubel's 'In Re Walt Whitman,' which contains some new things for him, and he is glad to see the old ones in such a handsome dress. He adds:

[1] It has sometimes been incorrectly stated that Whitman himself named O'Connor's pamphlet. Unquestionably Whitman was highly pleased with the title. Horace Traubel, in *With Walt Whitman in Camden*, quotes him as saying, '... the "good gray" — William's other name for me'; and Ellen M. Calder, formerly Mrs. William D. O'Connor, asserts unequivocally: 'Mr. O'Connor gave Whitman the name of the "Good Gray Poet" by which he is known, and always will be known.' See *Walt Whitman as Man, Poet, and Friend*, compiled by Charles N. Elliot (Richard Badger, 1915, page 61).

For other reference to this title, see page 241.

I enjoyed your essay on 'Walt Whitman and his Recent Critics' very much — perhaps as much as anything in the book. I was much interested in George Whitman's account of Walt's early years. I was considerably amazed, however, at his statement about you, William, and myself. He says we called ourselves 'Bohemians.' He has evidently confounded our pious little circle in Washington with the Pfaff crowd in New York. I am afraid he is not very good authority on the character of Walt's companions when he was away from *home.*[1]

Have you seen Symonds's book on Walt? A part of it reaches the high water mark of criticism, but a part of it is abominable, and contains the very worst things ever said about Walt. It seems that 'Calamus' suggests sodomy to him, and, from some remarks he makes, I judge that he was suspicious about Walt's relations with Peter Doyle. It appears that Walt made an indignant denial of any such construction of his poems, but, not-withstanding all, Symonds puts it in. Truly, I think much learning, or too much study of Greek manners and customs, hath made this Englishman mad. Was ever such folly or madness shown before by a professed friend? Walt's favorite figure about the cow who gave a pail full of rich milk, and then kicked it all over, is applicable to him with terrific force. If you have seen the book I would like to know what you think of it all.

The longer I live, and the more I read, the more Walt's greatness grows upon me. What sanity of mind! what breadth of vision! Where is it equalled among his contemporaries, or even among his predecessors?... How is your book about Walt coming on?

Concerning Symonds's deductions from the 'Calamus' poems, one thinks of Whitman's injunction:

> I charge you forever reject those who would expound me,
> For I cannot expound myself.

Symonds never met Whitman, but was one of his most steadfast and scholarly appreciators, and yet, through him were circulated two reports about him which, in the absence of fuller information, have proved exceedingly mischievous. Seemingly in refutation of Symonds's own conjectures concerning the Calamus poems is a portion of a letter he wrote in 1892, I cannot recall to whom, in which he said: 'But he [Whitman] also made me love my brethren and seek them out with more perhaps of passion than he would himself approve' — a significant comment, though somewhat contradictory.

[1] In this connection, see 'Walt Whitman at Pfaff's,' by Howells, in *The Conservator*, June, 1895, and 'A Few Impressions of Walt Whitman' [at Pfaff's] by David E. Cronin, in *The Conservator*, June, 1895.

Burroughs asks a correspondent, Miss Ludella Peck, if she noted his article in the 'Critic' for March 17, containing his passage at arms with Maurice Thompson, adding: 'I may touch him up again, as he beats the air so wildly. I am not in any of the places where he plants his blows, and the issue between us is not there. He is always snapping and snarling at the heels of Whitman and Tolstoy like a whiffet dog at the heels of a bear, and I thought for once I would shy a pebble at him.' He refers to Thompson's article in the March 'Atlantic' of that year, 'The Sapphic Secret,' and to his own article in the 'Critic' where, quoting Thompson's title for his heading, he says that Thompson's spiteful stabs at Whitman with a pocket-knife cannot reach the vitals of so great a man, and that if Whitman were living he probably would not know that he was being killed at all. Thompson had grouped the works of Ibsen, Tolstoy, and Whitman as 'a dirty wash of imitation.' Burroughs asks caustically if in his heart Thompson would not be glad if he could do a little of this 'Anna Karenina' sort of 'imitation,' and adds, 'I know some of his readers would, if he would not.'

In the Journal, March 22, Burroughs writes:

A passage omitted, on second thought, from my essay in last 'Critic' on the Sapphic Secret:

Discursive and experimental writers, like Mr. Thompson and myself — the mere nibbling mice of criticism — should temper their wrath when they sit in judgment upon the great ones — the lions who make the paths through the jungles of the world. It is no fault of theirs that they are not mice, but is it not our fault that we do not see them to be lions?

Mr. Thompson hits back in the 'Critic,' March 31 ('Again the Sapphic Secret'), taunting Burroughs with effrontery, since lacking a classical education, and therefore unable to read Greek literature in the original, he ventures to comment on the Greek influence in our literature. He implies that Burroughs is 'a sophisticated bumpkin.' And he makes a contemptible implication when he asks, 'But did Walt Whitman, fumbling with his boasted "phallic thumb of Love," reproduce the formative spirit animating American life, society, morals, religions, institutions?' He also says, 'True, if a man's world be a pigsty, he must as a poet sing the pigsty; but he is a nobler poet when the universe is his.' If the universe is not Whitman's, where in all literature has the universe been sung?

In May, dipping into Edmund Gosse's article on Whitman,[1] Burroughs confides to his Journal that he regards Gosse, though clever, as a very small critic — a man who has spent his days in overhauling and sorting the small potatoes of English literature, and who knows much about said literature that is not worth knowing, and that it would be a weariness to know:

> He sees nothing but a barbarous, unregenerated poetic nature in WW ... He thinks the secret of Whitman's attraction for certain minds is that they see themselves in him. Well, a poet in whom such men as Stevenson, Symonds, Emerson, Thoreau, and others, see themselves, must be something or somebody.... In Mr. Gosse's poems we see only little Mr. Gosse. When we can all see ourselves in him, he will have increased immensely in size and importance.

One can but smile at the now caustic critic of Mr. Gosse when recalling how that same critic had found him quite engaging a few years before. Let any one but tread on Whitman's toes, and Burroughs was there to chastise unsparingly. I am reminded of what he once said of some other critic of his bard:

> There is one ground on which I'll forgive a man for not seeing anything in WW — Let him produce something great himself, and then I'll forgive him — *but he never will do it* [added with asperity].

Burroughs's Journal for October 1 has this significant entry:

> If we come to Whitman in a critical frame of mind merely, in a frame of mind begotten by books, and not by life, as a professor and a judge, both critic and subject will fare poorly. Because in WW the professional poet is not uppermost; it is not the literary adept, got up for the occasion, that you meet first; but the real man as he lives and breathes, and as he walks the streets, whom you first face — a figure divested of artificial and conventional vestments, symbolized by the coatless portrait of the poet in the first edition of 'Leaves of Grass.' Your sense of real things, your grip of nature and life, are the first to be challenged. If you are looking for a poet instead of a man, you will probably be repelled at once. The poetry is there, of course, but it must be come at by a kind of indirection, a kind of sacrifice of our critical pride and equipment. We must take this man on his own terms, or not at all. We must divest ourselves of our theories and canons. We must seek him as a man and not as a poet. (See poem beginning 'Whoever you are, holding me now by the hand.') Hence the difficulties the professional critics have had with Whitman, the difficulties the

[1] Gosse: 'A Note on Walt Whitman,' *New Review*, April, 1894, reprinted in *Critical Kit Kats*, London, 1896.

minor poets have had with him. In the mind of the minor poet the sense of poetry as a craft, as something wrought, is stronger than his sense of life and reality. He values the shadow more than the reality. Third- and fourth-rate critics and poets almost invariably reject him. Men outside of literature accept him, and the greatest natures inside of literature. We find the poet in him in and through the man, in and through his human attributes and powers. The conventional poets all get themselves up for the occasion. Their language and posture are largely professional, like that of the lawyer or the priest. They feign and make believe a great deal. They speak through their forms, as the sea-captain through his trumpet. Not so with W. W. at all. You may like the poets very much and not like him at all. He is one step nearer you, nearer reality, than Tennyson. The usual literary veils and illusions are not in him. It is as if a living man touched you on the shoulder and walked by your side.

Yet if 'Leaves of Grass' is not good literature, good poetry, that ends it.

Among the group of later steadfast acceptors of Whitman was the scholar and archæologist Dr. Daniel G. Brinton, of Philadelphia, who made several interesting contributions in the 'Conservator,' notably an account of a visit to Whitman's birthplace, October, 1894, in company with Isaac Hull Platt and Horace Traubel ('A Visit to West Hills,' 'Conservator,' November, 1894), later published in the Whitman Fellowship Papers, Number 10; 'Walt Whitman and Science,' 'Conservator,' April, 1895, and 'Whitman's Sexual Imagery,' 'Conservator,' June, 1895. In the 'Arena,' September, 1894, the Reverend Minot J. Savage warmly espoused Whitman. Francis Howard Williams, in 'The Flute Player, and Other Poems' (1894) published two sonnets to Whitman; he also had one or more papers on 'The Poetry of Walt Whitman' in the 'American' in 1888. Whitman was fond of him and said to Traubel, 'In Frank's hands I am safe.' Of his stanch supporter Talcott Williams, Whitman said, 'The only thing that saves the Press from entire damnation is the presence of Talcott Williams.' When Traubel told Whitman that Mr. Harrison Morris regarded his meetings with him (W. W.) as epochs, the poet turned it off lightly, with some comment about his roses smelling good, but that Morris mustn't be too reckless with them. And when he learned that Mr. Morris was to have an article about him in the 'American' (1888), he told Traubel to caution him not to jeopardize his reputation too far by fooling with Whitman. After reading the article, he spoke of its friendliness and partial acceptance, and of the writer's evident intent to recognize in him 'some gleam of literary righteousness.' Not to be intimidated by Whitman's warnings, Mr. Morris has gone on writing about him, for example: a poem to Whitman in his 'Madonna, and Other Poems' (Philadelphia, 1894); and 'Walt Whitman,' Harvard University Press, 1929, which had already appeared in an Italian translation in 1920. In this book, giving reminiscences of the poet in his last years, Mr. Morris testifies to his sincerity and childlike naïveté, — probably much nearer the truth than the estimate of critics who see in Whitman only the poseur and the colossal egotist.

In 'Walt Whitman Again,' [1] Burroughs replied to an article by Edgar Fawcett in a preceding number. One paragraph from Burroughs's rejoinder follows:

> To the impeccable minor poet, with whom delicate fancies, petty feigning, faultless verse, etc., are all in all, what a shock Whitman must be! It were like taking a man where he lies languishing in a warm and perfumed bath and tossing him into the surf.

In the autumn of 1895 Burroughs held his house-warming at his rustic woodland cabin, Slabsides, a mile and more from his home on the Hudson. Thereafter he spent much time in the sequestered haunt, leisurely writing on his second book on Whitman, and communing with the spirit of his lost comrade. He came to realize, as never before, what peace and deep quiet joy Whitman's haunt on Timber Creek had yielded him. At a certain point in their careers, both men instinctively sought a retreat 'far from the clank of crowds,' where they could bathe in 'nature's primal sanities.' As winter set in, Burroughs was persuaded to do some public speaking — at Packer Institute, Brooklyn, on 'Observations of Nature,' at various schools and clubs, and at a Whitman dinner in Brooklyn. Of this last speech he wrote in his Journal that he was not well prepared and did not speak with much fullness and go. He was a variable speaker, sometimes feeling himself inadequate, again acquitting himself to his satisfaction.

Eldridge wrote Burroughs appreciatively in November about his papers in recent numbers of the 'Conservator':

[1] Burroughs: 'Walt Whitman Again,' *Conservator*, October, 1895. Burroughs: 'More Whitman Characteristics,' *ibid.*, November, 1895.

The piece named 'More Whitman Characteristics,' in the November number, struck me as the finest and broadest exposition of his work that Walt has yet received from anybody, and I was on the point of writing and telling you so when these papers came to hand, addressed in your well-remembered handwriting. I suppose the articles are a part of your forthcoming book on Walt, and give rich promise of a great treat in store for all of us....

My own book on Walt, which I design simply to be one of memories and not of criticism, still lags, and, like my fortunes, is 'still bound in shallows and in miseries.' Ill health and other disasters which have happened to me during the past year have prevented my going on with it.

Burroughs was highly gratified to come upon an article by Mr. Colin A. Scott, of Clark University, in the January number of the 'American Journal of Psychology' for 1896 — sound and discriminating, and speaking an enlightened word concerning the despised 'Children of Adam':

What we need at present is a modern phallicism, a religious and artistic spirit that goes out to meet the sexual instinct, and is able to find in it the center of evolution, the heart and soul of the world, the holy of holies to all right-feeling men.

Stedman wrote Burroughs, on February 12, of his delight that his 'dearest Burroughs' was going to speak to his Yale boys on Whitman. He spoke of his keen interest in Burroughs's 'Conservator' paper 'Two Critics on Walt Whitman,'[1] feeling honored thereby, and also instructed in many ways; and added: 'You are always honest and sincere, and I have often followed you as a teacher with happiness and sympathy.' Calling attention to page 353 in his 'Poets of America' to show Burroughs that he has misapprehended him somewhat, he continues:

From youth I have counted Whitman 'among the foremost lyric and idyllic poets,' and... cared more for him as a poet than as a hero or prophet.... I have always looked upon him, at his best, also as a great rhythmical and imaginative artist, by nature and by studied practice and self-training. Before he died, in fact, he rose to synthesis, and his final arrangement of his life-book is as beauteously logical and interrelated as a cathedral.

He explains that his 'Poets of America' had fewer quotations from Whitman than he would have used, owing to a monition from

[1] 'Two Critics on Walt Whitman,' *Conservator*, August, 1895. See also Burroughs: *Whitman: A Study*, pp. 142–46, 147–49.

a high authority, but that many more from W. W. will appear in
'An American Anthology' (as already in the 'Library of American
Literature'). And continuing:

Finally, you have always seemed to class me with the 'literary critics,'
and as one of those considering Whitman from the professional and
technical point of view. In this you show a difficulty in ever escaping from
a first impression — from an idea formed in earlier days. I have often
thought of trying to disabuse you of it, but have had a feeling that it would
be of no use — that you are sweet and strong and true, but lack a certain
flexibility. Now, as the scientists tell us, even the ice-glaciers and the
granite mountains do *flow*.

... Whitman has never 'puzzled' me as much as he has others, for I
knew him when he was relatively young and entering on his true mission.
Besides, is he deeper or more various than Homer, Shakespeare, the Bible?
So, if I ever criticized him technically, it usually was in his favor — but as
a minor consideration. I did, and do, think that, like several modern prose
realists, he violates Nature's laws by giving undue prominence to one class
of her functions. I would neither magnify nor depreciate any of Nature's
phases or processes, believing, with Whitman (and many another sage)
that all are equally in honor. My only quarrel with him was, in fact, that
his practice as a writer did not always carry out his own credo.

With more gracious and winning talk the genial Stedman chatters
on; his winsomeness recalls one of Burroughs's comments about him
in his Journal of that year, as being 'a lovable man... like a good,
frank, brave bright boy. A fine talker, who tells you you are a fool
in a way that does not hurt.'

The Journal, February 19, reveals the perturbed lecturer:

Go to New Haven to speak before the Phi Beta Kappa Society on Whitman.

Am dreadfully scared and worried, as usual, as I sit in my room at the
hotel; it seems utterly impossible for me to read that lecture. I could fly
to the moon easier. But when the hour strikes, and I find myself face to
face with the enemy, my courage and confidence mount, and I acquit myself entirely to my satisfaction. I speak about one-third of it and read the
rest. A fine audience, and appreciative.

He gives in the Journal a fragment of his opening remarks to the
Yale students. After telling them that Mr. Stedman had written
him that the Yale spirit is sturdy, democratic, unaffected, American, and so cosmopolitan that it is at home even in its own country,
he said he came to them with a theme that should appeal to all those
traits — Walt Whitman:

If it does not, the fault is in me, and not in it.

Mr. Stedman has himself written wisely and appreciatively of Whitman. Let me take this as a good omen, as a sign that the Yale spirit and the Whitman spirit are not so far apart as they might seem to be. But if it is so, if I have not your sympathy, then there is all the more reason why I should be true to myself and speak my own honest conviction about the man and his work. If, indeed, the Yale spirit is resolute, self-reliant, unaffected; if it is done with sugar-plums; if it has finished with illusions; if it can face the realities of life and the world; it ought to find much in Whitman to which it can respond. The example he set us of cheerful self-trust, of unshakeable determination to follow the inward light and go his own way in the world, ought to be an inspiration to every young man....

Of an autumn visit from Oscar Lovell Triggs to Slabsides, Burroughs wrote in his Journal:

We have had a day and a night in the Whitman land, and much talk and real intellectual intercourse. I think Triggs will yet strike out something new and valuable in the way of criticism — maybe formulate the principles of the new democratic criticism....[1]

I told him that Kennedy had written me that an old Yale professor of his had said recently that Whitcomb Riley was the true poet of democracy, instead of Whitman. We agreed that Riley was a true democratic poet, but not at all of commanding genius; he suggests nothing, is nothing, but Riley. He is a specimen, and not a genus, or tribe. He is a local flora, but not botany. There is no spiritual or intellectual stimulus in Riley. One welcomes his poems as he welcomes any real and genuine thing. But they are minor productions. They are light craft that do not draw much water, while Whitman's keel scrapes the deepest bars. He could do nothing in the waters in which the Hoosier poet disports himself.

Whitman is not the first or only democratic poet, but he is the first all-inclusive one — the first one in whom the democratic spirit has come to full maturity, and who proceeds to take possession of the world in its own right. He confronts the old types with an egotism equal to their own. Riley is a Hoosier poet, Whitman, a world-poet.

Again from the Journal:

[1] Triggs's contributions to the Whitman literature are:
Study of Browning and Whitman. Sonnenschein and Company, London; Macmillan, New York, 1893.
'Whitman's Lack of Humor,' *Conservator*, September, 1896.
'The Growth of *Leaves of Grass*,' *Conservator*, August, 1897.
'Walt Whitman: a Character Study,' *Conservator*, September–October, 1898.
Selection from the Prose and Poetry of Walt Whitman, with Introduction. Small, Maynard and Company, 1898.
'Variorum Readings of Leaves of Grass,' edited by Oscar Lovell Triggs, in *Leaves of Grass*, Doubleday, Page & Co., 1920, vol. 1.

Dec. 10. Probably the main thing about Whitman, after all, is his tremendous egotism, the thrust and power of the personal pronoun. At first this rather astonishes and irritates one. What a colossal egotist! we are apt to say, but by and by we come under its power, and see that it is not out of proportion — that the man makes his words good; that he is not above men, but of them, and would bring the whole race flush with himself. It is the egoism and ever-living presence that makes the 'Leaves' a man, in the same sense that no other book is. Of course it is the personal quality that tells in all writing, and in all action, too. How much of a man are you? Is the 'I' expressive of mere personal conceit, or of a deep, broad, natural egoism? We usually call it character, but, by whatever name, it is the man back of all.

Are Whitman's critical values greater than his literary or artistic values? But does not the ethical value of any piece of writing finally depend upon the literary value? upon the manner of presentation? A sermon aims at ethical value, but if its literary value be low, will its ethical value be high? I think not. Every page of Emerson has an ethical import which is enhanced by the poetic quality of the writing. The goody-good books are good ethics, but they do not strike home because they are poor literature. Whitman's ethical or patriotic or philosophic value will not save him. These things would not save the Bible. Only an effective presentation can embalm them. Matter and manner are equally important.... The matter is always in the man, in his personality, in the comprehensiveness of his relation to life and to Nature — in that something we call weight and authority....

On March 7 of that year the calm and reasonable Eldridge had written Burroughs in what, especially in the first paragraph, must seem to most of us an extravagant vein:

I was glad to know that you had been lecturing about Walt in Boston. Walt said to me on one occasion, referring to his works, 'I have either done a very great thing, or it is nothing at all.' Fully believing, as I do, that he has done 'a very great thing' — that this age will be chiefly remembered for his having lived in it — and that Emerson's chief title to fame will be that he recognized Walt's greatness when almost every one else was hostile or indifferent — I also think it is incumbent on all of us who knew him well to contribute what we can to the elucidation of his character and aims, for the benefit of succeeding generations. For he is going to be a great puzzle to succeeding ages, and if he is [as] great as we think he is, numberless will be the books that will be written about him to explain his books and his career.

Sometimes I am inclined to think that Dr. Bucke is right in claiming *especial inspiration* as the Key to the puzzle of the production of 'Leaves of Grass.' Look at his writings up to that time. As literature they are beneath contempt. The very commonest kind of newspaper and magazine writing, and in merit not up to the average of such stuff. Think of the man who wrote 'Franklin Williams, or the Inebriate's Doom,' under the stimulus, as he once told me, of relays of strong whisky cocktails, in order to keep the printer's devil, who was waiting, supplied with copy, afterward writing the sublime passage beginning, 'I am an acme of things accomplished, and I am an encloser of things to be!' — equal in majestic imagery to anything in the Book of Genesis, or Revelation, for that matter.

Walt once told me that the original piece entitled 'Walt Whitman' was produced in a mood, or condition of mind, that he had never been able to resume, and that he had felt utterly incompetent to produce anything equal to it since; that, in contemplating it, he felt, in regard to his own agency in it, like a somnambulist who is shown, during his waking hours, the giddy heights and impossible situations over which he has passed safely in his sleep.

William O'Connor, who, you know, was a devout believer in the Baconian authorship of the Shakespeare plays, told me that the career of Walt up to the production of 'L of G' (in his 36th year), was the only thing that had ever made him doubt that theory, or shaken his belief in it — the strongest basis, as you will remember, on which that theory rested, in his mind, was the impossibility of a man of Shakespeare's training, habits, and character producing that wondrous drama. Yet Walt's case seems almost as wonderful. Emerson said that he greeted him 'at the beginning of a great career which must have had a long foreground somewhere for such a start.' But was there any foreground which could adequately explain such a magnificent outburst?

... If I ever attain that condition of leisure and worldly prosperity which is necessary, I intend to resume my Reminiscences. As you are aware, for ten or twelve years I was about as intimate with Walt as anybody ever was, and although I could tell some things which might shock a rigid moralist, there was nothing in his conduct which from a large and generous standpoint was discreditable to him. His relations with women, so far as I had any knowledge of them, were always noble, and on the highest plane. Of course I shall have to practice a degree of reticence about some matters. In some cases, however, it will be hard to discriminate between what is purely private, as occurring in the confidences of friendship, and what his friends and admirers have a right to know.... [Here follow his comments on the estrangement between Whitman and O'Connor, quoted already on pages 97, 98.]

Again, April 4, Eldridge writes in part:

... I shall of course have to use a good deal of reticence in regard to things that Walt said to me in the unrestrained intercourse that we had, in order to spare the feelings of persons still living. For instance, meeting Walt at Camden, soon after ——'s article on him appeared... we spoke of it, and Walt said, referring to it, that he had recently been reading a new life of Lord Clive, the conqueror of India, and he sympathized with Clive's injunction delivered to somebody in his last days, 'Don't let my life be written by a d——d clerk.' This is pretty good, but of course it would never do to publish it. I would not wish to hurt ——'s feelings, and such a remark would probably wound him sorely. I agree with you that —— is a very lovable character, with many admirable qualities, but as a literary critic he seems to me very shallow — a certain superficial brilliancy he has, but he never gets to the root of the matter. He is capable of admiring the verbal felicities that occur in Walt's poetry, but of his 'great aim and scope' he has no appreciation whatever, in my judgment. The worst literary fault he has is his assumption that he 'knows it all.' Like Macaulay, he is 'cock sure' about everything.

I am glad that you also met Howells. I wrote him after his article in 'Harper's' magazine in which he spoke, as I thought, in a censorious manner about Walt's publication of Emerson's letter. I got a very pleasant letter from him in which he denied that he had intended any censure, but still indicated his opinion that the printing of any letter of the kind, although authorized, tacitly or expressly, would be in bad taste. Howells is a pretty good fellow, of whom great things might be expected, if Harvard College had not, at an early day, laid its icy finger on him and 'froze the genial currents of his soul.'[1]

I am thinking of writing an article for the 'Conservator' about the relations of Emerson and Whitman, and hope I shall be able to compass it. I hope to see your lecture on Walt in the next 'Conservator.' I am glad you had an opportunity to deliver it at Yale College, and trust the seed will have fallen on fruitful ground.

Eldridge's article here mentioned came out in the May 'Conservator' of that year. As for his Reminiscences, I cannot find any one who knows of the whereabouts of the notes and memoranda which he had made looking toward his book on Whitman. If ever his notes can be unearthed, they should prove treasure trove.

After reading Burroughs's address before the Yale students in the April 'Conservator,' Eldridge wrote him that he found two admissions toward its close to which, without further explanation, he must take exception, and that he would perhaps make them the text for an article in the 'Conservator' in the near future, but that he would like to hear from him further before printing anything, lest he had misunderstood him. He continues:

[1] As a matter of fact, Howells never went to Harvard, or any other college. Eldridge may refer to his connection with the *Atlantic Monthly*, which began in 1866 when he was twenty-nine.

You say: 'The home, the fireside, the domestic allurements are not in him.' Now it seems to me that the earlier poems, especially, are saturated with the love of home and domestic pleasures. Walt, as I knew him, was, as far as existing institutions are concerned, one of the most conservative of men. He was more passionately attached to the old fashioned family relations than any man I have ever known. This is indicated in so many places in 'Leaves of Grass' that I will not quote passages which must be as familiar to you as to me. Can it be possible that these passages do not convey the same significance to others as to me?

You say further, immediately following the above: 'Love, as we find it in other poets, is not in him.' This appears to me to concede too much, altogether — a hostile critic [1] said of Walt some years ago: 'There is a curious deficiency shown in him, almost alone among poets, of anything like personal and romantic love; of any elevated emotion toward an individual woman of his own age or generation his pages are bare.'

There is no doubt but that Walt thought that 'the love business,' as he would term it, was tremendously overdone throughout all modern literature, especially in the poets and novelists, and he desired to avoid that error; but in making his book he intended to give it its due and proportionate treatment, and I think he has done so. Was there ever written anywhere a more touching threnody of lost or hopeless love than is found in the piece entitled, 'Out of the Cradle Endlessly Rocking'? And there are other poems in which romantic and personal love is given a place, often by indirections, it is true, but it is there all the same.

And again on June 12:

In regard to your proposed treatment of the publication of the Emerson letter by Walt, as due to his want of knowledge of the conventions, the principal thing I have to say against it is, I don't think it will be quite true to treat it that way. Walt knew a great deal about the conventionalities in such cases. He must have known. He had been editor of two newspapers, the Brooklyn 'Freeman,' and the New Orleans 'Picayune.' These were not obscure country sheets, and, in conducting them, he must have had to decide many times on what was proper to be published, and what not. I don't think my proposition can be successfully assailed: that when a man sends a book, or a bicycle, to another, in the same circumstances that Walt sent 'Leaves of Grass' to Emerson, the reply is intended for publication, unless it should be marked 'private.' If this is true, then there was no violation of conventionalities involved in the case. I put the proposition to W. D. Howells, who had referred to the matter in his 'Harper's' article, and all he had to say in reply was, that there certainly was a difference in letters, but he thought better of a man who did not publish them in the way of advertisement, even when they were intended

[1] See T. W. Higginson's anonymous article on Whitman in the *Nation*, April 7, 1892.

for that. I send you his letter so that you may see exactly what he said. The blue pencil annotations are mine. He speaks of Emerson not showing *rancor*. This is a very infelicitous word. As though Emerson ever showed *rancor* about anything!...

The treatment of Walt as an unsophisticated child of nature may easily be pushed too far. It is true that he had many naïve characteristics to his dying day, which would suggest such a treatment; but he was many-sided, and had seen and absorbed almost every phase of life which America offers. I don't think he was very familiar with the parlors of Fifth Avenue, *but he had been in them*, and knew all there was in that superficial life. 'What he had seen once he had seen forever.'

I was gratified at your praise of my article in the May 'Conservator.' It [1] was not nearly as good as I might have made it if I had taken more time. There are some things in it that I think will be new to many of Walt's admirers. In my tribute to Wm. O'Connor I did not make any qualifications because that did not seem to be the place for it. Of course he had the defects of his qualities, and I sometimes wished he would not be so vehement. While it is true, I think, that he repelled a few persons by the strength of his statements, or the violence of his language, especially those of a cautious and conservative intellectual temperament, I believe the great majority were roused and convinced by that very means. I do not agree with you that he did not carry conviction, except as stated above. I notice that it is not the lawyers who make tepid and qualified statements who win their cases. William was a great *advocate* and ought to have been trained for the bar.

Every letter of Eldridge's that one sees makes one regret keenly that he did not publish his Reminiscences of Whitman — he was so calm and just, and knew Whitman so intimately from 1860 to 1892. The deep love he bore him reminds one of what Edward Dowden said of Whitman in 1871 — 'He called out the reverent affection of those nearest him.'

Excerpts from a letter of June 19, from Eldridge to Burroughs follow:

I do not expect you will agree with me always, and I am glad to hear that you will adhere to that statement in the lecture about Walt before Yale, if such is your final conviction. I don't know as I shall find time to write the article for the 'Conservator,' such as I spoke of, at present. I would suggest further, however, that if Walt had any intention in his poems it was to exploit the whole American 'human critter,' as he exists in the latter half of the Nineteenth Century. This intention was not only avowed again and again in his prose writings, but I heard him repeatedly

[1] Eldridge: 'The Personal Relations of Emerson and Whitman,' *Conservator*, May, 1896.

say the same thing in private conversation. This was his main defence for his introduction of things not usually spoken of in society. How could he pretend to portray man as he exists and ignore the sexual part? — so important and so vital? Now if he has failed to give due place to the domestic sentiments, and to love, as portrayed by other poets, he has so far failed in his portraiture of *man*. I do *not* claim everything for Walt, and am well aware that there are charms and allurements in other poets to which his work is a stranger. I am only anxious that you should consider these points before you print your book, for you have the ear of the literary and reading public much beyond any other Waitarian.

I think, with you, that Dr. Bucke is inclined to be a little 'cranky.' I should like to see how he makes it out that the first fifteen of the Shakespeare Sonnets are addressed to the 'Cosmic Consciousness.' To me those sonnets have always seemed to be addressed to some one who the author desired should marry and have a child. I would like very much to have some one explain to me what the Sonnets mean, anyway. I have studied them a good deal, but, beyond finding them to contain much magnificent poetry, the whole mass is to me an enigma, especially as to whom they are addressed to, or what purpose the author had in writing them.

In regard to the title for your forthcoming book, of the three you name I like 'A New World-Poet' the best. The 'Poet of Democracy' is good also, but it has been a good deal used in other connections, though, I believe, no book with such a title has ever been issued. I like 'A New World-Poet' because it suggests a new moral, spiritual, and intellectual world, as well as the geographical and physical.

It is strange that Burroughs finally decided on the title, 'Whitman: A Study,' for his book, since Symonds's book, already published (1893), had so similar a title — 'Walt Whitman: A Study.' A letter from Eldridge on July 23 is given in part:

I certainly agree with you that it was in very bad taste [of Whitman] to print a sentence from Emerson's letter in gilt on the back of his next edition; and the responsive letter, in which he addresses Emerson as 'Master' so many times, was in still worse taste. There can be no doubt that the reception of that letter made Walt, as the French say, a little *tête exalté*, or, as our boys would call it, gave him a case of the 'big head.' I don't think that Walt was perfect by any means, as my book, if it ever gets printed, will abundantly show; but still there was a valid excuse for the publication of that letter.

I shall be pleased and proud to have you quote in your book anything from my 'Conservator' article that may suit your purpose. I shall be delighted to receive the proofs you speak of sending me, and they will be returned at the earliest possible moment with my most candid criticism. I am grateful at the prospect of the early publication of your book. You have such a high standing as an author, in both England and America, that it is bound to be extensively reviewed in both countries, and will thereby revive the interest in Walt, which seems to me lately a little on the decline.

Regarding this moot question as to the propriety of Whitman using Emerson's letter, Isaac Hull Platt stoutly defends it in his little book, 'Walt Whitman' (pages 28–32), published in the Beacon Biography Series in 1904 by Small, Maynard and Company. He also points out that Charles A. Dana, then on the New York 'Tribune,' with his long history in journalism, urged its use. And concerning Whitman's letter to Emerson, which Whitman published in the 1856 edition of the 'Leaves,' Mr. Platt says understandingly (page 33): 'It was one of those acts which, under the influence of enthusiasm, everyone sometimes does, and feels sheepish about afterwards.'

As to the use of Emerson's letter, for which Whitman has been so criticized, I have often heard Burroughs say that Charles A. Dana, when urging it, said, 'It is the charter of an emperor.' Traubel, in volume 3 of 'With Walt Whitman in Camden' (pages 124–25), quotes Whitman's account of Charles A. Dana urging him to let them quote the Emerson letter in the 'Tribune.' Curiously enough Professor Holloway, in his 'Whitman' (pages 142–43), erroneously states that it was Richard Henry Dana, Jr. Both the Danas were friendly to Whitman, but it was not the 'Two Years Before the Mast' man, but the Dana of the 'Tribune' (and later of the 'Sun'), who helped get Whitman into that escapade for which he has so often been criticized.

Burroughs's book 'Whitman: A Study' came out in late November. He writes in his Journal, November 23:

The Whitman book came Saturday — think it has reality — that the reader will on the whole have the sense of having come in contact with real ideas and distinctions, and not with mere words. Could have made it much better if I had given another year to it.

When Eldridge received a copy of the Whitman book, he wrote Burroughs:

I am greatly pleased with it as a whole. You have made, *undoubtedly*, the ablest and most elaborate presentation of Walt as a poet and person that has yet been seen. All the purely personal part I think you have treated with great truthfulness, as well as unfailing tact. In regard to some points in your presentation of Walt's poetic scheme, I shall have to take exceptions, especially in what you say about the treatment of the 'love business' by him. If I ever get time I shall indicate my dissent, by some publication of your view of that matter. It would, however, be very strange if, in viewing the vast orb of poetry and philosophy he has created and bequeathed to us, there were not different perceptions of its character by different minds.

I wish to say now only that I have greatly enjoyed your work. At the lowest estimate it is a very juicy piece of criticism and exposition; and I hope it will have the success to which it is surely entitled by its literary merits alone.

Dr. Bucke wrote Burroughs enthusiastically, December 9, shortly after reading 'Whitman: A Study':

I have just had a letter from Kennedy, and I want you to know what it says about your book, as, of course, he speaks to me his real thought. He says: 'Burroughs's book is something to build on. I have written him my congratulations and praises. He has produced a fine piece of proselytising literature. It will do more in America to make Whitmanites than anything yet published. Foreigners will not swallow it so freely; it is too much of a whitewash. He has a splendid and firm conception of Walt Whitman as a great, natural, vital force in his day and generation — the embodiment of the spirit of the age and of the future in works of religion and art. This is a grand *motif* running through J. B.'s book. He does not treat the religion and the poetry *as art* at all fully, but much that he does write of is decidedly new and vital.'

On January 14 of the following year, Dr. Bucke wrote further:

I have been through your 'Whitman' again and read it with almost greater pleasure than before. I think fully as highly of it as I did at first, even perhaps a little more highly. You have never written a better book than this, or a book that will keep your name alive longer.

He then offers a list of a few errors he has noted, and tells Burroughs he thinks he has often quoted 'The Leaves' from memory, as some of his quotations are inaccurate; he urges him to go over all quotations before the next edition, since 'this book is so good in itself that its execution in type ought by rights to be perfect.'

Eldridge also writes on January 11:

I am not surprised that your book is making converts for Walt. Such a serious, able, and candid presentation of his claims has not heretofore been made. It rouses no antagonism, and could not have been executed in better temper or better taste. I think you did well to publish when you did. You might perhaps have improved it some by delay, but that is doubtful, while, as you remark, life is short and tempus foots it....

I have heard, of course, of Donaldson's book,[1] and Kennedy's, but have not seen them, and do not know whether I should care to own them. At any rate, I shall be glad to avail myself of your offer to lend them to me by mail. I will return them promptly and defray postage both ways. I have subscribed for the Peter Doyle book.[2]

I cannot report any progress on my book.... I have put but little on paper, but my mind is full of it.... In my opinion there is no immediate prospect that a book on such a subject, by an unknown author, could pay expenses....

One can but regret Eldridge's modesty which held him back from giving what must have proved a valuable contribution to Whitman literature. With those early years of companionship with Whitman, and with all that the association yielded him through the years, one of his keen mind and understanding heart could have made a book of inestimable value. But despite the richness of his qualifications, because he was unknown to letters, he feared to tread where others have rushed in with their distortions, conjectures, and imaginings, thus lifting their own names out of obscurity by linking them with Whitman's.

The grace with which Burroughs could tender a book as a gift is seen in his letter to Miss Ludella Peck, which accompanied his 'Whitman: A Study':

To make partial amends for my seeming neglect I come now with a book in my hand, which I suppose I have written for you as much as for anybody, or, rather *from* you, from the sympathy which I knew you and others like you would feel in my undertaking. The book has been on my hands for three or four years, and has caused me to neglect many other things. It ought to be a riper fruit than it is. I made it better each year, and at each re-writing, and probably could have kept on doing so; and one of these days I expect I shall regret that I did not wait a little longer; but life

---

[1] Thomas Donaldson: *Walt Whitman the Man.* Francis P. Harper, 1896. A contradictory, rather puerile book on the whole, though containing some interesting matter. Donaldson often flatly contradicts himself on the same page. He says, inexplicably, when there is abundant evidence to the contrary: 'Comradeship in its usual acceptance, had no charm for him. He did not smoke, and had no convivial or club habits. He did not like or use stimulants except as medicine, and even eschewed tea and coffee.' 'He could not be a "good fellow," in the general sense of the term, for it was not in him.' Whitman did not use tobacco in any form, but the other statements are surely wide of the mark.

[2] *Calamus* (Letters of W. to Peter Doyle), edited by Dr. Bucke. Laurens Maynard, 1897.

is short and art is long, so I have taken the irrevocable step of publication.

I shall welcome any criticism you may be moved to make of it. I always profit by any frank opinion of my friends. A sincere judgment never wounds, however adverse....

I have spent the season in the wilderness, in a rustic house I built last fall. I am writing you from this Whitman land, but the cold will soon drive me out....

Burroughs's honest-mindedness is shown in a journal entry (November, 1896):

I shall never be able to tell how much I am warped or biased in Whitman's favor, so that I am barred from taking an independent view of him. I would give anything to be sure that I see him as he is; to be his judge, and not his attorney. I early fell into the way of defending him, and it may be, *may be*, that I can only take an *ex parte* view of him. The moment I begin writing about him I become his advocate. My mind slides into the old rut at once. I must think further about this.

One singular thing about Whitman was that common, unlettered persons did not feel that he was separated from them — they looked upon him as one of themselves, with a difference that they did not quite understand, but which did not disturb them. My hired man, Smith Caswell, took to him greatly, and Peter Doyle and Walt were real loving comrades. Some would consider this trait a defect, but I consider it a great merit. Without the breadth of relation to mankind which this implies, Whitman would not be the inevitable democrat he is claimed to be.

In his Journal, January 4, is this passage about his recent book on Whitman:

To a certain critic: Can't you see that Whitman admits of and justifies this kind of statement — Can't you see that it is all made out of him, and that, therefore, the substance of it must be in him? Can't you see that it is no outside, cut and dried eulogy, but a sympathetic drawing-out and restatement of his intrinsic values? Could I have written the book had not the subject suggested it, or begot it upon me, as it were? You might as well say I eulogize Nature in my other books. I give you the result of the contact of my mind and spirit with Nature, and in this book I give you the result of the contact of my spirit with Whitman's. Whatever there is there comes from him through me. Could I have said these things of Tupper?

Among the many cancelled, and so unpublished, passages in Burroughs's 'Whitman: A Study,' the original manuscript of which is now owned by the Pierpont Morgan Library, the following trenchant comments on Whitman are here transcribed:

Whitman himself used to urge that poets of the refined and scholarly type of our New England poets, are among the choicest treasures of a young and crude nation like our own; how barren would New England seem without her scholars and poets! As barren as the middle and western states now seem, having as yet no adequate singers.

Emerson was less given to snubbing people's prejudices and convictions, much more careful of giving offense [*i.e.* than Ruskin, who had said that he would not mind his letters being published]. Then Whitman had used the letter to float the book. But if the book was what the letter declared it to be, 'the greatest piece of wit and wisdom America had yet contributed,' why should it not be [thus floated]?

The contents of the letter no doubt subjected him [Emerson] to a good deal of unkindly comment among Cambridge and Boston literary men. Then, on further acquaintance, Whitman's tremendous poetical democracy seems to have been rather more than Emerson could stand. Emerson's notions of fine manners embraced the traditional aristocratic element. In this, as in many other respects, Whitman contrasted with Emerson, who was always on the hunt for intellectual game.

Colonel Robert G. Ingersoll wrote Burroughs characteristically as follows, shortly after the publication of 'Whitman: A Study':

Accept my best thanks for your beautiful book on Whitman. You understand Whitman and his work perfectly. You appreciate his elemental quality, his sunburnt philosophy, his appalling candor, his rude naturalness, his kinship with Nature in all her forms, his perfect courage, and, above all, his sympathy. You have written a great book, and have built a lasting monument to the memory of your friend. I read every page with delight; all are filled with thought, poetry, philosophy. You have exhausted the subject, and have said the final word about Whitman and his work....

In a subsequent letter Colonel Ingersoll wrote:

Of course I do not agree with Whitman's philosophy. I think the world is full of failures, and have no confidence in the all-for-the-best creed. Neither do I see design in Nature that tends to prove benevolence, and what is called Providence. It is sad to be an orphan, but it is worse to have a bad father.

Better than anything else that Ingersoll has said about Whitman, was the final fervent sentence which he uttered at the poet's burial, in which he seemed insensibly to reflect Whitman's unquenchable belief in survival after death — 'I loved him living, *and I love him still.*' [1]

[1] Ingersoll's lecture 'An Oration on Walt Whitman' was published in pamphlet form (London, 1890), by the Progressive Publishing Company. It was delivered in Horticultural Hall, New York, on October 21, 1890.

XVIII

THE EMBERS THAT STILL BURN

(1897–1922)

Thou hast but taken thy lamp and gone to bed;
I stay a little longer, as one stays
To cover up the embers that still burn.

LONGFELLOW

IT would seem that with Whitman gone, and Burroughs's book about him well launched, the story of their comradeship would be at an end, but with Whitman's soul marching on, and with Burroughs surviving him as many more years as they had known each other, there remains an aftermath to be gleaned and garnered still. At the evening's close, in the Nest at Riverby, where Burroughs made his home with me in the last years, as he would cover the embers of the dying fire, he would often repeat wistfully the tender lines from Longfellow quoted above. Well may we apply these lines to Whitman's passing, while his comrade lingered on to cover the embers, and, when need should arise, to fan them into flame.

Before his own passing Burroughs was to have the satisfaction of seeing his country absorb the poet to a considerable degree, as surely, if not as lovingly and comprehendingly, as the poet had absorbed it. But he was also still to witness many covert and open attacks upon his comrade, and we shall find him keeping his own armor ready and burnished in Whitman's defense.

On April 12, 1898, Burroughs wrote in his Journal:

What a thorn, or sheaf of thorns, Walt Whitman is in the side of Edgar Fawcett. Poor Edgar! I hope Whitman does not keep him awake o' nights. I think I have seen at least half a dozen spiteful allusions to Whitman from his pen the past year, and now, in the last 'Collier's Weekly,' he has a long, carefully worded outburst. Think of it! This rude, uncouth bard of Democracy, hailed in Europe as a great poet and prophet, and poor Edgar, with his faultless verse, not hailed at all! If faultless verse, Edgar, made poets, poets would be as plenty as blackberries. But it requires a man, too, and in this respect, I suspect you are not much.

The article which had so incensed Burroughs ('Walt Whitman,' by Edgar Fawcett, in a March number of 'Collier's Weekly') provoked a reply from Dr. Bucke, 'An Open Letter to Edgar Fawcett,' which came out in the 'Conservator' for June.

An April letter from Eldridge shows him as sensitive as was Burroughs to the indignities directed toward Whitman:

I have read and enjoyed your juicy bit of criticism on Matthew Arnold in the May 'Atlantic.' Speaking of Matthew Arnold always reminds me of what he is reported to have said in regard to Walt when he was on his lecturing tour in this country. Some one asked him what he thought of Walt and he replied by asking, 'What does Longfellow think of him?' Indeed! how important! What does the sparrow think of the eagle? What does the rabbit think of the lion? I presume you have noticed in the same number how Higginson goes out of his way to pour his old venom on Walt. I suppose he can't help the rancorous dislike he contracted for Walt and his book during his 'seasick trip' from Fayal, but he ought to be ashamed to lug it in on all possible occasions.[1] He ends with his old sneer about Walt's not enlisting in the army instead of going into the hospitals. I wish you would take up the point incidentally in some of your writings, and try to show how malignantly unfair Higginson is in this matter. You can do it better than any one else, besides getting a wider audience. Perhaps you remember that William O'Connor replied to a similar attack of Higginson's in his contribution to Dr. Bucke's book. (See page 80.) But I don't think he showed his usual felicity in that retort. He used Longfellow as his foil, whereas, I should have used Lowell as the best instance: Lowell was born in 1819, same year as Walt, and consequently was, like him, of lawful age for enlistment at the outbreak of the War. Lowell was a furious patriot as well as a poet. Why did he not enlist? Has any one ever been mean and foolish enough to hurl it at him as a reproach because he did not? Excuse me for writing so much on this theme, but Higginson is so exasperating that I cannot help expressing my indignation to some one.

In his Journal, September 24, 1898, Burroughs wrote:

You may light your candle by mine, you may light your reason by mine, but not your faith, nor any purely personal emotion or aspiration. How I have tried to kindle my faith in immortality by Whitman's great torch, but I cannot. I am warmed by his tremendous faith, but it is only as fire warms iron. I very soon cool off again. There is no combustive material in me of that kind in which the spark can take.

[1] In connection with Higginson associating the *Leaves* with his seasickness, it is noteworthy that in his *Nation* article, April 7, 1892, he comments on 'some of the more nauseous passages' of the poems.

I do not recall what new deliverance of Higginson occasioned the following comment in Burroughs's Journal, in November, 1900:

Of course Higginson cannot endure Whitman. Higginson is essentially aristocratic; he tends to the elegant, the polished, the refined; he aspires to the scholarly, the witty, the distinguished; while in Whitman there is something rankly common, like freckles and sweat; he is democratic through and through; he makes no account of the social and elegant ideas; he is larger than they, and includes them.

My own association with Burroughs, and consequently my deepening interest in Whitman, began in the autumn of 1901. At that first meeting he talked engagingly of Whitman and their long comradeship, and gave me this ineffaceable word-picture of the poet:

Whitman was a child of the sea, nurtured and cradled by the sea, and he gave one the same sense of invigoration and illimitableness. He never looked so much at home as when on the shore — his gray clothes, gray hair, and far-seeing blue-gray eyes blending with the surroundings. And his thoughts — the same broad sweep, the elemental force and grandeur and all-embracingness of the impartial sea.

At the request of J. H. Johnston, of New York City, Eldridge wrote a most interesting letter for the dinner of the Whitman Fellowship, held on May 31, 1902. This was extracted from the 'New York Times Literary Supplement,' June 7. Excerpts are given here:

It will surprise some of Walt's admirers to learn that, as revealed by his conversations, he was one of the most conservative of men. He believed in the old ways; had no faith in any 'reforms,' as such, and thought that no change could be made in the condition of mankind except by the most gradual evolution.... He delighted in the company of old fashioned women; mothers of large families preferred, who did not talk about literature or reforms. No man ever honored motherhood or true womanhood more than he did. Anything like free love was utterly repugnant to his mind, and he had no toleration for the Mormons. In the early sixties there was an organization of free lovers in the upper part of New York City, well known to those familiar with the Bohemian life of New York in those days. One of our circle was lead astray and abandoned his wife and children in Washington to join this unsavory crowd. Walt met this man once after this happened, and he gave him as severe a verbal castigation as ever a man received. As William O'Connor said, he actually 'knouted' him. Words did not seem adequate to express his contempt for such a crowd and their practices.

He was likewise very hostile to anything like anarchy, communism, or socialism. At one time after the War Albert Brisbane, perhaps the ablest exponent of Fourierism in this country, spent the winter in Washington, and was often a visitor at O'Connor's, and met Walt. They had many talks together which I listened to, but Walt never yielded an inch of ground to him. He thought that any such ready-made plan for reorganizing society was ridiculous and not quite sane. Our form of government he thought about as good as could be under present human conditions. He was in favor, however, of strengthening the Executive branch, which he thought not quite powerful enough. He strenuously opposed the impeachment of President Johnson as an unwarranted attack upon the independence of the Executive. In the headlong impetuosity of youth, I was warmly in favor of it, but the lapse of time has convinced me that Walt was right.

For the abolitionists he had no sympathy. While opposed to slavery always, he thought that they considered the subject too all-important, and were incendiary in their methods. O'Connor and I, who were always ardent abolitionists, had many a 'hot time' with him over this subject. Of the Negro as a race he had a poor opinion. He said that there was in the constitution of the negro's mind an irredeemable trifling or volatile element, and that he would never amount to much in the scale of civilization. I never knew him to have a friend among the negroes while he was in Washington, and he never seemed to care for them, or they for him, although he never manifested any particular aversion to them. In defence of the negro's capabilities I once cited to him Wendell Phillips' eloquent portrait of Toussaint L'Ouverture, the pure black Haytian warrior and statesman.... He thought it a fancy picture much overdrawn, and added humorously, paraphrasing Betsy Prig in 'Martin Chuzzlewit,' 'I don't believe there was no such nigger.'

In June, 1902, Burroughs was trying to persuade himself to supplement his 'Poet and Person,' and his 'Whitman: A Study,' by a 'Life' of Whitman, which his publishers, Houghton, Mifflin and Company, were urging him to write. Eldridge, urging him on, offered him the use of his material, suggesting, too, that Mrs. Ellen Calder, formerly Mrs. William O'Connor, would doubtless put at his disposal whatever she had pertaining to Whitman. When Burroughs definitely decided not to write the life, he gave Professor Perry access to much of his Whitman material.

Eldridge commented to Burroughs, in a letter of June 19, on the sumptuous subscription edition of Whitman's complete works, which G. P. Putnam's Sons were about to bring out. This was to contain a 'sort of official biography' by his literary executors,

Harned, Bucke, and Traubel. Professor Triggs furnished an exhaustive bibliography for the Putnam edition, which is contained in
volume 10. A briefer Bibliography by him is found in his 'Selections
from the Prose and Poetry of Walt Whitman.'

Eldridge's letter continues:

Have you heard about the story that Walt had *six* children? In the
'Literary Digest' of April 12, 1902,[1] there appeared a digest of an article
written by Edward Carpenter for the 'London Reformer,' in which this
statement was made. His authority was a letter written by Walt to Addington Symonds in August, 1890. I could not have been more astonished,
when I heard of it, if I had been hit with a brick. I immediately wrote
to Traubel and he said they had known of it for some years prior to Walt's
death, and he always wondered how much I knew. He said that he had the
original of the letter to Symonds. It appears, however, that Walt never
gave any particulars of how or when or where or by whom he had these six
children, or whether they still lived; and, when pressed by Harned and
others to say more, was always too much distressed to do so. In my opinion no such thing can possibly be true. There were evidences that he was
not in his right mind for the last two years of his life, and this is one of
them.

Astounded as was Burroughs at this disclosure about Whitman's
children, with Whitman's letter to Symonds as evidence, he at first
credited it, or tried to, as will be seen in an excerpt from a letter
which he wrote Gilder in 1906:

One mystery in his [Whitman's] life can now never be cleared up — the
mystery connected with his children. I am disturbed, as you are, by his
failure to recognize them. If I only knew his reasons! He loved children,
he was deeply attached to the child of his brother George, and greatly
grieved at his death. There *must* have been some circumstances or conditions that were beyond his control that made him apparently ignore his
own offspring.

However, the more Burroughs ruminated on the known facts of
Whitman's life, and the detailed knowledge of his whereabouts, and
comings and goings, the more he was strongly inclined to consider
the story of Whitman's children as a figment of his disordered
imagination — the wish being, as it were, father to the thought.
Once when speaking to me about this he said:

I have often thought this statement may have been the result of Walt's

[1] *Literary Digest*, vol. 24, no. 15, p. 499.

disease — he was not exactly himself at times toward the last. It is all inexplicable; but that Walt would desert his own children is preposterous for anyone to believe who knew him. We shall never know the truth of it. I really doubt Walt's ever having had a child of his own — more's the pity! I'd like to think there were men and women in the world today with Whitman blood in their veins.

It is noteworthy that Eldridge, Burroughs, and Kennedy, each of whom had known Whitman long and intimately, ultimately came to the same conclusion about Whitman's reputed children, namely, that there had been none. In support of this opinion, arrived at by his intimates after considering the subject from many angles, is the fact that unconscious fabrication is exceedingly common in elderly persons afflicted as Whitman was in his later years. His letter to Symonds had been written in his seventy-second year, after several paralytic attacks accompanied with transitory confusion and clouding of consciousness. It would seem that Conway held a view similar to the one here advanced of a pathological fabrication. Just recently I have seen a statement from him in the Bliss Perry Whitman Collection in which he styles it 'Walt's giving way to a senile temptation to pose as a papa.' In that collection is also a communication from Stedman in which he speaks of his doubt as to the genuineness of that letter of Whitman to Symonds, despite the almost unmistakable Whitman phraseology of it. Later he decided, 'Even if Walt wrote it, it was for effect merely,' but still later, after discussing the point with a trustworthy friend of Whitman's later years, Francis Howard Williams, who had told him it was correct (but how did Mr. Williams know?) he was inclined to credit it, adding, 'There is no reason why it shouldn't be true.' It is probable that whatever Mr. Williams had learned had come through Harned or Traubel, and not direct from Whitman. Harned told Burroughs that he had once heard Whitman speak vaguely and confusedly of 'five or six children,' but that on trying to get him to be definite about it he said, 'Some other time, some other time.' And the time never came. In his books Traubel tells of frequently trying to get the story from Whitman. He says that at times he really wondered if there was any foundation for the statement. All of which fits into the picture of a pathological fabrication. There is another possible explanation of the fabrication than that on a pathological basis — namely, an intentional fabrication — 'for reasons.' It is well known that Symonds, saturated with Greek culture and customs, had persistently plied Whitman with queries as to a homosexual basis for the Calamus poems, even after Whitman had repudiated such an interpretation. And Kennedy and others have thought that this letter to Symonds may have been Whitman's ''cute way' of effectually defending himself of the charge of 'man-love,' thus silencing Symonds on that score. Still the explanation hardly explains, since many homosexual persons have fathered and mothered children. Whitman, however, may not have been aware of that fact. Today a more enlightened and sympathetic attitude toward the intermediate sex obtains than in Whitman's time, but, in any case, he would naturally have shrunk from the inferences Symonds drew from his Calamus poems, hence, as some think, may have offered the mythical children as, to him, a convincing refutation.

In his 'Walt Whitman,' Mr. Bliss Perry points out that in one respect only Whitman seems to have failed in the finer obligations of friendship, instancing his acceptance of the homage and defense of his friends, while keeping from them such significant facts as the story of the children. (It seems generally agreed that if that story be true, the children must all have been fathered before 1862.) Mr. Perry adds, 'There is abundant evidence that from 1862 onward his life was stainless so far as sexual relations were concerned.' [1]

[1] I offer the following hitherto unpublished testimony from Whitman himself in regard to his children, for what it is worth. As utterances, both written and verbal, made upon what was practically his death-bed, they may be credited as perhaps the most authentic and sincere testimony that Whitman has left anywhere on record as to the vexed question of his paternity.

On May 23, 1891, Whitman wrote to Dr. Bucke: 'The burial house in Harleigh well toward finished — I paid the constructor $500 last week — (as far as I can see I am favored in having Ralph Moore as my *alter ego* in making it) — I wish to collect the remains of my parents and two or three other near relations and shall doubtless do so — I have two deceased children (young man and woman — illegitimate of course) that I much desired to bury here with me — but have ab't abandoned the plan on account of angry litigation and fuss generally, and disinterment from down South.' Dr. Bucke made the following MS. note of a conversation with Whitman, December 23, 1891: 'I asked him if he did not want to say something to me about "that Southern matter." He said, "My children?" I said, "Yes." He said, "Well, I guess not." I said, "Harned thinks someone ought to know the main facts in case of any trouble arising after ——" He said, "Money matters, you mean?" I said, "Yes." "Oh," he said, "there will be no trouble of that kind," and went on to say that the people were of good family and would of themselves never come forward and claim connection.' These statements are copied from the originals in the Bucke Whitman Collection. — C. J. F.

On reading what Mr. Perry thought of Whitman's failure 'in the finer obligations of friendship,' Burroughs said:

Walt never talked of himself, and we didn't expect it of him. He wasn't given to confiding things, as one woman confides to another. It wouldn't have been in character. Whatever secrets there were in his life, he kept to himself. That was Walt. It was really his relation to the universe that interested and occupied him. [And later:] I doubt if any of the others — O'Connor or Eldridge — any more than I do, resented Walt's reticence as to his own history, as Mr. Perry seems to do for us.

The truth as to this phase of Whitman's life may never be disclosed. He chose to leave it obscured. A legitimate interest attaches to it, for, as Edward Carpenter has said, a man's relations to the question of sex are an important part of his mental outfit, his temperament, and his personality; but, lacking a knowledge of the facts, since nothing can be proved, we must be content to remain baffled.

In his Journal, January 28, 1903, Burroughs is again stirred up by another attack on Whitman from Higginson:

I see that Higginson, in his Lowell Institute lectures, continues his efforts to belittle Whitman....

Think of belittling him because he did not enlist as a soldier and carry a musket in the ranks! Could there be anything more shocking and incongruous than Whitman killing people? One would as soon expect Jesus Christ to go to war. Whitman was the lover, the healer, the reconciler, and the only thing in character for him to do in the War was what he did do — nurse the wounded and sick soldiers — Union men and Rebels alike, showing no preference. He was not an athlete, or a rough, but a great tender mother-man, to whom the martial spirit was utterly foreign.

In 1905, W. H. Trimble, of New Zealand, wrote a book entitled 'Walt Whitman and Leaves of Grass' (Watts and Company, London). He wrote Burroughs of his lectures and other work on Whitman in New Zealand. Later he and his wife made a Whitman Concordance, and published an interesting article, 'Concordance Making in New Zealand,' in the 'Atlantic Monthly,' September, 1909. That year they gave their Concordance into the keeping of Horace Traubel and Isaac Hull Platt. When Platt died, they had the Concordance sent to Mr. Henry S. Saunders. He bound the sheets in seven volumes, but has never succeeded in getting the work published. Trimble also had two pages on 'The Making of a Concordance' in the 'Conservator,' April, 1907. Annie E. Trimble wrote a book, 'Walt Whitman and Mental Science: an Interview,' which was published in Melbourne, Australia, 1911.

Much more has been said and printed about Dr. R. M. Bucke and Horace Traubel than about Whitman's other literary executor, Thomas B. Harned, yet Mr. Harned's services to the poet were exceptionally efficient, far-sighted, and unwearying, while his appreciation of the man and his work were of the highest. I shall never forget the fervor with which he read 'The Prayer of Columbus,' and the concluding part of 'Passage to India,' one evening in his own home, where John Burroughs and I were guests — Harned, a hard-headed, practical lawyer, being moved to exaltation by the mystical meanings enfolded in those sublime poems. He was always looking forward to a 'Life' of the poet yet to be written. In a letter to me of January 3, 1905, he wrote, in part:

Even Burroughs's last Study of Whitman is not entirely satisfactory to me.... I think Burroughs fails to recognize the tremendous spiritual force of 'Leaves of Grass.' He appreciates Whitman altogether on the intellectual side. What I think is the immense thing about Whitman is his unrestricted faith, and his imperturbable optimism. He justifies the ways of God to man as no other writer ever did.

When so much was being made of Whitman having ordered an expensive tomb for himself, while being helped financially by friends, Mr. Harned did his best to counteract the misleading statements which had been printed about it. He sent me a copy of the letter he had written to Mr. Perry to set right false statements, unwittingly made — the gist of his letter being that Whitman's plan was simply to have a rough granite tomb made at a cost of a few hundred dollars; [1] that his idea in building it was as much for his family as for himself; and that Whitman was aghast when the bill was presented to him for the completed tomb. Harned modestly said:

I knew he had been imposed upon and I took charge of the matter and relieved Whitman from all further anxiety. I do not feel called upon to

[1] Binns states in his *Life of Whitman* that the tomb was built after a well-known design by William Blake. His authority is probably a letter written by Whitman (August 23, 1890) to Dr. Bucke: 'Did I tell you that a monument designer, Philadelphia, has bro't me a design for the cemetery vault (do you remember Blake's "Death"?).'

make any further statement with regard to the tomb, except to protect the memory of Whitman against the statement that he deliberately incurred so large an expenditure.

As the years passed, however, and Harned found Whitman still being criticized for the tomb, he felt it necessary to make more explicit statements. On seeing a reported interview with John Burroughs, written by John Black, for the 'Brooklyn Daily Eagle,' May 31, 1919, in which many gross misquotations and misrepresentations occurred, Mr. Harned wrote me, June 3, as follows:

The statement that W. W's friends raised a fund of $5000 to go to the purchase of a home and that Walt diverted it to the building of a tomb is out of whole cloth. Whitman already had a 'home' clear, and he paid $1700 for it out of his royalties. At a later period some New England friends sent him $700 to buy a seashore bungalow, but he preferred to stay in Camden. I'm sick of this talk about a tomb. Walt never thought of a tomb until ten years after his mother's death. Through me the Harleigh Cemetery Company gave him a lot. I hold the deed in my hand, dated Apl 15, 1890, less than two years before his death. I went with him when he selected the lot. It was on slight rising ground and he said to me, 'I think I will go into the woods.' Some stone masons got him to order the tomb which he thought would cost a few hundred dollars. They got $1500 out of him. About a year before he died I found him greatly worried. An enormous bill was presented to him. He had hived some money from various sources, and was keeping it to make sure that his invalid brother, Eddie, should be properly cared for. I took the bill, and told the stone masons they could take their damned old tomb — that they had no right to impose on a man who had no idea of values. A few days after, I told Walt not to bother his head about the matter. With tears in his eyes he said, 'Tom, General Grant never did anything greater than that.' *This is not for publication.*[1] Suffice it to say that the bill was greatly reduced and settled. About this time he conceived the idea to have his immediate relatives buried in the tomb, and now all eight spaces are filled. You know how attached he was to his family. I laughed at the idea of the tomb at the time, but Walt had the right vision. He knew that he could not be skipped. The time will come when this tomb will be as significant as Mahomet's — a veritable mecca.

Of course Mr. Harned knew that John Burroughs was not responsible for the misstatements about the tomb in the reported interview with him, any more than he was for some other very

[1] This letter, and others from their father, is now printed with the permission of Mr. Harned's children.

absurd comments attributed to him by the interviewer. For example, he was reported as complaining that the literary men of the day did not attend Whitman's funeral, and among those he was quoted as naming were Longfellow and Emerson, both of whom had long been dead! As to the tomb, Harned himself met the remaining cost, after having exacted as much of a reduction of the exorbitant bill as he could compass.

When Traubel's first volume, 'With Walt Whitman in Camden,' came out, Burroughs wrote me about it, March, 1906:

I am reading the Traubel Whitman book.... There is too much of it. It should have been edited. It is too choppy and staccato. After a while this tires one. It might have been equal to 'Eckermann's Conversations with Goethe,' if there had been an Eckermann instead of a Traubel to do it. Some of my own letters should have been edited. And then the book only covers a few months instead of years.... I understand what Walt meant in that remark about me to which you refer. He saw me more or less in the light in which he saw Gilder and Stedman and Howells, because I was so often associated with them in the magazines, and because I so thoroughly accepted Arnold. I had not grown cold toward him, but saw less of him, and was not so active a disciple as I had been. I had absorptions of my own. Then the crowd that surrounded him was not altogether to my liking.... Elsewhere Walt says, 'John cannot let himself go,' and that 'on the convivial side he is not one of us.' That is true. I am not, as a rule, social with men.... I have no gift of self-abandon,... I have courage and self-assertion in the intellectual sphere, and courage in the physical sphere, but not in the moral and human sphere.... I am too prudent and conservative. I could not upset the table and smash the dishes, and go on a regular jamboree. I wish I could. My books would have more tang and wildness, and I should have written better poetry. Even Walt could not teach me to be a 'bold swimmer.'

The remark which I had quoted to Burroughs from Traubel's book occurs on pages 348–49 of volume 1:

Burroughs is still what he was in the early days — true to 'Leaves of Grass' and his original instincts. Of late years something has been added to him — sophistication, I may call it. He has mixed too much with the New York literary crowd — has been influenced by them, not always for good. Still, John is too deeply rooted — the soil in him is too firm, not to resist the pressure of that gang; he is too natural, too truly endowed. John's style has grown somewhat more refined — perhaps a little more literary, bookish — with time, but is still essentially rooted in the woods... — the first-hand cause and effects. John was with the original 'Leaves of

Grass' — in the first rank (the body guard) — and has never wavered, that I know of.

A sheaf of letters about Whitman, written in 1906, chiefly by Burroughs and Richard Watson Gilder, are extracted from here. They had been provoked by Perry's and Traubel's recently published books on Whitman. Mr. Gilder's first letter (to me) had been accompanied by a copy of his book 'In the Heights,' which contained a recent poem on Whitman called 'A Wondrous Song.'

[*R. W. G. to C. B., April* 23, 1906:]

I wrote of Whitman in a poem with full praise during his life, so I did not wait until his death to have my feelings about him known... nevertheless, I do not accept Whitman throughout. He had a charming and kindly personality, and he wrote, it seems to me, great poetry, or great lines, whether they are strictly poetry or not. It always seemed to me that they were, and there is something more than art in the rush of his language. He never seemed to understand art, and therefore naturally had no place in his mentality for a poet like Dante; and his saying that Shakespeare's plays were not written by Shakespeare *the actor* proves his literary criticism to be negligible, although often shrewd and sound and always admirably expressed. Because a man has intense emotions which he learns to express with force and beauty, it does not follow that he is all wise and all good. We have all to be grateful for Whitman — for the intense pleasure he gives to sensitive minds, and for his trumpet calls to the spirit. If he lacked in certain nobilities and finenesses, it is no wonder; but to deny that he did so lack seems to me a denial of the eternal verities. His self-consciousness and self-esteem were abnormal and sometimes ignoble, and to set him on a pedestal, as some do, as a demigod, morally and in every way — well, I cannot join in that, as much as I honor him.

My glimpse at the end of your evening at the studio [Eugene Heffley's] last night was delightful. How thrilling that sea piece of Mac Dowell's! We cannot be mistaken in recognizing unusual genius in his 'art.' There, there! I have used the word that made Walt 'sick at his stomach,' and I use it in exactly the sense that I always have used it, and in exactly the sense that raised his ire. If it had not been for *his* art, what figure would he have cut in our literature? He would have been a strident and soon-forgotten pamphleteer, for even his prose would have lacked.

[*R. W. G. to C. B., April* 23:]

... As to Whitman you must take what I write in my letter along with what I have written, at least twice, in rhyme, about him.[1] I owe him

---

[1] One of the instances referred to is probably the fifth stanza of 'Our Elder Poets,' Gilder's *Complete Poems*, page 139, beginning, 'He also in whose music rude.' The other is probably 'A Wondrous Song.'

much. He seems to me great — but if I compare him in character to — say — Emerson, I find him greatly lacking. But I am used to taking artists and philosophers and all the great at their height. Mankind is in a constant flux of evolution and the race has thrown off few perfect characters. Emerson was absolutely one — so was my mother — probably so was yours. I myself am fearfully lacking in perfection.

All I object to about Whitman is the following him as an exemplar of character. He was wonderful in traits, in abilities, in inspirations, in visions, in the power of expression. But morally he had failures; poetically, that is, artistically, he had failures; critically he had failures (as when he failed to appreciate Dante, and believed that Shakespeare, the *actor*, was not Shakespeare the dramatist and poet).

I have just been reading a MS. essay of that giant infant, Tolstoy, to prove, God forgive him, that Shakespeare was not up even to the average of his time! I consider Tolstoy one of the greatest human beings alive, but regard him insane in his criticism of art and as to the matter of non-resistance. I think [George] Barnard one of the most imaginative sculptors of our day, but deplore the occasional monstrosities which mar his plastic expression.... Some artists are marred by sentimentalism, some by unintellectualisms; some by one thing, some by another — but if truly artists and creators of beauty, we must be grateful for them and proclaim them to the world.

The next in the sheaf was a letter from Gilder to Mr. Bliss Perry (October 21), of which Gilder sent a duplicate to Burroughs:

I cannot tell you how much I have enjoyed and am grateful to you for writing your Whitman life.... This summer has been full of Whitman to me. I have read over 200,000 words of Traubel's unpublished Reminiscences, also your book, Burroughs's new and revised book,[1] and a lot of Whitman's poetry again — and I have talked with some of those who knew him.

It is strange that with all one's knowledge of his early incontinence, of his early and late money peculiarities, of his outrageous self-puffery, still my memory of the old man is of a lovely, affectionate, clean character. The good in him was more powerful than the bad — just as the good in his book is more powerful than the absurd, the pompous, the animality, and the poetical failure. The fact is that the dear old man who stood holding my hand outside of the church at Bryant's funeral is the one I love — not the self-conscious semi-hobo; and the poet that stirs, astonishes, thrills and uplifts me is not the ranting theorizer, reagitating (in prosaic and sometimes comical verse) the Emersonian doctrine like a madman; and stripping off his clothes in half animal and half religious frenzy.

[1] He refers to *Whitman: A Study*, but it had not been revised, and had been published in 1896.

For years I have been comforted by a new realization of the old doctrine of the defects of the quality. The way I have often put it is that, especially in our day, it is rare that a man makes a tremendous impression in any line without having vastly too much of the thing that gives him his success. Whitman could not have reacted so effectively from conventions, and with such great artistic results, if he had not had a tremendous push — and this push simply sent him too far. And again, men of letters as well as men of action work most effectively on some theory — like Wordsworth, like Whitman. Whitman's philosophy was at fault; but it was his 'working hypothesis.' There is no reason, however, that others should accept *his* 'working hypothesis.' That is the mistake of his 'hot little prophets' (good for you!).

Your book, showing his artistic origins, and his care in composition, confirms my view of him as an artist. For instance, what he says himself about 'Drum Taps' (p. 150). ('Drum Taps' was my first love, by the way.) Had he not been a poet, and in his way an artist, he might have been a shrieking and forgotten pamphleteer.

Perhaps the cleanliness that we felt in him, personally, came from that kind of repentance which is the best of all, namely, absolute change of conduct. If, with his physical makeup, he put all sexual uncontrol behind him, he did something noble, and the nobility was felt by his friends and associates who, like myself, are surprised and shocked at his confessions — which at least seem to include a tragic lack of responsibility for his own offspring. This was surely not noble, and so to the end his character was mixed, and far from offering an example of the highest manliness.

I can see that Whitman, from his point of view, may have been right in not taking Emerson's advice about omissions. And yet it was open to him to say — 'I meant these passages in all sincerity, but I find they are misunderstood — they are in danger of doing harm to souls; and they retard my message. Therefore, on advice of my friend and master, I withdraw them.' He refused to do so — and what has happened: Emerson has inspired, ennobled generations of men and women in his own country and throughout the world; while Whitman, today, stirs here and there a handful. His absolute disciples say he will have the future — his greater poems doubtless will have wider acceptance — but by the time that larger numbers are prepared for him, perhaps a stouter and saner poet will take his place. It is possible that he will miss fire. Who knows? but, at any rate, his eighty lines or more of attempt to change the instinctive privacy of mankind will always stand in the way of the acceptance of the body of his work. He himself begged a friend (Harned) *not* to have his book handsomely bound and placed on his center table! And why should not people object? Christ said to the woman taken in adultery — 'Go and sin no more.' Whitman said to the sinning woman — 'Go and prepare yourself to sin with me.' He probably did not mean what he said — but he had no business to say it.

I like extremely your exposure of his fault in the lack of appreciating degrees of excellence. He did not lay enough stress upon the climbing soul. As to form — it would not be hard to prove that he had form — as Stedman maintains, and as I said of him in the words you quote. Even his misuse, or invention, of words was a sort of ornamental form — he must have that word, wrong or right — it suited his line as well as expressed his thought. It was part of the music of his verse. He would in this go to greater lengths than any other poet — he ravished the language to bring it to his uses....

I am glad you said a good word for Traubel. Especially the second volume impressed me by its evidence of complete devotion to the old poet. And there is something of the Whitman charm about him. He is as sure of being remembered as Severn is, if for nothing else, for his kindness to the old poet....

When I asked Whitman, at Mr. Johnston's house in New York, whether he thought his form would one day be accepted as one of the forms of verse to be used by others, he said he rather thought not — that what people liked was the individuality, personality, urge, go, etc., etc., as used by him.

In writing to Traubel the other day I praised his extraordinary out-Boswelling of Boswell. It is a marvellous piece of reporting — some of which I will use. [In the 'Century Magazine.'] But some of it he has no business to print. (I don't think he will, in fact.)...

I also said to Traubel that Whitman's preaching of the animal side of life was unnecessary. Self-control is the only thing it is necessary to *preach* — (as in Tennyson's great line). — Animals we all are. The rigidity and repression of puritanism have passed — they never could long dominate any community. But we are always animals evolving into balanced, responsible human beings. To preach letting loose to a race of procreators is as useless as William James declares the preaching of fighting to the survivors of battles and descendants of warriors — which we all are. If it were not that he magnified his soul, also, he would have been a ghastly impertinence in literature.

But at his best what a poet he is! He takes the color out of most poets — just as the ocean takes the color out of everything but the truest art. He said that the ocean could not be described but was a standard to test one's verse by — his own verse is a standard for other poets in respect to force, vitality, forthrightness. His own poetry is oceanic. After a while we will stop analyzing it, and content ourselves with plunging into it, sailing over it, gazing out upon it, breathing its salt and saving breath. But because you have just written a book about Whitman, is no reason why you should be compelled to read a whole one about him by me.

In reading the Reminiscences and Records of his talk, I find that he resented the cynicism [?] not only of Gilder, but of Dante, Shakespeare, Lowell, Arnold, Stedman, and Whitman!... But, as Miss [Cecilia] Beaux said to me the other day, 'How much better that he should have been a creator than a critic.' There is always value in his *real* criticism — not in his prejudices — as, for instance, his contempt for [Charles] De Kay (one of his greatest admirers, by the way), whose writing [William Vaughn] Moody said last winter was the strongest, most Whitmanesque that is in American literature outside of Whitman's own — which I have long believed....

Yesterday (October 24) Mr. Traubel was in. I wrote the above on the impression derived from your book. He says that there are some things otherwise. He gives a different idea about the children — also about the Parton affair, and the tomb. I hope his view will be confirmed — but I don't like the prodigal illegitimacy anyhow. What I do like is the evident repentance.

On reading Gilder's letter to Mr. Perry, which Burroughs, at Gilder's request, had sent on to me, I could not forbear protesting to Mr. Gilder concerning his distorted interpretation of Whitman's poem 'To a Common Prostitute.' It seemed incredible that he could have so misread the poem. He even misquoted it. Whitman did not say, 'Go and prepare yourself to sin with me.' He said,

> I charge you that you make preparation to be worthy to meet me,
> And I charge you that you be patient and perfect till I come.

What was this but a rescuing hand reached to the outcast — a call to the slumbering womanhood within her — to respond to his compassionate and uplifting help? Did Christ himself ever utter words more divinely human to an erring one than those of Whitman —

> Not till the sun excludes you do I exclude you,
> Not till the waters refuse to glisten for you and the leaves to rustle for you, do my
> words refuse to glisten and rustle for you.

How can one misread those words any more than he could that other poem of Whitman's, 'The City Dead-House' — so poignantly beautiful, so ineffably tender? To read it is to see the great compassionate mother-man gazing in divine pity upon the outcast's form —

> That house once full of passion and beauty
>
> . . . .
>
> Dead house of love, house of madness and sin, crumbled, crushed,
>
> . . . .
>
> ... dead, dead, dead.

The last words are as a sob wrung from his pitying heart.

On reading the foregoing letter of Gilder's, Burroughs wrote him, November 2:

I shall send Dr. Barrus your letter to Perry, as you suggest, tho' I know there are things in it that will pain her, as they did me. A public lecturer, and a great lover of Whitman [Anita Trueman] was here on Monday and I gave her your letter to read, but when she came to the 'semi-hobo' she was so pained that she refused to read farther. She said she would as soon call Christ a semi-hobo, which is my own feeling about it. Christ-like, Walt seemed to prefer the company of publicans and sinners to that of the 'best society' of his time. He doubtless found more reality there, as Walt did; the cant and hypocrisy of the 'best society' are intolerable to such natures. Walt identifies himself with publicans and sinners in his poems in a way that to me does not suggest the semi-hobo, but suggests the God. I love to dwell on his divine commonness — his rich endowment of all the fundamental human traits and qualities. He was a tramp in the sense that all the great prophet-poets have been — he was near to common things and to universal humanity. As a man I did not find any suggestion of the 'hobo' in him, nor of the madman; neither did I, nor do I, as a poet. He is the sanest of the sane. I do not hesitate to say that no other work has ever been produced in this world so much in the spirit of Creation itself as 'Leaves of Grass.' This feeling grows upon me with age.

You compare him to his disadvantage with Emerson, but in power, in sweep and mass, in that pristine elemental push and energy, what comparison is there between them? Whitman was a world-poet, Emerson was a New England poet-prophet. Emerson has already had his day — a rare and precious spirit to whom you and I owe a great debt, but he can never be to our children, or to their children, what he was to us. I turn to him now (his essays) as to a reminiscence, to try to call up those days of my youth. I turn to Walt as to the sea, or the starry heavens, to expand my soul. After the New England poets the lift of Walt's lines is like the surge of ocean billows, compared to the ripple of an inland lake.

I have occasion to be astonished more and more frequently at the way his soul is marching on. I meet people wherever I go, especially among the women, who are coming under the spell of his great spirit. The other day at East Hampton, last summer at Byrdcliffe, recently at Hyde Park — young girls to whom I would not have dared to speak his name, married women who know motherhood and the realities of life, women teachers in girls' colleges — among all educated classes, I find the same growing, awakening interest in Whitman. Emerson's star is setting. Whitman's is rising.

In fifty years from now how antiquated will seem the epithets you apply to him in the first part of your letter — 'semi-hobo,' 'ranting theorizer,' 'half-animal and half-religious frenzy!'

One thing I plume myself upon in this world, and that is that I saw the greatness of the poet from the first — that no disguise of the common, the man, the rough, the tramp, could conceal from me the divinity that was back of all and challenged me to the contest. Familiar intercourse with him as a man did not blur this impression. That head, that presence, those words of love and wisdom, convinced like Nature herself. I pitied those who saw him, and yet saw him not. At times I used to be impatient with you, because you were more or less under the public delusion that he was a common vulgar person, and only now and then a poet. Your conventional training and associations stood in your way. You will not see his like again. The gods never come back.

One mystery in his life can now never be cleared up — the mystery connected with his children. I am disturbed, as you are, by his failure to recognize them. If I only knew his reasons! He loved children. He was deeply attached to the child of his brother George, and greatly grieved at his death. There *must* have been some circumstances or conditions that were beyond his control that made him apparently ignore his own offspring....

I am glad you could say a good word for Traubel. His own writing makes me sick, but he is a wonderful reporter, as I knew long ago. He can take the moment on the wing....

Always your friend
JOHN BURROUGHS

After having read Mr. Perry's 'Walt Whitman,' John Burroughs wrote me as follows, November 19 — a spontaneous letter which, to me, contains some of his finest writing about Whitman:

I was much interested in what you had to say of Mr. Perry's Whitman. Of course it leaves much to be said, but it comes the nearest to being an adequate account and estimate of Whitman of any life of him that has appeared.

I do not think there is any force in that comparison with Rousseau. I read Rousseau's 'Confessions' forty or more years ago, and they made little impression upon me except of the weakness and futility of Rousseau's character. Rousseau was weak, weak — at times a maudlin sentimentalist, at others almost a fool. Whitman was strong, strong, always calm and sane; always at his ease in the world; carried plenty of ballast, and cut his way deeply and steadily through the waves in the face of many adverse winds. Some of his ideas may have been the same as those of Rousseau, but I doubt if he was at all influenced by him. It is character that finally influences us, and not ideas — the man behind the idea. Whitman had no doubt read Rousseau. Indeed, I find one phrase in the 'Leaves' that seems to have been boldly taken from the 'Confessions' — 'behavior lawless as snowflakes.' This sentence doubtless stuck to Walt from his reading of the 'Confessions'; but I fail to see the mark of anything deep and formative upon him from Rousseau.

Ransack the world for Whitman's forbears and you only find hints here and there — vague, faint hints at that. The thing he did not *learn*, and could not *learn*, and which he did to an unprecedented degree, was to put a live man in a book — and a very great man, with candor and courage and love like that of a god. His book is not a confession, it is an incarnation, and does not, to me, suggest Rousseau any more than it suggests Thoreau, with whom he had many loves and attractions in common. Shall we say that Whitman got his local pride, his love of the open and of primitive things — the hut, the shore, the animals — from Thoreau? Did Thoreau's Essay on Walking inspire 'The Open Road'?

The origin of a poet's ideas is a secondary matter: to what extent does he make them his own, bone of his bone, and flesh of his flesh? Does he wield them as a master, or only as a tyro? Whitman's personality and soul-power so dominate his book that the intellectual propositions are like the bones under the flesh — you have to feel for them.

Whitman, at least during the hey-day of his powers, was certainly lacking in something which society much prizes, and cannot well get along without — taste — a delicate perception and appreciation of the finer relations of men in the social organism. But if he had had taste in this sense he would not have written 'Leaves of Grass.' He was a barbarian — entirely of the open air as opposed to parlors and libraries — and ignored, or was insensible of, the conventional proprieties and reticences and modesties that make social life possible. This is the price he paid for that elemental power and quality of his work that makes it so much in the spirit of creation itself.

Try to think of Emerson, or any other man who is so largely the product of the life of the family, the college, the church, making the avowals that Whitman does, identifying himself with the common, the near, even with the sinful and criminal. It is unthinkable. The apostles of the gospel of the cultured, the choice, the refined, play their part; we must have them if society is not to relapse into barbarism. But to say this is not to condemn 'Leaves of Grass.' The book does not make for coarseness or crime or anarchy — it makes for largeness, health, robustness, charity, love, contentment, faith, fatherhood, motherhood, and freedom for every slave on the face of the earth. Its oceans of love and sympathy save it. Its essential religiousness is like the sky over all. It does not, as has been charged, blur the difference between good and evil; it finds good in all, even in evil.

The 'semi-hobo' which Mr. Gilder saw in Whitman shows the narrowness of Mr. Gilder's vision, and I cannot agree with Mr. Perry that, with Whitman, 'the gentleman was no higher than the man, the saint no finer product than the sinner,' and that 'with a soul that instinctively cried, "Glory! Glory!" he nevertheless did not perceive that the glory of the terrestrial was one, and the glory of the celestial was another.' It was only in Whitman's large view, the cosmic sweep of his vision, that these things were equal. The earth is a star with the rest, tho' our senses do not take in the fact. The terrestrial and the celestial *are* one, unless our astronomy is at fault; though St Paul's eloquence long ago persuaded us they were not; and the saint and the sinner are alike embosomed in the same universe of mystery and wonder, and are equal, when contemplated in their absolute and eternal relations — the relations in which Whitman viewed them.

He did not discount the gentleman, but he put a premium, so to speak, on common humanity. Personally, he liked both, if they were genuine. He liked culture and refinement if they were not had at the expense of the native human traits. He was certainly strongly drawn to the common people, and was probably most content in their society. They seemed to give him something he missed in the higher circles; and he no doubt felt them nearer akin to his own father and mother. His most intimate friends in Washington, when I knew him, were William O'Connor and Charles Eldridge, both men of culture and refinement, but both very racy and human. True, he clung to the unlettered car-driver, Peter Doyle, at the same time, but Doyle was himself a kind of 'mute inglorious' Whitman, and a manly and lovable character.

Whitman glorified Lincoln, but it was not for his gentlemanly qualities. He glorified the common soldiers, too, on pretty much the same grounds; but one could not well infer from his poems that he looked upon both as of the same degree of glory.

I strenuously deny that he lost sight of the different degrees in the scale of human values. Readers constantly forget that it did not enter into his scheme to appraise the social, or cultural, or even the conventional moral values, but the fundamental human values upon which our lives (and the life of the state) finally rest — love, comradeship, religiousness, fatherhood, motherhood, manly endeavor, freedom, equality, and the divine average. The special, the exceptional, he did not fix his eye upon, but upon the universal average, and that which all may have upon the same terms. He did not celebrate the specially beautiful things in Nature, after the manner of so many poets, but rather was he fired by the contemplations of the earth as a whole, and of the cosmic laws and processes, and the beauty and power in which we are daily embosomed. In like manner it was not the special, choice, human traits that engaged him — heroism, devotion, the fine lady, the fine gentleman, and all the rest of it — but our common humanity, the soul, the body, sex, and the final sources of our moral and physical well-being.

You have only to enlarge your vision, and exalt your faith, enough, when all things become divine and beautiful; you have only to key your humanity up to the proper pitch, when all men and women become your brothers and sisters; you have only to look deep enough, and high enough, to see that 'all's right with the world'; and that there is 'no failure or imperfection in it.' But in our ordinary moods we do not see these things.

The poet-seer, in his extraordinary moods, sees them. Of course if Whitman does not take us with him to his mount of vision and make the competent reader see what he sees, then that is a serious failure. That he occasionally fails to do this, I shall not dispute.

We did not know till Whitman came what it really meant to carry the democratic spirit into literature. We see now how the attempt has exposed him to misinterpretation, even of such appreciative readers as Gilder, Perry, Mabie, and others; and to his being looked upon as a 'semi-hobo,' because of the fervor and all-inclusivenes of his love, and his affiliation with all types of mankind, finding 'lovers and equals everywhere,'... — an all-inclusiveness and sympathy like that of God himself. The way Whitman identifies himself with outcasts and criminals — the unfaltering, unblushing way in which he does it — is, to me, more than human.

Well, I started to write you a letter about some exceptions to things in Perry's book, and have written you an essay.... Can you pardon me?... When I begin to write about Whitman I cannot easily stop. I began forty years ago and am far from the end of him yet. He lures me on and on.... I can never read him long aloud without visible or invisible tears. His book is the man, and all my love and reverence for him in those long-gone days come back, and I miss him anew.

To a correspondent much disturbed over the growing disbelief in immortality Burroughs wrote that same year:

I think you are needlessly exercised on this subject.... What matters it? If our conscious identity does not continue after death, we shall never know it.... If it does continue, so much the better. No argument can satisfy you or me. Whitman once said to me that he would as soon hope to argue a man into good health, as to argue him into a belief in immortality. He said he *knew* it was so without proof; but I could never light my candle at his great torch.

He then recommends the correspondent to read Whitman's poem on 'Burial' — later called 'To Think of Time.'

Naturally, Thomas B. Harned, being one of the 'hot little prophets' mentioned by Mr. Perry in his book on Whitman, found much in that book to take exceptions to, not, however, on personal grounds. Reference has already been made to the corrections he made concerning misconceptions as to the tomb, but there were other matters which disturbed him — statements poorly authenticated, and wide of the mark. Early in 1907, writing me about Mr. Perry's book, the many excellences of which he praised, Mr. Harned said:

Perry deals out truth with penurious frugality.... He writes as if literature ought to be all pound cake and honey. The unevenness of Whitman disturbs him. This really is his greatness — to account for the valleys as well as the mountains, the deserts as well as the fruitful soil, the rattlesnake, as well as the humming-bird. The Lord saw that it was *all* good.

In a late edition, Mr. Perry set right some of the misstatements in his book, basing his corrections and modifications on facts submitted to him by Mr. Harned. But certain Whitmanites took up the cudgels in the poet's defense, notably Traubel and W. S. Kennedy, whose articles were printed in current 'Conservators.' Burroughs, in his 'Field and Study,'[1] publishes a discriminating critique on Mr. Perry's Whitman, which was probably written shortly after the publication of Mr. Perry's book. One sentence particularly in that article shows the consistency of Burroughs's attitude toward Whitman as held since the beginning of his comradeship:

He distils nothing, he confronts me with the immeasurable universe, and makes me feel how the ground I walk upon is a part of the solar system.

While Burroughs never tried to cram Whitman down the throats of others, when any one showed interest, he waxed enthusiastic. In the winter of 1908 Mr. Richard Le Gallienne wrote Burroughs:

I shall always retain a vivid picture of you as you stood with us, waiting for the train, talking to us of Walt Whitman, with snow in your hand, and aglow with the walk from Slabsides.... That day with you was a dream of boyhood come true, and both Ozias and I shall always treasure its fulfillment.

Doubtless Mr. Le Gallienne found a ready passport to Burroughs because of his having testified on several public occasions to his keen appreciation of Whitman. In a speech before the Whitman Fellowship, March, 1898, he had pointedly asked the assembled company: 'Are you true to Whitman's best? or only dilettante, amateur Whitmanites?'

When in Honolulu, in 1909, Burroughs was gratified to find many appreciators of his poet. At a celebration there on Whitman's birthday, much zeal was shown, and after the rhetorical readings and set speeches were over, the offhand talk by Burroughs was enthusiatically received. A few evenings later, at a beach party,

---

[1] Burroughs: *Field and Study* (Houghton Mifflin Company, 1919), pp. 225-32.

Burroughs was led into speaking of Whitman, but, the following day, dissatisfied with what he had said, he wrote a letter to the wife of Governor Frear, who had started him talking by confessing her inability to appreciate the 'Leaves.' His letter follows:

In return for your charming little poem, 'My Islands,' which has no doubt sung itself into many hearts, I am sending you an autograph copy of my poem 'Waiting,' which has seemed to give comfort to a good many persons. It was about my first poetic effort, and was written forty-seven years ago. In it, you see, I keep to the conventional metre and rhyme, of which I spoke rather flippantly, if not contemptuously the other night on the beach. In fact, I can do nothing in the way of poetry outside of these conventional forms. One would like to have a form of his own, if it could be an organic form, as Whitman's is, but few persons are equal to that; at least I am not.

The remark I made about the conventional forms, and the frills and ruffles of popular poetry, in commenting on Whitman, was ill-advised. What I should have said is that Whitman does not write poetry in the usually accepted sense of that term. When you take up 'Leaves of Grass,' if you fancy you have in hand a volume of poetry, as that word is usually understood, you are doomed to disappointment. Hence the great majority of persons who open Whitman are likely to ask in derision, 'Do you call *this* poetry?'

We may have to invent some other word to characterize his work. A great deal of it does not differ so much from prose, except that it is dithyrambic and ejaculatory. His work usually proves a sore trial to the reader whose taste has been founded upon current poetry, or even upon the masterpieces of English literature. It deserves to be called democratic poetry only in the sense that it is freer from ornamentation and highly-wrought artistic character than standard poetry is. One can hardly call it poetry in undress, because of the many verbal felicities, and memorable musical phrases, it contains; but it is poetry reduced to the bare essentials, to an extent that is not true of the work of any other man of like calibre.

Whitman's poetry is primitive and elemental to a remarkable degree. He does not so much aim at finished verse as at suggestive verse. He does not take a theme, say, as you and I do, and elaborate it — work it up into a finished artistic whole, so that it will be complete in itself and afford the satisfaction which gems and jewels and highly-wrought carving or sculpturing does. He says,

'I finish no specimens, but shower them by exhaustless laws, fresh and modern continually.'

The unity and value of his work is to be found in the extent to which it expresses the personality of a living, breathing, modern man, and not in any independent artistic design.

I have never been able to state in words my sense of the immanence of Whitman himself in his poems. I think there is nothing like it in the whole range of literature — the sense of a living, breathing personality. The poems, whatever the theme, are about himself. They revolve about him, and convey his quality to the reader to an unprecedented degree; and, whether you like it or not, his volume is more man than it is book. Of all things, it is work suggestive and kindling. A musical composer [1] once told me that Whitman stimulated him, for example, more than Tennyson did, because he left so much for him to do, while Tennyson left nothing.[2] I think it is for the same reason that Whitman has meant so much to many of the poets. He abounds so in hints and suggestions which kindle their poetic faculties.

'I turn upon you a passing glance, expecting the main things from you.'

If you have not read Whitman much, I caution you to go slow and not be hasty in your judgments. You will be repelled by many things, if not shocked. He is to be wrestled with and conquered. It is literally true, as he says, that he has arrived to be wrestled with as he passes, for the solid prizes of the universe.

But I did not mean to write you an essay. I only wanted to restate more clearly some of the things I said in a haphazard way the other night on the beach....

In connection with what Burroughs said in the foregoing letter concerning the form of Whitman's work, one is reminded of a significant letter which Hiram Corson wrote Whitman in 1886: Corson was eager, he said, to have a long talk with him concerning language-shaping, and the modern tendency toward impassioned prose, which he believed would be the poetic form of the future, 'and of which your "Leaves of Grass" is the most marked prophecy.' Whether this particular talk ever materialized, I do not know, but there were several meetings between Whitman and Corson and some correspondence. The first meeting, in 1885, had been brought about through Horace Howard Furness. Then Corson had endeavored, in vain, to convince Whitman that Browning was 'his man.' Traubel quotes Whitman as saying of Corson: 'He accepts me in a general way, without vehemence. Corson is judicial.'

Mr. Waldo R. Browne compiled an admirable collection of outdoor scenes and thoughts from the prose and poetry of Whitman, in

[1] Dr. Frederic L. Ritter, Musical Professor at Vassar College.

[2] Mr. George Chadwick, who has set 'Darest Thou Now, O Soul,' to music, tells me that he finds Whitman easier to set to music than any other poet. — C. J. F.

1912, which was published by Houghton Mifflin Company, under the felicitous title 'The Rolling Earth,' for which John Burroughs wrote an Introduction, a few excerpts from which follow:

His thoughts dwelt with the spheres — not as the scientist thinks of them, but as the poet and prophet thinks of them. I believe it was a personal conviction with him that in the future life he would be 'eligible' to visit the spheres. I remember that often in our walks by starlight he would suddenly stop and gaze long and intently at the sky, and then pass on without a word.... Over and over he turns his gaze upon the sky and upon the midnight constellations, and seeks to draw courage and composure from them. His panoramic style comes largely from his habit of contemplating the earth as a whole, 'swift swimming in space.' He sees processions and mass movements, continents and oceans, races and peoples flowing by him. I doubt if any other poet's imagination so revelled in thoughts of the whole scheme of things....

In March, 1913, Burroughs sent me an old 'Chap Book,' dated July 15, 1897, which contained an article on Whitman by John Jay Chapman, accompanying it with this statement:

This Chapman is a great egotist, but a small man; hence he feels Whitman's colossal egotism as an insult, an outrage. How he maligns him, and completely misses him, except here and there, as Gilder did. If Whitman was what Chapman thinks he was, neither you nor I could stand him for a moment. Chapman's mind is purely academic, and is as foreign to Whitman as the painted sky in the Grand Central station is to the real sky. I think every great egotist is angered by Whitman's egoism.

Writing Burroughs in 1914, J. W. Wallace, of Lancashire, England, who collaborated with Dr. J. Johnston in 'Visits to Whitman in 1890-1891,' expressed appreciation of the many letters and tokens of comradeship received from Burroughs throughout the years, adding:

No wonder that you were so great a friend of Walt, and that you have done such great service to his cause, for you have so much in common with him; and no wonder, let me add, that we who love Walt so deeply, and to whom his name is so incomparably sacred and dear, love you also with no small measure of the supreme love and veneration we give him.

If Burroughs waxed indignant at the 'glow-worms of literature,' he was always highly gratified by discriminating and penetrating criticism of Whitman, such, for example, as came out that year in a book by John Cowper Powys [1] which has this to say of Whitman's much ridiculed catalogues:

It is absurd to grumble at these Inventories of the Round Earth. They may not all move to Dorian flutes, but they form a background — like the lists of Kings in the Bible, and the lists of the Ships in Homer — against which, as against the great blank spaces of Life itself, 'the writing upon the wall' may make itself visible.

And his warning to modern poets who would create a new poetic form:

It is the fierce, tenacious, patient, constructive work of a lifetime, based upon a tremendous and overpowering Vision! Such a vision Walt Whitman had, and to such constant inspired labor he gave his life — notwithstanding his talk about loafing and inviting his soul!

Burroughs must have highly approved of the two following passages on Whitman in Mr. Van Wyck Brooks's chapter 'The Precipitant,' [2] since they are marked as he marked passages for approval and rereading:

The real significance of WW is that he, for the first time, gave us the sense of something organic in American life. Whitman was himself a great vegetable of a man, all of a piece in roots, flavor, substantiality, and succulence, well-ripened in the common sunshine. In him the hitherto incompatible extremes of the American temperament were fused.... For having all the ideas of New England... he came up from the other side with everything New England did not possess: quantities of rude emotion and a faculty of gathering human experience almost as great as that of the hero of the Odyssey. Living habitually among world ideas, world emotions, world impulses, and having experienced life on a truly grand scale, this extraordinary person, innocent as a pioneer of what is called urbanity, became nevertheless a man of the world in a sense in which ambassadors are not; and there is every reason to suppose he would have been perfectly at home in the company of Achilles, or Erasmus, or Louis XIV (pages 112–13).

Whitman... precipitated the American character. All those things which had been separate, self-sufficient, incoördinate — action, theory, idealism, business — he cast into a crucible; and they emerged, harmonious and molten, in a fresh democratic ideal, which is based upon the whole personality. Every strong personal impulse, every coöperating and unifying impulse, everything that enriches the social background, everything that enriches the individual, everything that impels and clarifies in the modern world owes something to Whitman (pages 118–19).

[1] Powys: *Visions and Revisions*. G. Arnold Shaw, New York, 1915. 281 pages.
[2] Brooks: *America's Coming of Age*. B. W. Huebsch, 1915.

One afternoon in mid-November, 1915, Mr. Burroughs came over to the Nest at Riverby, from his Bark Study, bringing several pages of smoothly written manuscript about Whitman on which he had been occupied for two forenoons. As he signed and dated it, he said, on handing it to me, 'I shall never get done with Whitman any more than with the birds.' These pages form the concluding parts of his essay 'The Poet of the Cosmos' — the last essay in 'Accepting the Universe.' Let me quote one passage from that essay:

It was my rare good fortune to know this quiet, sympathetic, tolerant man for more than thirty years, and to walk or saunter with him at all seasons and hours.... He was an easy-going, lethargic man — nothing strenuous about him, never in a hurry, never disturbed or excited, always in good humor, cleanly, clad in gray, with a fresh, florid complexion, large, broad, soft hands, blue-gray eyes, gray-haired and gray-bearded. He was fond of children and old people. What a contrast were his placid and easy-going ways to the astronomic sweep and power of his poems, his spirit darting its solar rays to the utmost bounds of the universe. When I was with him I did not feel his mighty intellect, I felt most his humanity, his primitive sympathy, the depth and intensity of his new democratic character, perhaps also that in him which led Thoreau to say that he suggested something a little more than human.[1]

A paragraph in that manuscript, omitted from the book, is given here:

To pick flaws in Whitman is like picking flaws in Nature herself. We do not look at the orbs, or at the earth, with a microscope; and to get at the good there is in Whitman we must bring to him a candor, a charity, and a spiritual robustness equal to his own, and that 'inner, never lost rapport we have with earth, light, air, trees,' and all created things.

The following passage occurs in Burroughs's Journal, September 15, 1917:

When I casually open 'Leaves of Grass' after the book has long been closed to me, it is like coming suddenly upon the ocean, after years of absence from it. I have been reading the verses in the magazines, or in the volume of some recent poet, and opening Whitman is like coming from an enamelled bathroom to the ocean beach. Such large, free ways, such elemental force, and simplicity, such freedom from the subtle and the over-refined, such fundamental statements, and absence of elaboration, such magnitude, and, at times, such absolute justness of phrasing! Emerson in

[1] Burroughs: *Accepting the Universe* (Houghton Mifflin Company, 1920), pp. 321–22.

his Journals may well speak of 'its Alleghany lift and sweep.' It is like the forest primeval, like the great plains, like the mountain-peaks, yet steeped in humanity and brotherly love. It is refined as the sky is refined, as the Great Lakes are refined, as the rain and the dews are refined. It is not culture, or poetry, or art, as we commonly use the terms — it is something greater, and better.

One April evening in 1919, at the Nest, as John Burroughs laid aside 'Leaves of Grass' from which he had been reading aloud, he exclaimed: 'What cheap stuff other poets seem compared with this voice out of the universal!' And shortly after he was quite thrilled to come upon Mr. Edgar Lee Masters's description of 'Petit, the Poet,' who was ticking off his little iambics

> Seeds in a dry pod, tick, tick, tick,
> . . . .
> While Homer and Whitman roared in the pines.

Consequently, since Mr. Masters was to give the address on that occasion, Burroughs attended the Vassar College celebration of the Whitman Centenary with lively anticipation. The students, too, were to give a pageant in the outdoor theater, founded on 'Leaves of Grass,' entitled 'The Call to Unity and Democracy.'

On the way over to Poughkeepsie, Mr. Burroughs had insisted that, as his physician, I stress the point that he must not be asked to speak on that occasion. He objected even to sitting on the platform until assured by President McCracken that he would not be called upon. But when Mr. Masters finished, and sat down, to the surprise of everybody, Mr. Burroughs jumped up, unasked, and gave a delightfully spontaneous, concrete talk of his friendship with Whitman in Washington, and in later years. He told of Whitman's visit to Vassar in the eighteen-seventies, when they had driven over from West Park in a buggy, with a lame white horse, no one at the College then, except Dr. Ritter, the professor of music, seeming to know anything about the poet. He spoke of Dr. Ritter then telling Whitman that to read the 'Leaves' set his brain and fingers all a-tingle. He spoke also of being at Vassar some years later with Herbert Gilchrist, the artist, and said that when Gilchrist, in lecturing, mentioned Whitman's name, a look of unconcealed disgust appeared on the face of one old gentleman of the faculty — a striking contrast, he pointed out, to the present-day attitude when the young women teachers and their students were finding in Whitman a guide to a wholesome and elevating attitude toward the facts of life, and, above all, toward a clean and sane understanding of wifehood and motherhood. Afterwards, when Burroughs was rallied about his unsolicited speech, he said, 'You were no more surprised than I was; but I couldn't keep my seat.... I wanted some touch of the real man there, even if I had to give it myself.'

When Harned wrote Burroughs of the forthcoming celebration in Brooklyn of the Whitman Centenary, and urged him to attend and read a paper, he added:

The New York and Chicago meetings during the last few years have been largely attended by socialists and radicals who gave a false impression to the public as to Whitman's attitude toward governmental and socialistic questions. Of course 'Leaves of Grass' includes them all, but I have always contended that his teachings are mostly constructive, and oftentimes conservative in the best sense of the term. He certainly was not an unconditional outlaw as some try to claim. Traubel has worked the socialistic racket, much to my exclusion and disgust. Some of these people are now in jail, and I protest against any effort to make out Walt as an unreasonable pacifist. His would have been a mighty voice of protest against the brutal and savage Hun, with a clarion call to arms against such destructive forces.

At the time of the Brooklyn Centenary, Burroughs was not well, his eighty-two years were beginning to weigh him down, and public speaking had always been a bugbear to him, but, the requests for him to participate being urgent, he said: 'I shouldn't fail Walt on this occasion — I must try to write something — but I never can read it.' After finishing his paper, and hearing it read aloud, he said, 'I'll go, if you will go and read it for me.' And that is what happened. The Centenary was celebrated, May 9, 1919, at the Brooklyn Academy of Music, under the auspices of the Brooklyn Institute of Arts and Sciences — the meeting being preliminary to the further celebration on the poet's birthday, May 31, at his birthplace, West Hills, Long Island. There were afternoon and evening sessions, both of which were presided over by Dr. Charles D. Atkins. Those who took part in the commemorative programmes were: John Burroughs, Thomas B. Harned, Dr. Samuel McChord Crothers, Professor William Lyons Phelps, Mr. Edwin Markham,

Mr. Hamlin Garland, Mr. Louis Untermeyer, Mr. Arthur M. Howe, and Mr. Clayton Hamilton.

The appearance of Burroughs on the platform at both sessions was warmly welcomed. His paper, 'Whitman as I See Him,' read in the evening, was enthusiastically received. This was printed, May 10, in the 'Brooklyn Daily Eagle,' and the entire programme was printed in the Whitman Memorial Number of the 'Eagle,' May 31.

Mr. Harned's tribute was full of intimate touches of Whitman's everyday life in Camden. His own introduction to him had come about through the poet's cheery 'Howdy' as they passed on the street. Although he gave no hint of it, many persons know that during those Camden years Harned and his family were unwearying in their devotion to Whitman's comfort and well-being. In his talk Harned emphasized Whitman's scrupulously clean and refined ways, and added: 'He has often been slandered about his habits. He was the personification of sobriety; — four ounces of liquor lasted him a year. He never used tobacco.' And continuing:

> Whitman believed in law and order, and more than once gave offense to some of his devoted followers [not so believing].... Of course he believed in popular government, and that the world could get along much better without czars, emperors, and kings. He had no toleration for the connection of Church and State. He has been claimed by the individualists, socialists, anarchists, spiritualists, and all other 'ists.' My own view is that he baffles classification. He had unrestricted faith and an imperturbable optimism, and he believed absolutely in the virtue and intelligence of the common people...; that the object of government was the preservation of liberty.... He condemned the exploiting of the many for the benefit of the few. He disliked the arrogance of the politicians, great and small. He had the poet's dream that comradeship was the solution for social and political ills. With all his faith and optimism he was never blind to many existing conditions.

Dr. Crothers pronounced Whitman's work 'a great spiritual revelation of a new order. No Hebrew writing — those ancient Psalms — ever spoke of Jerusalem so religiously and devoutly as Walt Whitman spoke of America.' Mr. Markham said, in part: 'He flung forth his "Leaves of Grass." How did the world receive it? With jeers and sneers. Now that the shouting is quieted down, we may gather from the echoes.' Mr. Howe's presentation of

Whitman's early journalistic career was especially welcome with its contribution of much fresh information. In summing up he said of Whitman's editorial writing:

... He wrote with sincerity and courage, but without distinction of thought or style. He could be denunciatory, he could be sarcastic, but he was never bitter or vitriolic.... He conveys the impression of one who regarded his occupation in journalism as something to which he was compelled by circumstances rather than as a vocation for which he had any positive affection. Yet the belief that he was invariably indolent and indifferent to his editorial obligations... is not sustained by the printed records of his work on the *Eagle*, at least. If the quality was not above the average of his time, if it has added nothing to his reputation, it represents nothing for which apology need be made.

Describing Whitman's appearance on meeting him in 1888, Mr. Hamlin Garland said:

He was one of the noblest figures that I had ever seen. He sat there like a stranded sea-dog.... He was poor, he was old; he was stricken, and he was misunderstood by the world, and yet he had no despair in his heart.... He was the greatest optimist I had ever known. I cannot follow him, and I am not big enough, but I wish I had the same wonderful outlook on life and death that he had.

Mr. Untermeyer pointed out that the new literature in these States, in France, and in England owes its very being to Whitman:

He revealed the great glory of the commonplace. For him ugliness was fused in a vast harmonious counterpoint.... It was his use of rich verbal material that he found in the street that made his influence so valuable.... I sometimes think that 'Leaves of Grass' is not poetry, but a language experiment. It is merely an effort to give the language new words.

Contrary to his long-held attitude toward Whitman, Professor Phelps gave a surprising eulogy on this occasion, saying, in part: 'When a true pioneer begins to work, it is the strangeness rather than the greatness of his work that makes the most sharp impression.' Here he quoted Dean Swift: 'When a new genius appears in this world, you may know him by this infallible sign, that all the dunces are in confederacy against him.' And, concluding:

He had four qualities that gave him permanence: a splendid imagination, absolute universality of feeling, a personality of extraordinary power that breathed into all he wrote, unbounded vitality, and the art to express himself at intervals in perfect words.

A few passages, much condensed, are culled here from Burroughs's paper. After rapidly tracing the change of attitude that had come about since he first knew Whitman up to the Centenary, he said:

But in our time Whitman is fast coming to his own. The change is like that of placing a golden seal upon that which before had only a paper label. We are all labelled and put in our places, but the golden approval of Time is put upon few. Be assured it is given to all who merit it. It has certainly been placed upon Whitman.

Burroughs referred to Whitman's sense of humor having been frequently questioned, and instanced lines and poems to show how really keen was his sense of humor. Though pointing out that his main gifts were epic and lyric, he named several poems in which there is plenty of dramatic action. He continued:

'Leaves of Grass' is like a world in the making. It is full of the germs of things; it is fluid and formative; it is suggestive and creative; it is a world of growing things.... Without metaphysics, it has a metaphysical background; its science is like the blood in the veins; it flows, it nourishes, it colors. The whole theory of poetry and art can be drawn from its pages.... The intellect is subordinated to the intuitions, and vision takes the place of reasoning.... The peculiar elemental music in his lines, like the winds or the waves, is one of their charms....

Whitman's composure and self-balance were constant. I never saw him ruffled or hurried or irritated or excited. He was a saunterer through life. He took everything as it came. I never saw him impatient. During his long years of lameness and, at times, almost helplessness, I doubt if he was ever known to complain, to fret, or to show any spirit of rebellion against his fate. He never lost his poise, and he never seemed to strive to keep it, or to be conscious of it. He answered in his daily life his own prayer:

'O, to be self-balanced for contingencies,
  To confront night, storms, hunger, ridicule, accidents, rebuffs,
    as the trees and animals do!'

He was a singularly restful nature. His friends basked in his presence as in sunshine. To the sick and wounded soldiers in the hospitals he brought this quieting, soothing spirit. His very presence was healing.... In fact, he was a self-constituted Red Cross in his own person....

Burroughs quoted Thoreau's comment about not being disturbed by any brag or egoism in the 'Leaves' since he had seen the author. He added:

We accuse Thoreau of narrowness, but a man who could accept two such men as John Brown and Walt Whitman had breadth of mind and heart sufficient to make a room full of such men as those contemporaries who saw nothing but two rebels in that hero of granite and iron, and that poet of universal love and charity.

Whitman did not merely sing or chant the praises of democracy; he *was* Democracy, the very incarnation of its spirit. It made his blood red, and his touch gentle. It was not a cloak which he put off and on; it was the marrow in his bones — yea, the bones themselves.... His commonness was so abounding and fundamental that it rose to the uncommon and suggested something God-like.

After stressing Whitman's cosmic qualities, Burroughs concluded by saying that he had been unable to interest Roosevelt in Whitman; that both men were

equally hail-fellow-well-met with all kinds and classes of men, but that one was in his very essence an autocrat, a leader, a ruler of men, while the other was in very essence a democrat whose interest in men was not to organize or to rule them,... or to reform them — all of which he knew the importance of — but to enrich and expand their souls and foster their religious sentiments through a revelation of what life in this stupendous universe had brought to him. Of course the strenuous life could not appeal to Whitman personally, and equally, of course, the leisurely, half-indolent, sauntering life of contemplation and enjoyment could not appeal to Roosevelt. That two such widely diverse types should be the fruit of American democracy is full of meaning, and is, I trust, a good omen for the future.

The crowning touch of the evening was given by Mr. Clayton Hamilton's reading of the Death Carol from 'When Lilacs Last in the Dooryard Bloom'd.'

Burroughs summed up the Whitman celebration in his Journal a day or two later:

Afternoon session not very well attended — two or three hundred people, mostly women. A fine speech by Garland. Crothers disappointed me — no charm, little humor, little valuable intellectual content. The pulpit spoils any man for serious thinking. Harned talked, Markham spoke — he saw more in Whitman than I expected he had.... A young Jewish poet, Untermeyer, spoke well. Dinner at Mrs. Mc Carroll's — daughter of J. H. Johnston [Whitman's intimate friend].

Evening session well attended. Phelps the best speaker. He used to despise Whitman, but now has met with a change of heart. His speech was fine and did my heart good. Dr. Barrus read my short paper.... The audience was very attentive. Mr. Howe, editor of the 'Brooklyn Eagle,' spoke admirably... on W's editorial career, a very valuable paper. Harned spoke entertainingly of his long acquaintance with W.... Clayton Hamilton, the critic, read some of W's poems admirably. On the whole a great time.

At last the literary world had acknowledged Whitman, and Burroughs, who had espoused his cause when he was despised and rejected, now had the satisfaction of seeing him duly honored at his Centenary.

Harned wrote exultantly a few days later:

... I hope you and Oom John got home all right.... The 'Brooklyn Eagle,' May 10, printed his paper in full, and I read it with complete approval. The whole affair was a triumph. It is now time for the granitic pudding-heads to quit carping forever. The fight is over. Walt has won. 'Leaves of Grass' triumphs!

Even so, things about Whitman which rankled occasionally got into print. In July and August, 1920, Burroughs was highly incensed at a series of articles, 'As I Remember,' which came out in the 'Saturday Evening Post,' written by Jefferson Winter, the son of William Winter. These were reminiscences of his father, in which quotations from Winter, the elder, showed that he had persisted in his long-held abuse of Whitman to the end of his life, his son carrying on the abuse. Burroughs was so furious at these late revelations of Winter's malice toward Whitman that he accused himself of lacking in backbone, in that he had treated Winter with consideration on the few occasions when he met him in his old age. 'He was always contemptible toward Walt,' he said, 'and it was contemptible of me not to show him that I resented it.'

But abuse from such a source could hardly affect him long. He was highly gratified on reading Mr. Perry's chapter on 'Poe and

---

[1] At the time of writing comes the news that the Hall of Fame in New York City has at last done itself the honor of admitting Walt Whitman to its august corridors. He had been voted upon at three previous elections. This time he just squeezed in, getting the required number of votes, 64, and no more. As Christopher Morley says in the 'Saturday Review of Literature,' 'Walt's delay in arriving was undoubtedly due to his not following the instructions always printed on the official announcements:

'*To Reach the Hall of Fame, take Broadway Express, 40 minutes.*'

Walt sauntered too slowly along the 'populous pavements,' but at last he can reiterate, 'I sit content.'

Henry David Thoreau is still outside the pale.

Whitman,' which came out that same year,[1] one passage of which is quoted here:

Walt Whitman, like Poe, had defects of character and defects of art. His life and work raise many problems which will long continue to fascinate and baffle the critics. But after all of them have had their say, it will remain true that he was a seer and a prophet far in advance of his own times, like Lincoln, and, like Lincoln, an inspired interpreter of the soul of this Republic.

A notebook kept by Burroughs in 1920 has this April entry:

The words 'divine,' 'holy,' 'sacred,' 'heavenly,' are born of our reactions from this world — they are proof that we do not find this world divine or sacred and have no practical belief that we are in the heavens on this planet. Probably the main spring of all doctrinal religions is dissatisfaction with this world. Only one man, so far as I know, has insisted upon religion, and yet not discounted this world at all, and that is Whitman. W. saw no better or greater God than himself, no world more divine than this, no more heaven or hell than there is now and here, and yet he saw it all for Religion's sake. He accepted all, he condemned nothing, he did not want the constellations any nearer, and declared that no man had yet been half devout enough. This is the new religion, the religion of science and of democracy, imbued with human passion.

In May:

Whitman was a new type of man, his like never before appeared in the world, at least in literature. The startling thing about him is his everyday, commonplace character suddenly transformed into such bardic and prophetic power, as if the trees and animals and rocks and rivers spoke. He is as aboriginal as the earth itself, and yet he is of today, and of America, in the fullest sense.

He was such a man as myths and legends grow up about. If he suggested something more than human to such a keen observer as Thoreau, what would he have suggested to the men of a more credulous age!

In October:

The only poet who has got any poetry out of astronomy is Whitman. The emotion of grandeur which the heavens awaken is a barren emotion. There is no suggestion of life or of man in the midnight skies. The celestial mechanics go their ceaseless rounds, grinding out suns and systems, but with no hint of anything human. W., of all the poets, is not overwhelmed by them. He easily dominates them. He strings the orbs on his thoughts as beads on a string. Take such a passage as the one beginning,

[1] Perry: *The American Spirit in Literature.* Yale University Press, 1920.

'I open my scuttle at night and see far-sprinkled systems,'

or the one that begins,

'This day before dawn I ascended the hill and looked at the crowded heavens,'

He is not exploiting astronomy, he is exploiting himself — the human soul.

In October, 1920, Mrs. Carolyn Wells Houghton wrote Burroughs an inquiry about Whitman's sense of humor, quoting him to himself as having said somewhere that Whitman was deficient in humor, and asking him if he could not modify that decree: 'Did you never notice the humorous intent which seems to me to crop out here and there in his personal relations with his friends?'

She added that from various sources she had seemed to find a vein of merriment in Whitman and hoped to prove a sense of humor tucked in among his greater characteristics, and to write an article, perhaps a book, on the subject. Burroughs replied on October 5:

I do not think you will succeed in making much of Whitman's humor; he was too serious-minded, too religious, of altogether too high a purpose to indulge in any flights of humor as such. There is now and then a humorous twinkle in his eye, as in the Boston Ballad, but there is much more sarcasm and contempt than humor. I am glad he had no greater sense of humor. It would often have stood in his way. He enjoyed a humorous story, and could laugh as heartily as any one, but I never remember hearing him tell one. I never heard him indulge in levity of any sort. The shady stories that many men delight in never amused him, and never passed his lips. He never treated the subject of women or sex with levity. The human form to him was so divine that he did not like to see it caricatured.

I was with him a great deal during the ten years I knew him in Washington, and often afterwards, during his illness. He was tolerant of every body and everything, yet could be a harsh and savage critic of men and measures. But his habitual tone was one of acceptance. I do not see how even a magazine article could be got out of his humor. To you, whose sense of humor we all know and appreciate, this may seem very strange. When we think of Lincoln, whom Walt Whitman admired and celebrated as no other poet has, with his sense of humor always active, and serving as a foil to his seriousmindedness, and to the burdens he carried, we can see what an important part humor may play in life....

Cordially yours

JOHN BURROUGHS

To my inquiry if she had ever prepared the article contemplated, Mrs. Houghton replied, 'No, I never wrote the article about Whitman's Sense of Humor, as I found it was much like the snakes in Ireland.'

A handy little Bibliography of Walt Whitman, prepared by Frank Shay in 1920, was sent to Burroughs that year by the compiler. Léon Bazalgette, the same year, brought out his 'Walt Whitman: The Man and his Work,' translated from the French by Ellen Fitzgerald, and published by Doubleday, Page and Company. One sentence in the Author's Introduction to this volume, a copy of which was sent by him to Burroughs, is marked by Burroughs: 'Through him a whole continent is suddenly an exultant voice.'

Strange to say, it was through Burroughs that my own appreciation of Whitman developed, and through Whitman that my personal association with Burroughs began. One evening in 1901, after having spent some hours in reading from the 'Leaves,' and later from Burroughs's 'Preliminary' in 'Whitman: A Study,' I impulsively wrote Burroughs a letter in which I tried to thank him for what he and, through him, Whitman, had done for me. Probably this was the best possible passport to his friendship. In his reply he said, 'If I have helped kindle your love for Nature, and deepen your appreciation for Whitman, it is a comfort to know it.' A subsequent letter carried a gracious invitation to Slabsides. On the occasion of my first visit there, after he had talked engagingly of his comradeship with Whitman, and had told me of Anne Gilchrist, he gave me the Small, Maynard and Company (1897) edition of the 'Leaves' and Elizabeth Porter Gould's 'Anne Gilchrist and Walt Whitman' (1900).

In the twenty years' association following that meeting, the experiences and privileges which came to me by reason of Burroughs's abiding love for Whitman, and his wide connections with other Whitman appreciators, are among the most deeply cherished of my life. The meetings, the talks, the readings, the friendships, the correspondence with other 'Whitman men' and 'Whitman women,' have all been deeply satisfying and enriching. Nor do these cease. It is an ever widening stream. Since the passing of Burroughs, many rare friendships growing out of the Whitman-

Burroughs interests have come, and are continually coming, to me, the tie that binds being 'the institution of the dear love of comrades.' With Burroughs I visited some of their old Washington haunts, looked from the windows in the Treasury Building where they had worked in early manhood, looking out upon the Potomac; with Burroughs I ate oysters at Harvey's, perched on the high stools, just as 'Walt' and 'Jack' did in the old days; and visited the 'house that Jack built' on V Street, where Ursula Burroughs gave the poet those delectable Sunday breakfasts. I stood with Burroughs beside the grave of O'Connor. I met some of the surviving members of the old Washington circle — Major Saxton (a centenarian in 1930 — sole survivor today of that glorious failure, the Brook Farm experiment), Aaron Johns, the John Pattens, and the Frank Bakers. And I listened while they and Burroughs recalled the long-gone days.

In the Harned home in Germantown the family talked of Whitman's comings and goings there, and pointed out a picture of a stranded ship in their dining-room, a favorite of Walt's, who used to say it reminded him of himself. Harned gave me many books, photographs, and mementoes that had been in Whitman's room at the time of his death. Later he accorded me the privilege of reading the original letters of Anne Gilchrist to Whitman, several years before he published them. There, too, I saw the precious notebooks kept by Whitman during the Civil War, which, with much other priceless Whitmaniana, Mr. Harned gave later to the Library of Congress. Through correspondence extending over many years, I came to know some of the little band of Whitman devotees in the north of England, chiefly Dr. J. Johnston and J. W. Wallace; likewise also, Elizabeth Dowden, the talented widow of Edward Dowden, whose friendship I cherish, and whom I have twice visited in her Dublin home. Through correspondence also I became acquainted with Léon Bazalgette, who, with his compatriot, Gabriel Sarrazin, has so ably interpreted Whitman to France.[1] And I have

---

[1] W. S. Kennedy (pages 45-46, and 281, in *The Fight of a Book for the World*) gives these data of Sarrazin's Whitman contributions:

Four chapters in *La Renaissance de la Poesie Anglaise*, 1798-1889. Paris, Perrin et Cie, 1889.

His estimate first appeared in *La Nouvelle Revue*, 1888 and 1889. An English translation of Sarrazin's contribution, by Mr. Harrison S. Morris, with Sarrazin's French vera treasured memory of rare hours with Edward Carpenter in his little shack at Guilford, and in his library. There in his old age, his beautiful life, then nearing completion, rose like a lambent peak suffused with ineffable grace and calm. A few months after that visit, Mrs. Charles Holden, an English friend, gave me this charming glimpse of Carpenter in her letter of August 31, 1926:

On Sunday morning we were in Surrey for the week-end at the James Bone cottage. James Bone, Charles, and I called on Edward Carpenter to wish him a happy birthday, his 82d. The little round man from Wigam opened the door a very little way and looked as though he feared I would put my foot in the opening, or make a forced entrance.

I asked for George Merrill, who was 'not down,' but who soon appeared. I said we just wanted to wish Mr. Carpenter a happy birthday. So he said, would we not see Mr. Carpenter? And then he took us round to the hut which you know. There he sat in the sunshine busy with pen and paper. He looked well and fragile and alert and whimsical and gay. He was beautiful. He looked smaller than when I last saw him. Perhaps he is like the people in the fairy stories who get smaller every day until one day they are just not there. He says his sight is bad, and his memory. Maybe! He says it is an advantage not to have too good a memory — one can forget so many of the painful things in a not-too-good-at-present world. How clear his eyes are, and how shapely and expressive his hands! Mr. Bone told him that C. P. Scott of the 'Manchester Guardian' was 80, and

sion of many passages from the *Leaves*, is given on pages 159–94, *In Re Walt Whitman*. The same contribution, translated by William Struthers, was printed in *The Conservator*, January, February, and March, 1899. Kennedy also states that he translated Sarrazin's paper on Whitman for Whitman, who printed it as a broadside in 1888, along with another translation of the same, by Dr. Bucke, as another broadside, the same year. Bazalgette's contributions on Whitman, the data of which are furnished me by H. S. Saunders, are:

Walt Whitman: l'Homme et son Œuvre. Paris, *Mercure de France*, 1908.

Feuilles d'Herbe. Paris, *Mercure de France*, 2 vols., 1909.

Poèmes de Walt Whitman: version française. F. Rieder et Cie, Paris, 1914.

Le Panseur de Plaies. Poèmes, Lettres et Fragments de Walt Whitman sur la Guerre, Édition de la Revue Littéraire des Primaires 'Les Humbles.' 1917.

Ode à la France: Poème de Walt Whitman (Traduction). Traduit par Léon Bazalgette. Se Trouve: à la Belle Édition. Paris, 1917.

Walt Whitman: Calamus Poèmes. Version Nouvelle. Édition du Sablier. Génève, 1919.

The Sleepers. A poem by Walt Whitman (published in both France and England.) François Bermonard, Paris, 1919.

Le 'Poème Évangile' de Walt Whitman. *Mercure de France*, Paris, 1921.

Feuilles d'Herbe (practically a new translation). *Mercure de France*, Paris, 2 vols., 1922.

Walt Whitman. Pages de Journal. *Mercure de France*, Paris, 1926.

Walt Whitman: The Man and His Work. Translated by Ellen Fitzgerald. Doubleday, Page and Company. 1920.

EDWARD CARPENTER
At Millthorpe, Guildford, August 7, 1924

that he cycled to and from his office every day and played tennis. Mr. Carpenter said he could not compete with that.

I said to him, 'I am going to write to Dr. Barrus this week.' He said, 'Clara Barrus! I liked her. I would not have missed her.' And I told him how diffident you are, and how we had to push you to see him, although you were so anxious to do so, but afraid lest you might intrude. He was surprised,... and said you had no need to be shy. But I think he likes you best shy.... When we were leaving he said, 'Give Clara Barrus my love.'

It is a happy memory. This man who has perhaps made one of the most permanent marks on the intellectual world, quietly, gracefully fading out of life, sitting high up, drinking in as much sunshine and freshness of air as he can get. I shall think of him when the wind blows and wonder if it is not too much for his frail body.

Mr. Bone's account of the same visit, in the 'Manchester Guardian,' said that Carpenter was then working on a book to be called 'Light from the East' — a collection of letters from his friend Arunachalam upon the esoteric lore of Ceylon.

On August 13, 1928, Margaret Holden again wrote me:

You may have heard that dear old Edward Carpenter seems to be drifting toward the other shore. His body is very feeble, and his mind, but he has occasional sparks of light glinting from it.... George Merrill is dead, but the other man you saw is kind and careful and capable. It cannot be a long way that gentle inspired traveller has to tread.

And it was not. He died on June 28, 1929.

Another unforgettable experience growing out of my association with John Burroughs was a house-party in Atlantic City in 1907 in the home of William Vanamee, a keen appreciator of Whitman, and an intimate of Burroughs. There for certain hours each day Burroughs reread with me Whitman's letters to him — many of which are quoted in this volume — while I noted his running comments on them. Unforgettable also the hours, 'after the supper and talk,' when Burroughs and the gifted pianist Mr. Eugene Heffley would read aloud 'Sea Drift' and other poems, within sound of the husky-voiced sea. And then Burroughs would talk as only he could when in the midst of a few congenial friends. Mr. Heffley would then play the superb sea pieces of MacDowell, after which gentle Patty Stair sat long and long at the piano in the gathering twilight, softly improvising, till we were wrapped in the 'tender and growing night,' while outside were 'the earth and the sea half-held by the night' — 'night of the large few stars.'

I recall, too, rare hours with Whitman friends in California, and in far-off Hawaii, when little circles listened while Burroughs read or talked of his comrade to the accompaniment of the Pacific's endlessly rocking waves. Treasured hours include also those spent in the homes of J. T. Trowbridge and William Sloane Kennedy, listening while the venerable friends revived their memories of Walt till he seemed in the very midst —

> Be it as if I were with you. Be not too certain but I am now with you.

Still other hours in my own home when Burroughs and the J. H. Johnstons recalled the years when they and Walt used to meet in the Johnston home in New York City. Besides these, especially significant were pilgrimages with Burroughs to Whitman's birthplace at West Hills; to the humble Mickle Street house in Camden; to the poet's haunts along Timber Creek (and conferences with surviving members of the Stafford family); and to the tomb, a few miles from Camden, where the great one lies.

Since the passing of Burroughs there has appeared a sketch of him in the 'Dictionary of American Biography,' by Mr. Norman Foerster, which contains a curiously untenable statement, that Burroughs in his last book, 'with admirable integrity recants the greatest emotional enthusiasm of his life, his devotion to Walt Whitman.' Never was there the slightest recantation of that enthusiasm or devotion. Moreover, never had Burroughs been able, try as he would, to accept Whitman's belief in personal immortality. On the contrary, with the 'admirable integrity' that characterized him, he confessed regretfully that he could not follow Whitman in this belief, but this was no new confession. The passage to which Mr. Foerster refers is on pages 285–88 in 'The Last Harvest,' and is called 'Facing the Mystery,' two sentences of which run thus: 'Whitman's indomitable faith I admire, but cannot share. My torch will not kindle at his flame.' But how far was this admission from showing the least wavering in his early and late enthusiasm for, and devotion to, his comrade!

We may well close this survey of the period covering the comradeship of Whitman and Burroughs with excerpts from Burroughs's last utterances about the poet. It is especially significant that, after his long and close association with the man, Burroughs could, almost at the close of his own life, write such a splendid, sweeping and sincere estimate of Whitman as is found in 'The Poet of the Cosmos,'[1] one passage from which is quoted here:

The world has had but one poet of the cosmos, and that was Whitman. His mind, his sympathies, sweep through a wider orbit than those of any other. I am bold enough to say frankly that I look upon him as the greatest personality — not the greatest intellect, but the most symbolical man, the greatest incarnation of mind, heart, and soul, fused and fired by the poetic spirit — that has appeared in the world during the Christian era.

Another passage from the same book[2] — the last of his books to be published during his lifetime — blends his own and Whitman's attitude toward the Whole:

'It is all right,' said Walt Whitman to me as I was leaving his death-bed and hearing his voice for the last time — 'It is all right.' Of course it was all right, and it will be all right when each and all of us fall into the last eternal sleep. Else it would not be. Our being here is all right, is it not? 'Friendly and faithful,' says Whitman, 'are the arms that have helped me.' And friendly and faithful must be the arms that bear us away. If it is good to come, it will be good to go — good in the large, cosmic sense, good in that it is in keeping with the spirit of the All.

In the spring of 1921 Burroughs was borne away by the faithful and friendly arms of which his great comrade had sung. His body was given back to Mother Earth on his eighty-fourth birthday. The attitude with which he faced the Great Mystery is shown in 'Accepting the Universe' (page 252):

I shall not be imprisoned in that grave where you are to bury my body. I shall be diffused in great Nature, in the soil, in the air, in the sunshine, in the hearts of those who love me, in all living and flowing currents of the world, though I may never again in my entirety be embodied in a single human being. My elements and my forces go back into the original sources out of which they came, and these sources are perennial in this vast, wonderful, divine cosmos.

From 'The Last Harvest,' a posthumous book in 1922, a brief

[1] Burroughs: *Accepting the Universe*, page 316.
[2] *Accepting the Universe*, pages 291-92.

quotation, on page 209, will suffice to show the steadfastness of Burroughs's espousal of his comrade and his comrade's book:

We go to Whitman for his attitude toward life and the universe; we go to stimulate and fortify our souls; in short, for his cosmic philosophy incarnated in a man.

THE END

Bibliography of Burroughs and Whitman

BIBLIOGRAPHY OF BURROUGHS ON WHITMAN

Book-notices of 'Drum Taps,' *Commonwealth*, November 10, 1865.

'Walt Whitman and his *Drum Taps*,' *The Galaxy*, December 1, 1866, vol. 2, pp. 606–15.

NOTES ON WALT WHITMAN AS POET AND PERSON, first edition, American News Company, New York, 1867. Second edition, with Supplementary Notes, J. S. Redfield, New York, 1871.

'More About Nature and the Poets,' *Appleton's Journal*, September 10, 1870, vol. 4, pp. 314–16.

Two paragraphs about Whitman in Burroughs's critique of Emerson, *The Galaxy*, February and April, 1876; later incorporated in BIRDS AND POETS, 1877.

'The Birds of the Poets,' *Scribner's Monthly*, September, 1873, vol. 6, pp. 565–74; later incorporated in BIRDS AND POETS (1877), pp. 17–21.

'Walt Whitman's Poetry,' *New York Tribune*, April 13, 1876.

'The Flight of the Eagle,' BIRDS AND POETS, 1877.

'Nature and the Poets,' *Scribner's Monthly*, December, 1879, vol. 19, pp. 285–95; also in PEPACTON (1881), pp. 107–09.

'Nature in Literature,' *The Critic*, July 16, 1881, vol. 1, p. 185.

'Mere Egotism,' *Lippincott's Monthly Magazine*, February, 1887, vol. 39, pp. 298–306.

'Walt Whitman's Seventieth Birthday,' *The Critic*, June 8, 1889, pp. 287–88. (Contains excerpts from a letter by Burroughs.)

'Camden's Compliment to Walt Whitman,' edited by Horace Traubel (Philadelphia, 1889), pp. 55–56. (Contains a letter from Burroughs, a part of which was published in the June *Critic*.)

'Mr. Howells's Agreement with Whitman,' *The Critic*, February 6, 1892, vol. 20, pp. 85–86.

'At the Graveside of Walt Whitman,' edited by Horace Traubel, Philadelphia, 1892. (Contains a contribution by Burroughs, pp. 22–24.)

'Walt Whitman, Poet of Democracy,' *Christian Union*, April 2, 1892, vol. 45, pp. 636–37.

'Walt Whitman,' *The Critic*, April 2, 1892, vol. 17, pp. 199–200.

'Walt Whitman After Death,' *The Critic*, April 9, 1892, vol. 17, p. 215.

An article on Whitman in the *Chicago Interocean*, April or May, 1892.

'The Poet of Democracy,' *North American Review*, May, 1892, vol. 154, pp. 523–40.

'A Boston Criticism of Whitman,' *Poet-Lore*, August–September, 1892, vol. 4, pp. 392–96.

IN RE WALT WHITMAN, edited by his literary executors, Philadelphia, 1893. (Contains two articles by Burroughs:) 'Walt Whitman and his

Recent Critics,' p. 93; 'Walt Whitman and the Common People,' pp. 363–65.

'Whitman's and Tennyson's Relation to Science,' *The Dial*, March 16, 1893, vol. 14, pp. 168–69; see also WHITMAN: A STUDY, pp. 252–56.

'A Glance into Walt Whitman,' *Lippincott's Monthly Magazine*, June 18, 1893, vol. 51, pp. 753–58.

'A Poet of Grand Physique,' *The Critic*, June 3, 1893, vol. 22, p. 372.

'Walt Whitman and his Art,' *Poet-Lore*, February, 1894, vol. 6, pp. 63–69. A letter from Burroughs commenting further on subject of preceding article, *Poet-Lore*, November, 1894, vol. 6, p. 577.

'Whitman's Self-Reliance,' originally published in the WALT WHITMAN FELLOWSHIP PAPERS, 1894, No. 9. Reprinted in *The Conservator*, November, 1894, vol. 5, pp. 131–34.

'The Sapphic Secret' (a reference to Whitman), *The Critic*, March 17, 1894.

'Democracy and Literature,' *The Outlook*, February 16, 1895, vol. 51, pp. 266–67.

'Emerson and Lowell's Views of Whitman,' *The Conservator*, June, 1895, vol. 6, pp. 51 ff.

'Two Critics of Whitman,' *The Conservator*, August, 1895, vol. 6, pp. 84–87.

'Walt Whitman Again,' *The Conservator*, October, 1895, vol. 6, pp. 116–19.

'More Whitman Characteristics,' *The Conservator*, November, 1895, vol. 6, pp. 131–33.

'Whitman's Relation to Morals,' *The Conservator*, April, 1896, vol. 7, pp. 19–22; see also WHITMAN: A STUDY, pp. 169–204.

'Whitman's Relation to Culture,' *The Conservator*, June, 1896, vol. 7, pp. 51–53; see also WHITMAN: A STUDY, pp. 205–27.

WHITMAN: A STUDY, Boston, 1896 (published November 21).

'Walt Whitman and the Younger Writers'; an Interview with Burroughs by Walter Blackburn Harte, *The Conservator*, July, 1896, vol. 7, pp. 69 ff.

'The Poet and the Modern,' *Atlantic Monthly*, October, 1896, vol. 78, pp. 563–66.

'On a Dictum of Matthew Arnold's,' *Atlantic Monthly*, May, 1897, vol. 79, pp. 713–17.

John Burroughs and Thomas Donaldson on Whitman — Reviews in *The Book Buyer*, vol. 14, p. 1. 1897.

Introduction to *Walt Whitman Selections*, by John Burroughs, *Library of the World's Best Literature*, edited by Charles Dudley Warner, vol. 27, pp. 15885–891. New York, 1896, 1897, 1898.

'The Secret of Whitman's Following,' *The Critic*, March 19, 1898, vol. 32, pp. 189–91.

'Walt Whitman as Man, Poet, and Friend,' edited by Charles N. Elliot,

Boston, 1915. (Contains a letter from Burroughs, written April 7, 1898, concerning the last time he saw Whitman, pp. 55–57.)

Sketch of Walt Whitman in *Encyclopædia Britannica*, Tenth Edition, 1902, vol. 23, pp. 840–41.

POEMS (LEAVES OF GRASS), with Biographical Introduction by Burroughs. Crowell's Poet Series, New York, 1902.

LAFAYETTE IN BROOKLYN, by Walt Whitman, with an Introduction by John Burroughs. George D. Smith, New York, 1905.

Walt Whitman, *Encyclopædia Britannica*, Eleventh Edition, 1911, vol. 28, pp. 610–11.

THE ROLLING EARTH; Outdoor Scenes and Thoughts from the Writings of Walt Whitman. Compiled by Waldo R. Browne, with an Introduction by John Burroughs. Boston, 1912.

'Whitman as I See Him,' for Whitman Centenary, *Brooklyn Daily Eagle*, May 10, 1919.

Letters about Whitman, from John Burroughs to Clara Barrus, and to Richard Watson Gilder, *The Modern School*, April–May number, 1919.

'The Poet of the Cosmos,' ACCEPTING THE UNIVERSE, pp. 316–28. 1920.

Letters from Burroughs to Egmont H. Arens, quoted in 'The End of a Literary Mystery,' by F. P. Hier, *American Mercury*, April, 1924, vol. 1, p. 471.

'Whitman and Burroughs as Comrades,' by Clara Barrus. *Yale Review*, October, 1925, vol. 15, pp. 59–81. (Contains excerpts on Whitman from letters, notebooks, and journals by Burroughs.)

LIFE AND LETTERS OF JOHN BURROUGHS, by Clara Barrus. Boston, 1926. (Contains many letters and journal excerpts about Whitman by Burroughs.)

THE HEART OF BURROUGHS'S JOURNALS, edited by Clara Barrus. Boston, 1928. (Contains many excerpts on Whitman.)

In addition to the foregoing, there are many passages about Whitman in the following books by Burroughs. No mention, however, is made here of the other books in which Burroughs has merely quoted from Whitman:

WINTER SUNSHINE, 1875; BIRDS AND POETS, 1877; SIGNS AND SEASONS, 1886; INDOOR STUDIES, 1889; LITERARY VALUES, 1902; TIME AND CHANGE, 1912; UNDER THE APPLE-TREES, 1916; FIELD AND STUDY, 1919; ACCEPTING THE UNIVERSE, 1920; UNDER THE MAPLES, 1921; THE LAST HARVEST, 1922.

INDEX